BENITO MUSSOLINI AND THE ART OF TYRANNY

BENITO MUSSOLINI AND THE ART OF TYRANNY

FASCIST ITALY'S INFAMOUS DICTATOR

WILLIAM NESTER

FRONTLINE
BOOKS

BENITO MUSSOLINI AND THE ART OF TYRANNY
From WW2 into the Cold War

First published in Great Britain in 2026
by Frontline Books
An imprint of
Pen & Sword Books Ltd
Yorkshire - Philadelphia

ISBN 9781036147716

A CIP catalogue record for this book is available from the British Library

Typeset by Lapiz Digital
Printed and bound in the UK by CPI Group (UK) Ltd,
Croydon, CR0 4YY.

Printed on paper from a sustainable source by
CPI Group (UK) Ltd, Croydon, CR0 4YY

The Publisher's authorised representative in the EU for product safety is Authorised Rep Compliance Ltd., Ground Floor, 71 Lower Baggot Street, Dublin D02 P593, Ireland.
www.arccompliance.com

For a complete list of Pen & Sword titles please contact
PEN & SWORD BOOKS LTD
47 Church Street, Barnsley, South Yorkshire, S70 2AS, England
E-mail: enquiries@pen-and-sword.co.uk
Website: www.pen-and-sword.co.uk
or
PEN & SWORD BOOKS
1950 Lawrence Rd, Havertown, PA 19083, USA
E-mail: uspen-and-sword@casematepublishers.com

CONTENTS

List of Plates vi
Acknowledgments vii
Tables viii

Introduction 1
Chapter 1 The Upbringing 19
Chapter 2 The Radical 28
Chapter 3 The Fascist Movement 40
Chapter 4 The Fascist State 61
Chapter 5 The Roads to Empire 93
Chapter 6 The Axis Pact of Steel 116
Chapter 7 The Military and Economic Power 145
Chapter 8 The Roads to Humiliating Defeat 162
Chapter 9 The Overthrow 196
Chapter 10 The Salo Republic 211
Chapter 11 The Legacy 235

Notes 257
Bibliography 282
Index 299

LIST OF PLATES

1. Mussolini at age 14.
2. Mussolini as a young man.
3. Mussolini speaking before a crowd.
4. Mussolini and family.
5. Mussolini after nose wounding by Violet Gibson.
6. Mussolini as Blackshirt speaker.
7. Mussolini in Libya, 1937.
8. Mussolini swimming.
9. Mussolini at his desk.
10. Mussolini with Neville Chamberlain.
11. Mussolini with Hitler.
12. Galeazzo Ciano and Edda Mussolini.
13. Mussolini and Carla Petacci's corpses, Milan, 29 April 1944.
14. The Mussolini crypt at Predappio.

ACKNOWLEDGEMENTS

I would like to express my deep gratitude and pleasure at having had yet another opportunity to work with the outstanding publishing team of John Grehan, Lisa Hoosan, Stephen Chumbley, and Martin Mace, who were always as kind as they were professional.

TABLES

2.1 Defence Spending of Europe's Great Power in British Pounds Sterling ... 37
3.1 First World War Great Power Military Casualties ... 47
3.2 Italian Prime Ministers, December 1909 to October 1922 ... 54
4.1 Benito Mussolini Cabinet, October 1922 ... 62
4.2 List of Fascist Party Secretaries, Tenures and Party Names, 1919–1945 ... 66
4.3 New Ministries, Initial Ministers and Founding Dates ... 71
4.4 Italian Economic Indexes, 1929–1939 ... 80
4.5 Industrial Worker Nominal and Real Earnings, 1929–1939 ... 81
4.6 Comparison of European Great Economic Power Per Capita Income (1960 dollars) ... 83
7.1 Italian Chiefs of Staff, May 1925 to May 1945 ... 146
7.2 Italy's Economy and Military Spending, 1938–1943 ... 148
7.3 Comparison of Military Spending as Share of Economy, 1939–1944 ... 149
7.4 Military Spending Service Shares, 1938–1943 ... 154
7.5 Great Power Gross Domestic Product, 1938–1945 (1990 dollars in billions) ... 158

INTRODUCTION

> We permit ourselves the luxury of being aristocratic and democratic, conservative and progressive, reactionary and revolutionary, accepting the law and going beyond it, according to the circumstances of the time, place and environment. In a word, of the 'history' in which we must live and act.
>
> (Benito Mussolini)

> War alone keeps all human energies at the maximum tension and sets the seal of nobility on those peoples who have the courage to face it.
>
> (Benito Mussolini)

> [T]he individual exists only insofar as he is subordinated to the state and as civilization becomes more complex, so the liberty of the individual must be increasingly restricted.
>
> (Benito Mussolini)

> The Fascism State, as a higher and more powerful expression of personality, is a force, but a spiritual force. It sums up all the manifestations of the intellectual and moral life of man.
>
> (Benito Mussolini)

> It is really simpler to give orders myself instead of having to send for the minister concerned and convince him about what I want done.
>
> (Benito Mussolini)

Art is a creative way to overcome a challenge whether it be painting a landscape, composing a symphony or running a country. Indeed, there is an art of tyranny that involves the aspirant taking and keeping uninhibited, arbitrary power. Tyrants have been around as long as humans and have usually made life miserable for those under their thumb whether they were organized as a family, village, tribe, state or empire.

Benito Mussolini is among the world's most recognizable tyrants with his scowl, jutting jaw, bald dome, booming voice, chopping fists, squat body and wide stance.[1] He founded the Fascist movement dedicated to transforming Italy's liberal democracy into a regime that mingled authoritarianism, nationalism, populism, corporatism, vigilantism and imperialism, with himself the all-powerful charismatic '*Duce*' or leader. By threatening to march on Rome with his Blackshirt militia, he bullied King Victor Emmanuel III into naming him prime minister. He ruled Italy from 30 October 1922 until 25 July 1943. Just 13 months after taking power, he pressured a majority within the Chamber of Deputies into passing the Acebo Law whereby a political party with the most votes that exceeded 25 per cent of the national total received 65 per cent of seats. His Fascist Party with allies surpassed that in the April 1924 election, winning 64 per cent of votes and 374 of 535 seats. With that overwhelming legislative majority, he issued decrees and had laws approved that granted him dictatorial powers, outlawed all political parties except for his Fascist Party, and jailed or drove into exile his opponents. He replaced the Chamber of Deputies with the Chamber of Fasci and Corporations in 1939. He also established the Fascist Grand Council whose twenty-eight Party members rubber-stamped his decrees and laws.

Yet Mussolini's dictatorship was limited as the king remained the head of state with the latent power to dismiss him as prime minister backed by the need and courage to do so. That time eventually came. The Fascist Grand Council and Victor Emmanuel collaborated to depose Mussolini in July 1943, after he dragged Italy into a series of disastrous wars.

Until the war years, most Italians enthusiastically embraced Mussolini's dictatorship because his economic and nationalist policies boosted their living standards, hope and pride. Mussolini oversaw a corporatist economy where the state partnered with industrial, agrarian, labour and energy groups to expand production, productivity, wages and quality of life. He explained that: 'As far as economics is concerned, we are liberals because we believe that the national economy cannot be usefully entrusted to collective or governmental and bureaucratic organizations.'[2] Private property and managed markets prevailed. Mussolini pushed through such reforms as an eight-hour working day, overtime pay, maternity leave and old age pensions. His regime invested in building or improving roads, schools, hospitals, electricity grids and sewage and water systems, draining the malarial Pontine Marshes and converting them to farmland, and promoting national patriotism and unity. Italians summed up Mussolini's practical feats with the refrain, 'He made the trains run on time'.

Appearances and feelings, of course, can be deceiving. Economically Italian Fascism actually lagged compared to other times and countries. The economy grew an average 1.9 per cent under Mussolini from 1922 to 1938, behind Sweden's 4.1 per cent, Germany's 3.8 per cent and Britain's 2.2 per cent and also behind the 2.7 per cent average growth under Italy's liberal democracy from 1897 to 1913. Average Italian productivity rose 3.5 per cent annually from 1901 to 1925 and a dismal 0.8 per cent from 1925 to 1940.[3] Yet most Italians were unaware of those differences and compared their dismal conditions during the First World War to their better lives under Mussolini's regime.

Mussolini ultimately failed catastrophically as a tyrant when he tried to fulfil his promise to make Italy as great a modern imperial nation as Ancient Rome. He actually shelved that dream during his first decade as Italy's *Duce* while he focused on monopolizing power and developing the economy. The emergence during the 1930s of two other imperialistic fascist great powers – Japan and Germany – reawakened Mussolini's ambition.

Japan initiated fascist imperialism when its army conquered China's north-eastern region of Manchuria in September 1931 and the League of Nations responded with nothing more than an investigation and protest. Thereafter Japan, Italy and Germany took turns invading weak countries and eventually formed an alliance, called the Axis or Pact of Steel, in 1939. Hubris, the belief of the Axis leaders that they were invincible, eventually led to the destruction of themselves and their regimes by provoking the overwhelming alliance of America, Britain and the Soviet Union against them.

Mussolini's first attempt at conquest appeared to succeed when the Italian army overran much of the African kingdom of Abyssinia after invading it in October 1935 and capturing the capital Addis Ababa in May 1936. Then Mussolini allied with fellow tyrant Adolf Hitler and together they sent military forces to support General Francisco Franco who led the army's revolt against Spain's republican government; the civil war lasted from July 1936 to March 1939 and resulted in Franco's triumph and establishment of a fascist dictatorship over Spain.

After that, Mussolini carried out a series of what became disastrous invasions of France, Greece and Egypt. The first failed militarily but succeeded diplomatically because Hitler's military machine, the Wehrmacht, decisively defeated the allied French, British, Belgian and Dutch armies and forced the French government under Marshal

Philippe Pétain to cede the northern and western halves of the country to Germany and a small portion of the south-east to Italy; Pétain's government became a Fascist puppet state under Berlin's supervision. The Greeks and the British defenders of Egypt routed the Italian invaders and each time Hitler sent German armies to rescue Mussolini's armies from complete defeat. Then Mussolini sent an army to join the German invasion of the Soviet Union that from June to December 1941, succeeded in routing the Red Army and fighting east as far as the outskirts of Leningrad, Moscow and Rostov before bogging down in the Russian winter. After that, year after year, the Red Army punched back the Axis forces, with Italy's army among those it decimated.

Meanwhile, Japan's military invaded the rest of China led by Generalissimo Chiang Kai-shek's regime from July 1937, then took over northern Indochina from France after its defeat in 1940 and southern Indochina in 1941. Mussolini dutifully joined Hitler in declaring war against the United States on 11 December 1941, four days after waves of Japanese carrier-based bombers devastated America's fleet at Pearl Harbor, Hawaii. Mussolini and Hitler exulted as over the next half year Japan's military conquered a vast Pacific and South-east Asian empire against the American, British, Dutch and Australian militaries defending parts of those regions.

America's entrance into the war was decisive for the eventual defeat of the Axis powers, starting with Mussolini's regime. American and British troops led by General Dwight Eisenhower landed in Morocco and Algeria in November 1942, to drive eastward against a German-Italian army led by Field Marshal Erwin Rommel that a British army led by General Bernard Montgomery had routed at El Alamein in western Egypt in October 1942. The Allied armies eventually crushed the Axis forces and captured 250,000 troops in northern Tunisia in May 1943.

The successful invasion of Sicily in July 1943 by American and British armies led respectively by Generals George Patton and Montgomery led to Mussolini's overthrow. The Fascist National Council debated his fate for nine hours from 24 July into the early hours of 25 July, when it voted nineteen to eight with one abstention that he resign. Later that day, King Victor Emmanuel III summoned him, announced that he would replace him as prime minister with General Pietro Badoglio and had him arrested and imprisoned.

The Allies completed their conquest of Sicily by 12 August. Montgomery's army invaded the Italian peninsula's toe on 3 September and began fighting up the foot. Secret negotiations with the Allies led to the king and Badoglio agreeing to surrender Italy on 8 September, but then they fled to safety behind Allied lines as an American army led by General Mark Clark landed at Salerno while part of Montgomery's army seized Taranto. After the coup, Hitler sent more German divisions to bolster those already deployed in Italy, and had deployed them near Italian divisions. When Italy's king announced the armistice, Hitler had most of his divisions disarm the Italian divisions, send the soldiers to prison camps and factories in Germany, then join the other German divisions battling the Allied armies in southern Italy. The war for the Italian peninsula lasted 18 devastating months.

Mussolini's incarceration was brief. On 12 September, Hitler dispatched a commando team to rescue him then imposed him as his puppet dictator of the so-called Fascist Salo Republic in German occupied northern Italy. Allied armies slowly ground their way up the Italian peninsula. A civil war erupted between mostly Communist led partisan guerillas and Italian troops still loyal to Mussolini and allied with the German army. Allied invasions of France's Normandy coast on 6 June 1944 and the Riviera on 15 August 1944, linked in eastern France in September 1944 to form the 450-mile Western Front from the North Sea to Switzerland. Meanwhile, the Soviet Red Army steadily drove back German-led Axis forces on the vast Eastern Front. Across the Pacific, American offensives captured strategic islands and destroyed Japanese naval and army forces toward the Japanese homeland.

Mussolini's end was swift, brutal and humiliating. As Allied forces approached, he tried to escape with his mistress into neighbouring Switzerland on 27 April. Partisans captured him on the morning of 28 April, executed him and his mistress and hung their bodies upside down in a Milan square. Two days later, Hitler and his mistress committed suicide in a Berlin bunker as Soviet troops closed in. His successor Admiral Karl Dönitz had subordinates surrender to Western Allied forces on 7 May and Soviet forces on 8 May. Japan's fascist regime held out for another three months and even after the atomic bombings of Hiroshima and Nagasaki the War Cabinet split over whether to surrender or fight to the last Japanese man, woman and child. The emperor backed those who wanted to surrender, broadcasted his intention on 14 August and his government formally surrendered on 2 September 1945. The Second World War ended with the destruction of all three major Fascist regimes, that of Italy, Germany and Japan along with minor Fascist allies like those of Hungary, Romania and Yugoslavia.

As a tyrant, Benito Mussolini's character and personality were as split as his mostly constructive economic policies and disastrous geopolitical policies. He exuded machismo, charisma and confidence that attracted followers. He was a narcissist who expected others to adore and obey him. He genuinely believed that he was infallible: 'often I would like to be wrong, but so far it has never happened and events have always turned out just as I foresaw'.[4] He described himself as 'like a cat, cautious and prudent, but when I jump I am sure of landing where I wish'.[5]

Yet he poorly hid traits that could alienate others. He was sullen, taciturn, prideful and hot-tempered. He was a bully and braggart who concealed a deep sense of inadequacy and inferiority. He was relatively short – five foot, five inches – the same height as fellow tyrant Joseph Stalin. Whether his diminutive stature swelled his pathologies is unknowable but likely. Regardless, he described himself as '*un animale poco socievole*' that can variously be translated as an anti-social lone wolf or, clinically, a sociopath.[6] He overcompensated with delusions of grandeur that he was an infallible genius. He was vindictive and violence-prone with festering rage and resentment. During his school years he stabbed two classmates and later when he was 19 a married woman with whom he was having an affair; although the wounds he inflicted were shallow his pathology was bone-deep.

Mussolini was a misanthrope contemptuous of humanity as emotional, ignorant, fearful, vengeful and hateful and so easily manipulated by strong leaders. Looking back, he explained where that view originated: 'Journalism led me to understand the human material from which politics was made.'[7] His natural introversion influenced his ruling style. He explained that: 'One must accept solitude . . . A chief cannot have equals or friends. The humble solace gained from exchanging confidences is denied him. He cannot open his heart. Never.'[8]

He was courageous. He fought stoically if not with exceptional heroism in the First World War from August 1915 to August 1917, when he received an honourable discharge and a prolonged hospital stay after being severely wounded by a grenade during a training exercise in February 1917. He learned to fence and fought numerous non-fatal duels with rapiers that ended with the first blood. He learned to fly and survived a crash in March 1921. He also enjoyed swimming in the sea and horseback riding. He suffered chronic ulcers that worsened his natural irritability. To alleviate his ulcers, he spurned tobacco and alcohol from 1923. His diet was mostly fruit, milk and antiacids that he wolved down in several minutes.

He was bright but ill-schooled and unrefined. With men, barracks-talk crudities tended to prevail. He bore little sense of humour or irony. Yet he did enjoy reading renowned books and attending plays, concerts, operas and films. He played the trombone and violin. He was a prolific writer as a journalist who aspired to create literature. He wrote three plays about respectively Napoleon, Caesar and Cavour, with the theme a great man betrayed. His two novels had anticlerical themes. He scorned Catholicism and other religions and feared no divine retribution for his sins and crimes. Yet, he was superstitious and worried about his enemies casting the evil eye on him.

He was a control-freak who sought to dominate everyone and everything. To that end, he was not just prime minister but by 1929 headed eight of thirteen ministries. In addition, he chaired the Fascist Party, Fascist Grand Council, Supreme Council on Defence, Council of State, Court of Accounts, Army Council, Supreme Council of Statistics, Permanent Committee on Cereal Production and Committee on Civilian Mobilization. In the Second World War, he was the military's commander-in-chief. He was a workaholic who put in 14-hour days on the job whatever and wherever that might be. His diverse duties and long hours exhausted him into deep sleeps that could last eight hours, although often insomnia plagued him.

As dictator, he was the decider in chief. He explained that: 'It is really simpler to give orders myself instead of having to send for the minister concerned and convince him about what I want done.'[9] The trouble was that countless choices came from gut instinct or whim rather than a careful cost-benefit analysis by experts. Often one decision complicated or contradicted an earlier decision. Atop that he failed to ensure that his underlings implemented his decrees, which often was not or poorly done. For subordinates, he favoured sycophants and shunned experts who might challenge him.

His wife Rachele knew his at times kinder, gentler and also gullible, indecisive, prevaricating sides:

> [H]e was susceptible to persuasion in that the last speaker usually left the most indelible impression. He was trusting to the point of naivete, thinking that anyone who agreed to work with him could never betray him. Basically kind-hearted, he was opposed to hurting people, always finding an excuse to forgive whether it was his children or his ministers. His philosophy of man was such that he felt a more intimate bond with some like Gandhi or Saint Francis (whom he worshipped and had made the Patron Saint of Italy), than someone like Stalin or Hitler (whom he admired to some degree but whose brutality and violence he'd always condemned).[10]

Among his self-defeating weaknesses one made him especially vulnerable. He eagerly sought the esteem and devotion of others. He revelled in being addressed with a title, like *professore* (teacher), *cavaliere* (literally knight, commonly upper-class gentleman) and, eventually, *duce* (leader). That rendered him an easy mark for manipulative, ambitious sycophants and flatterers.

Biographer Denis Mack Smith explained the challenge in analysing Mussolini:

> One difficulty in understanding him is that, though he had a host of admirers, he was a very private person and at no moment in his life possessed a friend who could pass on to posterity a balanced and convincing assessment of his personality, nor was there any close associate to whom he revealed himself naturally and unambiguously. Always in his relations with other people he was . . . on stage acting a part or rather acting a continual and baffling series of parts that are not always easy to disentangle and reconcile. As well as being a gifted actor, he possessed superlative ability as a propagandist whose public statements and private comments were often intended to conceal the truth as much as to reveal it; and this faculty, though it served him well enough at first, was eventually his undoing.[11]

Mussolini had complex, often conflicted views of and relations with women.[12] He grew up in a traditional society and naturally accepted its conservative views. His daughter Edda explained that: 'My father believed that a woman should remain a virgin until her marriage, then take care of the house, bear children and . . . be willing to accept her husband's infidelity.'[13] Despite that, over time his mind broadened as he met a series of brilliant modern women in the Socialist movement. He publicly endorsed giving women the right to vote and stand in elections, although he preferred that they stayed home and had large families to strengthen Italy. So, after he took power, he never granted women civil rights but did establish programmes that encouraged them to have as many children as possible.

Mussolini was twice married, for just a few months to Ada Dalser from December 1914 to February 1915 and from 17 December 1915 to Rachele Guidi. He had one child with Ada, born in 1915 and five children with Rachele, Edda born in 1910, Vittorio in 1916, Bruno in 1918, Romano in 1927 and Anna Maria in 1929. He was an aloof, stern father who hectored rather than playfully chatted with his children. He did adore Edda for her stubbornness, impetuosity and outspokenness that reflected his own.

Mussolini had a powerful sex drive and his machismo, power and fame attracted countless women. Among those smitten was Clementine Churchill, Winston's wife. During their meeting in March 1926, she gushed that he was 'one of the most wonderful men of our times' and found him 'quite him simple and natural, very dignified . . . [with] beautiful golden brown eyes which you can see but can't look at'.[14]

Over the decades, Mussolini had numerous fleeting sexual relations with women and several lengthy mistresses. He boasted of 'bedding' over 400 women, although countless landed on a couch or the floor.[15] The mistress who most entranced him was Leda Rafanelli, a feminist, socialist, novelist, poet, journalist and Muslim convert. After one especially heady sojourn, he wrote her that: 'Yesterday I spent three wonderful, swiftly dwindling hours with you. We spoke about everybody and everything. We have the same sympathies and antipathies in politics, in art, in philosophy, about the weather. We love solitude.' Another time, he wrote: 'With you I feel miles from Milan, journalism, politics, Italy, the West, Europe . . . Let's read Nietzsche and the Koran together. Listen. I am free every afternoon. Write to me when I can come and I shall be there, punctual and discreet.' She adored him just as much. She glorified him in an essay for *La Liberta*, an anarchist weekly as 'the socialist of heroic times. He is one who still feels, still believes in a virile and powerful way. He is a man.' She authored a novel with a disguised version of Mussolini as its hero.[16]

In stark contrast, his very traditional housewife Rachele endured Mussolini's bullying, boorishness and philandering, but he did not impress her. Long after his death, she revealed that 'he seemed like a lion, but really was a *pover uomo*, a poor chap'. She may have seemed like 'an abandoned wife, submissive to Benito and resigned to his infidelities . . . I admit that three women cause me great unhappiness – Ida Dalser, Margherita Sarfatti and Clara Petacci. But where is the man who does not deceive his wife at one time or another? Anyone in the *Duce*'s position was bound to attract attention.'[17]

What explains Mussolini's mass political appeal? He developed a polemical and demagogic speaking style that whipped audiences into zealous adoration. His speeches manipulated the frustrations, fears, hatreds and hopes that animated most people, identifying common enemies that they would vanquish together. He explained that 'one must always know how to strike the imagination of the public: that is the real secret of how to govern'.[18] His fiery theatrics obscured the banality of his crowd-pleasing bromides.

Mussolini profoundly understood psychology and sociology and carefully crafted his personality, behaviour, speeches and Fascist Party symbols and promises to entice and manipulate people. He knew that emotions, not reason, guide behaviour. People's loves and hates, desires and fears shape their choices, not strict calculations of costs and benefits. They want to be reassured, not challenged. They crave soothing myths and even prefer lies to hard facts that contradict their prejudices and dreams. They seek the comfort of the crowd rather than the spotlight of the podium or stage. Most people helplessly exist their entire lives in dreary routines subject to powerful others. Fatalistically, they accept what they cannot change. Indeed, they prefer security, not freedom with its dilemmas and duties. They will zealously follow a leader who appears strong even if he is wrong to a leader who is right but appears weak. They are content to live vicariously through the deeds of the charismatic leader they admire.

With that understanding of human nature in mind, Mussolini developed a personality cult (*Ducismo*) for himself as the all-powerful, all-knowing, infallible, great leader. His photograph adorned government offices, schoolrooms and military barracks, his poster walls and his statues in public squares across the nation. 'Mussolini is always right' was the key slogan the regime repeated endlessly. Like any popular 'Big Lie' loudly and repeatedly announced by leaders, publications and radio, gullible people immediately embraced it while knowledgeable people scoffed. Yet, with time, even most sceptics tolerated it even if they knew it was false.

His popularity traversed class lines, although ill-educated workers and peasants most enthusiastically embraced him. Countless women thrilled at his machismo and dreamt of being his lover. Men lived vicariously through his power, triumphs and mistresses. His followers believed that he genuinely cared about and sought to uplift their lives.

Any populist tyrant is inseparable from the people he inspires to grant him power and loyalty. Journalist Curzio Malaparte initially backed Mussolini and Fascism, but the Party expelled him in 1933 for his critical views. He explained the dynamic: 'It is not possible to draw a portrait of Mussolini, without drawing one, too, of the Italian people. His qualities and his defects are not his own. Rather they are the qualities and defects of all Italians.'[19]

A key value of Italian political culture enhanced Mussolini's appeal. '*Bella Figura*' or 'Beautiful Appearance' is style's triumph over substance. Just what Mussolini may have said was not as important as the theatrical way he said it. His utterances may have been false, bland or absurd but people accepted them if he put on a good show and looked good doing it. Mussolini quipped that governing Italians demanded 'only two things, policemen and bands playing in the street'.[20] During the war, he increasingly despaired at worsening opposition and the passive resistance of most Italians: 'The Italian race is a race of sheep. Eighteen years is not enough to change them . . . We must keep them disciplined and in uniform from morning until night . . . To make a people great it is necessary to send them into battle even if you have to kick them in the pants.'[21]

Mussolini had genuine political skills beyond oratory. The greatest challenge he faced and overcame was unifying an array of mutually antagonistic political groups under his firm leadership after the king named him prime minister in October 1922. Two decades later, he recalled just how onerous that was:

> If you could only imagine what an enormous effort it was to reach an arrangement that would not create conflicts between mutually jealous and suspicious rival powers, the government, the party, the monarchy, the Vatican, the army, the Militia, the prefects, party officials, heads of various national associations, powerful trusts, etc. . . . these are the indigestions of totalitarianism . . . It was an effort to overcome the traditional and specific shortcomings of the Italian people who are both great and petty, who have changed only externally after twenty years of steady therapy.[22]

What did Mussolini believe? Like most people, his beliefs evolved with time. His father was a devoted Socialist who indoctrinated him in that revolutionary ideology. Later as a 20-year-old journalist in an essay for the Lausanne newspaper, *The Worker's Future,* Mussolini expressed what most appealed to him about that creed: 'Socialism means the elevation and purification of the individual conscience and its achievement will be the result of long series of efforts. Everyone, indeed, from the professional man to the worker, can bring a stone to the edifice, doing a socialist deed every day and so prepare for the overthrow of existing society.'[23]

Mussolini condemned liberal individualism and humanism. He asserted that: 'the individual exists only insofar as he is subordinated to the state and as civilization becomes more complex, so the liberty of the individual must be increasingly restricted.'[24] Yet people willingly accept that subjection because the state personifies and protects the nation and thus gives its members an esteemed collective identity and meaning.

The core of Mussolini's beliefs was the Social Darwinian notion that groups struggle incessantly against each other to survive, prosper and subdue others. That struggle is progressive because groups with superior powers of leadership, organization, culture, cohesion, innovation, invention and fighting prowess vanquish their lessers and eventually uplift them. War ultimately brings out the best in groups and the individuals who compose them. He explained: 'War alone keeps all human energies at the maximum tension and sets the seal of nobility on those peoples who have the courage to face it.'[25] War was the ultimate test for manhood and nationhood. A man or nation was only as great as its ability to fight and conquer others.

Mussolini adored military pageantry, the officers with riding crops and jackets adorned with glittering medals; the immaculately uniformed troops shouldering rifles briskly goose-stepping past; the rumbling tanks with their long barrels. The phallocentrism and homoeroticism is unmistakable. The trauma of fighting on the front line in the First World War warped the lives and outlooks of countless veterans in Italy and elsewhere. Giovanni Gentile, Italian Fascism's leading philosopher, explained their psychology: 'For us the war has never come to an end. We simply replaced external enemies with internal ones'.[26]

Eventually, Mussolini abandoned International Socialism and embraced National Socialism, which he called Fascism.[27] Ideologically the idea of civil and international war was as vital for fascism as class and inter-class war was for communism. Mussolini noted that key contrast while addressing Communists in the Chamber of Deputies on 1 December 1921: 'I recognize that between us and the Communists there are no political affinities but there are intellectual affinities. We, like you, consider necessary a centralized and unitary state which imposes an iron discipline on all individuals, with this difference, that you arrive at this conclusion via the concept of class and we arrive there via the concept of nation.'[28]

French scholar Raymond Aaron explored the dynamic history between Communism and Fascism as each influenced and emulated the other:

> [I]n spite of their evident differences, Fascist and Communist regimes . . . have analogous origins and converging lines of evolution. The former move from an exacerbated nationalism to a kind of socialism; the latter, starting out from revolt and in the name of freedom, have resulted in a regime of authoritarian government and patriotic exaltation. The two forces . . . thus end in a paradoxical and perhaps

> odious reconciliation, thanks to 'the almost limitless powers which the modern structure of the state places at the disposal of revolutionaries and men of action'.[29]

Mussolini asserted Fascism's essence: 'the Fascist conception of the state is all-embracing; outside of it no human or spiritual values can exist, much less have value. Thus understood Fascism is totalitarian and the fascist state – a synthesis and a unit inclusive of all values – interprets, develops and potentiates the whole life of a people.'[30] Paradoxically, to achieve that fascism was a shapeshifting concept that varied with political expediency. Mussolini explained: 'We permit ourselves the luxury of being aristocratic and democratic, conservative and progressive, reactionary and revolutionary, accepting the law and going beyond it, according to the circumstances of the time, place and environment. In a word, of the "history" in which we must live and act.'[31] He insisted that 'we are not those who embalm a past. We are those who anticipate the future.'[32] To that end, paradoxically, he restricted his regime's political, economic and social power, explaining: 'No state is more totalitarian and authoritarian than the Fascist state; no state is more jealous of its sovereignty and prestige. But it is precisely because of that that the Fascist state does not feel required to interfere in matters beyond its competence and foreign to its nature.'[33] In other words, pragmatism would prevail over dogmatism, unlike in the Soviet Union where Joseph Stalin imposed a truly totalitarian communist regime.

By 1932, Mussolini insisted that Fascism not only fulfilled humanity's practical needs but also its spiritual yearnings:

> The Fascism State, as a higher and more powerful expression of personality, is a force, but a spiritual force. It sums up all the manifestations of the intellectual and moral life of man . . . The Fascist State is an inwardly accepted standard and rule of conduct, a discipline that permeates the will no less than the intellect . . . it dwells in the heart of the man of action and of the thinker, of the artist and of the man of science: soul of the soul.[34]

Thus did Mussolini's Fascism develop over time. Before October 1922, he asserted a radical, militant, violent Fascism to devastate rival parties and eventually bully the king into naming him prime minister. As the government's chief, his Fascism initially emphasized coalition-building and problem-solving that encouraged the Chamber of Deputies to grant him emergency, temporary power to better get things done. From January 1925, he had enough legal and political power to transform himself into an outright tyrant who outlawed all other political groups and politicians. From the invasion of Abyssinia in October 1935, the creation of a glorious Italian empire became Fascism's core expression.

Mussolini's Fascist movement and takeover of Italy in October 1922 inspired Fascists elsewhere across Europe and beyond. In November 1923, visiting Spanish General Primo de Rivera delighted Mussolini by gushing that: 'Your figure is not just an Italian one. You are the apostle of the world campaign against dissolution and anarchy . . . Fascism is a universal phenomenon that ought to conquer all nations . . . Fascism is a living gospel.'[35]

Mussolini sought to encourage Fascism's spread through 'parallelism' or communication and assistance among movements and governments in different countries to emulate and surpass each other. For instance, after Greek General Ioannis Metaxas suspended the constitution and asserted dictatorial powers on 4 August 1936, Mussolini sent him this blueprint for establishing a fascist regime: '1. to organize a single governing party. 2. to create a single organization of Greek youth. 3. to create a single organization of employers and workers recognized by law and entailing a collective work contract with legal standing. 4. to create a *dopolavoro* [afterwork leisure organizations] on the Italian mode.'[36]

Il Duce can be compared insightfully to countless dictators throughout history, best with his fellow Fascist tyrant north of the Alps.[37] Benito Mussolini and Adolf Hitler had bullying fathers who warped and stunted their emotional development, rendering them angry, histrionic, mistrustful, aggressive, manipulative and domineering.[38] Both compensated for a deep sense of inferiority and inadequacy by projecting supreme confidence in themselves and scapegoating other individuals and groups as enemies to be scorned and repressed. Both became skilled demagogues that whipped crowds into frenzies of adoration and devotion to themselves. Both were draft dodgers before serving in the army, although Hitler volunteered and Mussolini was drafted. Both were found guilty of sedition and served prison terms. Both composed their own speeches and wrote at length about their views, but relied on a key intellectual to elaborate his political philosophy, Giovanni Gentile and Alfred Rosenberg, respectively. Both symbolically exemplified his version of autocracy, Mussolini Fascism, Hitler Nazism,

Both were obsessed with being all-powerful but getting fabulously rich disinterested them. Both lived frugally even after becoming wealthy, Mussolini from his newspaper *Il Populo d'Italia* and Hitler from his bestselling autobiography *Mein Kampf* (*My Struggle*). Both wielded state funds to corrupt and coopt key political or business leaders but diverted relatively little to themselves or their cronies. Hitler had a handful of relatives who he ensured had comfortable, secure lives. Mussolini had a huge extended family through himself and his wife that he helped with stipends and jobs.

Eventually they deeply bonded, although their relationship's dynamic seesawed with time.[39] Hitler adored and emulated Mussolini as a demagogue and populist who founded and developed the Fascist movement that took over Italy and became its dictator. His Nazi Party with himself its supreme leader was his version of the Fascist Party, but initially failed to take political power. Loyal police and soldiers crushed his Nazi Party's 'March on Berlin' in October 1923 and a court sentenced him and most of his inner circle to prison. Behind bars, Hitler wrote in *Mein Kampf* that:

> In this period . . . I conceived the profoundest admiration for the great man south of the Alps, who, full of ardent love for his people, made no pacts with the enemies of Italy, but strove for their annihilation by all ways and means. What will rank Mussolini among the great men of this earth is his determination not to share Italy with the Marxists, but to destroy internationalism and save the fatherland from it.[40]

In other ways, Mussolini and Hitler starkly contrasted. Mussolini was a workaholic with 14-hour days in which he chaired key policy committees; Hitler was in the office at most half that time and often did not bother showing up until late morning. Mussolini had a successful career as a journalist before entering politics; Hitler was a failed artist who spent years in Bohemian poverty in Vienna and Munich. Although both fought in the First World War, Mussolini endured 18 months at the front before being hospitalized and eventually honourably discharged after being wounded by a grenade's accidental explosion during a training exercise; Hitler was a genuine hero with nearly four years in the trenches during which he won two Iron Crosses. Mussolini took power on his first try; Hitler's first attempt was a disaster that landed him in prison. Mussolini was a womanizer with numerous mistresses and offspring beyond his wife and five children with her; Hitler apparently had a low sex drive, few girlfriends and no known offspring.

Of the two, Hitler was more decisive and ruthless. Worried that Ernst Röhm, who headed the Brownshirt Storm Troops (*Sturmabteilung*, SA) militia, might overthrow him, Hitler had him and around 200 other suspects arrested on 30 June 1934 and shot then or later. In contrast, Mussolini fired or reassigned to distant posts those he feared might usurp him. His ministers and advisors rarely lasted more than a year or so. Hitler was the German military's commander-in-chief. According to Italy's constitution, the king was the commander-in-chief and throughout his regime Mussolini struggled to assert that power for himself.

They differed over the targets of their initial imperialism. Mussolini was an opportunist who sought to expand Italy's empire with 'easy' conquests like Ethiopia and Albania. Irredentism or liberating and uniting German speakers within the Third Reich primarily motivated Hitler to take over Austria in March 1938, the Sudetenland from Czechoslovakia in September 1938 and Poland in September 1939. Yet a key imperial goal that united them was acquiring 'living space' (*lebensraum, spazio vitale*) for their excess populations.

Morally, the crucial difference was the number of people each had murdered. Mussolini established a Special Tribunal for political crimes like treason including espionage and plots for coups and assassination in 1927; from 1927 to 1943, the Special Tribunal condemned 42 people to death and executed 31 of them and found 13,547 others guilty of lesser crimes for which they altogether received 27,742 years in prison, although most got off with reprimands.[41] Arguably, those convictions were lawful, not arbitrary. Then there were the hundreds of brutal murders and thousands of beatings and tortures committed by Fascist thugs against political enemies from 1919 to 1945; Mussolini ordered some of those crimes and encouraged the rest. While Mussolini may have been relatively restrained in fighting European enemies, he was utterly ruthless toward Africans who opposed him. Tens of thousands of Libyans and Ethiopians died resisting Italian imperialism, while starvation and disease may have killed a hundred thousand or so more. Yet, however horrific Mussolini's crimes were, two other tyrants of that era far surpassed him. Hitler had millions of people murdered either in his concentration camp system or by death squads that followed his armies' conquests. Stalin had hundreds of thousands of people murdered, millions imprisoned on treason charges and millions murdered through starvation or being worked to death in his Gulag concentration camp system.

Biographer R.J.B. Bosworth noted key differences with Mussolini:

> A bully, a coward and a failure . . . Promiscuity, boasting, strutting, vanity, petty cruelty, incompetence – these were the words most associated with Mussolini and they have painted him as more a figure of fun than of the sort of dread reserved for his fellow dictators, Hitler and Stalin. These latter were fearful totalitarian tyrants. Mussolini, though it was he who

> first announced the intention of building a 'totalitarian state', was but a 'Sawdust Caesar', no more than a buffoon.

Bosworth further observed that: 'Mussolini, unlike what remains the received understanding of "friend" Adolf Hitler, was . . . a man not so different from many another. In his crass vainglory, his appalling sexism and racism, his innumerable sins of omission, his sad Darwinism, there . . . went numbers of Italians of his generation, and there go . . . many of us.'[42]

After Hitler took power in 1933, their relationship flipflopped over the next dozen years. Initially, Hitler was a fawning supplicant while Mussolini was sceptical, aloof and privately disdainful. From 1938 to 1941, Mussolini was increasingly dazzled by Hitler's diplomatic coups whereby Germany engulfed Austria and Czechoslovakia then his Wehrmacht blitzkriegs that conquered Poland, Norway, the Low Countries and France and overran most of the western Soviet Union, capturing and killing millions of enemy soldiers. Hitler was increasingly contemptuous of Mussolini for his inept dictatorship and military whose follies in North Africa and the Balkans had forced him to divert German armies to the rescue. Mussolini joined Hitler in declaring war against the United States after their ally Japan attacked Pearl Harbor and the Philippines. Both dictators became increasingly desperate, despairing and deluded as the Allies racked up victory after victory on the Soviet Front, North Africa and Sicily. Mussolini became Hitler's puppet after the Italian government arrested him, a German commando team rescued him and the *Führer* set him up in the 'Salo Republic' in northern Italy. They died within two days of each other in April 1945 as their regime collapsed around them, Mussolini and his mistress killed by partisans and Hitler and his new wife by suicide. What each thought of the other during their last moments was unrecorded but likely mingled the deepest regret and disgust.

Another apt comparison is Mussolini with Franciso Franco who endured in power from the time he won the civil war in 1939 until his death in 1975. The most vital reason for Franco's longevity was that he did not involve Spain in any wars during that time, unlike the catastrophic series that Mussolini and Hitler blundered themselves into that led to the extinction of themselves and their regimes. Biographer Paul Preston lauded Franco's brilliance in massing and wielding 'powers that were comparable to those of Hitler and greater than those of Mussolini' who had the 'ability to calibrate almost instantly the weakness and/or price of a man' and 'with consummate skill, striking decisively at his outright enemies but maintaining the loyalty of those within the Nationalist coalition with cunning and a perceptive insight into human weakness worthy of a man who learned his politics among the tribes of Morocco'.[43]

Benito Mussolini and the Art of Tyranny explores the nature of the dictator and his regime and their strengths, weaknesses, triumphs, disasters and legacies. That is not just fascinating in itself, but provides valuable insights and lessons for contemporary politics. Fascism did not die with Mussolini, but endured and recently is spreading to ever more countries. The 'Legacy' chapter reveals why Fascism is increasingly so virulent and appealing to people around the world.

Chapter 1

THE UPBRINGING

> I was an arrogant and violent child. Some of my schoolmates still have scars on their faces from the stones that I threw at them.
>
> (Benito Mussolini)

> My greatest love was for my mother. She was so quiet, so tender and yet so strong . . . To displease her was my one fear.
>
> (Bentio Mussolini)

> When she got up weeping and humiliated she insulted me by saying I had robbed her of her honour and it is not impossible that she spoke the truth. But I ask you, what kind of honour could she have meant?
>
> (Benito Mussolini)

> One day Italy will be afraid of me.
>
> (Benito Mussolini)

Benito Amilcare Andrea Mussolini was born on 29 July 1883, to Alessandro and Rosa Maltoni Mussolini. His birthplace was the hamlet of Dovia near Predappio, a village in the Apennine Mountain foothills 10 miles south of Forli, the provincial capital. Alessandro was a domineering Italian patriot and local socialist leader, active since 1874. The authorities arrested him for his radicalism in 1878 and kept him under house arrest until they released him for his pending wedding. He named his son Benito for Benito Jaurez, Mexico's president who resisted and eventually overcame the French invasion and imposition of Emperor Maximilian I, an Austrian Habsburg prince, in 1864; Jaurez and his followers overthrew Maximilian's regime in 1867. The other two names came from his socialist comrades Amilcare Cipriano and

Andrea Costa; Costa became the first socialist elected to Parliament in 1882. Benito's devout mother Rosa got her husband briefly to set aside his anticlericalism and have their son was baptized in the local church.

The Mussolinis enjoyed a lower middle class income with Alessandro a blacksmith and Rosa a teacher. Two younger siblings eventually joined Mussolini, Arnaldo in 1885 and sister Evige in 1888. Mussolini was close to both. Arnaldo became Mussolini's most trusted political advisor and his death in 1931 deeply depressed him.

Their mother Rosa was highly intelligent, attended an academy that taught education and became a schoolteacher among the few professions open to women at that time. To the school's administrators, she explained her methodology:

> In teaching geography I follow the most rational method and avoid the formality of complex naming which simply loads the mind with abstract and so useless, ideas. Such concepts hang around for a while in a pupil's mind but soon just disappear. In regard to history, I understand the sentiment involved, seeking above all to foster character in children, as well as reinforcing their resolution and determination.[1]

Mussolini did not begin to speak until he was three years old. Rosa took him to a doctor at Forli who found nothing physically wrong and reassured her: 'Don't worry my good woman, soon he will talk too much'.[2] Biographer Richard Bosworth attributed Mussolini's arrested linguistic development to turmoil between his father and mother.[3] Both parents were strong-willed, outspoken and unaffectionate; his father was controlling, manipulative, critical and a firm believer in the 'spare the rod and spoil the child' upbringing for his children, especially rambunctious and aggressive Benito. For Mussolini, 'My greatest love was for my mother. She was so quiet, so tender and yet so strong . . . To displease her was my one fear.'[4]

Decades later, Mussolini admitted that he was a troubled and troubling youth: 'I was an arrogant and violent child. Some of my schoolmates still have scars on their faces from the stones that I threw at them. A nomad by instinct, I wandered long the river from morning until night, robbing birds' nests and stealing fruit . . . I followed my mother. I helped my father in his modest work.' At one point, he presciently warned his mother that, 'One day Italy will be afraid of me'.[5]

When Mussolini was nine, his parents sent him to the Salesian Order's boarding school at nearby Faenza. He was a poor student who ranked in his class's bottom third. He was unhappy there with its silent meals, wretched food, strict discipline and daily mass. He was vindictive, vengeful, cruel and violent. By one account, he 'sought quarrels for their own sake and because he needed to dominate; if he won a bet he asked more than his due, if he lost he tried to avoid payment'.[6] Two years later he was expelled after stabbing a student in the hand with his penknife.

His parents were able to get him admitted to a state high school called the College Giosue Carducci at Forlimpopoli. He began studying dutifully, scored higher grades and was not expelled after threatening a classmate with a knife. He did best in pedagogy, language and literature and less well in maths and agriculture. He learned to play the trombone. He became a skilled orator and in 1901 the College selected him to give a speech commemorating the composer Giuseppe Verdi. He penned poems that he tore up and essays that he submitted to publications. His first publication was a discourse on the Russian novel that appeared in a local teachers' magazine in December 1901.

He began seducing girls and swelled with pride at his conquests. In his autobiography, he admitted raping one girl: 'I caught her on the stairs, throwing her into a corner behind a door and made her mine. When she got up weeping and humiliated she insulted me by saying I had robbed her of her honour and it is not impossible that she spoke the truth. But I ask you, what kind of honour could she have meant?'[7]

Mussolini graduated from the high school in 1901 and sought to become a teacher. He suffered rejections for being too young until February 1902, when he received his first job at a small elementary school in the village of Pieve Saliceto. His father reacted not with congratulations but with condemnation: 'What a dreadful state of affairs! A teacher . . . An educated young man reduced to being a mere servant.'[8]

Despite such a remote school with its young students, Mussolini revelled in his title '*professore*' or teacher. Yet the administration rejected his attempt to get his contract renewed in June 1902. His morals likely had as much to do with that dismissal as his pedagogy. He spent his off hours drinking and gambling with cronies and pocketed a knife and brass-knuckles for protection. He caused a scandal by having an affair with a soldier's wife whose husband was posted elsewhere. He gloated by how he treated her: 'I accustomed her to my exclusive and tyrannical love; she obeyed me blindly and let me dispose of her as I wished.'[9] He stabbed her in a quarrel between them. He was just 18 years old.

He sought to escape his past and a likely pending army draft notice on 9 July 1902 by boarding the first of several trains that carried him to Lausanne, Switzerland. Shortly after arriving he learned that his father had been arrested and would serve a half-year prison term, although why has been lost. He spent his 19th birthday in exile. He would stay in Switzerland for most of the next two years during which he became highly proficient in French and German and experienced a political and philosophical awakening.

The Italian state that Mussolini fled was just two generations old.[10] Before that, the last time that the peninsula was politically united was the fifth century under the tottering Roman Empire. During those intervening thirteen centuries, Italy was nothing more than a 'geographic expression', Austrian Prince Klemens von Metternich's apt term for the shifting mosaics of states.

Napoleon Bonaparte was united Italy's grandfather. During his initial conquests then French occupation from 1796 to 1814, he consolidated the peninsula into three states: much of Piedmont, Liguria, Tuscany and the Papal States as French departments; much of Lombardy, Venezia and Romagna as first the Republic then Kingdom of Italy, with himself the king; and southern Italy as the Kingdom of Naples ruled first by his brother Joseph then by his brother-in-law Joachim Murat. Each realm received a French-style constitution, legal system and administration along with economic unification and subsidies for key war industries.

The Great Powers, Britain, Prussia, Austria and Russia, defeated, deposed and exiled Napoleon twice, first to the island of Elba n 1814, then after his escape and return to power in France, permanently following the Battle of Waterloo with his interment on the remote island of St. Helena in 1815. Meanwhile, the Great Powers convened a Congress of all Europe's states at Vienna with the goal of returning the continent to the monarchical values and states that prevailed before the radical French Revolution's liberalism and nationalism erupted in 1789. Thereafter, Austria, Russia, Prussia, France and Britain formed a Concert of Europe that met occasionally at various cities to coordinate military efforts to crush revolutionary liberal and nationalist revolts.

In Italy, the Great Powers restored nine of the pre-1796 states, with the most important the north-west Kingdom of Piedmont-Sardinia with its capital at Turin; the southern Kingdom of the Two Sicilies with its capital at Naples; the Papal States with their capital at Rome; and the Austrian Empire with its capital at Vienna and control over north-eastern Italy split among autonomous provinces, with the most important Lombardy, Venezia and Tuscany.

Three brilliant leaders were crucial for Italy's unification, Giuseppe Mazzini, a revolutionary; Giuseppe Garibaldi, a general; and Camille

Benso, Count Cavour, a statesman. Mazzini led the way with his 'Young Italy' or 'Resurgence' (*Risorgimento*) movement of liberalism and nationalism that he promoted through pamphlets and secret organizing. Revolutionary groups called Carboni committed to a unified Italian republic mushroomed across Italy. Those ideals inspired Garibaldi, a merchant from Nice who journeyed to Latin America to help those countries fight for independence from the Spanish and Portuguese empires. Cavour rose through the ranks of Piedmont-Sardinia's government with his own vision for his realm creating a unified, modern, economically dynamic Italy.

The turning point was 1848, when liberal and nationalist revolutions spread across Europe including in Turin, Milan and Naples. Most of the Italian states crushed the revolts with reactionary zeal. However, Piedmont-Sardinian King Carl Albert did so by granting his subjects a 'Statute' (*Statuo*), essentially a constitution, on 4 March 1848. The Statute bound the monarchy by law, established an appointed Senate, an elected Chamber of Deputies and an appointed Council of Ministers headed by a prime minister officially known as President of the Council and granted his subjects civil rights that effectively made them citizens. Nonetheless, the king reserved executive power for himself. The Statute's Article 5 clearly states that: 'To the King alone appertains Executive Power. He is the Supreme Head of the State; he commands all the Armed Forces on land and sea; he declares war, makes treaties of peace and alliance.' That Statute governed first the Kingdom of Piedmont-Sardinia then, after unification in 1861, the Kingdom of Italy until 1946.[11]

When Italian patriots in Milan and Venice revolted against Austrian rule and declared independence in March 1848, Carl Albert joined forces with them in what became the First Italian War of Independence. Initially, the Italians expelled the Austrians but Austrian commander Joseph Radetsky massed reinforcements, crushed the revolts, defeated the Piedmont-Sardinian army at the Battle of Custoza and restored Austrian rule by August 1948. Carl Albert abdicated in favour of his son Victor Emmanuel II. The new king embraced his father's ambition for Piedmont-Sardinia and Italy. He launched a war against Austria in early 1849, but the Austrians defeated his army at Novara in March.

Cavour was elected to the Chamber of Deputies. Victor Emmanuel II recognized his brilliance and named him Agriculture and Trade Minister from 1850 to 1852, Finance Minister from 1851 to 1852 and finally Prime Minister from 1852 until his death in 1861. Cavour recognized that the revolutionary forces of liberalism and nationalism could not be crushed for long, only coopted. As he rose through the government ranks, he talked Victor Emmanuel into a new attempt to unify Italy, this time in alliance with France.

Thanks to a massive French army, the Kingdom of Piedmont-Sardinia won the Second War for Italian Independence as the allied army defeated the Austrians at the battles of Magenta on 4 June and Solferino on 24 June 1859; Garibaldi played a crucial role in this war. The peace terms took nine months to negotiate, but on 22 March 1860, Piedmont-Sardinia annexed Tuscany, Modena and part of the Papal States while France took Nice and Savoy and the Austrians retook Lombardy and Venezia. In early 1861, Garibaldi led a thousand 'Redshirts' to invade Sicily then southern Italy as Victor Emmanuel advanced south with his army to crush the Kingdom of the Two Sicilies. Victor Emmanuel II declared himself the King of Italy on 17 March 1861.

Victor Emmanuel took advantage of a war between Austria and Prussia to capture Lombardy and Venezia from 20 June to 12 August in 1866, then annexed those regions to Italy. In a brief war with the Papacy, the Italian army conquered Rome on 20 September 1870 and annexed that city and the rest of the Papal States. Italy's first capital was Turin where parliament recognized Victor Emmanuel as Italy's king on 17 March 1862, then Florence from 3 February 1865 to 3 February 1871 and finally Rome ever since.

State-building involves reforming or creating political institutions in a system that protects and develops the inhabitants. Nation-building involves uniting a people who share a common or similar language, values, traditions and aspirations. The latter is far more challenging than the former because it involves changing often deep-set mentalities rather than institutions. It was Massimo d'Azeglio, prime minster from May 1849 to November 1852, who famously said, 'We have made Italy, now we must make Italians'. Nearly all Italians did not identify as such, but instead identified primarily with their clan and village or city neighbourhood. Their ruler and realm were abstractions. The most recent versions, Victor Emmanuel II and Italy, puzzled most people. Language was a critical impediment to making Italians. The peninsula and large islands of Sicily and Sardinia were mosaics of hundreds of dialects. Only about 2.5 per cent of Italians spoke the official language in 1860. A national school system was the best way to instil standard Italian, but that process would slowly evolve over generations.

Italy's ruling elite gradually, steadily transformed the political system into a democracy.[12] Plebiscites in 1860, 1866 and 1870 expanded the electorate and rights. A big jump came with a 1882 law that tripled the number of qualified voters from 600,000 and 2.18 per cent of the population to over 2,000,000 and 6.97 per cent. Yet by 1900, Italy trailed well behind other democratizing countries in the portion of adults that could vote with 8 per cent compared to 15 per cent in Russia, 16 per cent in Romania, 18 per cent in Britain, 22 per cent in Germany, 23 per cent in Serbia and Belgium and 29 per cent in France, although above 6 per cent in Hungary.[13] Meanwhile, Italy's population expanded from 26 million in 1871 to 37 million in 1914, despite losing 10 million to emigration overseas, mostly to the United States just from 1896 to 1915.[14] Five times more men immigrated than women.

The economy steadily modernized with a railway system, electrical, sewage, fresh water and telephone grids in cities and beyond, and mass-production factories.[15] The industrial core was the triangular region among Turin, Milan and Genoa. Italy's economy expanded an average 2.8 per cent from 1896 to 1913, faster than France's 1.9 per cent and Britain's 1.7, but behind Germany's 3.2 per cent.[16]

Yet, overall Italy lagged far behind the other great powers by most economic measures. Italy's population and thus potential mass market in 1913 was 35.1 million compared to France's 39.7 million, Britain's 45.6 million, Japan's 51.3 million, Austria-Hungary's 52.1 million, Germany's 66.9 million, America's 97.3 million and Russia's 175.1 million. If Britain's per capita industrialization level in 1900 was 100, by 1913, Italy's was 26, compared above 20 for Russia and Japan but behind Austria-Hungary's 32, France's 59, Germany's 85, Britain's 115 and America's 126. With Britain's total industrial potential 100 in 1900, Italy's 22.5 in 1913 was last compared to Japan's 25.1, Austria-Hungary's 40.7 per cent, France's 57.3, Russia's 76.6,, Britain's 127.2, Germany's 137.7 and America's 298.1. Italy's 2.4 per cent share of world manufacturing in 1913 was far behind Austria-Hungary's 4.4 per cent, France's 6.1 per cent, Russia's 8.2 per cent, Britain's 13.6 per cent, Germany's 14.8 per cent and America's 32.0 per cent.[17]

What those numbers do not reveal is the varying and often vast discrepancies in each country between the upper, middle and lower classes, with abysmal poverty afflicting those at the bottom. Of those countries, most people had comfortable middle or opulent upper incomes only in America, Britain and Germany, roughly even numbers of middle and upper incomes to lower incomes in France and Austria-Hungary and mostly lower incomes in Italy and Russia. In every country, those discrepancies had increasingly severe political consequences.

A radical, militant alternative to liberalism and nationalism emerged in the mid-nineteenth century and became increasingly virulent during the late nineteenth century. Karl Marx and his partner Friedrich

Engels developed what was variously called Marxism, Socialism and Communism through publications and organizations. Their 'Communist Manifesto' of 1848 called for revolution of the working class (proletariat) against their business owner (bourgeoisie) oppressors; that publication coincided with and helped fuel the revolutions that erupted across Europe that year by masses of impoverished, exploited and desperate mostly city-dwellers. Authorities in each country managed to crush the revolutionaries or to co-opt them with promised reforms. Marx, Engel and other socialist leaders formed the First International of socialist parties in 1864 that lasted until 1876, when it broke up between socialists and anarchists. Socialist leaders formed the Second International that banned anarchists in 1889; it lasted until 1916, when it broke amidst the First World War as workers fought in their national armies' ranks against each other rather than against their respective governments.

Filippo Turati led the Italian Socialist Party's founding at Genoa in 1892.[18] He was elected to the Chamber of Deputies in 1896. He represented the Socialist Party's 'Reformist' majority dedicated to bettering working peoples' lives through laws and regulations within the democratic system. Fiercely opposing the 'Reformists' were the 'Maximalists' who advocated violent revolution; Mussolini was a Maximalist before he became a Fascist.

With unification, Italy was considered among the six Great Powers along with Britain, France, Russia, Germany and Austria-Hungary.[19] A movement led by parliamentarians Sidney Sonnino and Pasquale Mancini called for Italy to emulate Europe's other great powers by conquering an empire.[20] Prime Minister Francesco Crispi embraced that movement, arguing that Italy, like Germany, wanted an imperial 'place in the sun' or overseas empire for wealth, power, prestige, excess population and native soldiers, labourers and consumers. As latecomer unified states, Italy and Germany fought for territorial scraps left after previous conquests by other great powers.

Italy joined the 'Scramble for Africa' in the late nineteenth century that within a generation carved that continent into swaths of colonies. The Great Powers were united in wanting to peacefully resolve the 'Eastern Question', how to divvy tup he declining Ottoman Empire. Russia's victory over the Ottoman Empire in a war from 1877 to 1878 led the Great Powers to meet in Berlin to sort out who got what. The Russians, British and French respectively took Cyprus and Tunisia. The great powers rejected Italy's demand to take the Ottoman North African provinces of Tripolitania and Cyrenaica.

Like other European powers with overseas empires, trading companies took the first imperial step for several colonies. For instance, Italy's colony of Eritrea began when a merchant firm purchased land bordering Assab Bay from the local sultanate in 1869.[21] Italy declared Assab a colony in 1882 and over the next three years annexed ever more of the northward coast. In January 1885, a battalion of troops landed unopposed at the Red Sea port of Massawa, 370 miles from Assab.

From Massawa, the Italians pushed inland into Abyssinia (Ethiopia), the last independent African kingdom. Abyssinian Emperor Yohannes ordered his army to repel the invaders. The Abyssinian army wiped out 500 Italian troops at Dogali in 1887. Yohannes died two years later. With the Treaty of Wachale, Emperor Minilik II ceded his realm's northern tip to Italy in March 1889.

The Italians united their Red Sea territory into a colony they called Eritrea on 1 January 1890. Prime Minister Francesco Crispi declared Eritrea's importance as the first stage in Abyssinia's eventual conquest: 'Ethiopia extends its hands to us . . . A vast region has been opened to our industry and commerce without any sacrifice of blood . . . Vast zones of land for settlement would in the foreseeable future be offered to the fecund Italian.'[22]

Crispi's government authorized Eritrea's governor General Oreste Baratieri to take over more land on the long road to Addis Abada, the Abyssinian empire's capital. Menelik massed 73,000 armed men and overwhelmed Baratieri's 17,500 troops at Adwa on 1 March 1896, killing 5,900 and capturing 2,000, while suffering 3,886 dead and 6,000 wounded.[23] Baratieri led his army's remnants back to Eritrea. Forty years later, Benito Mussolini would avenge that humiliating disaster.

Chapter 2

THE RADICAL

> Let us have no more talk of battleships, barracks, cannon, at a time when thousands of villages have no schools, roads, electricity or doctors, but still live tragically beyond the pale of civilized life.
>
> (Benito Mussolini)

> What we must do is not study the world but transform it . . . The interests of the proletariat are opposed to those of the middle class. No agreement between them is possible. One or the other must disappear.
>
> (Benito Mussolini)

> Twelve years of my life in the party are or ought to be sufficient guarantee of my socialist faith. Socialism is in my very blood.
>
> (Benito Mussolini)

In Lausanne, Benito Mussolini talked his way into being a journalist for the weekly socialist journal, *The Future of Workers* (*L'Avvenire del Lavoratore*). The chief editor was Tito Barbone who headed Switzerland's Italian Socialist Party. Over the next half year, Mussolini got nine articles published in the journal and also penned essays for other publications like *The Proletariat* (*Il Proletario*). He gave rousing radical speeches before various socialist audiences. He acquired a swelling reputation for being a political firebrand and leader. He was exultant when the liberal Rome newspaper *La Tribuna* described him as a '*grande duce*' (major leader) in April 1904.[1]

The revolutionary rhetoric that Mussolini used during his public speeches and his other illicit activities got him arrested and deported, first in 1903 from Berne where he spent two weeks in jail for publicly calling for a general strike before being transported to Italy. He was soon back agitating in Switzerland. He was arrested again for falsifying his Swiss visa's expiration date in Geneva and expelled on 6 April 1904, then slipped back.

Nonetheless, Switzerland and most of its cantons were relatively more tolerant of radical views than other realms like Russia, Austria-Hungary and Germany. Radicals from those countries fled to safety in Switzerland because it was democratic, neutral and multinational. Vladimir Lenin and Leon Trotsky were the most notorious of scores of hardline Russian Communists that formed communities in Zurich, Geneva, Berne and other Swiss cities.

Switzerland had a parliamentary system established in 1848. Delegates from the cantons devised the Federal Constitution that established a National Assembly, with a National Council elected by qualified voters with 111 seats distributed proportional among the canton's populations and a Council of State with delegates elected by canton governments. Switzerland was a multinational state whose cantons split among speakers of German north and east, French west and Italian south; in some cantons one language dominated, while others had two or three mingled languages. The cantons remained autonomous, each with its own laws, regulations and police force, including a secret branch that spied on political dissidents.

During a socialist gathering at Geneva in March 1904. Mussolini befriended Angelica Balabanoff, a Russia communist. Until then he had only read the revolutionary pamphlet 'The Communist Manifesto', by Karl Marx and Friedrich Engels. Balabanoff tutored Mussolini in Marxism and a broader array of radical views including those of Friedrich Nietzsche, Louis Blanqui, Karl Kautsky, Peter Kropotkin, George Sorel and Arthur Schopenhauer. Amidst these heady days, he learned of his Italian army draft notice in March 1904. He ignored it and when he did not appear the army declared him a draft dodger. He enrolled in the University of Lausanne's Department of Social Science in May 1904. His most influential class was taught by Vilfredo Pareto, a brilliant social scientist on leave from the University of Florence.

What explains Mussolini's radical beliefs and the zeal with which he asserted them during those exile years and thereafter?[2] In her autobiography, Balabanoff observed the sources of Mussolini's radicalism as 'more the reflection of his early environment and his own rebellious ego than the product of understanding and conviction; his hatred of oppression was not that impersonal hatred of a system shared by all revolutionaries; it sprang rather from his own sense of indignity and frustration, from a passion to assert his own ego and from a determination for personal revenge'.[3]

Biographer Denis Mack Smith elaborated those insights:

> Some of his fierce talk was an affectation adopted by a person still trying to discover himself, but throughout his life much of the real Mussolini was hidden by a succession of poses, many of which reveal aspects of his character. The frequent changes of opinion do not necessarily mean that he was an intellectual light-weight, but rather that he placed little value on ideas. He appeared to adopt opinions merely because they fitted some new attitude or would help his career. He sometimes seemed to change his whole philosophical outlook overnight and would justify the fact as an example of an inner intuition that he came to consider as infallible.[4]

Mussolini learned that the Italian government was granting amnesty to draft dodgers who joined the army. He chose to accept the amnesty and report for duty at Bologna. He served in the 10th Bersagliere, an elite light infantry regiment, at Verona from January 1905 to September 1906. He was just a month into his service when he received a furlough to rush to his mother who was afflicted with meningitis and mourn her death on 19 February 1905. Her death devastated him: 'For many days I was lost. From me had been taken the one dear and truly near living being, the one soul closest . . . My mother had suffered . . . because of my wanderings and pugnacious life.'[5]

With deep sorrow, Mussolini returned to his regiment. During his 18 months of military service, he began questioning but still retained his socialist anti-militarism, anti-nationalism and internationalism. After his honourable discharge in September 1906, he decided to stay in Italy rather than return to Switzerland's radical exile communities.

Mussolini passed a University of Bologna test that qualified him to teach French in November 1907. He got a teaching post at the small fishing port of Oneglia, on the Ligurian coast in March 1908. At Oneglia, he wrote essays for various socialist publications. In July 1908, he resigned his post and journeyed to Trento, in the Austro-Hungarian empire, where he became the Labour Chamber's secretary and edited the weekly socialist newspaper *The Future of Workers* (*L'Avvenire del Lavaratore*), the same publication he had worked on in Lausanne.

A month after arriving in Trento, police arrested him for suspected theft and while searching his apartment discovered seditious writings. Although a jury acquitted him on 24 September, the Austrian authorities expelled him. In an editorial commemorating Karl Marx 25 years after his death, Mussolini asserted these revolutionary communist maxims: 'What we must do is not study the world but transform it . . . The interests of the proletariat are opposed to those of the middle class. No agreement between them is possible. One or the other must disappear.'[6]

He returned to Forli where his father owned a restaurant. He became editor of the Socialist Party's weekly four-page newspaper *The Class Struggle* (*La Lotta di Classe*) on 9 January 1910. Over several months, he boosted subscribers to over a thousand and revelled that his fiery editorials attracted those eager readers.

He fell in love with Rachele Guidi, the daughter of his father's girlfriend.[7] Rachele described what they looked like then: 'I was slim with blond hair and small mischievous blue eyes. No one was better at climbing trees or caching birds . . . He'd grown a moustache and a small beard and wore a loose neck-tie, a big black hat and a threadbare suit, with newspapers sticking out of the pockets. But what struck me most of all was the gleam in his eyes, which seemed larger than ever.' As for their courtship:

> Each time we met on subsequent Sundays, our affection for each other grew. Not that Benito ever played the great lover . . . We went for long walks in the countryside, hardly speaking. Now and again, Benito would kick a stone out of the way as if he were dismissing an idea or an opponent, then turn to me and say: 'We'll get rid of them in the end. We'll chase out the bourgeois, the rich landowners who get a good living from their estates'. I had my own revolutionary ideas but his forcefulness made me uneasy. I said: 'They'll put you in prison, Benito, as they did before'. . . . Benito and I went dancing. He was a fine dancer . . . Benito played the violin and we danced. I discovered what a fine musician he was.[8]

Rachele fell in love with Mussolini for many reasons but especially for 'his fearlessness in facing and overcoming obstacles . . . the kindness behind his apparent gruffness and pride . . . his youthful confidence in his future and I must admit that I was overjoyed to be so ardently desired . . . I felt quite maternal toward him . . . that tender feeling which is the secret of a woman in love'.[9]

He got her pregnant and she gave birth to their daughter, Edda, on 1 September 1910, but they did not then marry. Rachele explained that he had promised to marry her but angrily broke it off when he learned 'of a particular male companion' of hers and he 'made me burn his letters'. He confronted her other lover and warned him never to see her again. He then asked her to marry him but this time she refused because she reasoned that 'a man who spent all his time in political demonstrations or in prison was no husband for me'.[10]

He set Rachele and Edda up in a two-room apartment in Forli and lived off and on with them over the next five years. He was

> devoted to his daughter. He would rock her, spend hours watching her sleep . . . Like all babies, Edda would sometimes wake and cry in the night. Whatever the time, he would play the violin until she when back to sleep . . . Later when she was just three, he took her everywhere – even the newspaper office. So by the age of four, she already knew the alphabet and used to write it proudly with chalk on the kitchen floor.[11]

He wrote a novel called *Claudia Particella: The Cardinal's Mistress* with an anticlerical theme that was published first in Italy then translated into several other languages including English. He also got published a polemical anticlerical pamphlet called 'John Hus, the Man of Truth'. He attended the Socialist Party conference in Milan in October 1910. At age 56, his father died on 19 November 1910.

Italy suffered worsening political turmoil. An anarchist murdered King Umberto I on 29 July 1900 and his son took the throne as Victor Emmanuel III. Labourers were increasingly militant and organized to demand better pay and work conditions; strikes and violence were increasingly common. Rural socialists established the peasant National Federation of Agricultural Workers (*Federterra*) from 758 local groups with 152,000 combined members in 1901. Urban socialists formed the General Confederation of Labour on 1 October 1906. In reaction, corporate leaders established the General Confederation of Industry (*Confindustria*) on 5 May 1910.

The Socialist Party steadily expanded its number of Chamber of Deputies seats, although they attracted a smaller share of voters than in most other democratizing European countries, 17.6 per cent in 1913 compared to 16.8 per cent in France in 1914, 22.0 per cent in Belgium in 1912, 25.4 per cent in Austria in 1911 and 34.8 per cent in Germany in 1912, although well above the 6.4 per cent in Britain in 1910.[12]

Liberal Party chief Giovanni Giolitti was the dominant political leader with stints as prime minister from 1903 to 1905, 1906 to 1909 and 1911 to March 1914. His policy of Transformation (*Trasformismo*) emphasized practical, centrist political trade-offs and reforms. He got the king and parliament to approve an electoral law bill in 1912 that expanded eligible voters from 3 million to 8.5 million.

During these years, Mussolini sought philosophically to reconcile two opposed world visions asserted by Friedrich Nietzsche and Karl Marx. Nietzsche condemned the drone-like, mindless conformity of most people trapped in political, economic, social, cultural and religious institutions that they could not comprehend, let alone change. Only a few gifted individuals, 'Supermen' (*Übermensch*), had the intelligence, knowledge, character and will to liberate themselves. As such, only supermen were fit to rule the rest of humanity. For Marx, history's heroes were the masses of workers and peasants who struggled to liberate themselves from the repression and exploitation of the economic and thus political, social, cultural and religious elite. He called for violent revolution: 'Workers of the world unite! You have nothing to lose but your chains!'

Eventually, Mussolini took elements of both outlooks and meshed them with other ideas to develop the political philosophy of fascism. Until then, these 1903 thoughts characterized his world view's essence:

> The collective spirit is not yet entirely formed and is torn between the old and the new, between modern ideals and ancient beliefs . . . The superman is the symbol, he is exponent of this anxious and tragic period of crisis that the European consciousness is undergoing in the search for new sources of pleasure, beauty and ideal . . . He is the sunset but also the sunrise. He is above all a hymn to life – to life experienced with all the energies in a continual tension that is striving to something higher, something finer, something more tempting.[13]

Mussolini became an avid reader and occasional essayist for the journal *La Voce* (*The Voice*), founded by Giuseppe Prezzolini in 1909. *La Voce* was Italy's leading cultural review. Prezzolini celebrated Italian creativity and nationalism. He developed the notion of '*Uomo Vociano*' (Vocian Man) who dynamically expressed the best elements of the modern world and traditional Italy, of aesthetic beauty and civic duties. That was Prezzolini's solution to the contemporary world's oppression, exploitation and alienation of humanity:

> Modern man lives without the faith of the past and without any faith in the present and often without any faith in a faith of the future. Destined to live in a new civilization, he feels that he has been sacrificed, yet without having any self-awareness of the cause, which might render him great. He feels his own tragedy, yet cannot climb high enough intellectually to turn himself into Fate and master his own dilemma. Whence the sense of dismay, the darkness, the nihilism of so many souls.[14]

Futurism was an antidote to that deep pessimism, at least for the handful of knowing, daring, exceptional individuals who could realize its ideals.[15] Futurists were a group of painters, poets and essayists who celebrated the modern world's 'creative-destruction' that shattered political, economic, social, cultural and religious institutions, behaviours and beliefs that straitjacketed and exploited humanity. They were iconoclasts and anarchists and some were violent militants. They embraced the automobile and the aircraft as thrilling symbols of the modern world that carried passengers with unprecedented speed and lurking danger to their desired destinations.

Futurists viewed the present and future with excitement and optimism. Umberto Boccioni expressed their outlook; 'We Futurists are giving an example of an enthusiastic human adherence to the form of civilization that is forming before our eyes . . . We are ecstatic in the face of modernity and feel the innovative delirium of our epoch.' Their 1910 Manifesto declared:

> Italy is being reborn. Its political resurgence will be followed by a cultural resurgence. In the land inhabited by the illiterate peasant, schools will be set up; in the land where doing nothing in the sun was the only available profession, millions of machines are already roaring; in the land where traditional aesthetics reigned supreme, new flights of artistic inspiration are emerging and dazzling the world with their brilliance.[16]

As such, Futurists viewed the modern world completely different from Marxists. They saw liberation and fulfilment where Marxists saw alienation and oppression. Leading Futurist artists included Boccioni, Filippo Marinetti, Carlo Carra and Gino Severini whose paintings had loud, thick pigments and jagged lines denoting rapid movement and often depicted trains, planes and automobiles. The Futurists held major exhibitions of their art at Milan in 1911 and Paris in 1912.

Mussolini embraced Futurism as a revolutionary force breaking up political and social morality and mores: 'We feel ourselves attracted to a life that is multiplex, harmonious, vertiginous, global . . . The word that epitomizes and renders the unmistakable rote of our century is "movement" . . . Movement everywhere and acceleration of the rhythm of life.' After taking power, he expressed his proud political debt to those visionaries: 'I formally declare that without Futurism there would never have been a Fascist revolution'.[17]

Italian imperialists called the Ottoman Empire's two North African provinces of Tripolitania and Cyrenaica in Libya, 'Italy's fourth shore'.

In September 1911, a quarter century after Italy's government first claimed Libya, Prime Minister Giovanni Giolitti forged a consensus in the Chamber of Deputies for issuing the Ottoman Empire an ultimatum for their possession.

As the government's declaration of war appeared imminent, Mussolini protested that in an editorial in *The Workers' Future* on 23 September and called for a general strike on 25 September. Many workers at factories across the region walked off the job while a group of radicals sabotaged the railway at nearby Meldora, delaying troop trains. Police attacked strikers and arrested many. Mussolini lauded the strikers and saboteurs in an editorial.

Giolitti issued the Ottoman Empire an ultimatum on 27 September that war would result unless Italy received Tripolitania and Cyrenaica within 24 hours. When the Turks refused, Parliament voted to declare war against the Ottoman Empire on 28 September. In North Africa, Italian troops invaded and captured Tripolitania and Cyrenaica. In the Aegean Sea, they invaded and captured Rhodes and eventually eleven other Dodecanese Islands. The Turks ceded those conquests to Italy with the Treaty of Ouchy (Lausanne) signed on 28 October 1912.[18]

Meanwhile, police arrested Mussolini and his socialist coterie on 14 October 1911. He went on trial on eight counts whose most serious included sedition, sabotage, violently resisting arrest and inciting insurrection on 18 November. Throughout the trial, he was defiant, not contrite, at one point asserting: 'If you acquit me, you shame me; if you convict me, you honour me'.[19] Although the jury 'honoured him', he was not sentenced to prison for life, just one year, and was released early on 12 March 1912.

Mussolini attended the Socialist Party's thirteenth conference at Reggio Emilia from 7 to 14 July 1912. On 12 July he gave a speech so rousing and radical that the editorial board of the Socialist Party's newspaper *Avanti!* (*Advance!*) named him editor-in-chief. Mussolini moved his family to Milan where *Avanti!* was published and assumed that post on 1 December 1912. Within a year and a half, he raised the paper's circulation above 100,000 and made a profit by firing incompetent printers and writers, investing in cutting-edge print technology and ensuring the articles were crisply written and relevant to people's interests. He joined the Lombardy Association of Journalists (*Associazione Lombarda dei Giornalisti*) founded in 1890.

Three radical women played a vital role in Mussolini's life during these years. For assistant editor, he tapped Angelica Balabanoff, his former radical tutor in Geneva. Leda Rafanelli was a feminist, socialist, novelist, poet, journalist and Muslim convert, with whom Mussolini had a torrid affair. Another lover was *Avanti!*'s art critic Margherita Sarfatti, a Jewish feminist, mother and wife of Cesare Sarfatti, a lawyer and socialist.[20] She was part of the Futurist community and was especially close to Umberto Boccioni. She probably talked him into dressing elegantly, shaving his moustache and enhancing his appreciation of art, theatre, literature and music. From her, Mussolini learned a key political lesson that 'you can't govern without art and artists'.[21] After he formed the Fascist movement, she donated him money. He diverted some or much of that to flying and fencing lessons and a four-cylinder Alfa Romeo automobile. She wrote *The Life of Benito Mussolini*, published in 1926.[22]

Mussolini was among the Socialist Party's candidates in the 1913 Chamber of Deputy elections with the first round on 26 October and the second on 2 November. Since the previous election in 1909, Parliament passed and King Victor Emmanuel III promulgated a law that expanded the electorate to all literate men 21 years and older and all illiterate men 30 years and older. That more than tripled the number of eligible voters from 2,930,473 to 8,443,205. Twelve parties won seats among 508 contested. First place went to Giovanni Giolitti's Liberal Union Party with 2,387,947 votes or 37.62 per cent and 270 seats, down 59. Second was Constantino Lazzari's Italian Socialist Party with 883,409 votes or 17.62 per cent and 52 seats, up 11; Mussolini was among the losers. Third went to Ettore Sacchi's Radical Party with 522,522 votes or 10.42 per cent and 62 seats, up 14. Gerrymandering explains why the Radical Party garnered more seats with fewer votes than the Socialist Party.[23] The king reappointed Giolitti the prime minister.

An international crisis erupted on 28 June 1914, when Serbian terrorist Gavrilo Princip shot to death Austrian Archduke Franz Ferdinand and his wife Sophie in Sarajevo, the capital of Bosnia-Herzegovina, a province the Austro-Hungarian empire annexed in 1908. Austrian police captured Princeps and his comrades in their Black Hand group. Interrogations revealed that Serbia's government, with its capital at Belgrade, had created the Black Hand group to undermine Austrian rule over Bosnia-Herzegovina with its mostly Serbian population. On 23 July, Vienna issued Belgrade a ten-point ultimatum that would result in war if the Serbs rejected it or failed to reply within 48 hours.

A war would likely soon involve all Europe's Great Powers along with many smaller countries. Russia was allied with Serbia bilaterally and with France and Britain into a Triple Entente. Germany was allied with Austria and Italy in a Triple Alliance that would activate if one or more of them was the victim of an attack, but not the aggressor.

Fear explained why those alliances existed. War was as old as humanity in Europe, but in the late nineteenth century modern technological marvels like railways, steamships, telegraphs, telephones and mass assembly line production had rendered warfare's scale and destruction far greater than before.[24] The side that mobilized more troops quicker to attack the enemy would likely prevail and the favourable odds swelled with the power of one's allies and their angles of attack. During the late nineteenth century, the Great Powers had sublimated territorial and ethnic conflicts within Europe by cooperating in carving up most of Africa and Asia as colonies. Those spoils were consumed and being digested. Now all the old animosities over where to draw territorial lines across diverse, restive peoples within Europe reemerged, nowhere worse than in the Balkans with its ethnic and religious mosaic. Exacerbating tension was a naval arms race in which Germany sought to catch up to Britain in the number of cutting-edge battleships called Dreadnoughts, thus challenging Britain's overwhelming naval power. Germany could afford that buildup because its economy had surpassed Britain's in size and dynamism, with their respective share of world manufacturing 8.5 per cent and 22.9 per cent in 1880 and 14.8 per cent and 13.6 per cent in 1913. That naval arms race between Britain and Germany was part of a broader military buildup race among all the great powers. Despite that, military spending as a share of the economy for the great powers was fairly modest, with Italy and Russia the highest with 5.1 per cent, France 4.8 per cent, Germany 3.9 per cent and Britain and Austria at 3.2 per cent.[25]

2.1 Defence Spending of Europe's Great Power in British Pounds Sterling[26]

	1894	1913	Money Rise	Percent Rise
Britain	33.4	72.5	19.1	117.1
France	37.6	72.0	34.4	91.5
Russia	85.8	101.7	15.9	18.5
Germany	36.2	93.4	57.2	158.0
Austria	9.6	25.0	15.4	160.4
Italy	14.0	39.6	25.6	182.9

Serbia's government replied on 25 July to Austria's ultimatum with a point-by-point diplomatic response that agreed to comply with each one except the demand that Austrians oversee Serbia's investigation and prosecution of the crime. Austria declared war on Serbia on 28 July, as both countries mobilized their armies. Against Germany's warning not to do so, Russia began mobilizing its army on 31 July. Germany began its own mobilization and declared war against Russia on 1 August and took over Luxembourg and formed a secret alliance with the Ottoman Empire on 2 August. France began its mobilization on 2 August. When Germany invaded Belgium on 4 August, Britain declared war on Germany. Meanwhile, Prime Minister Antonio Salandra declared on 1 August, that Italy was not obligated to join its Triple Alliance partners in war because Germany was the aggressor and so would remain neutral.

The German army initially succeeded in overrunning much of Belgium then invading France from the north in an attempt to circle and destroy most of the French army deployed along the eastern border with Germany. A small British army blunted that advance at Mons in Belgium, then fell back into northern France. A hastily assembled French reserve army at Paris was conveyed eastward by the city's requisitioned trucks and taxis to slam into and push back the German right flank at the battle of the Marne from 5 to 14 September. Thereafter each army dug in along the front that stretched 400 or so miles from Switzerland to the North Sea. In the Balkans, the Serbs repelled the initial Austrian onslaught and each side entrenched. On the Eastern Front, the Germans demolished two Russian armies at the battles of Tannenberg and Masurian Lakes. The Austrian and eventually the Turkish armies advanced against Russian armies along their stretches of frontier. The Eastern Front soon stabilized along a zigzagging, shifting 600-mile line between the Baltic and Black Seas.

Two technologies made each front relatively stagnant for the next four years, machine guns and barbed wire. Two men manning a machine gun, with one man pulling the trigger and the other feeding it long belts of ammunition from within a sandbagged bunker could slaughter hundreds of troops armed with rifles struggling through barbed wire rolls before them. Mass attacks usually failed and were deemed a success if they captured a few hundred yards of front, even at the cost of thousands of lives.

Mussolini initially expressed through *Avanti!* articles the Socialist Party's official view that the war was wrong and that Italy should stay neutral, cut military spending and boost spending for needy people: 'Let us have no more talk of battleships, barracks, cannon, at a time when thousands of villages have no schools, roads, electricity or doctors, but still live tragically beyond the pale of civilized life.'[27]

Yet, soon Mussolini leaned toward morally supporting the Entente Allies. In the 13 September 1914 edition, he published an article by

Sergio Panunzio who made that argument. He guardedly expressed that view himself in the 30 September edition and called for Italy to shift from 'absolute neutrality to an active and working neutrality'.[28] He criticized Marxism and its adherents for putting abstract theories before human nature and needs. He argued that 'a party which wishes to live in history and, in so far as it is allowed, to make history, cannot submit at the penalty of suicide, to a line which is dependent on an unarguable dogma or an eternal law, separate from the iron necessity [of change] over space and time'.[29]

Mussolini asserted his heretical views during a meeting of the Socialist Party executive in Bologna on 20 October 1914. Hardline Socialists angrily condemned his views. Mussolini resigned as *Avanti!*'s editor. He was stunned, saddened and humiliated when the Socialist Party expelled him. He replied: 'Whatever happens you will not lose me. Twelve years of my life in the party are or ought to be sufficient guarantee of my socialist faith. Socialism is in my very blood.'[30] But Mussolini soon completely abandoned socialism for a new creed.

Chapter 3

THE FASCIST MOVEMENT

It was a victory for the whole Italian race. After a thousand years, we, awakened, were again giving a tangible proof of our moral and spiritual valour. We were living again on warlike tradition. We felt our formidable weight in the future of a new Europe.

(Benito Mussolini)

Fascism draws its sword to cut the Gordian knots which tie and burden Italian life.

(Benito Mussolini)

[E]ither we are allowed to govern or we will seize power by marching on Rome to take by the throat the miserable political class that governs us.

(Benito Mussolini)

Benito Mussolini converted from championing Karl Marx's communism and internationalism to nationalism and militarism that mixed the outlooks of Giuseppe Mazzini, Friedrich Nietzsche, Social Darwinism and Futurism. A week after his expulsion from the Socialist Party, he wrote: 'Reality is moving with an accelerated rhythm. We have had the singular privilege of living at the most tragic hour in the history of the world. Do we want to be . . . mere spectators of the great drama? Or do we want to be – in some way and in some sense – protagonists?'[1] Mussolini's very public expulsion and outlook inspired countless Italians, especially Futurists. Carlo Cara proclaimed this about Mussolini: 'In him, there is the drama of our entire generation'.[2]

Mussolini did not invent the Fascist movement of nationalism, authoritarianism, corporatism and imperialism but adapted it from other militant groups along with blackshirted militia and the stiff outstretched right arm and open-palmed salute.[3] Fasces were the ancient Roman Republican symbol of a bound bundle of arrows and an axe exuding authority, unity and strength. Their first modern expression was by the Workers' Associations that mushroomed across Italy after the first at Palermo in May 1892.

To develop and promote that outlook into a distinct political philosophy, Mussolini founded the newspaper *Il Populo d'Italia* (*The People of Italy*) whose first edition appeared on 15 November 1914. He called for a 'Fasces of Revolutionary Action' (*Fasci d'Azione Rivoluzionaria*) in *Il Populo d'Italia* on 11 December 1914, issued a constitution for the group on 6 January 1915 and held the first meeting in Milan on 24 January. He called on Italy to join the Entente and win Trentino and Trieste from Austria-Hungary. 'Work, Obey and Fight' became the Fascist motto. The initial result was a loose roster of affiliated nationalist groups that collectively numbered over 5,000 members with Mussolini the nominal leader with Alceste De Ambris and Michele Bianchi his deputies.[4]

He got Filippo Naldi, a rich industrialist, partly to underwrite both *Il Popolo* and Fasces of Revolutionary Action. Soon they began receiving donations from an array of others, most prominently Giovanni Agnelli of Fiat, Carlo Esterle of Italian Edison Company, Pio Perrone of Ansaldo Manufacturing Company and Giuseppe Bruzzone of *Unione Zuccheri* (the Sugar Combine). But they also took secret foreign funds. Mussolini and Naldi journeyed to Switzerland to meet French intelligence officers and eventually received 20,000 francs through the French Institute in Milan and its director Julien Luchaire.[5]

A volatile mix of violence and honour mingled in Mussolini's psyche. To a reporter who asked how he felt about being expelled from the Socialist Party, he asserted: 'As long as I have a pen in my hand and a revolver in my pocket, I fear no man. I am strong even when I am alone and indeed because I am alone.'[6] Yet, from now, as a public figure, he avoided the bullying and brawls of his youth. Instead, he fought duels with socialists who offended his honour, three rapier rounds with Lino Merlino in February 1915 and eight rounds with Claudio Treves in March 1915, during which he inflicted three wounds and sustained one.[7]

Prime Minister Antonio Salandra, Foreign Minister Sidney Sonnino and other key leaders were willing to ally Italy with that side which promised the most post-war territory. They hoped to get Nice, Corsica, Tunisia and Malta by siding with Germany and Austria or the Tyrol, Trieste, Istria and Dalmatia by siding with Britain, France and Russia. Sonnino began negotiating with the Austrians on 9 December 1914, but they rejected his demands. He journeyed to London to open talks with British, French and

Russian diplomats on 4 March 1915. After five weeks of haggling, they signed the secret Treaty of London on 26 April, that granted Italy's wish list of Tyrol, Trieste, Istria, Fiume, Dalmatia and the Dodecanese islands. Despite that, King Victor Emmanuel hesitated to go to war.

Meanwhile, Mussolini through his *Il Popolo* newspaper and Fasces of Revolutionary Action demanded that Italy join the Triple Entente against the Central Powers to gain the very territories that Sonnino had secretly won through negotiations. On 13 May, Mussolini taunted the king by declaring: 'We want war and if you, sire, who under Article V of the Constitution can send all our soldiers to the frontiers, refuse it to us, you will lose your crown'.[8]

Threats from Mussolini and other radical leaders intimidated King Victor Emmanuel III who feared: 'I must make war; otherwise there will be revolution'.[9] On 16 May, he authorized Salandra to introduce a war resolution in Parliament. The Chamber of Deputies voted 407 to 74 for war against Austria-Hungary on 24 May. A broad political consensus backed Italy's entrance into the war although the wartime prime ministers were all Liberal Union Party leaders, Salandra from 21 March 1914 to 18 June 1916, Paolo Baselli until 30 October 1917 and Vittorio Orlando until 23 June 1919.

On paper, the 850,000-man army should have been ready for the war. Since unification, the government had generously funded the military, with the army enjoying an average 17.4 per cent and the navy 6.3 per cent of the national budget from 1862 to 1913. In fiscal year 1913–14, Italy spent 650 million lira on the military to just 150 million for education.[10] More critically, army commanders had nine months to study the war from both sides of the trenches and understand the challenges that lay ahead and avoid earlier mistakes by the belligerents. Tragically, they did not do so. Indeed, the army had no contingency plans for war. Field Marshal Luigi Cardona the army chief of staff, had no combat experience and largely owed his rapid promotion up the ranks to being the son of Rafaele Cardona, a leading general of the unification wars. Atop all that, the army had depleted and not replenished its munition reserves during the war in Libya from 1911 to 1912.

Most vital of all, Italy's economy could not sustain the army even for months, let alone years; Italian factories and farms did not produce enough crucial military supplies. Italy would depend mostly on British and American factories for manufactured goods and on American farms for food. And to pay for all that, Italy would have to borrow more money from British and American bankers for its immediate expenses, then borrow more money to pay interest on its skyrocketing debt. That was doable in the short-term but would lead to a post-war economic crisis that would help Mussolini and his Fascist Party take power.

Nonetheless, Italy's economy did expand during the war. The number of factories specializing in war products rose from 221 in 1915 to 1,976 in 1918. Factories produced 382 warplanes in 1915, 1,255 in 1916, 3,861 in 1917 and 6,523 in 1918 and the number of manufacturers climbed from three to sixty-two. Artillery shell production soared from 14,000 a day in May 1915 to 50,000 a day a year later.[11]

The Italian front was a blood-soaked stalemate like the Western, Eastern, Serbian and Dardanelles fronts.[12] The Austrians mostly held higher ground along the 400 or so mile frontier that meandered between the Swiss border and the Adriatic Sea, with around 300 of those miles hilly or mountainous. The Austrians had heavily fortified their side and manned it with sixty-one divisions. Chief of Staff Field Marshal Luigi Cardona spent just three weeks hastily preparing fifty-eight Italian divisions before launching an offensive on 23 May. The Austrians blunted that offensive and numerous others over the next two years and a half years.

Mussolini was drafted into the army on 31 August 1915. He served dutifully in the 11th Bersaglieri at the front for the next two years, earning promotions from private to corporal and eventually to sergeant. On 22 February 1917, during a training exercise behind the lines, his grenade launcher overheated and the grenade exploded, killing several of his comrades and wounding him with forty-four steel fragments.

He needed months and numerous operations to recover. In the hospital, Mussolini briefly chatted with Victor Emmanuel III who was visiting the wounded. Although the king was well aware of Mussolini's radicalism and anti-monarchism, their brief exchange of words was cordial.

'How do you feel, Mussolini?'

'Not too well your Majesty.'

'Be brave, Mussolini. Try to resign yourself to your immobility and your pain.'[13]

If Mussolini thought, 'That's easy for you to say', he kept silent.

Of course, at the time, neither could imagine that within five years, the king would name Mussolini the prime minister and the two would meet numerous times over the next 22 years. Meanwhile, the army honourably discharged him in August 1917.

Mussolini was a married man when he was drafted. He got involved with Ida Dalser in Trentino and asked her to come to Milan to work on *Il Populo d'Italia*. He married her in late 1914 after getting her pregnant. At the front,

Mussolini got word that Ida had given birth to a son she called Benito on 11 November 1915. It is unclear whether he convinced a court to dissolve their marriage in exchange for him paying her monthly child support or that they remained married.[14] He received a month's leave in December 1915 to recover from typhus, first in a hospital then in Milan. On 17 December, he and Rachele finally married in a civil ceremony five years after she gave birth to their daughter Edda. They subsequently had four more children, Vittorio on 27 September 1916, Bruno on 22 April 1918, Romano on 26 September 1927 and Anna Maria on 3 September 1929.

Mussolini's Fasces of Revolutionary Action and Fascist newspaper withered while he was at the front. He revived *Il Populo d'Italia* with donations from Cesare Goldmann, a Jewish businessman from Milan, and the Ansaldo shipbuilding corporation. He organized a Parliamentary Union for National Defence (*Fascio Parlementare di Difesa Nationale*) attended by 152 deputies and 90 senators in December 1917. The meeting was essentially a pep rally for the war. Mussolini failed to talk any them into joining his budding Fascist Party.

Meanwhile, two decisive events convulsed the Great War. President Woodrow Wilson asked Congress for a declaration of war against Germany on 2 April 1917. Congress overwhelming approved by 82 to 6 against with 6 abstentions that same day and by 373 to 50 against with 8 abstentions on 6 April. The president and a vast congressional majority were infuriated by Germany's resumption on 1 January 1917 of unrestricted submarine warfare with three American ships sunk in March, and a message from German Foreign Minister Arthur Zimmermann to the ambassador in Mexico City, telling him that if Mexico went to war against the United States, Berlin would give Mexico as much military aid and advice as possible, which had been intercepted by the British, decoded and shared with Wilson.

Wilson appointed General John Pershing to command America's army in France. It would take 14 months of a steady buildup of conscripted, trained and equipped troops in France before that army was ready to fight alongside the French and British armies against the Germans.

Meanwhile, the Entente lost a crucial ally. Russia experienced two revolutions in 1917. From August 1914 to March 1917, Russia suffered over six million casualties, an imploding economy, worsening food shortages, malnutrition, disease and inflation. Tsar Nicholas II was at army headquarters acting as commander-in-chief to preside over endless defeats. Mass demonstrations erupted in Saint Petersburg, the capital, Moscow and many other cities in March. Police and soldiers killed over 1,300 protestors but the demonstrations grew in number.

A group of centre-leftist leaders in the Duma or parliament formed a provisional government and demanded that the tsar abdicate. On 3 March, Nicholas abdicated in favour of his brother Michael, but he did not want the throne so the Romanov dynasty ended that day after nearly four centuries in power.

Prince Georgy Lvov chaired the committee that headed the provisional government. He promised the Russian people that a constituent assembly eventually would be elected to draft a democratic constitution for Russia. Meanwhile, Russia would continue to honour its commitment to the Allies to war against the Germans, Austrians and Turks. That decision and another half year of more mass death from combat, disease and starvation led to the second revolution.

Russia's Communist Party, then called the Bolsheviks, had an underground organization in Russia that competed with an array of other political parties for adherents. Vladimir Lenin, the Bolshevik Party Chair, was in exile at Zurich, Switzerland. Hoping Lenin would provoke a revolution, the German government provided free train passage for him and his entourage across Germany to a port where they boarded a ship for Sweden and then trains to Saint Petersburg. Lenin realized that hope. After arriving in April, he mobilized the Bolshevik Party to overthrow the provisional government. The coup against the provisional government, now headed by Alexander Kerensky, came on 7 November, when Bolshevik militants seized key government offices, telephone exchanges and other key places in Saint Petersburg, Moscow and other cities. The Bolshevik promise that they would provide 'peace, bread and land' attracted countless supporters. On 3 March 1918, Bolshevik and German diplomats signed the Treaty of Brest Litovsk whereby Germany, Austria and Turkey took much of western Russia in exchange for peace. On the Western Front, the Germans raced to transfer troops there from the Eastern Front, hoping to overwhelm the Allied armies before America's army peaked in strength.

Meanwhile, the Austrian army inflicted a devastating defeat on Italy's army with a carefully planned offensive along the Isonzo River centred on Caporetto that raged from 24 October to 19 November 1917. The Austrians decimated the Italians, killing 13,000, wounding 30,000 and capturing over 250,000 at the cost of 70,000 casualties and punching the front line back 90 miles to the Piave River.[15]

Mussolini recalled the impact on him: 'Never in my life as an Italian and as a politician have I experienced a sorrow equal to that which I suffered after news of the defeat of Caporetto'. He vented his rage with fiery editorials demanding that the government assert 'severe action against slackers and whoever undermined the spirit of war. I called for the organization of a volunteer army. I insisted on the suppression of socialist newspapers. I asked for military rule in the north of Italy. I asked for a more humane treatment of soldiers. I campaigned for war discipline.'[16]

King Victor Emmanuel finally relieved the inept Cardona as chief of staff and replaced him with Marshal Armando Diaz on 9 November 1917. Over the next eight months, Diaz slowly rebuilt the Italian army then launched two victorious campaigns in 1918. The Italian army pushed back the Austrians at the Battle of the Piave River from 15 to 23 June and then advanced further during the Battle of Vittorio Veneto from 23 October to 3 November. On other segments of the front, Italian troops captured Trento on 3 November and a flotilla landed troops that took lightly-defended Trieste on 5 November.

Those successful campaigns coincided with equally decisive offensives on the Western Front. After the Treaty of Brest-Litovsk with Russia, Germany transferred around a million troops to the Western Front, where they launched five separate offensives between 21 March and 18 July; each captured a diminishing expanse of front before Allied reinforcements blunted the advance. The Allied French, American and British armies then began their own series of offensives from mid-July that by early November had punched back the German line from a dozen to 50 miles.

German Chancellor Max von Baden sent President Wilson a telegram requesting an armistice on 4 October. Wilson replied by demanding that Kaiser Wilhelm order his army to withdraw to Germany then abdicate. The Ottoman Turks signed an armistice with the Allies on 30 October. The Austrians signed an armistice with the Italians on 4 November. The Germans signed an armistice with the French, British and American Allies on 11 November. With the guns finally silenced on all fronts, the key question now was what peace terms the Allies would impose on the Central Powers.

Prime Minister Vittorio Orlando celebrated Italy's victory in a speech before the Senate on 15 December 1918. For him, the key triumph was the assertion and realization of national power:

> Italy is truly a great power today . . . because she has demonstrated capacity for action and resolution that genuinely identifies her with the great states of history and of the present. This, in my view, is Italy's primary and major gain, a gain that cannot be subject to any debate round an international table, that cannot be challenged or diminished or taken away.[17]

That 'gain' came at a horrendous human and economic cost. The war inflicted 578,000 Italian dead and 947,000 wounded. Swaths of north-east Italy were nothing but churned-up earth, rubble of former towns and villages and countless ill-buried rotting corpses. Italy's military dead and wounded were among the respective totals of 9,450,00 and 15,404,905 suffered by all the warring countries. Another six to thirteen million civilians may have died from violence, disease, starvation or despair.[18]

A financial crisis engulfed post-war Italy along with the other European belligerents.[19] The national budget soared from 2.5 billion lire in fiscal year 1913–14 to 30.8 billion lire in 1918–19 and the national debt with it. The war cost 148 billion lire, twice the total government budgets from 1861 to 1913. Italy's war costs were part of the $147 billion spent by Allied countries paid and the $61 billion spent by the Central Powers. From 1913 to 1919, the lira plummeted in value from 4.97 to the dollar to 19.30 to the dollar, while the cost of living index soared from 100 to 268. Italy owed America and Britain around $4.4 billion and could pay only token amounts of the interest due.[20]

3.1 First World War Great Power Military Casualties[21]

	Killed	Wounded	Prisoners	Total
Allies				
Britain	723,000	1,662,625	170,389	2,556,014
France	1,398,000	2,000,000	446,300	3,884,300
Italy	578,000	947,000	530,000	2,055,000
Russia	1,811,000	1,450,000	3,500,000	6,761,000
America	114,000	205,690	4,480	324,170
Total Allied	5,421,000	7,025,487	4,846,376	17,292,863
Central Powers				
Germany	2,037,000	4,207,028	617,922	6,861,950
Austria	1,100,000	3,620,000	2,200,000	6,920,000
Turkey	804,000	400,000	250,000	1,454,000
Total Central	4,029,000	8,379,418	3,078,000	15,486,963
Total	9,450,000	15,404,905	7,924,921	32,779,826

Allied totals include statistics from minor Allies Belgium, Portugal, the British Empire, Serbia, Greece and Romania.

Central Powers totals include Bulgaria's statistics.

Overall, the post-war income and living standards for most Italians were much worse than before. One exception was the countryside. There the socialist Federterra Movement politically mobilized sharecropper and tenant peasants to seize the agrarian estates that they worked. Landowners in the General Confederation of Agriculture (*Confederazione Generale del'Agricoltura*, Confagricola) collaborated with local police to suppress the peasants. Yet, faced with a violent takeover of their land, most owners preferred to sell off patches for nominal prices. The result was that from 1911 to 1921 the share of peasants who owned the land they worked rose from 38 per cent to 48 per cent.[22]

As partial compensation for the nation's human and economic losses, Italy's leaders were eager to reap the promises of territorial expansion promised by the secret 1915 Treaty of London with Britain, France and Russia. With those expectations, nearly all Italians would be outraged when Italy did not get all that was promised.

Mussolini exalted that Italy was among the war's winners: 'It was a victory for the whole Italian race. After a thousand years, we, awakened, were again giving a tangible proof of our moral and spiritual valour. We were living again on warlike tradition. We felt our formidable weight in the future of a new Europe.'[23]

When the war ended, Mussolini was 35 years old, married and the father of three small children. He spent little time at home, with the excuse that heading the Fascist movement devoured nearly all his time. He did devote his days and evenings to party work but managed to squeeze in interludes for pleasure. His chief mistress remained Margherita Sarfatti.

Mussolini's Fasces of Revolutionary Action was one of a score of similar paramilitary groups called 'Daring Squads' (*Arditi Squadre*) or 'Action Squads' (*Squadre d'Azione*) of 'militants' (*squadristi*) composed mostly of war veterans and local thugs. The oldest proto-Fascist group was the Italian Nationalist Association (ANI) with its newspaper *The Nationalist Idea* (*L'Idea Nationale*) founded in 1910, led by Enrico Corradini and Giovanni Papini. Veterans swelled its ranks after the war. The Nationalist Association called for expanding Italy's colonial empire. The Nationalist Association's militant wing wore blue shirts. Other prominent Fascist groups whose leaders hoped to unite the movement with themselves as *Il Duce* included Leandro Arpinati's Emilia Romagna headquartered at Bologna; Adelchi Serena's in southern Abruzzo at L'Aquila; Giacomo Acerbo's in northern Abruzzo at Chieti; and Roberto Farinacci's in northern Lombardy at Modena. Mussolini eventually subordinated all these leaders into a united Fascist Party. Ever more groups, including Mussolini's, dressed in black shirts and shouted *A Noi!*, meaning Italy 'For Us!' at rallies. Fighting often erupted between fascist and left-wing militant groups.

Mussolini invited sixty members of fascist groups from the region to a private meeting in Milan on 21 March 1919. They agreed to unite in a group called the Italian Combat Fasci (*Fasci Italiani di Combattimento*) with an Executive Council of a half-dozen members initially chaired by Ferruccio Vecchi but dominated by Mussolini. They then invited more fascists to a congress to endorse their group two days later. On 23 March 119 delegates crowded into a reception hall overlooking Piazza San Sepolcro formally to declare and join the Italian Combat Fasci. They approved its agenda, devised mostly by Mussolini, that called for a constituent assembly, a republic, abolition of the senate and nobility, the break-up of large agrarian estates and distribution of that land to the tenants who worked it and corporatist cooperation between business owners, managers and workers for their mutual profit and expansion.

Mussolini initially served as general secretary jointly with Attilio Longoni, an army pilot and factory worker until 1 August 1919, when he named Umberto Pasella, a worker's union leader. In all, a dozen individuals served as the Fascist Party secretary from 1919 to 1945, under its three names. He and the executive committee renamed their group the National Fascist Party (*Partito Nazionale Fascista,* PNF) on 10 November 1921. Meanwhile, Mussolini established auxiliaries including the journal *The Fascist* (*Il Fascio*) in August 1919 and the University Fascist Youth (*Gioventu Universitaria Fascista,* GRU) in 1920. Mussolini organized a bodyguard of his toughest fighters that he called his Action Squad.

Spearheading the fascist movement exhilarated him:

> I led a life of intense activity. I managed the *Populo d'Italia* and every morning I was able to give the political text for that day, not only to Milan but to the principal cities of Italy in which the political life of the nation found its source. I led the Fascist party with a firm hand . . . I gave some very strict orders. I had an ear open to all who came to Milan with communications about our organization in the various provinces. I watched the activities of our enemies.[24]

Mussolini envisioned fascism as a nationalist, authoritarian state led by his charismatic dictatorship dedicated to expanding Italy's power, wealth and prestige. Pragmatism, flexibility and opportunism determined just what policies best achieved that. To develop the economy, the state would bolster infrastructure like roads, railways, ports, electricity, sewage and fresh water systems, schools and hospitals and partner with private investors to expand strategic industries like steel, automobiles, shipbuilding, armaments and railways. All individuals and groups would devote themselves to the nation and state personified by the dictator who led it and revel in the subsequent glories.

Mussolini's most prominent rival then was Ferruccio Vecchi who expressed Fascist critiques and exhortations through his newspaper *L'Ardito* (*The Militant*). He called his Fascist version *Arditismo Civile* or Squadrism. In February 1919, Vecchi formed an alliance with Filipo Tomasso Marinetti, a Futurist painter and nationalist. Vecchi and Marinetti were autonomous Fascist Party members. On 15 April 1919, they led a march of combatants that attacked and destroyed the office of the Socialist newspaper *Avanti!*. In *L'Ardito.* Vecchi celebrated that sacking as fascism's first victory.

Mussolini sat on the sidelines during that assault. He had demurred their demand that he and his followers join them. Yet, he tried to take credit for the idea during an interview by a journalist whose article appeared in *Il Giornale d'Italia* on 18 April. He pointedly did not mention Vecchi while insisting that: 'Everything that happened at *Avanti!* was the product of a spontaneous mass action, action by the soldiers and the people, fed up with Leninist blackmail. We of the Fasci did not plan the attack on the Socialist paper, but we accept full moral responsibility for the incident.'[25]

The rivalry between Mussolini and Vecchi to head the swelling Fascist movement was overshadowed by a more famed, charismatic potential rival. Gabriele D'Annunzio was a decorated combat pilot who lost an eye in a flying accident, and a poet, womanizer and leader of his own Fascist group.[26] Among his wartime feats was flying solo over Vienna. He emerged from the war a colonel with five silver medals for exemplary courage.

Mussolini and Vecchi vied for his endorsement, hoping he would not displace them. Vecchi hailed D'Annunzio as Fascism's *Duce* in his *Arditismo Civile.* Mussolini's *Il Popolo D'Italia* published D'Annunzio's fiery essays and letters, most vitally his 'Letter to the Dalmatians' on 3 January 1919.

The peace conference to settle the Great War officially opened in Paris on 19 January 1919 and climaxed with the signing of the Treaty of Versailles at the Palace of Versailles a dozen miles west of Paris on 28 June 1919.[27] Although delegations from thirty-two states and nationalities attended, the Big Four leaders of American President Woodrow Wilson and prime ministers David Lloyd George of Britain, Georges Clemenceau of France and Vittorio Orlando decided all the key issues usually after prolonged and at times acrimonious debate. Wilson wanted 'a peace without victors' that would make the Great War 'the war to end all wars' whose details he articulated during his 'Fourteen Points Speech' before Congress on 8 January 1918. Eight of his points concerned specific territorial adjustments designed to alleviate long-standing international conflicts. The other six involved five general principles of open diplomacy, free trade, arms reduction, freedom of the seas and self-determination for all peoples to be guaranteed by an international assembly of all nations dedicated to collective security, 'all for one and one for all'.

Over the next six months, the leaders and their delegations painstakingly debated issues, compromised and constructed the treaty. The British, French and Italians wanted a vindictive peace that forced the losers, especially Germany, to pay huge reparations to the winner, while imposing strict limits on the German military's size and weapons. They forced Wilson to surrender each of his principles except for the League of Nations. In the treaty, Article 231 declared that Germany had started the war and thus had to pay reparations, whose amount a reparations committee would determine and thereafter could have an army with no more than 100,000 troops, a coast guard for a navy with no large warships and was forbidden to have an air force. The Germans protested those restrictions and penalties but ultimately signed the treaty when the Allies threatened to resume the war.

Prime Minister Orlando and most Italians protested the articles that affected Italy. Among Wilson's Fourteen Points was 'a readjustment of the frontiers of Italy should be effected along clearly recognized lines of nationality'. That conflicted with Italian territorial goals that faced rivals; Yugoslavia for Trieste, Istria and Dalmatia; Greece for Albania, Anatolia and the Dodecanese Islands; and Austria for the Upper Adige/Southern Tyrol. Wilson insisted that Dalmatia should go to the new Slavic state of Yugoslavia that the Big Four had designated. Orlando grudgingly yielded Dalmatia but insisted that Istria and the port of Fiume with its majority Italian population should rightfully go to Italy. With that same logic, Wilson opposed Italy's takeover of mostly German-speaking South Tyrol, although there Orlando finally prevailed; Italy would stretch north to the Brenner Pass. Wilson also yielded on Istria even though Slovenes slightly outnumbered Italians there. Among the Versailles Treaty's quirks was to reduce Austria to a rump state of six million German-speakers and concoct Yugoslavia with twelve million people split among six regions, four languages and three religions with the imposed King Peter I.

Italy won two regions from Austria, the South Tyrol and Istria that included the port of Trieste. Those were significant territorial gains. Yet, most Italians, especially Fascists, condemned Orlando's government for the 'Mutilated Victory' that failed to win Fiume and the Dodecanese islands in the Versailles Treaty.[28] Mussolini recalled the Versailles Treaty's impact on Italy as 'a complete shattering of ideals. We had won the war; we were utterly defeated in the political battle.'[29]

The Chamber of Deputies held a confidence vote on the government on 19 June and voted 262 to 78 against. Orlando and his cabinet resigned. Francesco Nitti formed a government on 23 June. The government eventually accepted the territorial changes initiated by the Versailles Treaty. With the Allies, Italy signed peace treaties with other enemies, Austria at Saint Germain on 10 September, 1919, Hungary at Trianon on 4 June 1920 and Turkey at Lausanne on 24 July 1923.

For Italians, the Versailles Treaty's worst flaw was not taking title to Fiume (Rijeka), a deepwater port on the Dalmatian coast with 49,000 mostly Italian-speaking inhabitants. Gabriel D'Annunzio led 200 or so militants to Fiume, bloodlessly took power and declared the city a free state on 12 September 1919.[30] He and his deputy Alceste De Ambris drafted a constitution they called the Carnaro Charter (*Carta del Carnaro*) for Fiume. Although Mussolini was deeply jealous of D'Annunzio, he celebrated the takeover in *Il Populo d'Italia* editorials. He published D'Annunzio's triumphant 15 September letter to him: 'My Dear Mussolini, I have risked all, I have given all, I have conquered. I am the master of Fiume . . . If half the Italians had the spirit of Fiumesi, we would be masters of the world . . . Either Italy or Death!' To that, Mussolini declared that: 'The Italian government is not in Rome but in Fiume. It is that government to which we owe obedience.'[31]

Mussolini flew to Fiume to meet D'Annunzio and observe his realm on 7 October. He invited D'Annunzio to join him at Florence for a conference of Fascist groups. There, Mussolini upstaged him with a speech in which he asserted that Fascism paradoxically but profoundly was 'not republican, not socialist, not democratic, not conservative, not nationalist' but was 'a synthesis of all negations and all positives'.[32]

D'Annunzio held a plebiscite on 26 November, on two related questions: should Italy annex Fiume and should the National Unity Party continue to govern the city. Of 10,331 eligible voters, 7,155 turned out and 6,199 embraced annexation.[33]

At Prime Minister Giolitti's urging, King Victor Emmanuel ordered Admiral Enrico Millo, who commanded Italian forces occupying Dalmatia, to withdraw them and General Enrico Caviglia to lead a task force to compel D'Annunzio and his army to leave Fiume. Caviglia had his warships blockade Fiume and sent a message to D'Annunzio to surrender by royal decree. He rejected the demand. On 26 December, Caviglia ordered the battleship *Andrea Doria* to fire a shell at D'Annunzio's headquarters at city hall. The blast narrowly missed D'Annunzio but killed thirty-five of his men and wounded dozens more. D'Annunzio sent word that he was willing to talk. Two days of haggling led to a deal whereby the task force evacuated D'Annunzio and his followers to Italy and let them return to their homes with the promise to give up militarism or risk long prison terms. That deal at once terminated the crisis for Italy and Mussolini's most charismatic potential rival. Italy followed that up with the Treaty of Rapallo, signed with Yugoslavia, then called the Kingdom of Serbia, Croatia and Slovenia, on 19 November 1920, whereby it received the eastern Adriatic Sea enclaves of Istria with the ports of Pula and Zara, while ceding Dalmatia to Yugoslavia and making Fiume a free city-state.

Meanwhile, Victor Emmanuel III and Parliament approved a constitutional amendment that established proportional representation on 14 August 1919. Each party would submit a list of candidates which would become deputies proportional to that party's share of the vote. The new electoral system heartened small political parties that previously had no chance of winning seats. The next Chamber of Deputies election would be held on 16 November 1919.

To mobilize for that pending election, Mussolini convened the Fascist Party at Florence on 8 October. Mussolini claimed that the Fascist Party numbered 148 Fasci with 45,000 total members; actually, there were just 56 Fasci with 17,000 total members.[34] The election results reflected those measly figures. Mussolini garnered just around 4,000 votes in his Milan district and none of his fellow Fascist candidates won a seat; in stunning contrast, the Socialist and People's Parties respectively won 176,000 and 74,000 Milan votes.[35]

Nationally, of 5,684,818 votes cast or 56.58 per cent of those eligible, the three top winners were the Italian Socialist Party (PSI) led by Nicola Bombacci with 1,834,792 votes or 32.28 per cent and 156 seats of 508 total, up from 104 and two new parties, Luigi Sturzo's Italian People's Party (PPI) with 1,167,354 votes or 20.53 per cent and 101 seats and Vittorio Orlando's alliance of Liberals, Democrats and Radicals with 964,195 votes or 15.91 per cent and 91 seats.[36] Nitti remained prime minister after forming a coalition government of the three largest parties. Giovanni Giolitti replaced Nitti as prime minister on 15 June 1920 and remained in power until 4 July 1921.

3.2 Italian Prime Ministers, December 1909 to October 1922

Leader	Tenure	Party
Sidney Sonnino	11 December 1909 to 31 March 1910	Conservative
Luigi Luzzatti	31 March 1910 to 30 March 1911	Conservative
Giovanni Giolitti	30 March 1911 to 21 March 1914	
Antonio Salandra	21 March 1914 to 18 June 1916	Liberal Union Party
Paolo Baselli	18 June 1916 to 30 October 1917	Liberal Union Party
Vittorio Orlando	30 October 1917 to 23 June 1919	Liberal Union Party
Francesco Nitti	23 June 1919 to 15 June 1920	Italian Radical Party
Giovanni Giolitti	25 June 1920 to 4 July 1921	Liberal Union Party
Ivanoe Bonomi	4 July 1921 to 26 February 1922	Italian Radical Socialist Party
Luigi Facta	26 February 1922 to 30 October 1922	Liberal Union-Liberal Party

Mussolini and his Fascist Party were sore losers. The day after the election, a Fascist militant threw a bomb at a Socialist Party victory parade marching through Milan and wounded nine people. Police raided *Il Popolo d'Italia*'s office and discovered the secret room called 'The Lair', where they found grenades and revolvers. The police arrested Mussolini, Filipo Marinetti and Ferrucio Vecchi. Mussolini's latest incarceration was brief. Prime Minister Nitti ordered the three Fascist leaders released with no indictments after receiving a phone call from Luigi Albertini, editor-in-chief of *Corriere della Sera,* Italy's most powerful newspaper. Albertini declared Mussolini was now 'only a has been, don't make a martyr of him'.[37]

Mussolini organized a Fascist Congress of 120 delegates from 22 to 25 May 1920, straddling the fifth anniversary of Italy's entrance into the First World War. Notably absent were Ferrucio Vecchi and Filipo Marinetti, who dropped their memberships. Mussolini managed to sideline D'Annunzio by getting him to retire to Vittoriale Palace at Salo overlooking Lake Larga.

Mussolini celebrated violence as Fascism's means and end:

> The iron law of violence . . . had been confirmed . . . The formation of squads and battling units which I had drawn up by institution had been accomplished. I had given them, in precise directions, well-specified tasks within clean limits. They began their work of discipline and retaliation . . . Among them was the best type of Italian manhood who . . . met and destroyed the social-communist spiders which . . . were exterminating . . . the Italian people . . . The black shirt – symbol of hardihood – was our uniform of war.[38]

Like the Fascist Party, the Socialist Party pursued dual electoral and militant strategies to take power. The Socialists explicitly declared their intention to impose a communist revolution on Italy with a resolution at their congress in Bologna in October 1919:

> the proletariat must have recourse to the use of violence for the conquest of power over the bourgeoisie . . . The existing institutions of local and national government cannot in any way be transformed into organs that will help liberate the people. Instead we must use new and proletarian organizations such as workers' soviets and we must adhere to the Third International.[39]

The Third International was the Communist International or Comintern, the Soviet Union's tool to foment communist revolutions around the world.

The two most popular political parties got most of their support from affiliated labour organizations, the Socialist Party with 2,150,000 members of the Italian Workers' Confederation (*Confederazione Italiana dei Lavoratori*, CGL) and the People's Party with 1,162,238 members of the Italian Workers Federation (*Federazione Italiana dei Lavoratori*, CIL). Each party's parliamentary strength at once reflected and shaped its labour affiliate's relative moderation, especially whether to declare a general strike that paralyzed the country.

The Socialist Party instigated or exacerbated waves of strikes and riots across Italy then united them under the Italian Workers Confederation to takeover factories in Turin, Milan and other northern industrial cities in August 1920. The Italian Workers' Confederation's membership skyrocketed from 249,000 in 1918 to 2,320,000 in 1920 along with the number of man-days lost to strikes from 906,000 to 14,200,000.[40]

Confindustria's corporations worked together to try to expel the strikers. Prime Minister Giolitti brokered a deal between *Confindustria* and the Italian Workers' Confederation, signed on 15 September, whereby employees would evacuate the factories on 27 September and return to work on 4 October in return for management recognizing a vague right of association to address wages, hours and other work conditions. Several months of mass strikes devastated the economy with bankruptcies and mass firings. Countless workers no longer had a place to work.

The mass strikes, disruptions and layoffs boosted the Fascist Party which condemned them. Increasingly, business owners and city mayors secretly turned to local Fascist Party branches for strike breakers. From January to May 1921 alone, 207 militants died and 891 were wounded in the fighting.[41] Mussolini instructed the Fasci to focus their attacks on the Socialist Party, especially their headquarters, meeting halls and printing presses, He argued in a November 1920 *Populo d'Italia* editorial that: 'The reality is this. The Socialist Party is a Russian army encamped in Italy. Against this foreign army, Fascists have launched a guerilla war and they will conduct it with exceptional seriousness.'[42] Street battles and assassinations among political parties, especially the Communists, Socialists and Fascists, resulted in 3,000 deaths, including 425 Fascists, from January 1919 to October 1922.[43]

Meanwhile, the Socialist Party split bitterly between moderates who emphasized gaining power within the parliamentary system and radicals who sought to destroy that system with a revolution like in Russia.[44] That came during the Socialist Party's congress at Livorno from 15 to 21 January 1921. The radicals introduced a 21-point revolutionary doctrine drafted by the Comintern in Moscow and demanded that the Socialist Party adopt it. Days of bitter debates culminated with a vote in which the moderates prevailed with 98,000 weighted votes to 58,000 radical votes and 15,000 for a compromise position. The radicals, led by Amadeo Bordiga, Antonio Gramsci and Nicola Bombacci, angrily stalked out. In a congress in a nearby hall in Livorno, they founded the Italian Communist Party on 21 January. Bordiga was the first general secretary. The Communist Party's birth and adherence to revolutionary Communist International (Comintern) orders emanating from Moscow, would boost Mussolini's Fascist Party as a countervailing force in the minds of countless Italians.[45]

Mussolini was thrilled when Prime Minister Giolitti called for a Chamber of Deputies election on 15 May 1921 and eagerly led his Fascist Party toward the vote. The political agenda that he and his inner circle devised for the Fascist Party included a progressive tax rate and inheritance taxes; the arms industry's nationalization; ending land tenancy by giving peasants what they tilled; the right for women to vote and run for office; a fixed minimum wage; and the abolition of the Senate. That progressive agenda enraged radical leftists because it appropriated their most popular ideas.

Mussolini's Fascist Party won 0.45 per cent of the national vote and two of 535 seats; he actually ran and won in two districts, in Milan with 124,918 votes and in Bologna with 172,491 votes.[46] Mussolini managed to entice militant converts from other parties and the Fascist Party soon had 35 seats. Giolitti actually welcomed Mussolini and his comrades into the Chamber of Deputies, lauding them for being 'young, for the most part, and animated by an aggressive spirit . . . I regarded that as a great advantage, because now Fascism represented a real force in the country.'[47] That 'aggressive spirit' would intimidate the king into naming Mussolini the prime minister just 15 months later and the Chamber of Deputies to grant him ever more powers until he transformed Italy from a democracy into a dictatorship.

Nationally, the top four parties were Giovanni Bacci's Italian Socialist Party (PSI) with 24.69 per cent and 123 seats; Luigi Sturzo's Italian People's Party (PPI) with 20.39 per cent and 108 seats; Giovanni Giolitti's new Democratic Bloc (BD) with 19.07 per cent and 105 seats; Francesco Nitti's Democratic Liberal Party (PLD) with 10.31 per cent and 68 seats. The newborn Italian Communist Party (CPI) won 4.10 per cent of the vote and 15 seats.[48] Giolitti could not hold his coalition government together and it collapsed on 27 June. Ivanoe Bonomi of the Italian Radical Socialist Party formed a coalition with himself as prime minister that took power on 4 July 1921.

Mussolini projected a conciliatory image for himself and the Fascist Party during his maiden speech on 21 June. He called for more efficient government, fewer business regulations, good relations between the state and the Catholic Church and a truce with the Socialist Party. Two lines were especially striking. One rebuked the core Marxist belief: 'We deny that the history of mankind can be explained by economic determinism'. The other repudiated violence and offered peace: 'Violence is not a system . . . it is not a sport . . . We are ready to lay down our arms if you too will disarm and especially disarm your minds.'[49] His speech inspired loud applause from moderate delegates and grousing by Fascist Party hardliners led by Dino Grandi and Roberto Farinacci.

To solidify his leadership of the Fascist Party, Mussolini moved to Rome and lived in a suite at the Hotel des Princes in the Piazza di Spagna. Hardliners like Dino Grandi of Bologna, Pietro Marsich of Venice, Roberto Farinacci of Modena, Cesare De Vecchio of Turin and Achille Starace of Trento each led a faction that sought to depose Mussolini and make himself the leader. As their criticism of him grew, Mussolini insisted on 2 August, that: 'If Fascism does not follow me, no one can force me to follow Fascism'. They squared off during a congress with 541 delegates at Bologna on 16 August. Angered, Mussolini declared: 'It is not I who am resigning, but the others who are forcing me to leave'.[50] He still had a majority of followers on the Executive Council that on 19 August refused to accept his resignation.

Over the next six weeks Mussolini cut deals and played off his rivals. He organized a congress packed with his followers at Rome from 7 to 10 November 1921 and managed to subordinate his then most powerful rivals Grandi and Marsich. The three embraced on stage before the cheering delegates. The delegates overwhelmingly voted to officially name their party the National Fascist Party (*Partito Nazionale Fascista*, PNF). Michele Bianchi became the Fascist Party's secretary general.

The Fascist Party's membership soared from 20,615 to 218,453 in 1,333 Fasci or branches in just one year between December 1920 and December 1921. Of the branches, 62 per cent were in northern, 13 in central, 19 per cent in southern and 8 per cent in island Italy. A member survey found that 57.5 per cent were war veterans, 24.3 per cent peasants, 15.45 per cent workers, 13 per cent students, 12 per cent landowners, 9.8 per cent white-collar workers, 9.2 per cent artisans, 6.6 per cent lawyers, doctors and other professionals, 4.8 per cent bureaucrats, 2.8 per cent businessmen, 1.1 per cent teachers and 1 per cent seamen.[51]

Mussolini hoped to expand his prestige with diplomatic journeys in 1922. In January, he travelled to Cannes, France, to observe the inter-Allied conference led by French Prime Minister and Foreign Minister Aristide Bertrand and British Foreign Minister David Lloyd George. In March, he went to Berlin to meet Foreign Minister Walter Rathenau.

Mussolini sought to elevate himself and his creed to the Pantheon of the world's greatest philosophers and philosophies. For that he had to theoretically flesh out Fascism to compete as a coherent philosophy with Socialism, Liberalism, Communism and other political ideologies. To that end, he founded the journal *Gerarchia* (*Hierarchy*) in Milan to develop Fascism as a political philosophy, with the first issue appearing in January 1922.

He received ever more endorsements from mostly businessmen but also labour and peasant leaders. He was thrilled to hear about the alleged comments of Monsignor Achille Ratti, Milan's archbishop, to the writer Luca Valti: 'Mussolini is making great progress and he is going to invade everything with the strength of a natural force.

Mussolini is a remarkable man . . . he has the zeal of the novice that pushes a man forward . . . The future belongs to him.'[52] After Pope Benedict XV died on 22 January 1922, the College of Cardinals replaced him with Ratti, who took the name Pius XI on 6 February.

Mussolini bolstered the Fascist Party's electoral power by forming the National Confederation of Syndicates in Milan on 25 January 1922, which he renamed the General Confederation of Fascist Syndicates with Edmondo Rossoni the secretary general in December 1922. Membership soared to 700,000 by July before levelling off. The syndicates or groups included not just blue collar workers but also peasants and white collar workers. All along, Mussolini's Blackshirt militia steadily expanded. By October 1922, the *Fasci di Combattimento* had a group in over 7,300 communes across Italy. They held frequent rallies in main squares and parades through city streets.

A no-confidence vote of 295 to 107 forced Prime Minister Bonomi to resign on 17 February 1922. Liberal Party leader Luigi Facta cobbled together a centre-right coalition and the king named him prime minister on 26 February

The decision by Mussolini and his inner circle to take over Italy's government came during a Fascist Party conference at the San Carlo Theatre in Naples on 24 October. He announced that 'either we are allowed to govern or we will seize power by marching on Rome to take by the throat the miserable political class that governs us'.[53] He appointed Four Deputies (*Quadrumvirs*) to mobilize the coup, Cesare De Vecchi, Italo Balbo, Emilio De Bono and Michele Bianchi, who commanded the largest and most aggressive militias. He divided Italy into twelve zones, each headed by an inspector who would mobilize its Fasci. The march would begin at points near Rome, Tivoli, Santa Marinella and Mentana, each with a train station where Fascists would mass the day before. Mussolini returned to his headquarters at *Populo d'Italia*'s office in Milan where he would direct operations by telegram and telephone; Switzerland was a few hours away by train should the government crush his coup.

The *Quadrumvirs* established their headquarters at the Hotel Brufani in Perugia, a hilltop city 85 rail miles north of Rome. They printed and dispatched by train and truck across Italy thousands of copies of a poster to be glued on walls with these incendiary words: 'Fascisti! Italians! The time for determined battle has come! . . . Today the army of the black shirts . . . going directly to Rome, brings victory again to the glory of that Capitol . . . Fascism draws its sword to cut the Gordian knots which tie and burden Italian life'.[54]

On 26 October Mussolini publically issued his threat to lead his Fascist militants in a march to Rome if King Victor Emannuel III did not name him prime minister and let him form a government. The *Quadrumvirs* sent word to the Inspectors who disseminated word to local Fasci to mobilize their men to demonstrate, parade and take over government offices and telephone exchanges on 27 October. Vital mass rallies took place in Rome, Milan, Florence and Perugia. In *Populo d'Italia,* Mussolini claimed that 300,000 Blackshirts would converge on Rome; the real figure was one-tenth of that, around 30,000. He would also later claim that 'Three Thousand Fascist Martyrs' died fighting during the takeover. Actually, none did, although Blackshirts did kill three opponents in sporadic street skirmishes on that fatal day.

Prime Minister Facta and Chief of Staff Pietro Badoglio drafted a martial law decree, presented it to the king at 9.00 on the morning of 28 October and urged him to let the military crush the marchers. In Rome, General Emanuele Pugliese commanded 25,000 troops. The king refused, the first time in his 22 years on the throne that he rejected his advisors' consensus.[55] He believed Mussolini's 300,000 militants lie, when actually the army far outnumbered and outgunned the Fascists. He also worried about the loyalty of many officers and soldiers. He learned that military authorities in Venice, Padua and Trieste were collaborating with the Fascists.

Victor Emmanuel had Facta resign as prime minister, replaced him with Antonio Salandra and had Salandra telephone Mussolini and offer him four portfolios in a coalition government. Mussolini refused. He would be prime minister or else the March on Rome would proceed. The king had his military advisor General Auturo Cittadini inform Mussolini on 29 October that he had named him prime minister and summoned him to form a government.

Mussolini took the night train with General Secretary Bianchi from Milan to Rome. The train arrived at the central station in late morning. An honour guard and a special car awaited *Il Duce*. The car took Mussolini and Bianchi to Quirinale Palace, the royal residence. Before the king, Mussolini declared: 'I bring Your Majesty the Italy of Vittorio Veneto, consecrated anew by victory and I am Your Majesty's loyal servant.'[56] Victor Emmanuel gravely pronounced him prime minister.

Mussolini now headed Italy's government. What would the 39-year-old *Duce* and his Fascist Party do with that power?

Chapter 4

THE FASCIST STATE

> Everything within the state, nothing outside the state, nothing against the state.
>
> (Benito Mussolini)

> The Italian Nation is an organism having ends, life, superior methods of power and endurance than those of the divided and regrouped individuals which compose it. It is a moral, political and economic unity which realizes itself integrally in the Fascist State.
>
> (Benito Mussolini)

> I assume, I alone, the political, moral, historical responsibility for everything that has happened . . . If Fascism has been a criminal association, if all the violence has been the result of a determined historical, political, moral delinquency, the responsibility for this is on me, because I created it with my propaganda.
>
> (Benito Mussolini)

Looking back two decades later, Benito Mussolini asked and answered key questions about his coup's significance:

> What was the march on Rome? A mere governmental crisis, a normal change of ministers? No. It was something more than that. An insurrection? Yes. One which lasted on and off for about two years. Did that insurrection erupt into a revolution? No. Assuming that a revolution takes place not only when the system of government but also the constitutional framework is changed by force, Fascism did not cause a revolution in October 1922.[1]

Mussolini began his Fascist revolution two years later and it was bloodless.[2]

Immediately after taking power, Mussolini faced the enormous challenge of uniting a spectrum of rival political factions under his leadership. With only 35 Fascist seats out of 535 in the Chamber of Deputies, he had to entice rather than alienate the centrist and rightist political parties. To govern, he allied his National Fascist Party (PNF) with Luigi Sturzo's Italian People's Party (PPI), Giovanni Giolitti's Italian Liberal Party (PLI), Giovanni Colonna's Social Democratic Party (DPP) and Enrico Corradini's Italian Nationalist Association (ANI).

Mussolini ensured that his Fascist Party dominated the government by holding eleven of twenty-one cabinet posts and that his own power was overwhelming as prime minister, foreign minister and interior minister. Palazzo Viminale held the offices for the prime minister (President of the Council of Ministers) and interior minister, while initially Palazzo della Consulta then Palazzo Chigi held the foreign minister's office. Beyond himself, his Fascist Party picks were second-tier leaders. He pointedly did not tap Dino Grandi, Italo Balbo, Roberto Farinacci or Michele Bianchi to head any ministry. As Interior Minister, Mussolini appointed Fascist Party *quadrumvir* Emilio De Bono as Police Minister. Otherwise, he gave the Liberal Party three ministries, the People's Party two ministries and the Social Democratic Party two ministries. He had professionals head the War and Navy Ministries, General Armando Diaz and Admiral Paolo di Revel, respectively.

Mussolini succeeded in coopting the Italian Nationalist Association (ANI), the oldest such group, by tapping its chief Luigi Federzoni to be Colonial Minister.[3] His price for Federzoni was to dissolve the Nationalist Association into the Fascist Party and his Blueshirt militia into the Blackshirts. The Nationalist Association's top lawyer Alfredo Rocco handled that political and legal transition. Mussolini rewarded him by naming him the Justice Minister in 1925.

4.1 Benito Mussolini's Cabinet, October 1922

Post	Person	Party
Prime	Benito Mussolini	Fascist
Foreign	Benito Mussolini	Fascist
Interior	Benito Mussolini	Fascist
Treasury	Vincenzo Tangono	People's
War	Armando Diaz	Army General

Navy	Paolo di Revel	Navy Admiral
Grace and Justice	Pietro de Francisci	Fascist
Justice and Worship	Aldo Oviglio	Fascist
Public Education	Giovanni Gentile	Fascist
National Economy	Orso Corbino	Liberal
Industry and Commerce	Teofino Rossi	Liberal
Agriculture	Giuseppe D'Arzago	Liberal
Labour and Social Security	Stefano Cavazzoni	People's
Public Works	Gabrielo Camazza	Social Democratic
Colonial	Luigi Federzoni	National Association
Finance	Alberto De Stefani	Fascist
Post and Telegraph	Giovanni Colona	Social Democratic
Communications	Costanzo Ciano	Fascist
Lands Freed from the Enemy	Giovanni Giurnati	Fascist
Italian Africa	Alessandro Lessona	Fascist
Council of Minsters Secretary	Giacomo Acerbo	Fascist

Violence marred Mussolini's inauguration. On 31 October, he had 50,000 Blackshirts conduct a ceremonial March on Rome that he reviewed at Villa Borghese while the royal family observed at Quirinale Palace. As the column paraded through the working-class districts of San Lorenzo and Trionfale, fights erupted between Fascists and Communist and Socialist hecklers, with nine killed, nineteen wounded and the Socialist Party's newspaper office sacked. Mussolini issued orders whereby that night fifty special trains packed with Blackshirts departed from Rome to their home regions across the country.

Parliament reconvened on 16 November, with both houses packed in the Chamber of Deputies at Palazzo Montecitorio. Prime Minister Mussolini mingled threats and conciliation in his maiden speech before them: 'Gentlemen, what I am performing in this chamber today is an act of purely formal deference to you, for which I ask of you no sign of special gratitude. I declare that this revolution has its rights. I have refused to carry my victory to its final conclusion. I could do so.' He paused dramatically, then with a raised voice asserted: 'With three hundred thousand armed young men . . . prepared for everything, ready to obey me in almost mystic blindness, I could chastise all those who have slandered and sought to sully Fascism. I have set myself certain limits.'[4]

Most deputies and senators applauded, some enthusiastically, others for show, while many stared in silent fear. In their separate chambers, each voted to approve Mussolini's ominous message, the Senators by acclamation, the Deputies by 306 to 116 for this resolution: 'Having confidence in the destiny of the nation, the Chamber approves the government's statement and proceeds with the agenda.'[5]

Mussolini gathered twenty Fascist leaders at the Grand Hotel for two key announcements on 15 December 1922. First, he declared the creation of the Fascist Grand Council that would meet at ten o'clock the twelfth day of each month to discuss and approve policies. He then declared that he would consolidate the Fascist Party's array of affiliated militia groups into the Militia for National Security (*Milizia per la Sicurezza Nationale*, MSN), soon renamed the Voluntary Militia for National Security (*Milizia Voluntaria per la Sicurezza Nationale*, MVSN). The elite Blackshirt troops were the 'Always Ready' (*Sempre Pronto*) squads. The Roman Legion was the model for the Fascist militia which was hierarchically organized into cohorts, centuries, maniples and squads, with three of each forming the unit above. There were 133 legions split among fifteen zones and organized into three-legion divisions. Militia swore allegiance to Mussolini, their Commander General. Mussolini got the king to issue a royal decree legalizing those changes and that power on 14 January 1923.

To further bolster the Voluntary Militia's legitimacy, he issued this decree in September 1923:

> It is significant that, as part of its duties to defend the revolution, the new Militia has been given the task of maintaining public order, thus taking away from the army a duty which distracted it from its proper functions and goals. But it cannot be denied that the Militia exists above all in order to permeate Italian youth with a new spirit, to train them in the use of weapons, to enlarge the basis which sustains the destinies of the Italian people . . . Wars today are not fought by regular armies only, they are fought by nations.[6]

Mussolini cut deals with the major party leaders with conventional political horse trading. However, for recalcitrant opponents he wielded terror to bully them into compliance by unleashing his Action

Squads to attack them and their followers. In the months following his takeover, his militants murdered fifteen opponents and severely beat over fifty.[7] The worst violence came on 25 December 1922, when Mussolini had Blackshirts led by Ferruccio De Vecchi destroy the office of the Communist Party's newspaper *The New Order* (*L'Ordine Nuovo*) in Turin; a dozen or so people died in the brawl and scores suffered injuries.

Mussolini worried about rivals within the Fascist Party who might build up power and displace him. He squared off with that threat during a Grand Council meeting on 12 January 1923. *Il Duce* asserted that 'the country can perhaps put up with Mussolini but not with several dozens'. He ordered all militant groups to join the national Fascist militia and declare allegiance to him. He also forbade militia leaders from being political leaders. During a speech on 26 March 1923, he declared that: 'Our great victory cannot be questioned. It is questioned only by those Fascists who do not accept our stern discipline and persevere in their idiotic and unheroic illegal ways which I am determined to suppress because they sully the purity of Fascism and endanger the future of the nation.'[8]

The most obvious potential rival was the Fascist Party General Secretary. Michele Bianchi held that post from 11 November 1921 until Mussolini asked him to resign on 13 October 1923, nearly a year after the coup and replaced him with Francesco Giunta. Fearing that Guinta was amassing too much power, he had him resign on 23 April 1924 and replaced him with the *Quadrumvirs* – Cesare De Vecchi, Italo Balbo, Emilio De Bono and Michele Bono – who had led 'the March on Rome'. The result was disunity and deadlock among those prima donnas. Mussolini replaced them with Roberto Farinacci, Cremona's charismatic, popular Fascist boss, on 15 February 1925.

Yet that boosted Farinacci's authority to realize his own dictatorial ambitions.[9] Over the next 13 months until Mussolini dismissed him on 30 March 1926, he consolidated power at the top by dismissing dissident or autonomous groups and individuals, packing ranks with dutiful loyalists, encouraging the growth of militia squads autonomous from loyalty to Mussolini and criticizing Grand Council decrees. That made the Fascist Party more Farinacci's creature than Mussolini's. That resembled what Joseph Stalin had done as the Communist Party's Secretary General in the Soviet Union. Farinacci, however, did not wield that power to overthrow Mussolini as Stalin had in purging his rivals.

Farinacci's attempts to form a private militia worried Mussolini, who issued him this rebuke on 13 October 1925: 'I will not tolerate squads of any kind and I will not tolerate that resolutions of the Grand Council be questioned . . . Whenever the prestige and authority of the government are involved I will not be questioned and I will employ all means. My order is clear . . . All squads are to be dissolved.'[10] Farinacci promptly stepped down and Mussolini replaced him with Augusto Turati.

4.2 List of Fascist Party Secretaries, Tenures and Party Names

Duumvirate	23 March 1919	1 August 1919	Italian Fasces of Combat
Umberto Pasella	1 August 919	10 November 1921	Italian Fasces of Combat
Michele Bianchi	10 November 1921	13 October 1923	National Fascist Party
Francesco Giunta	13 October 1923	23 April 1924	National Fascist Party
Quadrumvirate	23 April 1924	15 February 1925	National Fascist Party
Roberto Farinacci	15 February 1925	30 March 1926	National Fascist Party
Augusto Turati	30 March 1926	7 October 1930	National Fascist Party
Giovanni Giurati	7 October 1930	12 December 1931	National Fascist Party
Achille Starace	12 December 1931	31 October 1939	National Fascist Party
Ettore Muti	31 October 1939	30 October 1940	National Fascist Party
Adelphi Serena	30 October 1940	21 December 1941	National Fascist Party
Aldo Vidussoni	21 December 1941	19 April 1943	National Fascist Party
Carlo Scorza	19 April 1943	27 July 1943	National Fascist Party
Alessandro Pavolini	15 November 1943	28 April 1945	Republican Fascist Party

Mussolini and Victor Emmanuel III had a complicated relationship. Mussolini at once abhorred and needed the king. He disdained Victor Emmanuel for his weak will and diminutive stature but as prime minister served him and could be dismissed by him. Victor Emmanuel at once feared and despised Mussolini.

During Mussolini's 21 years as prime minister, he remained constitutionally subordinate to the king who was both the head of state and commander-in-chief. He dutifully attended the weekly morning audience on Monday and Thursday and stepped back when foreign heads of states visited to stand beside the king in formal settings. Mussolini may have originated nearly all the decrees that built and sustained his dictatorship, but the king co-signed each one, most enthusiastically, some reluctantly. Mussolini's Fascist Party may have eventually occupied every Chamber of Deputy seat, but the king still appointed all Senate seats, albeit eventually ensuring that they were Fascist Party members. Mussolini may have been the acting commander-in-chief during the war but the king never relinquished his symbolic authority and attended most military ceremonies.

Italian soldiers and civilians swore allegiance to both men, trying not to imagine what to do if they turned against each other. The oath to the King stated: 'I swear to be faithful to the King and his royal successors, to loyally observe the Statute and other laws of the state, to fulfil all the duties of my state, for the sole purpose of the inseparable good of the King and the patria.' The oath to Mussolini stated: 'In the name of God and of Italy, I swear to execute the orders of the *Duce* and to serve with all my strength and, if necessary, with my blood, the cause of the Fascist Revolution.'[11]

Mussolini recalled how their relationship changed over that time until the king dismissed him and had him arrested:

> Our relations were always cordial but never friendly. There was always something between us which prevented our reaching a relationship of real confidence. During the various wars, the King was only a passenger and vacillated perpetually. He was less so in the 1940 war, when he not only raised no objections of any sort but considered the war against France and Britain a necessary decision. As the war went on, the attitude changed.[12]

That was only partly true. Actually the king initially opposed and under pressure eventually yielded to Italy joining Germany in warring against Britain and France. And Mussolini does not mention his loathing for the king's timidity, vacillation and diminutive status.

The king was not just the commander-in-chief, a largely ceremonial post activated only in war. He directly commanded the Royal Carabinieri Corps (*Corpo dei Carabinieri Reali*), a paramilitary national police force dedicated to protecting him and following his orders. The Royal Guard were police that defended him wherever he went along with his many palaces. All troops and police swore allegiance solely to the king.

Critical for Mussolini's dictatorship was somehow subordinating the military. For that he engaged in a tug-of-war with Victor Emmanuel III over 21 years. One key way was periodically naming himself the army, navy and, from 1925, air force ministers and in 1939 naming himself acting commander-in-chief. Despite his efforts, eventually the king decisively won that struggle.

Mussolini's first critical stride on his path to dictatorship took place on 15 July 1923, when he got the Chamber of Deputies to vote 303 to 40 to grant him emergency powers for a year. With that, he and jurist Giacomo Acerbo devised a legal means of taking over the Chamber of Deputies. Acerbo drafted a law whereby any political party that won more than 25 per cent of the vote would receive 65 per cent of the seats. The Chamber of Deputies passed the Acerbo Law by 235 for and 139 against, with 77 abstentions on 21 July; the Senate approved it on 14 November; and Victor Emmanuel III ratified it on 18 November 1923.

The first election under the new system came on 6 April 1924. For that, Mussolini formed a National List of his Fascist Party allied with the Liberal, Social Democratic (former Radical) and Peasant Parties and former prime ministers Antonio Salandra, Giovanni Giolitti and Vittorio Orlando. When the votes were counted, Mussolini's National List won 4,305,936 votes or 64.94 per cent of 7,165,502 valid votes and 374 of 535 seats; support included around 50 per cent of votes in the north, 76 per cent in the centre and 81 per cent in the south.[13] The nearest runner up was Alcide de Gasperi's Italian People's Party (PPI) with 9.01 per cent and 39 seats, down 69. Then came Giacomo Matteotti's new Unitary Socialist Party with 5.90 per cent and 24 sears; Tito Nobili's Italian Socialist Party (PSI) with 5.03 per cent and 22 seats, down 101 and Antonio Gramsci's Italian Communist Party (CPI) with 3.74 per cent and 19 seats, up from four.[14]

With an overwhelming parliamentary majority, Mussolini could legally impose his Fascist revolution. Then a vicious murder nearly ended his march to dictatorship.

Giacomo Matteotti headed the Unitary Socialist Party and was Parliament's most outspoken deputy, frequently protesting Fascist Party corruption and vote-rigging. On 10 June 1924, Matteotti emerged from his apartment building facing the Tiber River and began walking along it. The police officer assigned to guard him was gone. Suddenly, five men jumped out of a car and dragged him into it. When he resisted, they stabbed him to death then drove his body 14 miles outside of Rome to a forsaken place where they decapitated him and left his remains.

Police detectives soon tracked down the killers. A nearby hotel concierge witnessed the abduction and recorded the getaway car's license plate number. The vehicle's owner was Filipo Filipelli, the editor of the Fascist-affiliated newspaper *Il Corriere Italiano* and a Mussolini advisor. Filipelli nervously explained that he had lent his car to Amerigo Dumini, Mussolini's bodyguard and a hit man suspected of assassinating at least a dozen other political opponents. Police soon arrested Dumini and four other suspects that included Fascist militant Albino Volpi, called 'the gorilla' and low-level thugs Amleto Poveromo, Augusto Malacria and Giuseppe Viola hired for the job. The five claimed they were innocent of Matteotti's abduction.

Word that Mussolini was likely behind the crime provoked outrage. Victor Emmanuel III resisted demands by many deputies, newspaper editors and other prominent voices to dismiss him from the government. Mussolini angrily denied any link with the crime. On the evening of 12 June, he appeared before the Chamber of Deputies to declare: 'I believe the Chamber is concerned with what has happened to Deputy Matteotti, who disappeared suddenly . . . in circumstances of time and place that are not yet altogether definite but can support the hypothesis of a crime that, if it has indeed been committed, can only arouse the indignation and the grief of the government and Parliament.'[15]

Parliament's houses both backed Mussolini, but differed greatly in their relative enthusiasm. On 26 June, the Senate voted confidence in Mussolini by 225 to 21, with 6 abstentions. On 27 June, 124 members of the Socialist, Popular, Republican, Constitutionalist and Communist Parties walked out of the Chamber, convened in a nearby hall and pledged not to return until the crime was thoroughly investigated and everyone behind it was prosecuted. Three of four of the remaining 411 deputies were Mussolini loyalists, outright Fascists or allies. The boycott by the dissidents, who called themselves the Aventinian Group, made getting approval for Mussolini's decrees much easier as only a handful of cowed opposition deputies remained. That empowered Mussolini confidently to declare that: 'If His Majesty the King should call me at the termination of this session and tell me that I must go,

I would stand at attention, salute and obey.'[16] He knew that Victor Emmanuel was too timid and isolated to dare do so.

Mussolini's only fear was that he would not just be deposed but prosecuted for murder if the assassins confessed. He tersely told his inner circle that 'if I get away with this we all survive; otherwise we shall all sink together'.[17] On 17 June, he appointed Nationalist Association leader Luigi Federzoni as Interior Minister and asked him to conduct a thorough investigation. Meanwhile, behind the scenes he bought the silence of the five for at least 2.37 million lire. He also paid compensation to Matteotti's widow and children.[18]

Charges against the five suspects turned to murder when police found Matteotti's decapitated body on 16 August. Yet, Mussolini got away with that murder. The killers kept silent. Dumani, Volpi and Poveromo received six-year prison sentences, while Viola and Malacria were acquitted because they sat in the front seat while the other three murdered Matteotti in the back. On 32 July 1925, the king granted the three murderers amnesty after they served just two months in prison.

Meanwhile, Fascist deputy Armando Casalini was gunned down on 12 September 1924. Mussolini accused the Communist Party of committing the murder, yet publicly declared that the Fascist Party Blackshirts would not launch retaliatory attacks without proof. At least, not yet.

Mussolini felt politically secure enough to exchange his conciliatory attitude to Matteotti's murder for defiance during a Chamber of Deputies speech on 3 January 1925:

> I assume, I alone, the political, moral, historical responsibility for everything that has happened . . . If Fascism has been a criminal association, if all the violence has been the result of a determined historical, political, moral delinquency, the responsibility for this is on me, because I created it with my propaganda . . . Fascism, the Government, the Party, is at its highest efficiency.

He recognized the right of the Chamber of Deputies under the Constitution's Article 47 to vote to indict him and for the High Court of Justice to try him. but 'I am not looking for this vote'. He ended by declaring: 'Italy, Gentlemen, wants peace, wants quiet, wants work, wants calm; we will give it with love, if that be possible or with strength, if that be necessary . . . We all know that this is not a personal fancy, not lust for government, not base passion, but only infinite and powerful love for my country.'[19] With those carefully crafted words, Mussolini brilliantly neutralized any deputies who hoped to depose him with a no-confidence or indictment vote.

Nearly ten months later, Mussolini announced that he was crossing the Rubicon from wielding temporary emergency powers granted by Parliament toward an eventual blatant tyranny in a speech before a packed audience at Milan's La Scala Opera House on 28 October 1925. To unite the Italian people 'in nationalism, common purpose and prosperity', he would establish 'a totalitarian state' or 'Everything within the state, nothing outside the state, nothing against the state'.[20]

Mussolini did not abolish the Chamber of Deputies, he ignored it. From 1924 to 1929, the Chamber of Deputies debated and voted on only 45 of 5,553 laws that Mussolini promulgated.[21] He did have the Chamber of Deputies rubber-stamp a bill on 18 November 1925 that transformed the constitutional power of the prime minister, officially known as president of the council of ministers, from first among equals in the cabinet to the government's highest executive, beholden only to the king. He followed that up with a law on 31 January 1926, that gave all his decrees the power of law.

He sought to monopolize power by heading as many ministries and committees as possible and mostly confining Fascist Party leaders to second tier or ceremonial posts. He was not just Prime Minister but named himself Foreign Affairs Minister from 1922 to 1929 and 1932 to 1936; Interior Minister from 1922 to 1924 and from 1926 to 1943; Colonial Minister in 1924 and from 1928 to 1929 and from 1935 to 1936; War Minister from 1925 to 1929 and from 1933 to 1943, Navy Minister from 1925 to 1929 and 1933 to 1943; and Public Works Minister in 1929. He created eight new ministries and picked Fascist Party loyalists to head them, including two for himself, Air Force from 1925 to 1929 and 1933 to 1943 and Corporations from 1926 to 1929.

4.3 New Ministries, Initial Ministers and Founding Dates

Ministry	Minister	Founding Date
Air Force	Benito Mussolini	30 August 1925
Corporations	Benito Mussolini	2 July 1926
Agriculture and Forestry	Giacomo Acerbo	12 September 1929
Press and Propaganda	Galeazzo Ciano	26 June 1935
National Fascist Party	Achille Starace	11 January 1937
Popular Culture	Dino Alfieri	27 May 1937
Exchange and Currency	Felice Guarneri	20 November 1937
War Production	Carlo Favagrossa	6 February 1943

Mussolini steadily revoked ever more civil liberties. On 24 December 1925, he decreed that state officials could be fired if they were not affiliated with the Fascist Party. On 31 January 1926, he decreed that the government could revoke the citizenship of anyone who actively opposed the Fascist Party. Mussolini made the 124 deputies of the Aventinian boycott permanent with a law on 9 November 1926 that stripped them of their seats. In 1928, he decreed that every newspaper editor and journalist had to be Fascist Party members.

He decreed the abolition of Rome's city council and transformation into an appointed governorship. He abolished local elections for mayor (*sindico*) for municipalities with fewer than 5,000 people and empowered himself to appoint what he called magistrates (*podesta*) for five-year terms with a decree on 4 February 1926. Magistrates had the combined power of mayors and city councils (*consiglio*). On 3 September 1926, he extended his power to appoint *podesta* to all city governments. He explained that

> by extending the office of *podesta* to the larger municipalities, we will eliminate, wherever they still linger, the seeds of discord that are rooted in the more or less secret desire to gain a municipal seat and that will free the mind of the Italian people from the disease of politics as the sole objective of life . . . [F]ascism will then have achieved one of the goals that most effectively assure the future of the nation: unity of command.[22]

Fascist Party membership was as much an indicator of the Mussolini regime's relative popularity as the stock market was of Italy's relative economic health. Fascist Party membership initially soared from 300,000 in October 1922 to 782,979 in December 1923. Membership then dropped to 642,248 in 1924, after Matteotti's murder and fell further to 599,998 in 1925. From reforms initiated by Roberto Farinacci's term as Fascist Party Secretary membership shot up to 937,997 in 1927 and 1,034,998 in 1929.[23]

The Fascist Party's pyramid hierarchy (*Gerarchia*) included the executive committee chaired by Mussolini, the party secretary, the Grand Council, then regional and finally local 'bosses' (*Ras*, an Ethiopian word that means chief). Journalists accounted for half of ministers and Grand Council members, twenty senior diplomats and sixty-eight deputies in 1930.[24] He sought to govern through expert specialists rather than party ideologues. For that, he established 'Technical Advisory Groups' (*Gruppi di Competenza*) for ministries and big problems.

Mussolini dodged several assassinate attempts. On 4 November 1925, police arrested General Luigi Capello and former socialist deputy Tito

Zaniboni for planning his demise. On 7 April 1926, Violet Gibson, a rich Irish woman, fired at Mussolini and nicked his nose. She was arrested but not charged with attempted murder. Doctors declared her insane and had British authorities return her to Britain where she spent the rest of her life in an asylum.

Mussolini exploited that near-death experience to enhance his political appeal. Later on the day of Gibson's shot, he appeared with a bandaged nose before a group of party officials and workers and declared: 'If I go forward, follow me. If I retreat, kill me. If I die, avenge me'. That evening before another crowd, he stated: 'I am the newest sort of Italian, one who is never thrown by events, but rather proceeds always straight down the road assigned by destiny'.[25]

Mussolini's next brush with death came in Rome on 11 September 1926, when anarchist Gino Lucetti threw a bomb at his passing car. Shrapnel from the explosion missed Mussolini but wounded eight pedestrians; Lucetti received a 30-year prison sentence for attempted murder. On 26 November, in Bologna, anarchist teenager Anteo Zamboni fired at Mussolini as his car drove past. Once again, Mussolini was uninjured but an angry mob murdered Zamboni.

Mussolini reacted by decreeing on 9 November 1926 the State Security Law that outlawed all political parties except the Fascist Party; allowed the state to arrest and deport anyone who opposed the state in word or deed to internal or foreign exile; established the secret police called the Organization for Vigilance and Repression of Anti-Fascism (*Opera Vigilanza Repressione Antifascismo*, OVRA) headquartered in Milan; reinstated the death penalty for those who conspired to murder or did murder the king, queen or prime minister and for espionage and treason; and founded the Special Tribunal for Defence of the State to try those cases. Previously, in September 1926, Mussolini had appointed hardliner Arturo Bocchini Chief (*Capo*) of the State Police (*Polizia di Stato*) and in November named him also OVRA's. Bocchini effectively served in both posts until his death in 1940, when Mussolini had Carmine Senise take his place. Mussolini replaced the conciliatory Luigi Federzoni as Interior Minister with himself on 6 November1926.

Mussolini immediately wielded the State Security Law to have the 124 opposition members in the Chamber of Deputies, mostly socialists and communists, expelled and stripped of their parliamentary immunity from prosecution. He had Communist Party leader Antonio Gramsci arrested and tried for treason; Gramsci received a life sentence and died in prison in 1926. The state arrested and exiled over 500 political opponents by the year's end.

In all, from its inauguration on 1 February 1927 to Mussolini's overthrow on 25 July 1943, the Special Tribunal conducted 720 'audiences' with 5,319 suspects, of which 5,155 received sentences to a total of 28,115 years or average five-year terms. The Special Tribunal condemned to death forty-two people, of whom thirty-one were actually executed, and imposed seven life sentences. The regular court system also tried thousands of people accused of political crimes. However, most of the sentences involved a 'reprimand' (*diffida*) or 'admonition' (*ammonizione*) with no jail time but a two-year parole during which the criminal had to keep a steady job and commit no more crimes. Then there were those sentenced to 'police detention' (*confine di polizia*) or internal exile for up to five years. Those condemned mostly were sent to the tiny islands of Lipari, Ustica and Lampedusa. Although they arrived in chains, they were unbound daily to receive ten lire for food, shelter and other expenses and could earn money in any legal way. OVRA eventually numbered 50,000 personnel and compiled files on over 130,000 Italians and others.[26] In 1932, Mussolini pardoned 22,173 political prisoners, nearly all those then under various sentence,s and kept only 337 in prison.[27]

Thousands of leftist radicals went into foreign exile (*fuorusciti*), either voluntary or coerced.[28] Paris was the magnet for most of them. France was a republic with regular elections and a viable multi-party system that included a Socialist Party and a Communist Party. Italy's Socialist and Communist Parties had their headquarters and conferences in France.

Mussolini amassed more power with three decrees in 1928. The Election Law issued on 17 May 1928 reduced the number of Chamber of Deputy seats to 400 that the Fascist Grand Council approved from a list of 800 candidates submitted by Fascist industry, union and other organizations. That list of 400 was then submitted to voters to accept or reject. But voters first had to approve that new system in a plebiscite. He decreed on 9 December 1928 that the Fascist Grand Council was the supreme state organ with a president, himself and twenty-eight members appointed by him. The Fascist Grand Council supervised and determined the outcomes of all other state institutions except the monarchy. With time, Mussolini bothered summoning the Grand Council less, 106 sessions from 1923 to 1929, 56 from 1930 to 1936 and 23 from 1937 to 1943.[29] His 9 December decree suspended the 1848 Statute (*Statuto Egidio*) or Italy's effective constitution issued by King Albert, first to his Kingdom of Piedmont-Sardinia to after unification adapted to the Kingdom of Italy in 1861.

Mussolini ensured that the plebiscite did not express the free will of Italian men. Only members of Fascist organizations or the military were eligible to vote with an official list of 9,638,657. Voters confronted this question: 'Do you approve the list of members approved by the Grand National Council of Fascism?' After submitting his identity to an election official at the poll, he received two ballots, one 'yes' with a tricolour flag and fasces symbol, the other 'no' on a white background. He entered the voting booth where he left his discarded choice then emerged to hand his choice to an election official who dutifully recorded it and who made it.

In the plebiscite held on 24 March 1929, 8,519,559 voters voted for the elimination of their power to vote and only 136,198 voted to keep that right. The 400-candidate list Chamber of Deputy election came on 28 March. Voters overwhelmingly endorsed the list, with 8,517,838 or 98.4 per cent in favour, 135,757 or 1.57 per cent opposed and 8,092 or 0.09 per cent submitting either a blank or spoiled ballot.[30]

Mussolini combined his offices at Palazzo Viminale (Prime Minster, Interior Minister) and Palazzo Chigi (Foreign Minister) into a grand room at Palazzo Venezia on 19 September 1929. Palazzo Venezia is a magnificent Renaissance building whose construction began in 1455. His desk was in the huge World Map Room (*Sala del Mappamondo*) 60ft on each side with a 40ft-high ceiling and a balcony overlooking Piazza Venezia. From the balcony, he delivered fiery speeches to huge crowds below. He had a broad avenue built from a corner of Piazza Venezia to the Colosseum a mile away. Near the Colosseum, he had erected four huge map panels that depicted the Roman Empire's expansion to its height.

Mussolini lived alone in Rome from 1922 to 1925, while his wife and five children first stayed in their cramped Milan apartment, then a country house called Villa Carpena near Forli and finally a six-room apartment back in Milan. During that time, he moved his residence from Hotel des Princes to the five-star Hotel Savoia, then an apartment at Palazzo Tittoni. Eventually, he recognized that appearing as a family man would enhance his political image. Mussolini and Rachele married in a Catholic church ceremony on 28 December 1925 and had their children baptized. In 1927, Forli's provincial government presented Mussolini with Rocca delle Caminate, a tenth-century castle just two and a half miles from Predappio, his boyhood home. He used Rocca delle Caminate as a summer residence and capital. On 15 November 1929, he moved his family to the opulent nineteenth-century Villa Torlonia surrounded by a vast walled garden two miles from the king's

Palazzo Quirinale along Via Nometana. He did not own the mansion but rented it for a lira a year from its owner. Although Mussolini was frugal and simple in his personal belongings, he shamelessly wielded his power to enhance his own clan and Rachele's; from 1922 to 1943, he handed out varying stipends to 229 of his own relatives and to 105 of Rachele's.[31]

Rachele described his daily routine:

> He arose at six and, after physical exercises, immediately drank an orangeade or glass of grape juice. Then he went out for a [horseback] canter and had a shower on his return. Breakfast consisted of fresh fruit, milk with a little coffee and wholemeal bread . . . He had stopped smoking after the war . . . He was in his office by eight, broke off a few minutes at eleven to eat something and was back home at two. His meal invariably consisted of a little spaghetti with tomato sauce, fresh or cooked vegetables, a good deal of fruit, no coffee. Then into the study, where he went through the Italian and foreign papers. He even found time to study topical publications, when he was not engrossed in reading the classics. There was never any siesta. He was off to the office about six and back home about nine for supper, consisting of a clear soup, vegetables and soup. Wine and spirits he never touched. Meals were a matter of a few minutes. He never lingered at the table or grumbled about the food, provided it was simple and natural . . . He went to bed about ten-thirty. He was always a heavy sleeper.[32]

Despite that relatively healthy lifestyle, the stress of being *Il Duce* inflicted him with a duodenal ulcer and insomnia. His eyes weakened but he was too vain to wear reading glasses in public. For speeches, he had a special typewriter built that typed letters large enough for him to read. He tried to stay in shape by swimming and tennis in his spare time.

The popularity of Mussolini and Fascism depended on whether people believed that they were wealthier and happier. Accomplishing that depended on devising and implementing policies that ameliorated the severe economic problems plaguing Italy. The economy was disjointed with relatively advanced and internationally competitive financial, industrial, transportation and communication sectors and a largely inefficient agrarian sector with relatively few landowners and many landless peasants and vast gaps between the rich, the middle class and the poverty-stricken masses. The population split roughly even between urban and rural inhabitants. Most modern businesses were in the north, with some in the centre and few in the south. That explained why average incomes were highest in the north and lowest in the south. That maldistribution of wealth reflected and shaped school systems. Italy's illiteracy rate for people over six years old in 1931 was 20.9 per cent, with 10.0 per cent in the north, 21 per cent in the centre and 39 per cent in the south and the islands.[33] Organized crime was another problem plaguing some southern regions, most notoriously the Cosa Nostra in Sicily, the 'Ndrangheta in Calabria and the Camorra in Campania.[34] To varying degrees, corruption and patron-client ties (*clientelismo*) afflicted every region.

Mussolini's regime depended on the support of business leaders.[35] Among Italy's most powerful industrialists were Giovanni Agnelli of Fiat (*Fabrica Italiana Automobili Turino* or Italian Automobile Maker at Turin); Adriano Olivetti of Olivetti Company that made typewriters and other business machines at Ivrea; Magneti Marelli of Magneti Marelli Company that made a variety of industrial products at Sesto San Giovanni; Alfa Romeo of Alfa Romeo near Milan that made cars, trucks and tanks; Guido Donegani of Montecatini chemical complex near Livorno; Alberto Pirelli of Pirelli rubber and chemical complex near Milan; Giorgio Falk of Milanese Steel complex near Milan; Vittorio Cini of the Cini shipping company at Venice and hydroelectric system in Alpine rivers flowing south to the Po River; and Giuseppe Volpi di Misurata of Port Marghera chemical and manufacturing complex near Venice.[36] Those corporations and scores of others were members of the General Confederation of Italian Industry (*Confederazione Generale dell'Industria Italiana* or *Confindustria*) established in 1919.

Il Duce's economic policies did uplift both large corporations and most Italians. Certainly, everyone benefited from government investments that improved or expanded roads, railways, electricity grids, schools, hospitals and sewer and water systems. Corporate investments and profits rose with government tax cuts and subsidies. Land reclamation and distribution bettered the lives of peasant recipients. Around 1927, Mussolini and other Fascist spokesmen referred to four related economic 'Battles' of the Lira, Land, Grain and Births or, respectively, a strong, stable currency; land distribution for peasants; expanded food production; and population increase.

Corporatism is a system in which managers and workers cooperate to resolve conflicts over production, pay, hours and safety. Mussolini had Justice Minister Alfredo Rocco cut a deal with *Confindustria* to accept corporatism. Under the Palazzo Vidoni Pact signed on 2 October 1925, *Confindustria* did so in return for independent labour unions abolished, strikes and lockouts banned and only Fascist unions or syndicates allowed. On 1 July 1926, a decree established the Corporations

Ministry and National Council of Corporations to manage industry. By 26 August 1926, the government had established twelve national unions or cartels for major industries including manufacturing, finance, insurance, transportation and agribusiness. Eventually twenty-two cartels emerged with greatly varying degrees of cooperation among the members and adherence to government guidance.

The most important corporatist institutions were the Confederation of Fascist Corporations (*Confederazione delle Corporazioni Fascisti*) and the National Confederation of Fascist Unions (*Confederazione Nationale dei Sindacati Fascisti*). Several institutions were critical for raising and lending money for key corporations and projects. Mussolini nationalized the private *Instituto di Credito Cooperazione*, founded in 1913 and renamed it the *Banca Nationale del Lavore e della Cooperazione* in May 1927. Finance Minister Guido Jung and financial wizard Alberto Beneduce headed from their respective inceptions the Credit Consortium for Public Works (*Consorzio di Credito per le Opere Pubbliche*, Crediop) founded in 1919 and the Credit Institute for Public Utility Companies (*Instituto di Credito per le Imprese di Publica Utilita*, ICIPU) founded in 1924. With Mussolini's approval, they established the Italian Credit Institute (*Instituto Mobiliare Italiano*, IMI) in 1931 and the Institute for Industrial Reconstruction (*Instituto di Ricostruzione Industriale*, IRI) in January 1933.

Mussolini co-opted blue-collar workers with the Law on Corporations of 3 April 1926. The government abolished demanding, strike-prone labour unions and replaced them with syndicates that cooperated with their managers with both devoted to helping build a greater Italy.[37] He explained his vision for them: 'Fascist syndicalism stands for class collaboration . . . capital and labour are not two contradictory terms, they are terms that complement each other . . . A single hour – only one, I tell you – lost from work in a factory is already a grave injury of a national character.'[38]

Mussolini recognized that all work and no play made for exhausted, unreliable Fascists. He established the National Afterwork Club (*Opera Nationale Dopolavoro*, OND) for leisure groups led by Mario Giani in 1925.[39] Two years later, Mussolini replaced Giani with Augusto Turati who made that organization a Fascist Party auxiliary. By May 1933, Fascist trade unions had 3,820,000 members and afterwork organizations had 1,800,000 members.[40]

With Mussolini's approval, Giuseppe Bottai and Augusto Turati drafted a Labour Charter and issued it on 23 April 1927. Like most other Fascist policies and doctrines. the Labour Charter claimed to liberate people by suppressing them. The preamble asserted and justified the subjection of people to the Nation via the State: 'The Italian Nation is an organism having ends, life, superior methods of power and endurance than those of the divided and regrouped individuals which compose it. It is a moral, political and economic unity which realizes itself integrally in the Fascist State.' To that, Mussolini elaborated: 'It is only the State that gives people a consciousness of itself'.[41]

The Labour Charter actually explained Fascist corporatism:

> The corporative State considers private initiative in the field of production the most effective and useful instrument in the interest of the Nation . . . State intervention in economic production takes place only when private initiative is lacking or insufficient or whenever the political interests of the State are involved. Such intervention can assume the form of control, encouragement and direct management.[42]

Two American business innovators inspired Mussolini and other Fascist leaders. Henry Ford revolutionized productivity with the assembly-line system he established for his Ford Automobile Company. Frederick Taylor worked his way up the hierarchy of several businesses and along the way developed and wrote books about 'scientific management' that maximized each employee's efficiency. Mussolini encouraged Italy's businesses to adapt Fordism and Taylorism for their workplaces.

Italy's worst chronic economic problem was inflation that diminished or wiped out business profits and wage hikes. Mussolini understood that inflation's most vital source was the lira's weak value that raised import costs while boosting Italian exports. He declared: 'The fate of the regime is tied to the fate of the lira. It is necessary to consider the battle of the lira as absolutely decisive.'[43] He reestablished the gold standard and set the lira at 19 to the American dollar and 92.46 to the British pound in December 1927. Wholesale prices dropped from 129 in 1926 to 100 in 1929, but inflicted lower growth and exports and higher joblessness.

The Great Depression wiped out much of the economic progress that Italy had made during the 1920s. It began when New York's unregulated stock market collapsed and with it America's economy in October 1929. Congress and President Herbert Hoover then globalized America's depression in 1930 with the Smoot-Hawley Act that raised tariffs 50 per cent to protect beleaguered domestic industries. Italy and other countries retaliated by raising their own tariffs. World trade imploded and with it every nation's economy.

Italy's economy declined from 1929 to 1934, with national income's value dropping from 124,621,000 lire to 118,523,000 lire, per capita income from 3,079 lire to 1,829 lire, the manufacturing index from 90 to 80, the manufacturing employment index from 90 to 71, the wholesale price index from 100 to 65 and the living cost index from 102 to 78. Mussolini worsened those declines by slashing civil servants wages by 12 per cent, factory wages by 8 to 10 per cent and farm labourer wages by 10 to 25 per cent to save money for the bureaucracy and profits for businesses.[44]

4.4 Italian Economic Indexes, 1929–1939[45]

Years	National Income in Lira	Per Capita Income in Lira	Manufacturing Index	Manufacturing Employment Index	Whole Price Index	Living Cost Index
1929	124,621,000	3,079	90	90	100	102
1930	116,024,000	2,845	85	88	90	99
1931	116,019,000	2,823	77	80	78	90
1932	120,585,000	2,916	77	71	73	87
1933	119,369,000	2,868	82	72	67	82
1934	118,423,000	1,829	80	75	65	78
1935	129,672,000	3,075	86	85	72	79
1936	128,280,000	3,022	86	86	80	84
1937	137,995,000	3,228	100	94	94	93
1938	137,877,000	3,201	100	100	100	100
1939	145,115,000	3,360	109	103	104	104

Mussolini maintained his deflationary policy until 1934, when he imposed import restrictions on finished or semi-finished products while cutting tariffs for raw materials. That at once stimulated domestic production and jobs at the cost of shortages, higher prices and often poorer-quality homemade goods. The economy steadily expanded to 145,115,00 lire, per capita income to 3,360 lire, the manufacturing index to 109, the manufacturing employment index to 103, the wholesale price index to 104 and the living cost index to 104 in 1939, each above the amount a decade earlier.

Mussolini devoted half the national budget to the military and imperialism from 1934 to 1940. Increased military spending stimulated the economy from 1935 to 1940. Mussolini's wars in Ethiopia and Spain demanded large rises in armament and equipment production. From 1934 to 1939, national income rose from 118,523,000 lire to 145,115,000 lire, per capita income from 2,829 lire to 3,360 lire, the manufacturing index from 80 to 109, the manufacturing employment index from 75 to 103, the wholesale price index from 65 to 104 and the cost of living index from 78 to 104.[46] Italy's budget deficit soared from 2,117,000,000 in fiscal 1934 to 1935 to 12,687,000,000 in 1935 to 1936 and to 16,230,000,000 in 1936 to 1937.[47] Business profits varied enormously during the Great Depression. Net profits were 0.8 in 1931, a negative 1.38 per cent loss in 1932, then rose to 2.18 per cent in 1933, 4.10 per cent in 1934, 5.74 per cent in 1935 and 7.28 per cent in 1936.[48]

4.5 Industrial Worker Nominal and Real Earnings, 1929–1939[49]

Years	Hourly Earning Index	Monthly Earning Index	Living Cost Index	Real Hourly Earning Index	Real Monthly Earning Index	Average Monthly Hours
1929	99.5	100.6	101.6	97.9	99.0	182
1930	98.6	95.8	98.4	100.2	97.4	175
1931	92.9	87,7	88.9	104.5	98.7	170
1932	91.0	84.9	84.9	107.1	100.0	168
1933	88.6	85.6	81.4	108.8	105.1	174
1934	85.7	81.9	77.2	111.0	106.1	172
1935	84.3	74.5	78.3	107.6	95.1	159
1936	89.5	78.1	84.2	106.3	92.7	157
1937	100.5	91.0	92.2	109.0	98.7	163
1938	107.6	95.1	99.3	108.3	95.8	159
1939	117.8	104.6	103.7	113.4	100.8	160

To rescue failing corporations with cash infusions, buyouts and restructuring, Mussolini created the Italian Industrial and Financial Corporation (*Societa Finanzaria Industriale Italiana,* Sofindit), the Italian Securities Institution (*Instituto Mobiliare Italiano,* IMI) and the Industrial Reconstruction Institute (*Instituto di Ricostruzione Industriale,* IRI). As a last resort, he nationalized bankrupt but important corporations including 90 per cent of merchant shipping, 80 per cent of shipbuilding, 75 per cent of pig-iron production and 45 per cent of steel. In all, by 1940, the state owned about one-quarter of Italy's economy, the largest share of any government beyond the Communist Soviet Union.[50]

Mussolini's policies at once alleviated and worsened worker conditions. To reduce business costs, he pressured the official unions to accept wage cuts that ranged from 10 per cent to 20 per cent in October 1927, cross-the-board 8 per cent cuts in December 1930 and cross-the-board 7 per cent cuts in May 1937. To reduce mass poverty and joblessness, he inaugurated sick pay in 1928, social security in 1929 and year-end bonuses and extended severance pay in 1938. Social security included health, accident and pension funds paid by employers by 5.75 per cent of average salaries and by workers with 3.25 per cent of their wages; in 1939, those contributions respectively rose to 19.50 per cent and 4.5 per cent. He permitted wage increases from July 1936 to February that ranged from 4 per cent for textile manufacturing to 11 per cent for machine manufacturing, with an average 10 per cent rise for all industrial workers. The result was that from 1936 to 1939 the hourly wage index rose from 106.3 to 113.4 and the monthly wage index rose from 92.7 to 100.8.[51]

Italian consumption patterns varied with the prices for various products. On average, Italians spent 49.5 per cent on food and 30.4 per cent on other goods and services from 1925 to 1930 and 45.5 per cent on food and 34.1 per cent on other goods and services from 1936 to 1940. Food consumption per person varied notably. Average annual meat consumption was 20kg from 1921 to 1925, 22kg from 1926 to 1930 and from 1931 to 1939 below 20kg; average daily fat consumption 70g from 1926 to 1930 and 60g from 1930 to 1939; average daily calories 2,800 from 1926 to 1930 and 2,600 to 2,700 from 1936 to 1940.[52]

Among Mussolini's catchier slogans was 'to reclaim the land and with the land the man and with the man, the race'. His reclamation point man was the agronomist Arrigo Serpieri who served as an Agriculture Ministry undersecretary in several divisions from 1922 to 1935. Serpieri sponsored the Land Reclamation Law that Mussolini signed on 13 February 1934.

For reclamation, Mussolini notably claimed one extraordinary feat that had eluded previous ambitious rulers going back to Emperor Augustus – draining the 200,000-acre malarial Pontine Marshes and converting most of it to farmland and the new towns of Littoria, Sabaudia and Pontinia. Health Minister Alessandro Messe drafted the plan that Mussolini inaugurated in 1929. It took a decade and 125,000 workers to construct the system of canals, dykes and pumping stations along with towns with Latina the new province's capital in 1932.

4.6 Comparison of European Great Economic Power Per Capita Income (1960 dollars)[53]

	1913	1929	1933	1938
Italy	441	517	492	551
Germany	757	770	716	1,126
France	695	982	846	936
Britain	996	1,038	995	1,161
Russia/USSR	326	293	340	458

A regular theme of a Mussolini harangue was that a nation's security strengthened as its population grew larger, healthier and more literate.[54] He unfavourably compared Italy's 40 million people with 80 million Germans and 200 million Slavs. He wanted Italy's population to rise by a third to 60 million by 1950. He explained that: 'It is necessary to watch over the destiny of our race with others with seriousness. It is necessary to make the race healthy, beginning with issues involving mothers and infants.'[55]

To those related ends, Mussolini founded the National Agency for Maternity and Infancy (*Opera Nazionale per la Maternita ed Infanzia*) in 1925. He outlawed contraception advocates in 1924, imposed a tax on bachelors in 1926 and outlawed homosexual acts in 1931. In 1927, he declared a 'Battle for Births' that encouraged more children by eliminating taxes for families with six or more. He granted a subsidy for each child starting with the second in 1927 and the first in 1935 and doubled benefits in 1941. He founded Rural Housewives (*Massaie Rurale*) in 1935 to advise agrarian women how to better their homes' efficiency, hygiene and gardens and their children's education and health. He founded the Section for Female Labourers and Homemakers (*Sezione Operaie e Lavorati a Domicilio*, SOLD) in 1937 that reached a million members by 1940. Each year Mussolini invited to Palazzo Venezia the ninety-five most prolific mothers and their families for a small monetary award and health insurance that from 1939 included a silver medal.[56]

Augusto Turati was among Mussolini's inner circle and served a stint as Fascist Party Secretary. He expressed the view of not just the Fascist Party but traditionalists everywhere when he declared: 'The family is the basic cell of the State, the Nation and the people. It is the only possible safeguard, the only trench defending us against the corrosion coming from the various amoral, immoral and dissolvent forces around.'[57]

Despite all these policies, Italy's birth rate slightly declined and population growth stalled. The average birthrate dropped from 29.8 per thousand people from 1921 to 1925 to 23.1 per thousand from 1936 to 1940. By 1937, Mussolini complained that he had lost fifteen potential army divisions from the births that did not happen.[58] Fascist Party members did not practice what Mussolini preached. Most members had two children.

One way to boost population was to discourage Italians from emigrating and entice back previous emigrants. From 1880 to 1920, around 16 million Italians moved to foreign countries, where around 9 million settled, while 6 million returned. Most of those who stayed sent remittances to their families and lenders and most of those who returned brought back money and skills. Around 1.5 million Italians left their country during Mussolini's first five years in power, from 1922 to 1927.

Mussolini sought to rally the loyalty of immigrants, stem the outflow, encourage more remittances and undercut anti-fascist groups. To those ends, he announced the formation of Italian Fasci Abroad (*Fasci Italiani all'Estero*) on 1 May 1921, but did not actually establish an organization until 14 August 1922 and begin dispatching the first 'delegates' to mobilize foreign Italian communities until December 1922. He had Giuseppe Bastianini head Italian Fasci Abroad. Each Fascio or branch was open to all men and women respectively over 20 and 17 years old, with high moral standards and no affiliation with other political groups or parties. Members had to obey both the law in their adopted country and dictates of Mussolini and Fascist Party headquarters in Rome. Mussolini dissolved the earlier, competing association, the Italian League, established in 1920. He established the newsletter *Fasci Italiani all'Estero* in May 1924 and renamed it *Il Legionario* in January 1925. The number of Fascio steadily expanded to 280 by 25 October 1925, when Bastianini convened the first international conference of Italian Fasci Abroad at Rome and Milan.

Foreign Ministry professionals considered Italian Fasci Abroad not an ally but a rival that could undermine their diplomacy on specific issues. Bastianini talked Mussolini, who was foreign minister, into imposing these rules: all Italian diplomats had to be committed Fascists; all Italian anti-Fascists abroad were stripped of their citizenship; Italian Fasci Abroad was the sole representative of Italy aboard and controlled the Department of Emigration.[59]

The United States harboured the largest and most affluent number of Italian emigrants and their descendants.[60] They were among 20 million immigrants to the United States from 1880 to 1920. Difficulties in housing, educating and assimilating those foreigners along with worsening poverty and crime prompted Congress to impose quotas by nationality with the 1921 Emergency Quota Act and more sharply with the 1924 Immigration Act. That stemmed Italian immigration to America but not their growing political, economic and cultural influence.

By 1930, Italian American immigrants and their descents numbered 18,000,000 or 5.4 per cent of America's population and 1,000,000 New Yorkers or 17 per cent of that city's population. In 1933, Italo Balbo declared before a packed crowd at Madison Square Garden coliseum: 'Italians of New York, we bring you the greetings of Italy and Mussolini . . . Be proud that you are Italians . . . And especially you, workers of untiring hands and simple hearts . . . Mussolini has ended the era of humiliations. To be an Italian is a title of honour.'[61]

Relations between America and Italy shaped and reflected relations between Italian Americans and their maternal country.[62] Mussolini's regime looked to Washington and Italian Americans for diplomatic and financial support. Most Italian Americans looked back across the Atlantic with mingled pride and shame. As Italian crime organizations mushroomed in American cities because of alcohol prohibition from 1919 to 1933, Italian Americans suffered worsening suspicion and acrimony from many other Americans. After becoming president in March 1933, Franklin Roosevelt's corporatist economic policies resembled Mussolini's. As the threat from Fascist Japan, Italy and Germany imperialism grew more virulent during the late 1930s, Roosevelt's administration searched for ways either to deter or entice Mussolini. During the Second World War, Washington used Italian Americans as intelligence officers and cut deals with Mafia leaders like Charles 'Lucky' Luciano to aid America's occupation of Italy.

Mussolini understood that a political revolution could triumph only if a cultural revolution accompanied it.[63] For that, he declared war against those elements of traditional Italian culture that he viewed as anti-Fascist:

> We must scrape and pulverize, in the character and mentality of the Italians, the sediments deposited by those terrible centuries of political, military and moral decay . . . It is an immense labour. The Risorgimento was but the beginning because it was the work of tiny minorities; the world war, instead, was profoundly educational. Now it is a matter of continuing, day by day, the reworking of the national character of the Italians.[64]

He sought to transform Italians into 'New Men' and 'New Women'.[65]

For inspiring the general population, Mussolini explained:

> [T]he masses are nothing but a herd of sheep as long as they are unorganized. I am nowise antagonistic to them. All that I deny is that they are capable of ruling themselves. But if you lead them, you must guide them by two reins, enthusiasm and interest . . . .The mystical and the political factors condition one another reciprocally.

For that he 'creates new forms, new myths and new rites . . . He must create new festivals, new gestures, new forms, which will themselves become traditional'.[66]

The key to Italy's cultural revolution was creating a modern secular religion of myth, ritual and creed that celebrated the Italian state and nation exemplified by *Il Duce* as the all-powerful, all-knowing, brilliant, infallible leader. Mussolini explained in 1922 that: 'Only the myth can give strength and energy to a people to construct its own identity.'[67] In 1926, he explained that Fascism was a political religion for all Italians to embrace: 'Fascism is not only a party, it is a regime, it is not only a regime, but a faith, it is not only a faith, but a religion.'[68]

To that end, Mussolini and his underlings wielded the power of government and mass media to develop a personality cult (*Ducismo*) for himself as *Il Duce*, Fascism's dynamic, visionary, courageous heart, mind, body and soul. He developed himself as a charismatic, populist dictator by studying works by Friedrich Nietzsche, Gustav Le Bon, George Michels and George Sorel. Those writers emphasized the psychology of controlling and manipulating others, including the mass populace, one's immediate followers and business, labour, peasant, cultural and religious leaders.

Mussolini's photograph adorned every government office, school room and countless businesses and homes and statues of him public squares across Italy. In all, Mussolini was photographed in over 2,500 poses and 30 million copies were distributed.[69] Hundreds of photos of Mussolini depicted him mingling with the people, working at construction sites and farm fields, greeting prominent foreign visitors or skiing, horseback riding, fencing or swimming. Italians were repeatedly reminded that 'Mussolini is always right'.

'Believe, Obey, Fight' (*Credere, Obbedire, Combattere*), the most apt and succinct Fascist slogan, was belatedly conceived by Achille Starace and popularized by Mussolini in 1934. That was a notable improvement on the refrain, 'Better to live a day as a lion rather than a hundred years as a sheep' (*Meglio vivere un Giorno da leone che centro anni da pecora*) that Mussolini coined two years earlier. Although neither slogan specifies just what or for whom one is believing in and fighting for, implicitly that was the Italian state and nation personified by *Il Duce*. Mussolini explained what membership meant and demanded: 'The Fascist Party is an army or, if you wish, an order. You only enter it to serve and obey.'[70] As for Fascist symbols, Mussolini made the Fasces icon of an axe in a bound bundle of arrows and the outstretched salute mandatory for all government, military and political personnel in 1922 and the official state emblem on 30 December 1926. He required all formal government and military meetings to begin with the 'Salute to the *Duce*' from 12 December 1931.

He sought to make the public square (*piazza*) the centre of Fascist expression much as the church was for believers and the home was for families. For that, he sponsored national Fascist celebrations or 'gatherings' (*adunate*) and encouraged local bosses to hold their own celebrations for local achievements and efforts.[71] The new festivals included Birth of the Fasci di Combattimento (23 March), Birth of Rome (14 April), Foundation of the Empire (9 May), Birth of the Nation and Entry into the Great War (24 May), March on Rome (28 October) and Victory (4 November). Of those, the most important was the annual 'March on Rome' commemoration. For the March on Rome's tenth anniversary, he had the 'Exhibition on the Fascist Revolution (*Mostra della Rivoluzione Fascista*) open at Rome's Exhibition Hall initially for half a year, then extended it to two years.

During the March on Rome's fifth anniversary in 1927, Mussolini reflected on all the changes that he and his followers had imposed on Italy since then:

> Fascism has confronted the problem of the modern State, its character and its function. In this creation of a new State, that is authoritarian, not absolutist, hierarchical and organic – that is open to people of all classes, categories and interests – is the great revolutionary originality of Fascism and it provides a lesson, perhaps, for the entire modern world, that oscillates between the authority of the State and the excessive power of the individual, between State and anti-State.[72]

Mussolini wanted every art form to celebrate and develop Fascism.[73] He explained: 'In the Fascist state, art acquires a social function, an educational function. It must translate the ethics of our time. It must give unity of style and greatness of line to communal life. Art, therefore, returns to being what it was in the highest periods and amid the highest societies: a perfect moment for spiritual government.'[74]

Mussolini had Victor Emmanuel decree the Royal Italian Academy's creation on 7 January 1926, although it was not inaugurated until 28 October 1929. The Italian Academy's role was 'to promote and coordinate Italian intellectual movement in the fields of science, literature and the arts, keep the national character pure in accordance with the genius and traditions of the stock and favour the expansion and influence [of this national spirit] outside the confines of the state'.[75] The King and *Duce* chose the sixty members who received monthly 3,000-lire stipends and competed to win one of the four annual Mussolini prizes. Among the leading members he appointed were Futurist painter and poet Filippo Marinetti, composer Pietro Mascagni, playwright Luigi Pirandello, physicist Enrico Fermi and inventor Guglielmo Marconi who became the president. One notable omission was the conductor Arturo Toscanini, who joined the Fascist Party in 1919, but fell out with Mussolini and emigrated to America to head the New York Philharmonic Symphony in 1926.

Mussolini established other cultural organizations including the Fascist Cultural Institution, renamed the National Institution of Fascist Culture in 1937, the National Fascist Federation of Theatrical, Cinematic and Related Industries, the National Confederation of Fascist Syndicates of Professionals and Artists and the National Fascist Union of Musicians. The Dante Alighieri Society was founded to promote Italy's language and literature culture at home and abroad in July 1889; Mussolini's regime contributed funds to boost its overseas branches.

Mussolini had teams of architects develop Fascist architecture of stark, whitish, monumental, symmetrical buildings.[76] The showpiece was the Rome Universal Exposition (*Esposizione Universale Roma*, EUR), a building complex developed west of Rome as a business and cultural centre from 1935 for a World's Fair scheduled for 1942. The central building was the Palace of Italian Culture (*Palazzo della Civilita Italiana*), with six stories of nine arches each. The most important architects were Giovanni Guerrini, Ernesto La Padula and Mario Romano. Fascist architecture was the austerity and mystery of Georgio de Chirico's paintings.

To promote Fascist literature, several leaders started their own political and literary journals including Giuseppe Bottai's *Critica Fascist*, Francesco Coppola's *Politica*, Franco Ciarlantini's *Augustea*, Edmondo Rossoni's *La Stirpe*. Among the more prominent novels that promoted Fascist themes were Alberto Moravia's *Gli Indifferenti* (*The Indifferent Ones*, 1929); Umberto Barbaro's *Luce Fredda* (*Cold Light*, 1931), Enrico Emmanuelli's *Radiographia di una Notte* (*X-Ray of a Night*, 1932);

Romano Bilenchi's *Il Capofabbrica* (*The Foreman*, 1935); Elio Vittorini's *Conversazione in Sicilia* (*Conversation in Sicily*, 1941).

A few writers dared to explore problems caused or exacerbated by Fascism like Alba De Cespedes in his *Nessuno Torna in Dietro* (*There's No Turning Back*, 1938) and Moravia in his *La Mascherata* (*The Masked Ball*, 1941). Carrado Alvaro was initially among a few dissident writers who dared express themselves. He subtly questioned Fascism through his short story collections *L'Amata alla Finestra* (*The Loved One at the Window*, 1929) and *Gente in Aspromonte* (*The People of Aspromonte*, 1930). However, he did so from the safe distance of Berlin, where he fled in 1929. Mussolini appreciated not just the subtlety but the beauty of *Gente in Aspromonte*. After *Il Duce* publicly praised his stories, Alvaro returned to Italy and praised Mussolini as 'a genius' who devised 'solutions to the modern problems of Italian life'.[77] His next celebrated novel was *L'Uomo e Forte* (*Man Is Strong*, 1938).

Mussolini assigned a group of writers to compose a *Dictionary of Politics* with definitions that celebrated Fascism and denigrated rival political philosophies. He sponsored the Institute of the Italian Encyclopaedia with Giovanni Treccani its director and Giovanni Gentile its editor-in-chief in 1926. The encyclopaedia eventually expanded to 35 volumes with 60,000 articles and 50 million words. Many thinkers contributed to Fascism's development as a political philosophy, none so voluminously or profoundly than Giovanni Gentile.[78] Among scores of articles and several books, his most accessible and key writings were 'The Manifesto of Fascist Intellectuals' (1928) and 'The Doctrine of Fascism' (1932).

Mussolini developed a network of propaganda institutions. He had the king decree the founding of the Italian Radiophonic Union (*Unione Radiofonicaa Italiana*) as the government's radio broadcaster at Turin on 27 August 1924. That same year, he founded the Educational Film Union (*L'Unione Cinegrafica Educativa*, LUCE), which in turn established the Newsreel (*Gionale Luce*) that created propaganda newsreels that every film theatre had to show before the main features. He renamed the Press Office the Secretariat for Press and Propaganda in 1934, then the Ministry of Popular Culture in 1934, with the power to censor and shape the content of all publications, films and broadcasts. He named his son-in-law Galeazzo Ciano the minister the first year followed by Dino Alfieri, Alessandro Pavolini and Gaetano Polvorelli for short terms through July 1943.

LUCE's most extensive propaganda campaign came during Adolf Hitler's May 1938 visit to Rome, Naples and Florence. A team of a 120 or so artists, writers, designers, decorators, photographers and film-makers produced dozens of newsreels, 30,000 photos and 50,000 postcards.[79]

For Mussolini, film was 'the regime's most powerful weapon'.[80] Leo Longanesi, a journalist, essayist, reviewer and screenwriter, explained how movies surpassed literature as the most politically powerful artistic genre for the newest generation: 'Today films have replaced novels as the source of new models for youth. The situations, gestures, physiognomies and environments they see, like the words they hear, enter into their memories as real, lived experiences; they stir up fantasies, stimulate dreams and can even form characters, Many youth today possess a temperament that might be defined as cinematographic.'[81] Yet, a film could backfire on the regime if it was too ham-handed and provoked derision rather than inspired loyalty.

Nearly all leading screenwriters, directors and producers made films that did not challenge Fascism and some that extolled it.[82] Among the more lauded films with Fascist themes were Alessandro Blasetti's *Sole* (*Sun*, 1929), *Resurrectio* (*Resurrection*, 1931) and *Terra Madre* (*Mother Earth*, 1931); Mario Camerini's *Kif Tebbi* (1930), *Uomini, que Mascalzoni!* (*Men, What Rascals They Are!*, 1931), *Il Grande Appello* (*The Great Call*, 1936) and *Rotaie* (*Rails*, 1936); Augusto Genina's *Il Camino dei Eroi* (*The Road of Heroes*, 1936) and *Lo Squadrone Bianco* (*The White Squadron*, 1936; Giulio Brignone's *Sotto la Croce del Sud* (*Under the Southern Cross*, 1937); Umberto Barbaro's *L'Ultimo Nemica* (*The Last Enemy*, 1938); Francesco De Robertis's *Uomini sul Fondo* (*Men on the Bottom*, 1941); and Luchino Visconti's *Ossessione* (*Obsession*, 1942).

All along most people preferred light-hearted or adventure-themed Hollywood movies no matter how the regime's film reviewers denounced them. Mussolini understood that outright banning American films would spur a popular uproar. Instead, he had a law passed in 1927 that forced theatres to reserve 10 per cent of their showings for Italian movies. The 1938 Alfieri Law gave the regime a monopoly over buying and distributing foreign films and imposed high tariffs on imported films.

Mussolini encouraged a group of investors in 1935 to establish the National Film Industry Entity (*Ente Nazionale Industrie Cinematografiche*, ENIC) to produce and show films. The Entity had twenty-nine film theatres in 1935 and ninety-four in 1941. The Entity's most acclaimed film was *Scipio Africanus: The Defeat of Hannibal*, directed by Carmine Gallone in 1937.

Mussolini recognized that transforming young people into Fascists was critical for the regime's future.[83] Teachers were the key to making that happen. He decreed in October 1931 that all university professors and lower school teachers must declare a loyalty oath that partly included: 'I swear to be faithful to the king . . . to the Fascist system . . . to fulfil my duties as a teacher with the purpose of training industrious, honest citizens devoted to the Fatherland.' He required all professors and teachers to join the Fascist Party from 1933 and forced all teachers to wear a Fascist uniform from 1934.

He encouraged the creation of Young University Fascist Groups (*Gioventu Fascista Universitaria*, GUF) on campus. Three short-lived Fascist journals targeted young people, *Saggiatore* published in Rome from 1930 to 1933, *Orpheus* in Milan from 1932 to 1934 and *L'Universale* in Florence from 1931 to 1935; they soon died because virtually all youths preferred light-hearted entertainment to ponderous polemics. The biweekly magazine *Corrente di Vita Giovanile* was less academic but little more popular and lasted from 1938 to 1940.

Outside of school, he established a series of organizations that socialized children in Fascism. When a boy had his sixth birthday, he could join the *Ballila* and wear a Fascist uniform and sing Fascist songs and play games. From age 8 to 12, boys could join the *Ballila Escursionisti* or Campers, from 12 to 14 the *Ballila Moschettieri* or Musketeers, from 14 to 16 the *Avanguardisti Moschettieri* or Advanced Guard Musketeers and from 16 to 18 the *Avanguardisti Mitraglieri* or Advanced Guard Machine Gunners. At each meeting, boys recited this oath: 'I believe in the genius of *Il Duce* and Our Lord Fascism. I believe in the Communion of the martyrs of Fascism, Lord, thou who lights every flame, Lord thou who rules every heart, Revive in me each day, My passion for Italy.' There was also the Fascist Ten Commandments to recite. Once a boy was 18, he could join the Fascist Party and the Blackshirt militia.[84]

Mussolini established a School of Fascist Mysticism at Milan, a Faculty of Fascist Studies at Perugia University and an International Centre of Fascist Studies at Lausanne. Of the three, he spent the most time with Nicolo Giani and Milan University's Fascist group to establish the 'School of Fascist Mysticism' (*Scuola di Mistica Fascita*) on 11 April 1930. Giani was the first director and Vito Mussolini, *Il Duce*'s nephew and Arnaldo's son, the first president. The school promoted the concept that Fascism was as much a spiritual as a political movement and served as a finishing school for leaders. Giani explained: 'Our task must focus only on coordinating, interpreting and processing the thought of the *Duce* . . . to develop and specify the new values that are in the Fascist work of Mussolini.' *Il Duce* decreed in 1936 that the study of Fascism was mandatory in all philosophy classes.

For Mussolini, transforming Italians into ideal Fascists seemed to be an endless Sisyphean struggle. He often despaired at getting lackadaisical Italians to conform to his dictates: 'I am making superhuman efforts to educate this people and I know I shall succeed. They must realize that they can come of age only by accepting obedience. When they have learnt to obey, they must and will believe what I tell them and then they will march in compact ranks at my command.'[85]

Chapter 5

THE ROADS TO EMPIRE

> Italy finally has its empire . . . It is a Fascist empire, an empire of peace, an empire of civilization and humanity.
>
> (Benito Mussolini)

> I repeat my authorization to your excellency to initiate and systematically conduct a policy of terror and extermination and against rebels and populations in complicity with them. Without the law of ten eyes for one we cannot heal this wound in good time.
>
> (Benito Mussolini)

> National Socialist Germany and Fascist Italy will be friends for tens and tens of years or at least until I die.
>
> (Adolf Hitler)

Militarism and imperialism were core values of Benito Mussolini's Fascist creed. He had long dreamed of being a modern-day Julius Caesar and conquering vast territories to expand the Italian empire. For him, colonizing other peoples was the ultimate test of a nation's virility, akin to a real man vanquishing a series of initially resistant comely women. He was dead set to create a modern version of the Roman Empire: 'It is destiny . . . that Rome again takes her place as the city that will be the director of the civilization of all Western Europe. Let us . . . make . . . Italy one of the nations without which it is impossible to conceive the future history of the world.'[1]

Mussolini's vision faced some key challenges. Ideally, an empire enhances the imperial state's strategic, economic and cultural power. Historically, colonies usually became liabilities rather than assets. Atop the upfront costs of conquest, the state invested ever more human, financial and material resources in the colonies while usually extracting a fraction in revenues to pay for all that. That was certainly true of Italy's colonial governments that depended on state subsidies for half to three-quarters of their budgets. Often the conquest was never completed; native forces continued to resist, forcing the imperial state to deploy ever more military forces against them. Nonetheless, a few favoured businesses usually profited and often reaped vast fortunes by exploiting plantations, mines, shipping and other privileges. Over the long term, ever more subject natives themselves become colonists as they migrated to the imperial country.[2]

Imperialism, of course, diametrically opposed international relations since the Versailles Treaty signed in June 1919 and the League of Nations, inaugurated in 1920. The victorious Allies, including Italy, established the League dedicated to realizing President Woodrow Wilson's dream of making the First World War 'the war to end all wars'. Its 'Covenant' or constitution outlawed aggressive war and required all members to resolve conflicts peacefully rather than violently; if a state or states threatened to attack others, League members would unite first to impose diplomatic and economic sanctions that ideally deterred the aggression and if deterrence failed, unite militarily to crush the aggressor. Those who drafted the Covenant hoped that 'collective security' or 'one for all and all for one', by members would appear so politically, economically and militarily overwhelming that no would-be imperialist leader or regime would dare break the peace.

Ironically, America's Senate did not ratify the Versailles Treaty that committed signatories to establish the League of Nations. Nonetheless, American presidents sought to uphold world peace parallel to the League's efforts. President Warren Harding sponsored the Washington naval arms reduction conference from 12 November 1921 to 6 February 1922. Three key treaties emerged that appeared significant steps toward reducing military strength and international tensions. The Five Power Pact established naval tonnage limits among America, Britain, Japan, France and Italy in a ratio of 5-5-3-1.75-1.75. To fulfil that deal, each member either had to scrap existing warships or their plans to build new one. The Four Power Pact between America, Britain, Japan and France required them to recognize and not violate the territories of each in the Pacific Ocean and resolve any conflicts through negotiations, not force. The Nine Power Pact between America, Britain, Japan, France, Italy, China, Portugal, Belgium and the Netherlands required each to respect each other's territory in the Pacific Ocean, especially China where Britain, France, Japan, Germany and Russia had imposed 'spheres of influence' over the previous half century.

Mussolini took power when that League of Nations and Washington Treaty world was developing. With imperialism a core value and policy, Fascism was diametrically opposed to that world. Mussolini, however, shelved imperialism for now. His priority was consolidating and expanding power for himself as Italy's *Duce* and his Fascist Party in parliament and regional and local governments across Italy. But he was also eager for the great powers and the rest of the global community to respect him. He would embark on imperialism only after he amassed dictatorial powers in Italy and two other great powers, Japan and Germany, also embraced Fascism and imperialism.[3]

Mussolini assumed the duties of Foreign Minister from 31 October 1922 to 12 September 1929, from 20 July 1932 to 11 June 1936 and from 6 February 1936 to 25 July 1943. After his behaviour at several early foreign conferences provoked scathing foreign news reports about his vulgarity and lack of sophistication Mussolini stayed home and insisted that foreign leaders visit him. His only exception was fellow Fascist and tyrant Adolf Hitler. Mussolini and Hitler met numerous times at cities or remote sites in each other's realms from 1934 to 1944.[4]

Mussolini's first foreign diplomatic journey was to Lausanne for the peace conference that began on 20 November 1922. The governments of Britain, France and Italy hastily organized the gathering after General Mustafa Kemal Ataturk overthrew the Ottoman government and repudiated the Treaty of Sèvres on 1 November, which the victorious Allies, Britain, France and Italy, had forced the Ottoman Empire to sign on 11 August 1920, reducing Turkey to a rump state and gave some of its provinces to Greece while Britain and France took its Middle East provinces as 'mandates' and Italy kept the Dodecanese Islands that it captured from Turkey during a war from 1911 to 1912.

For eleven weeks, negotiations deadlocked between the three European powers that wanted to reimpose the harsh terms and the Turks who insisted that they return the territory they took. Eight months later, diplomats finally resolved most issues. Under the Treaty of Lausanne, signed on 24 July 1923, religious freedom would prevail in those countries, Turkey surrendered its claims to Arab lands and the Dodecanese Islands but took control of western Turkey that it had captured from the Greeks.

Mussolini stayed only a few days at the Lausanne Conference before turning over negotiations to a foreign ministry diplomatic team. His goal was to make a strong showing. With an entourage of Blackshirts, he asserted his rank as prime minister to have British Foreign Secretary Lord George Curzon and French Foreign Minister Raymond Poincaré come to meet him at the Grand Hotel on 19 November, the day before the conference formally began. Later he made a speech before the assembled delegations. Mussolini failed to impress Poincaré, who privately referred to him as a 'swine', but Curzon lauded him as 'a young man, a great character and a great force'.[5]

Mussolini then journeyed to London to meet King George V, Prime Minister Andrew Bonar Law and other political and business leaders. Although Mussolini was politely received, he did not enjoy the British people, with their aloofness, dry humour and dreary weather. He dismissed them as akin to 'Germans who have travelled'.[6] Nonetheless, Mussolini helped Victor Emmanuel host King George V and Queen Mary when they visited Rome on 7 May 1923.

A crisis between Italy and Greece erupted on 27 August 1923.[7] General Enrico Tellini was with two aides, an interpreter and a driver in a car driving north from Ioannis in north-west Greece to the Albanian border. Tellini was Italy's chief delegate to an inter-Allied boundary commission surveying the Greek-Albanian frontier. The car stopped before a tree blocking the road. There either one or more gunmen shot all five men to death, but did not rob them.

The murders enraged Mussolini along with the Italian public. On 28 August, he had Ambassador Gulio Montagna issue Greek Prime Minister Stylianos Gonatas an ultimatum demanding an apology, a state funeral in the Catholic Cathedral in Athens, military honours for Tellini, 50 million lire in reparations and the arrest, trial and execution of the murderers. On 29 August, Mussolini had Montagna inform Gonatas that an Italian naval flotilla would occupy the island of Corfu if Greece did not agree to the ultimatum. On 30 August, Greek Prime Minister Stylianos Gonatas issued Montagna an official reply that expressed sorrow and promised to hold a solemn funeral for the deceased but rejected the other demands.

Mussolini had Naval Minister Thaon di Revel order a flotilla led by General Antonio Foschini to take over Corfu's capital Kerkira. When the local authorities rejected his surrender demand, Foschini ordered a bombardment of the citadel before landing troops to occupy the city; the shells killed sixteen civilians and wounded thirty-two, including children. Through the League of Nations, the British and French governments condemned Italy's invasion of Corfu and demanded that Mussolini withdraw those troops. London backed that demand by warning that all its warships in the Mediterranean Sea would converge on Corfu. On 1 September, Greece formally asked the League of Nations to resolve the dispute.

Mussolini had Italian Ambassador Antonio Salandra, the former prime minister, warn the League of Nations that he did not accept its jurisdiction and would withdraw Italy if it interfered. He insisted that the separate Conference of Ambassadors suggest a resolution. The League of Nations granted Mussolini's demand. On 8 September, the League's Conference of Ambassadors issued a nine-point resolution for Greece and Italy to sign. Although the resolution essentially echoed Mussolini's demands, Gonatas accepted them. Both prime ministers signed the resolution.

Mussolini had decisively won his first attempt at international brinksmanship. His popularity in Italy soared. He had revealed that the League of Nations was weak, divided and easily intimidated. On 27 September, he ordered Italy's task force withdrawn from Corfu. On 29 September, he publicly announced that he would return 10 million of the 50 million lire reparation to Athens, asking that it be donated to Greek and Armenian refugees. Countless people around the world admired Mussolini for being decisive, tough and generous.

Mussolini was well aware of Germany's right-wing militants who resembled Italy's *Squadristi*. He first learned about Adolf Hitler in September 1921, when his emissary, Kurt Ludecke, appeared at his *Popolo di Italia* newspaper office and asked to meet him. Hitler tasked Ludecke to 'size Mussolini up, estimate his chances for success, get his opinion on crucial matters, find out whether and how we could cooperate'. Ludecke found that:

> Even then, he had the habit of staging himself, placing his desk in the farthest corner, so that callers must approach him across the entire room. At the desk sat a square-cut man in a dark, shabby suit and untidy shirt, with a high dome of bald forehead and powerful almost frightening eyes. He welcomed me in a pleasant, resonant voice . . . I notice his hands. They were small and soft and showed how overstruck he was, for the nails were bitten . . . almost to the moons . . . The more we talked, the more I liked him.

Ludecke was disappointed to learn that 'Mussolini had never heard of Hitler'.[8] Ludecke explained that Hitler greatly admired Mussolini and partly modelled his own populist oratory, political philosophy, Nazi Party organization and paramilitary violence on *Il Duce*. That flattered Mussolini but he was not then prepared to form a formal tie between his Fascist Party and Hitler's obscure Nazi Party.

After Ludecke left, Mussolini had Adofo Tedaldi lead a Foreign Ministry team that investigated Germany's right-wing militant movement and compiled a report, submitted in November 1922. The report concluded that only Hitler's Nazi Party accepted the Versailles Treaty's transfer of Austria's mostly German-speaking South Tyrol to Italy, where it was called the Upper Adige region; all other militant groups opposed that transfer and demanded its return.

Ludecke returned to Italy in August 1923 and met Mussolini again. Mussolini was now Italy's prime minister, after having intimidated King Victor Emmanuel III into naming him the head of government after he threatened to 'March on Rome' with his Blackshirt army in October 1922. Hitler had given Ludecke the mission of secretly informing Mussolini that he would soon lead the Nazi Party on a 'March on Berlin' and would greatly appreciate any help he could give him. Ludecke found Mussolini 'courteous, but it was obvious that he would not commit himself in any way . . . Mussolini, being legally prime minister, in friendly relations with Berlin, could not officially take notice of the representative of a party opposing the government', let alone one committing to overthrowing and forming a Nazi regime.[9]

Hitler's 'March' ended in disaster. On 8 and 9 November 1923, he attempted a putsch or coup by his Nazi Brownshirts in Munich. The government crushed his revolt, arrested him and most of his inner circle and sentenced them to prison terms. After that, Mussolini forgot about Hitler for the next half-dozen years. Then Hitler reappeared on Germany's political stage and eventually caught up to and surpassed Mussolini in taking, holding and ultimately losing tyrannical power.

Among the Versailles Treaty's tenets was that Germany had to pay reparations to the victorious Allies, who formed an Inter-Allied Reparations Committee to determine the amount and schedule. In April 1921, the Committee declared that Germany owed 132 billion gold reichsmarks and issued a monthly payments schedule. Berlin paid the first billion gold reichsmarks then, in January 1923, informed the Committee that it could pay no more.

That default threatened to implode the global financial system and economy. The French, British, Belgians and Italians used reparations partly to repay their wartime loans from the United States that totalled $11 billion. Italy alone owed America and Britain respectively $2 billion and $2.5 billion.[10] If the debtor countries stopped those payments, they would likely bankrupt America's lenders and that in turn would provoke a domino effect of failing banks and industries around the world.

The governments of France and Belgium responded by sending troops into Germany's demilitarized Ruhr in the central Rhine River valley and took over factories and mines. Berlin reacted by calling on the workers to stop working. The Allied governments agreed that a compromise was essential to prevent a global depression. The Inter-Allied Reparations Committee formed a subcommittee to devise a settlement acceptable to all parties. Charles Dawes, a brilliant American banker and President Warren Harding's federal budget director, chaired the ten-man subcommittee with two members each from the United States, Britain, France, Belgium and Italy. The members examined data and debated what to do from 14 January to 9 April 1924, when they issued their report. What was called the Dawes Plan reduced the total amount and monthly payments and interest rate, lengthened the payments schedule and loaned Germany enough money to make those payments. The five Allies and Germany signed the Dawes Plan on 16 August 1924, after which the French and Belgium troops were withdrawn.

Mussolini played no direct role in the crisis and its resolution. He did fully back the Dawes Plan without complaining that Italy, like the other Allies, would get far less reparations. On 12 April, Dawes journeyed to Rome to meet Mussolini and explain the plan to him. Mussolini was gracious and embraced the plan. Dawes was accustomed to meeting the world's top political and business leaders but Mussolini especially impressed him. He later wrote: 'After leaving him I felt as if I had seen Julius Caesar'.[11] Of course, that is exactly the impression on his guests that Mussolini always intended.

Mussolini spoke often if vaguely of creating a new Roman Empire. He oversaw negotiations that expanded Italian territory in 1924 and 1926. The first was the acquisition of Fiume and a stretch of Dalmatian coast. Astonishingly, he achieved that long-standing Italian foreign policy goal by having his diplomats offer Yugoslavia's government three minor concessions, Port Baros, the Fiumara Canal and a 99-year concession of part of Fiume's port. Mussolini and Yugoslavia's envoy signed the Pact of Rome with those tenets on 27 January. For that, with deep gratitude, Victor Emmanuel declared Mussolini a Knight of the Annunziata and Gabriele D'Annunzio the Prince of Monte Nevoso. He then got British Foreign Secretary Curzon to cede Kenya's Juba valley to Somalia and Egypt's Jarabub oasis to Libya.

Mussolini then worked on consolidating Italy's existing colonies – Libya, Eritrea and Somalia. Rome's rule was most precarious in Libya.[12] Italy had seized Libya from the Ottoman Empire in 1912 after a two-year war. Just four years later, Italy withdrew nearly all its troops from Libya to fight in the First World War. The Senussi were an Islamist sect founded by Mohammad Ibn al-Senussi, the Grand Senussi at Mecca in 1837, then spread by him across Cyrenaica or eastern Libya after he journeyed there. When the Italians took over Libya, Umar al-Mukhtar headed the Senussi sect. He took advantage of Italy's withdrawal by preaching Jihad or Holy War against the Italians who remained. By 1918, the Jihadists had driven the Italians back to Tripoli, Benghazi and a handful of other towns along the coast.

After taking power, Mussolini ordered Libya's Governor-General Pietro Badoglio and General Rodolfo Graziani to do whatever was necessary to crush the rebels. Graziani deployed his 10,000 troops to attack Jihadist strongholds. Poison gas was among the weapons the army wielded against the rebels. Yet the army was unable to inflict any major defeats on the Jihadists who fought a classic guerrilla war of hit and run that inflicted casualties and drained morale.

Graziani changed his strategy in June 1930. He sought to split the rebels from the population by herding over 80,000 Cyrenaicans into five huge concentration camps where perhaps one in five died of starvation and disease. He sought to starve the rebels by slaughtering 90,000 head of livestock. The war turned in September 1931, when Italian troops captured and executed Umar al-Mukhtar. The surviving Senussi leaders agreed to lay down their arms and surrender half a million acres of land to Italy. The war cost as many as 100,000 Libyan and several thousand Italian lives. Yet, by 1933, the Italian government had enticed only 1,500 settlers to those Libyan lands.[13]

Mussolini achieved what every Italian statesman before him failed to do. He made peace with the Papacy.[14] The Vatican opposed Italian unification in the nineteenth century, especially after the government confiscated Church lands in territory it controlled. Pope Pius IX issued the Syllabus of Errors encyclical that condemned liberalism, nationalism, socialism and secularism in 1862. He then excommunicated King Victor Emmanuel II along with his army and political advisors on 1 November 1870, after a national plebiscite approved Italy's takeover of Rome and the Papal States. The Italian government subsequently nationalized the Catholic Church's remaining property in the Papal States, confined the papacy to Vatican City within Rome and secularized schools.

Although Mussolini was an agonistic who preached modernism and rationalism, he had solid political reasons for reconciliation. Most Italians remained devout Catholics who regularly attended mass and married and baptized their children before the altar. Mussolini initiated talks with the Vatican in May 1926. After three years of intermittent negotiations, Mussolini and Papal Secretary of State Pietro Gasparri signed the Treaty of Lateran Palace on 11 February 1929. The Vatican recognized Italy's territory and property seized from the Church in return for Rome recognizing the Vatican as a sovereign state, paying compensation and accepting Catholicism as the nation's official religion with Church-sanctioned marriages and compulsory school classes on Church theology.

That treaty bolstered Mussolini's power and prestige. Pope Pius XI lauded him as 'the man whom Providence has sent us'. The Vatican newspaper *L'Observatore Romano* declared that: 'Italy has been given back to God and God to Italy'.[15]

The honeymoon did not last long. Mussolini rattled the Vatican's faith in him when he banned Catholic Action youth groups in May 1931. He did so because they advocated faith in God and the Church and refuted Fascism, Socialism and Communism as 'Godless' ideologies. He wanted those young people to join Fascist youth organizations and become loyal followers of himself and his creed. Pius XI replied with the encyclical 'We Have No Need' (*Non Abbiamo Bisogna*) on 29 June 1931. He condemned the Fascist worship of the state (statolatry) as pagan and designed to convert young people from belief in God. He did not excommunicate Mussolini but did call him a Catholic in baptism only, but anti-Catholic through his beliefs and behaviour. Mussolini eased tensions when he paid a formal visit as head of state to Pius at the Vatican on New Year's Day, 1932.

The British announced that they would host a naval reduction conference between Britain, America, Japan, France and Italy at London in early 1931. The object was to impose limits on other types of warships not covered by the 1922 Five Power Pact.

Before the Grand Fascist Council, Mussolini explained his strategy for the conference: 'Italy will disarm only if everyone disarms . . . However, we must also be clear that we arm ourselves materially and spiritually for defence not aggression. Fascist Italy will never start a war.'[16] That stunning statement appeared to refute the obsession with military power, war and imperialism asserted by Mussolini and most other Fascists.

Hard practical political realities forced Mussolini to shelve ideological correctness for the time being. Taxes trailed further behind government spending, causing the national debt to soar which required more loans at higher interest rates to service. Cutting back naval expenditure would reduce the budget crunch. Mussolini's statement was designed to reassure Italy's bond and stock markets, especially the financial titans that dominated them.

The London naval conference lasted from 21 January to 22 April 1931. The result was a treaty among America, Britain, Japan, France and Italy that essentially extended the 1922 Five Power Pact's 5-5-3-1.75-1.75 ratio for battleship and heavy cruiser tonnage to light cruisers, destroyers and submarines, although the formula varied slightly.

Mussolini's most unusual diplomatic encounter was hosting Mahatma Gandhi at Villa Torlonia in December 1931. By then Gandhi was a world-renowned Indian independence leader who espoused non-violence for that and all political conflicts. Chatting amiably, Gandhi strolled in his robes leading his pet goat by a leash among the political, diplomatic and business dignitaries that Mussolini invited to the reception. Gandhi deeply moved Mussolini who gushed to Rachele that: 'He is a holy man, a genius and unique in that he uses goodness as a weapon. Perhaps he is one of the few people in the world who understands the British and their imperial policy. If India ever becomes free, she will owe it to this man . . . and he tells me he is sure of liberating his people in his own lifetime.'[17]

During his first decade in power, Mussolini went along with most international peace efforts and initiated a few. He authorized a trade treaty with the Soviet Union on 7 February 1924. Under the Geneva Protocol signed on 17 June 1925, Italy was among the signatories who pledged not to develop or use chemical and biological weapons. Mussolini would blatantly violate that treaty when he authorized the military to use poison gas in the war to conquer Ethiopia. Under the Treaty of Locarno signed by diplomats of Italy, Britain, France, Poland, Belgium, Czechoslovakia and Germany on 1 December 1925, Germany's boundaries with its neighbours and the demilitarized Rhineland were inviolable and upheld by the League of Nations.

French Foreign Minister Aristide Briand raised with American Secretary of State Frank Kellogg the idea of a non-aggression pact between France and America in 1928. Kellogg countered with the idea that they draft a treaty open to any country dedicated to international peace. The result was the Kellogg-Briand Pact whose official title was the General Treaty for Renunciation of War as the Instrument of National Policy, signed on 27 August 1928 by America, France and thirteen other states, including Italy, Germany and Japan whose imperialism would provoke the Second World War; by 1929, fifty-seven countries had signed the Kellogg-Briand Pact.

Mussolini's constructive foreign policies elicited praise from many foreign leaders he met. After talks with him in Livorno on

20 September 1926, British Foreign Secretary Austen Chamberlain returned to London and publicly stated: 'I have very great respect and very great admiration for Mr. Mussolini himself. He is a man with great strength of character and profound sagacity and in his personal conduct is marked by great charm and complete simplicity.'[18] On 18 February 1933, Winston Churchill declared before the Anti-Socialist League congress that:

> The Roman genius personified by Mussolini, the greatest living lawgiver, has shown many nations that the pressure of Socialism can be resisted; that spirit has pointed out the road that a nation can follow when it is bravely led. With the Fascist system Mussolini has established a central direction that countries engaged in a hand to hand battle against Socialism should not hesitate to take as their guide.[19]

Churchill's view of Mussolini and Fascism would change drastically over the next decade.

Japan's conquest of Manchuria, China's north-eastern region, defiance of the League of Nations and withdrawal from that international organization between September 1931 and February 1933 acutely reawakened Mussolini's dormant imperialist dreams and sharpened those of Adolf Hitler who took power in Germany. From September 1931 to September 1939, each Fascist regime's mostly unresisted aggressions only encouraged more until they provoked the Second World War.[20]

Japan's government was adopting a version of Fascism that included authoritarianism, ultranationalism, corporatism, militarism and imperialism, although it's version varied in two way. One was that Japan lacked a charismatic dictator; Emperor Hirohito was a meek if semi-divine symbol of Japan, while the war cabinet of the prime minister and five other ministers made policy by forging compromises among themselves then getting Hirohito's signature. Japan also lacked a mass Fascist party that animated the masses. In the emperor's name, the government promoted Fascist policies and unquestioning loyalty of the people without a political party.

Like Italy and Germany, Japan adopted a democratic political and constitutional monarchy in the late nineteenth century and expanded the electorate in stages to embrace all men aged over 20 in 1925. Yet Japan's liberal political system was grounded in an authoritarian political culture. Japan's military, with its samurai or bushido tradition, and most Japanese deplored liberalism for the same reasons that Western conservatives, Fascists and Nazis did. Like Italy and Germany,

Japan's government suspended the democratic system and civil rights in stages over years starting in 1925.

Japan seized limited economic control over Manchuria after defeating Russian in a war between them from 1904 to 1905. Previously, Russia had pressured China's government to grant it privileges to exploit Manchuria's vast forestry, agricultural, mineral and fisheries wealth, including building and protecting a railway to haul away all those resources. Japan had a 30,000-man army in Manchuria.

China had dissolved into civil war after the Ching Dynasty collapsed in 1911. By 1931, the Nationalist Party (Kuomintang, KMT) led by Generalissimo Chiang Kai-shek had unified much of the vast country, but warlords ruled Manchuria and other regions and the Communist Party controlled the northern region around Yanan near Mongolia. Radical officers in Japan's Manchurian army sought to conquer the region. On 18 September 1931, they detonated a bomb on the South Manchurian Railway, shot several Chinese and claimed that radical Chinese were the culprits. The Japanese government used that as the excuse to overrun Manchuria.

Chiang Kai-shek's ambassador protested to the League of Nations on 19 September. The League of Nations passed a resolution on 24 October, that called on Japan to withdraw its army by 16 November. When Japan rejected that resolution, the League formed a five-man commission led by Victor Bulwer-Lytton, Earl Lytton, to journey to Manchuria and investigate what happened. Meanwhile, American Secretary of State Henry Stimson announced that the United States would not recognize any change to Manchuria's legal status. On 14 January 1932, the Lytton commission disembarked at Shanghai and spent six weeks in China amidst six months in the Far East. Meanwhile, Tokyo established the puppet state of Manchukuo led by Puyi, the last Ching emperor, on 1 March 1932. On 2 October 1932. the League of Nations publicly issued the Lytton Report that documented Japanese imperialism in Manchuria and condemned that aggression but did not impose any economic sanctions. Japan withdrew from the League of Nations on 24 February 1933.

Japan's blatant imperialism in conquering Manchuria and defying the League of Nations electrified Mussolini. He viewed contemptuously the failure of Britain and France to uphold the League of Nations' collective security system and force Japan to withdraw from Manchuria. He saw those countries as declining powers with crumbling empires that Italy could feast on. Mussolini soon had a fellow Fascist ruler who shared his imperialist dreams, although three years would pass before they forged an alliance.

Adolf Hitler deeply admired Mussolini and emulated his ruling style of populism, demagoguery and pageantry, his ideology of authoritarianism, ultranationalism, corporatism and imperialism and even his 'March on Rome', although his 'March on Berlin' cost him a prison stint. In October 1932, Hitler declared that: 'National Socialist Germany and Fascist Italy will be friends for tens and tens of years or at least until I die'.[21]

Like Mussolini, Hitler took power legally. His Nazi Party won ever more seats in the Reichstag, Germany's lower parliamentary house similar to Italy's Chamber of Deputies: 2.62 per cent of the vote and 12 of 491 seats in 1928; 18.25 per cent and 107 of 577 seats in 1930; and 37.27 per cent of the vote and 230 of 608 seats in July 1932; before dipping slightly to 33.09 per cent of the vote and 196 of 584 seats in November 1932. Despite having a plurality of seats in 1932, President Paul von Hindenburg appointed two other leaders chancellor or prime minister, Franz von Papen and Kurt von Schleicher. Then, nearly a decade after Hitler's failed putsch, Hindenburg named him chancellor on 30 January 1933.

In power, Hitler wielded the same tactics as Mussolini to amass total power. He used the excuse of a fire at the Reichstag started by a communist on 27 February, to pressure Hindenburg to grant him temporary dictatorial powers under Constitution Article 48. Hitler used that power to suspend civil liberties and the Communist Party. He got the Reichstag and the upper house the Reichsrat to pass the Enabling Act that granted him the power to rule by decree on 23 March.

Despite sharing an ideology and being dictators, Mussolini initially was wary of Hitler. He worried that Hitler would unify Austria with Germany and try to take Italy's Alto Adige German-speaking or South Tyrol region that was among the First World War's spoils from Austria.[22] That fear inspired Mussolini on 19 March 1933 to invite diplomats from Germany, Britain and France to Palazzo Venezia to negotiate a non-aggression treaty. The result was the Four Power Pact signed on 15 July 1933. Italy, Germany and Britain subsequently ratified the treaty but France's parliament did not. Hitler announced on 14 October 1933 that Germany would withdraw from the League of Nations.

Meanwhile, Mussolini greeted Austrian Chancellor Engelbert Dollfuss at Palazzo Venezia on 19 April 1933. They discussed their common interest in preventing Germany from 'taking over Austria and informally agreed that Italy would militarily aid Austria against a German invasion. The chancellor greatly impressed *Il Duce* who recalled: 'Dollfuss, in spite of his miniscule size, is a man of ingenuity, possessed of real will. Together these qualities give a good impression.'[23]

Mussolini and Hitler first met in Venice from 14 to 15 June 1934. Hitler was dressed in a cheap business suit, Mussolini resplendent in his uniform. Hitler was 'radiant' to meet the *supermensch* who inspired his own Nazi acts and style. Nonetheless, Hitler submitted him to a two-hour harangue of his feats, goals, loves and hates. When Hitler caught his breath, Mussolini emphasized that he would not tolerate Germany's takeover of Austria or Italy's region of Alto Adige, the South Tyrol. Overall, Mussolini was not impressed with his fellow Fascist and afterward acidly quipped that the *Führer* looked 'like a plumber in a macintosh'. He dismissed Hitler's autobiography *Mein Kampf* (My Struggle) as an unreadable 'Hitler's New Testament'. He especially deplored Hitler's policies of eugenics and persecution of Jews and other 'inferior peoples'.[24]

Mussolini was furious to learn that Hitler was behind an attempted putsch by Austria's Nazi Party that murdered Chancellor Dollfuss on 25 July 1934. Austria's continued independence from Germany was obviously vital to Italy's security. Atop that, Mussolini liked Dollfuss so much that he invited him and his family to join his own family at Riccione, an Adriatic Sea beach resort. Their wives and children were already together and Dollfuss was about to leave to join them when he was assassinated.[25]

Mussolini mobilized four divisions on the Austrian frontier but did not send a specific warning or condemnation to Hitler. However, he did express contempt for Hitler's regime in a public speech: 'Thirty centuries of history allow us to look with utter disdain on certain doctrines from the other side of the Alps which are espoused by the descendants of people who were illiterate at a time when Rome had Caesar, Virgil and Augustus'.[26]

Italy's empire numbered just 50,000 colonists in 1930, spread thin among Libya, Eritrea, Somaliland and the Dodecanese islands. Those colonies all cost far more to administer, defend, develop and sustain than the meagre crops and minerals that farmers and miners gleaned from them and the minuscule government revenues from taxes and tariffs. Nonetheless, Mussolini sought to expand that empire.

For would-be conquerors, pickings on the African continent were sparse. By 1935, European powers had conquered every African realm but one, Ethiopia, then called Abyssinia, ruled by Emperor Haile Selassie. His kingdom was the latest to sprawl over that mountainous region of north-east Africa and source of the Blue Nile River. In the fourth century, Aksun King Ezana converted to Coptic Christianity. Jewish communities established by merchants emerged after that. Although Ethiopian tradition claims the Queen of Sheba who sent a caravan of riches to King Solomon, Yemen was that legend's more likely source. Ethiopia was a twentieth century anachronism, a medieval kingdom whose 14.6 million people included around 80 ethnic groups, four million serfs and two million slaves.[27]

The frontier between the Abyssinian and Italian empires was ill-marked with overlapping claims. Italy had two colonies in East Africa, Eritrea and Somaliland, both bordering Ethiopia but divided along the Red Sea by French Djibouti and on the Indian Ocean by British Somaliland. A 1928 Italian-Abyssinian treaty designated the border between Ethiopia and Eritrea as 73 miles from the coast. The Italians violated that treaty when they built a fort at Walwal oasis 81 miles within Ethiopia in 1930. King Victor Emmanuel III visited Eritrea in September 1932.

Haile Selassie was crowned Abyssinia's emperor on 2 November 1930. He tried to diminish the swelling Italian threat by forging relations with other countries.[28] In 1933, he welcomed a delegation of Japanese diplomats, military officers and industrialists to develop bilateral trade and attract investments. American and British companies also explored trade and investment possibilities.

Darkening Italian relations with Ethiopia was the Abyssinian army's destruction of an invading Italian army at Adowa in March 1896. Mussolini was determined to avenge that humiliating defeat by conquering Abyssinia, then transforming that realm into a prosperous, profitable colony.[29] During the early 1930s, he built up both a list of reasons for war and military forces in Eritrea and Somaliland. Mussolini sent Count Luigi Vinci as his ambassador to Abyssinia in 1933. Vinci complained of frequent raids by Abyssinian brigands against Eritrean settlements and supply trucks.

A crisis erupted on 22 November 1934, when an Ethiopian force of a thousand troops appeared before Walwal and its commander, Fitorari Shiferra, demanded that the Italian commander, Captain Roberto Cimmaruta, withdraw his force to Eritrea. Cimmaruta rejected that demand. On 5 December, the Ethiopians attacked but the defenders repelled them. Around 110 Ethiopians and 50 Italians died in the fighting.

Mussolini publicly declared on 30 December 1934 that: 'The problem of Italo-Abyssinian relations has moved in recent times onto a new plane. From a problem of diplomacy it has become a problem of force; a "historic" problem which must be resolved by the only means which ever resolve such problems – the use of arms.'[30]

On 7 January 1935 Mussolini and French Premier Pierre Laval signed a treaty that committed both countries to resisting German aggression and for France to cede some disputed territory to Italy near Libya and East Africa and guarantee Italian residents of Tunisia rights until 1965; secretly, Laval promised Mussolini 'a free hand' in East Africa against Ethiopia, although he later denied doing so.

Il Duce announced on 16 January 1935, that he had named himself the Colonial Minister and General Emilio De Bono the High Commissioner and Commander-in-Chief for East Africa. An Italian army corps bound for East Africa lifted anchor on 6 February, followed by two more divisions on the 11th.

Mussolini's dreams for Ethiopia were grandiose. He promised to 'raise an Ethiopian force of a million soldiers, build fifty or so airfields and a metallurgical industry, so that Ethiopia would find on its own soil everything necessary for military development. Then we can realize the link up with Libya and liberate ourselves from the servitude imposed by the Suez Canal.'[31] None of those dreams came remotely true.

Mussolini massed two armies to conquer Ethiopia. In Eritrea, General Emilio De Bono's army numbered 300,000 troops, one-third regulars, one-third Blackshirt militia and one-third natives. Native troops included 60,200 Eritreans, 20,000 Somalians and 20,000 Libyans. The Italians mobilized one of ten Eritreans or 40 per cent of the active male workforce for the army. In Somaliland, General Graziani's army numbered 285,000 troops.[32] The plan was for De Bono to drive straight for Addis Ababa while Graziani overran southern Ethiopia.

Behind those impressive paper numbers, the campaign's planning and implementation was abysmal, especially in Eritrea. The port of Massawa was so small that troops and supplies bottlenecked there to trickle onto the continent. At most the port could daily transfer 3,000 tons of supplies between ships and shore of the two million tons that eventually arrived. Drinking water was the worse deficiency. Three-quarters of the army's water was imported from Italy.

Anthony Eden, Britain's Minister to the League of Nations, flew to Rome to offer Mussolini a compromise. Ethiopia would swap a swatch of Ogaden desert for the right of transit over a stretch of Italian Somaliland to the port of Zella in British Somaliland. Mussolini rejected that offer and insisted on taking all of Ethiopia.

Without a declaration of war, both armies invaded Ethiopia on 3 October 1935.[33] De Bono's army routed the few Ethiopian troops in their way and marched into Adowa on 7 October and Makelle on 8

November. Meanwhile, Ras Tadessa Mulugeta led the Ethiopian army north from Addis Abada on 8 November. Believing that De Bono was moving too slowly, Mussolini promoted him to marshal and replaced him with General Pietro Badoglio on 16 November. Emperor Haile Selassie moved his headquarters to Dessie, Wollo Province's capital, on 18 November. On the southern front, Graziani's army crossed the frontier but fought defensively against a series of attacks by Ras Desta Damtu.

Meanwhile, fifty members of the League of Nations hoped to stop the Italian army in its tracks. On 10 October, they voted for a resolution that Italy was the aggressor in Ethiopia and the next day voted to impose economic sanctions against Italy that would begin on 18 November unless Mussolini withdrew his army.[34]

The sanctions proved to be symbolic not substantive. The British could have stopped Italy's conquest simply by denying Italian transport and supply ships passage through the Suez Canal. But they feared that too tough a stance against Mussolini would drive him into an alliance with Hitler. That essentially happened anyway. Hitler gleefully violated the sanctions with more German exports to Italy to capture the market share yielded by rivals, undermine the League of Nations and inspire Mussolini's gratitude. Most vital was the coal that fired factories, train locomotives and electricity grids; Germany's share of Italian consumption soared from 23 per cent in 1923 to 74 per cent in 1936.[35]

Foreign Ministers Samuel Hoare and Pierre Laval agreed on 8 December to offer to revoke the sanctions if Mussolini agreed to conquer only two-thirds of Ethiopia. The press learned of that 'Hoare-Laval Pact' and revealed it the next day. Ever more prominent editorial and political voices condemned that as appeasement. Hoare resigned on 18 December and Anthony Eden took his place as foreign secretary.

Winston Churchill then was a House of Commons 'backbencher', but had strong views on how to handle Mussolini derived a decade earlier when he was Chancellor of the Exchequer: 'On the two occasions in 1927 when I met Mussolini our personal relations had been intimate and easy. I would never have encouraged Britain to make a breach with him about Abyssinia or roused the League of Nations against him unless we were prepared to go to war in the last extreme.'[36]

Mussolini announced the 'First Wedding Ring Day' on 18 December 1935, during which patriotic Italian wives would exchange their gold wedding rings for steel ones. In Rome, Queen Elena and Rachele

Mussolini stood side-by-side before a huge crowd of women before the Tomb of the Unknow Soldier and were the first to cast their rings into a brazier. The Treasury Ministry melted the gold rings into bullion bars to help finance the Ethiopian War.

Both armies rested for much of the winter as reinforcements and supplies arrived. Graziani resumed his offensive on 1 January and fought Ras Damtu at Genale Doria from 12 to 20 January, defeated him and after nearly two months of stalemate advanced on 1 April, fought Damtu at Ogaden from 14 to 25 April and routed him again. Badoglio's army resumed the offensive on 1 February, fought Mulugeta's army at Amba Aradam from 10 to 19 February 1936 and finally crushed it. Badoglio's army marched on to fight the combined armies of Ras Kassa and Ras Seyoum at Tembien from 20 to 24 February, routed them then pushed on to engage Ras Imru's army at Shire from 29 February to 2 March and routed it. The decisive battle came at Maychew on 31 March, when Badoglio routed the Ethiopian army commanded by Emperor Haile Selassie. Guerrilla attacks on Italian supply convoys on both fronts slowed both army advances to crawls.

Haile Selassie and his royal entourage packed into a train and departed Addis Ababa for French Djibouti on 2 May 1936. Three days later, Badoglio's army marched unopposed into Addis Ababa, while the emperor and his court boarded a British warship bound for exile in Europe.

Word of those events inspired celebration in Italy. On 9 May, with Victor Emmanuel III beside him, Mussolini announced that: 'Italy finally has its empire . . . It is a Fascist empire, an empire of peace, an empire of civilization and humanity'.[37] *Il Duce* then decreed that: 'The title Emperor of Ethiopia shall hereafter be borne by the King of Italy and his successors'. The new Emperor awarded Mussolini the Grand Cross of the Military Order of Savoy, named General De Bono a marshal and replaced him with Marshal Rodolfo Graziani as his 'Viceroy of Ethiopia'.

Mussolini recalled that Victor Emmanuel was so elated that

> he suddenly got up and said, 'Mussolini, as a reward for the Ethiopian victory will you, in addition to my personal congratulations and the gratitude of our country, accept the title of Prince for yourself and your descendants?' 'Your Majesty . . . I wish to remain plain Mussolini, as I have always been'. The King, now Emperor, replied, 'But a peerage at least'. 'The Mussolinis have always been peasants and I am rather proud of that fact'.[38]

Not all Italians revelled in Ethiopia's conquest. In her memoir, Rachele Mussolini issued this warning to her husband:

> Remember Napoleon, Benito, since you admire him so much. True he was powerful; he mastered Europe and even ruled countries further afield. But what did he really do? As soon as he won one victory he looked for more, After each conquest, he still wanted a bigger empire. And what happened to him, Benito? He lost the lot! Everything crumbled under his feet, Don't be like him.

Mussolini angrily replied: 'What do you want me to do? Resign? Raise chickens in Romagna? You must be joking, Rachele.'[39] And so Mussolini, like countless other husbands since the dawn of human time, dismissed his wife's sage advice and ended up with the disastrous consequences that she predicted.

As Rachele warned, those victory celebrations proved to be premature. The Italian army may have occupied Ethiopia's capital Addis Ababa as the latest link in a chain of towns and oases leading back to Eritrea, but rebel guerrillas infested that route and other regions across the kingdom. The Italians could not begin to exploit the population and whatever meagre crops and minerals the land yielded until they crushed the guerillas. For that, Mussolini could only imagine the harshest means. On 5 June 1936, he issued this command to General Graziani: 'All rebels made prisoners are to be shot'. A month later when the Ethiopian resistance remained virulent, Mussolini elaborated his order: 'I repeat my authorization to your excellency to initiate and systematically conduct policy of terror and extermination and against rebels and populations in complicity with them. Without the law of ten eyes for one we cannot heal this wound in good time.'[40]

Ethiopian terrorists tossed grenades into an Italian crowd presided over by Graziani celebrating the birthday of Crown Prince Umberto on 19 February 1937. The explosions wounded around thirty people including Graziani. Enraged, Mussolini issued this directive: 'No persons arrested are to be released without my order. All civilians and [Coptic] clerics . . . are to be shot without delay.'[41] Graziani had Fascist Chief Guido Cortese unleash his Blackshirts for three days of systematic murder of Ethiopians. From 3,000 to 30,000 Ethiopians died in the slaughter. Blackshirts also sacked the Debra Lebranos monastery that held the most sacred texts of Ethiopian Christianity and history.

Among the invaders were two of Mussolini's sons, Vittorio and Bruno, his nephew Vito, son of his deceased brother Arnaldo, and his son-in-law Galeazzo Ciano. Of the four, Ciano had the highest rank as commander of the 15th Bombardier Squadron with Vittorio and Bruno as pilots. Their squadron initiated the war on 2 October, with a bombing attack on Ethiopian positions. Ciano flew numerous missions and twice was forced to crash land after bullets pierced his fuel tank. In December 1935, he was flown to Rome for an emergency operation for a severe nose and throat infection. In February 1936, he returned to Abyssinia to fly more missions and again survived being shot down. After he flew solo in a reconnaissance mission over Abyssinia's capital, Mussolini telegraphed him the message that 'I am very proud of your flight over Addis Ababa'. Ciano received two silver medals for courage during the campaign.[42]

Yet the horrors Ciano witnessed and helped inflict in Abyssinia disillusioned him. After one bombing mission against civilians, he admitted that 'we ha`ve carried out a slaughter'. He told Colonial Ministry undersecretary Alessandro Lessona that: 'A military victory can be ruled out, because in this mountainous terrain there cannot be rapid solutions. Meanwhile, we will be strangled by sanctions. We must have diplomatic talks with England and immediately. I see dark clouds on the horizon.'[43]

Italy's conquest cost relatively few Italian lives, 1,537 from combat and several thousand others from disease. The war was catastrophic for Ethiopians as perhaps a quarter of a million died from bombs, bullets, disease and starvation. Poison gas was used against the Ethiopians, even though Italy had signed the 1925 Geneva Protocol that banned chemical weapons. The military shipped 617 tons of poison gas for the campaign.[44] The merchant marine conducted the war's most efficient military operations by transporting 637,000 personnel and 2.1 million tons of supplies to Eritrea and evacuating 44,000 casualties. Italy's financial cost for the conquest from 1935 to 1940 was exorbitant – 77 billion lira of the 116 billion lira military budget. Italian exports to Ethiopia did rise from 248,000,000 lira's worth in 1931 to 2,500,000,000 in 1937, thus benefiting the companies that made those sales.[45]

Haile Selassie made a speech in his native tongue Amharic condemning Italian imperialism and asking for help before the League of Nations in Geneva on 12 May 1936. Italian journalists blew whistles drowning out the emperor's speech for 15 minutes until police arrested them. The emperor's appeal was poignant but changed nothing. The British and French had already unofficially accepted that conquest and they led the League. Britain announced that it would end economic sanctions against Italy on 18 June 1936 and soon nearly all other governments made their own announcements. Despite that the League of Nations condemned Italy's conquest of Ethiopia on 11 December 1937. Mussolini replied by announcing Italy's withdrawal from the League of Nations on 13 December 1937. That was little more than four years after Hitler announced Germany's withdrawal on 14 October 1933.

Mussolini organized Eritrea, Somalia and Ethiopia as Italian East Africa (*Africa Orientale Italiana*). He hoped that East Africa would flourish under Italian rule with hundreds of thousands of Italian immigrants.[46] That did not happen. Few Italians wanted to emigrate there and those that did could not prosper in such a desolate land and traditional, resentful culture. Only 3,200 Italian peasants settled in Ethiopia by 1941. In contrast, Eritrea's Italian population soared. There were only 4,188 settlers in 1931. Then, from April 1935 to May 1936, over 300,000 soldiers and 50,000 labourers disembarked. By 1939, after most troops and labourers departed, Eritrea's Italian population was 75,000.[47]

Italy's rule over Ethiopia was progressive in several ways. The Italians declared freedom for Ethiopia's two million slaves and four million serfs. The Italians also improved or extended the realm's long-distance road, railway, school, water, sewage and electrical systems. They expanded crop acreage and improved productivity.[48]

As in any colony, some colonists had relations with native women that resulted in mixed racial children. The Italian word for those relationships was '*Madamismo*', playing off the 'madame' used for native women. Mussolini issued on 19 April 1937 a decree that outlawed sex between Italians and African natives, with prison terms up to five years. Only Italians were culpable; natives suffered no penalty. To alleviate the frustrated demand for women among the colonists, the government recruited women, mostly poor, many prostitutes, and shipped them to Ethiopia as settlers; the shipments were called 'Venus Cars' (*Carri de Venere*).

Fascist leaders who inspected the colonies despaired at the quality of most colonists. Robert Farinacci complained to Mussolini that: 'The Italians present the indigenous with a quite unimperial spectacle'. Specifically, he cited their ragged appearance, servile attitude to natives, corruption, greed and incompetence. In his book *Il Governo delle Genti di Colore* (*Governing Peoples of Colour*, 1940), Raffaele Di Lauro called on settlers to realize the Italian value of '*Bella Figura*' or 'Cutting a Good Figure'.[49]

Mussolini sought to undermine British and French domination of the Middle East and Egypt. He sent up an Arab-language propaganda radio broadcast at Bari in May 1934. His core message was that Italy,

Fascism and himself respected Arabs and Muslims and that the British and French did not.

Mussolini visited Libya in March 1937. At Tripoli on 18 March, he performed the remarkable public ceremony before Italian and Muslim officials of unsheathing the 'Sword of Islam' to wield against Italy's enemies. What the Muslims thought of his embrace of Islamic Holy War was unrecorded, but likely mixed indignation, disgust and disbelief. Mussolini did pledge this: 'Fascist Italy wants to assure the Muslim populations of Libya and Ethiopia that it will provide peace, justice, prosperity, respect for the laws of the Prophet and also wishes to demonstrate with its legislation its solicitude for your better future.'[50]

Mussolini followed up that pledge with a stunning act. The Grand Council proclaimed that Libya was an integral part of the Italian kingdom on 26 October 1938 and extended Italian citizenship to Libyans and established the Muslim Association of the Lictor (*Associazione Musulmana del Littorio*) on 9 January 1939. In practice, Mussolini imposed strict education and wealth requirements for Libyans who applied for citizenship and restrictions on what government posts they could hold.

Mussolini did give the Muslim world a genuine gift in April 1939. His son-in-law Galeazzo Ciano was among countless Italians disturbed by his announcement that he would 'erect a mosque in Rome in view of the fact that 6,000,000 Italian subjects are now Mohammedans . . . at the Vatican they are horror struck at the idea . . . But the *Duce* has made up his mind and he is supported in this by the King . . . Personally I do not see any need for such a thing . . . In so far as this proposal concerns the Albanians, we realize that they are an atheistic people who would prefer a rise in salary to a mosque.'[51]

Fascism championed imperialism as a means and an end. The November 1938 edition of the Fascist journal *Partito e Impero* (*Party and Empire*) explained the significance of Italy's imperial expansion:

> Italy cannot yet consider itself successful . . . We must have the willpower to always strive for new goals . . . Whoever gives up will lose. This is the injunction of the party: never to allow the Italian people to rest, to urge them on, to foster among them the urge to expand indefinitely in order to survive, to instil in them a sense of the superiority of our race over the blacks . . . In short, we must give the Italian people an imperialist and racist mentality.[52]

Mussolini explained the key for Italy's imperial success in a secret speech before Fascist party leaders on 25 October 1938: 'The empire will be preserved only if we impress the natives with the fact that we are clearly and overwhelmingly superior'.[53]

Italy's government spent 249,500,000,000 lire from fiscal years 1934–5 to 1939–40, of which the military, colonies and wars in Ethiopia and Spain devoured 51 per cent. Italy's imports from its colonies were just 2 per cent of its total imports. The colonies had to import as much as half of their total food needs. That was largely because the Italians replaced countless acres of food crops with cash crops. Although Libya had enormous oil and gas reserves beneath its sands they were not discovered and exploited until after the Libyans freed themselves from Italian rule.[54]

Mussolini could not escape the core imperial dilemma. Like virtually all colonies throughout history, Italy's cost much more than they yielded in wealth.

Chapter 6

THE AXIS PACT OF STEEL

> These men are not made of the same stuff . . . as the Francis Drakes and the other magnificent adventurers who created the empire. These, after all, are the tired sons of a long line of rich men and they will lose their empire.
>
> (Benito Mussolini)

> Madrid has fallen and with the capital all the other cities of Red Spain. The war is over. It is a new formidable victory for Fascism, perhaps the greatest one so far.
>
> (Galeazzo Ciano)

> Here is one of those rare men . . . who are not made by history but by whom history is made.
>
> (Adolf Hitler on Benito Mussolini)

Tyrants face many dilemmas that aggravate their natural paranoia. The worst is who to trust and who to eliminate. They are haunted by fear of those eager to depose them. They want their regime to survive their eventual deaths but worry that designating an heir might empower him to make their demise sooner rather than later.

In all that, Benito Mussolini was a typical tyrant. He played off potential rivals against each other and ensured that none kept a position of power long enough to make it impregnable. With one exception and two partial exceptions, he had no genuine friends, only underlings. He despised his subordinates, condemning them as 'all rotten to the core'.[1] The exception was his devoted younger brother Arnaldo who became his closest advisor, the only person he truly trusted. After Mussolini took power, they spoke by telephone nearly every day. Arnaldo literally and figuratively followed in Benito's footsteps as a teacher then to Switzerland and the socialist movement. During the First World War, he fought valiantly and rose to the rank of captain. He became a journalist and took Mussolini's place as director of *Il Populo d'Italia* from 1923 to 1927. He was an environmentalist who headed the National Forest Committee. In 1930, Mussolini asked him to found the School of Fascist Mysticism in Milan to train Party leaders, but had his son Vittorio serve as president. Genuine grief engulfed Mussolini when a heart attack killed Arnaldo at age 46 on 21 December 1931. Mussolini had Vittorio replace Arnaldo as director of *Populo d'Italia*.

After Arnaldo died, Mussolini gradually became more dependent on his son-in-law Galeazzo Ciano as his closest advisor and possible heir. Ciano was handsome, bright, articulate, charming and a womanizer.[2] He studied law at the University of Rome, dabbled as a playwright, short story writer and journalist, but became a diplomat after passing the Foreign Ministry exam at age 22 in 1925. He then served at the Italian embassies in Brazil, Argentina and China, before returning to Rome in late 1929.

Ciano's father was Costanzo Ciano, a naval captain and war hero awarded four silver medals in the First World War, devoted Fascist from 1919, elected Fascist member of the Chamber of Deputies from 1921, among the 'March on Rome' leaders, Navy Ministry undersecretary and Merchant Marine Commissioner in 1922, Fascist Grand Council member in 1925, Posts and Telegraph Minister and Communications Minister in 1924 and Chamber of Deputy president from 1934; King Victor Emmanual III named him an admiral in 1923 and count in 1925. After Arnold, he was Mussolini's closest confident and possible successor. That possibility ended with Costanzo Ciano's death on 26 June 1939.

Ciano and Edda, Mussolini's eldest and most adored child, met at Rome in January 1930; he was 27 and she was 19 years old. Edda was high-spirited, outspoken and sensual, stigmatized by many for being born out of wedlock; her memoir published in 1977 offers fascinating insights into Mussolini and his Fascist regime.[3] With 400 guests, they married at San Giuseppe Church, went to St. Peter's Cathedral to kiss the foot of St. Peter's silver statue for luck and had their reception at Villa Torlonia, the Mussolini palace, on 24 April 1930. Initially, Ciano and Edda passionately loved each other. She called him Gallo (Cock). They drank, gambled and socialized much like Scott and Zelda Fitgerald. They had three children. Their passion later receded and they agreed to an open marriage with each ignoring the other's affairs.

Mussolini was generous to his son-in-law, naming him first Italian Consul at Shanghai from 1930 to 1934. During the Ethiopian campaign, Ciano commanded the 15th Bombardier Squadron, flew many missions, was shot down three times and won two silver medals. Mussolini recalled him to be Popular Culture Minister from June 1935 to June 1936. Mussolini transferred the foreign minister portfolio from himself to Ciano on 11 June 1936.

Ciano surpassed Mussolini's actual sons in approaching the type of man the *Duce* wanted them to be. After becoming Foreign Minister, Ciano advised Mussolini with polite candour and did not hesitate to disagree with him. Yet Ciano harboured flaws that potentially undermined the regime's security – garrulousness and a need to be admired and the centre of attention. Edda worried that 'he was often careless when he confided in people, especially pretty women, and that some of his remarks were repeated either to the Germans or the Fascist extremists'.[4]

Edda was aware that Ciano was mocked behind his back for 'passing himself as my father's heir and proudly emulating him to such an extent that he aped Mussolini's mannerisms and way of speaking'. She explained why: 'My husband seemed to simply because he met with him several times a day for years and so unconsciously adopted certain of his characteristics'. She admitted that: 'Certainly it was Ciano's ambition to become head of state one day'.[5]

Yet, Mussolini and Ciano had disputes that eventually estranged them. One was their views of Germany. Edda recalled that 'my husband never liked Germany or the Germans, not for political reasons in the beginning, but simply because he was a true Latin and therefore not attracted to their mentality . . . that they lacked a sense of humour . . . warmth and levity'. In contrast, Mussolini 'loved Germany . . . that Germany which had given birth not only to men such as Wagner, Nietzsche, Kant, Goethe, Schiller, Luther and even Marx, but also to great militarists like Frederick II and Bismarck. Everything related to Germany interested him, its poetry, its language, its customs and even its old traditions. And he had a special admiration for the Prussian Army.'[6]

The critical blows to their relationship came from Mussolini's war strategy whose worsening disastrous defeats steadily alienated Ciano. In July 1943, he joined seventeen other members of the twenty-eight man Fascist Grand Council to vote for Mussolini's ouster. Eventually, as *Il Duce* of the rump Salo Republic in northern Italy, Mussolini avenged what he called their betrayal. Ciano was among six members who voted against him that the Germans captured and handed over to his regime. A Fascist tribunal found the six guilty of treason, condemned Ciano and four others to death and a sixth to 30 years in prison. Mussolini rejected Edda's pleas to spare her husband and his son-in-law.

Historians are indebted to Ciano for the diary he kept when he was Foreign Minister from 1936 to 1943 that provides crucial insights into the nature of Mussolini and his regime.[7] Malcolm Muggeridge was a British journalist who knew Ciano and after the war edited his diary. He succinctly explained the nature of both: 'Ciano . . . was too vain to hide the true workings of his mind and the true character of his aspirations and too foolish to be aware of how completely he was giving himself and those about whom he wrote away. If he had been cleverer, his Diary would have been far less revealing.' Instead, Ciano 'records the mental processes, sudden rages, lechery and sentimentality, flashes of insight, inconceivable stupidities, ingenuousness and shrewdness of the buffoon who for a quarter of a century imposed himself on the Italian people . . . There the man is in all his folly and humanity.'[8]

One persistent Mussolini foreign policy sought to undermine exiled Italians who formed anti-Fascist groups that he condemned as 'outlaws' (*fuorusciti*).[9] Mussolini's ban of political parties starting with the Communist and Socialist Parties and assaults and arrests of its leaders forced tens of thousands of them to flee to foreign countries. Paris was the magnet for most activists although large communities resided in London and New York.

Socialist Party chief Pietro Nenni formed the Italian Antifascist Concentration (*Concentrazione Antifascista Italiana*, CAI) in Paris in April 1927 and it soon became the most powerful resistance group for eight years. The Antifascist Concentration published the weekly newspaper *La Liberta* from May 1927 to May 1934, when the organization imploded from animosities among its rival factions.

The Italian Communist Party, led by Palmiro Togliatti and Antonio Gramsci, was the most powerful resistance group during most of the Mussolini years. Gramsci was arrested in 1926 and sentenced to life in prison, where he died on 27 April 1937. Although Togliatti spent years in Moscow and was a Comintern agent, he retained autonomy for the Italian Communist Party. He was a leading proponent of the Popular Front strategy of allying with as many centre-left parties and groups as possible. In 1934 he established the Italian Popular Union as a coalition of anti-fascist groups dominated by the Communist Party. The Popular Union expanded to 45,000 members then imploded after Stalin allied the Communist Soviet Union with Adolf Hitler's Nazi Third Reich in

August 1939. The Communist Party had a deep underground in Italy throughout the Mussolini years that reemerged as partisan guerrillas that fought his Salo Republic and the German army.

Another resistance group was Justice and Liberty (*Giustizia e Liberta*), founded by Carlo Rosselli in 1929. Rosselli advocated reforms and rejected Marxism in his weekly newspaper *Giustizia e Liberta* and his book *Liberal Socialism* (*Socialismo Liberale*). He allied his group with the Italian Antifascist Concentration but reverted to independence after it dissolved. Mussolini viewed Rosselli's Liberty and Justice as the most dangerous group because his pragmatic centre-left political agenda had the broadest appeal.

Among Rosselli's roles was to enlist and send volunteers to the Garibaldi Brigade fighting on the Republican side against Francisco Franco's Nationalists backed by Mussolini. France's leading Fascist group was the Secret Committee of Revolutionary Action (*Comite Secrète d'Action Révolutionnaire*), called *Cagoulards* (Cowls or Hoods) for their attempts to cloak their identity. A group of them accosted Rosselli and his brother Nello while they were driving in Normandy and stabbed them to death on 9 June 1937. Circumstantial evidence links Italian Foreign Minister Galeazzo Ciano to the Cagoulards for the murders. Eventually French police captured the murderers and learned that they were commissioned by General Mario Roatta, Major Roberto Navale, a military intelligence attaché, Lieutenant Colonel Santo Emannuele, the Italian Secret Service chief, and Ciano's aide Filippo Anfuso. The French government issued a protest to Mussolini and demanded justice. Mussolini claimed that he knew nothing about the murders which he called 'an error'.[10]

Among the Versailles Treaty's restrictions on Germany was that no German military forces could be in the Rhineland region. On 7 March 1936, Hitler blatantly violated that clause when he sent 10,000 troops into the Rhineland. The British and French governments protested that act but did not rally the League of Nations to oppose it. That appeasement encouraged the three Fascist powers to commit increasingly blatant acts of international aggression.

Mussolini was determined to spread Fascism to other countries either through mass movements or coups. Spain appeared to be a promising field for Fascism. Political instability had plagued the realm ever since 1807, when Napoleon bullied King Charles IV to relinquish the crown to him, whereupon he enthroned his brother as Joseph I. What followed was thirteen decades of factions vying for power, often violently, with those who seized it failing to establish legitimacy and longevity.

Just from 1923 to 1936, a four-way tug among royalists, republicans, Communists and Fascists literally tore Spain apart. King Alfonso XIII feared the swelling popularity of labour and peasant movements led by radical leftists In 1923, he encouraged General Miguel de Rivera to take power in a military coup, suspend the 1876 constitution and parliament (*cortez*) and rule as Spain's dictator in collaboration with himself. Admiral Juan Anzar-Cabanas pressured Rivera to resign and took his place in 1930. Worsening unrest, demonstrations, strikes and riots at Anzar-Cabanas's harsh rule caused Alfonso XIII to hold municipal elections on 12 April 1931. Liberals and Socialists captured most city governments and called for the overthrow of Alfonso and Anzar-Cabanas. Alfonso fled to foreign exile and Anzar-Cabanas resigned.

A revolutionary group led by Niceto Alcala-Zamora took power and declared Spain's Second Republic on 14 April 1931, abolished the Senate and held elections for the unicameral legislature on 28 June. Of a score or more political parties that competed, the Socialist-Republican coalition led by Alcala-Zamora won one-third of the vote. Alcala-Zamora formed a coalition with an array of leftist parties. He resigned in October and Manuel Alzana became president. The Constitution, enacted in December 1931, formally established the republic. Alzana's policies of confiscating Catholic Church property and abolishing Catholic schools and charities alienated traditional Spaniards.

Mussolini first tried to manipulate Spanish politics by secretly sending arms to a group led by General Jose Sanjurjo that tried to overthrow Spain's republic in August 1932. Loyal army and police units crushed the revolt. Sanjurjo received the death penalty which was commuted to prison for life.

Jose Antonio de Primo de Rivera, the dictator's son, founded the Falange or Fascist Party on 29 October 1933.[11] Mussolini began sending Primo de Rivera a monthly 50,000 peseta subsidy to develop the Falange Party from June 1935. He ended the subsidy after Spain's Republic imprisoned Primo de Rivera in April 1936.

The Spanish Confederation of Autonomous Right-Wing Groups (CEDA) led by Jose Gil-Robes y Quinones won the November 1933 election and demanded to form a government. Alzana refused to name Robes prime minister and instead let Radical Republican Party leader Alejandro Lerroux form the government. CEDA pressured Lerroux to grant the party three ministries, with Gil-Robes the war minister in 1934. That provoked an insurrection by the Communist and Socialist Parties but the army crushed the rebels. The Popular Front of liberal, socialist and communist parties won the February 1936 election and formed a government led by Alzana.[12]

General Emilio Mola initiated a military conspiracy to overthrow the government and restore the monarchy and a conservative government to power. Generals Francisco Franco and Jose Sanjurjo were key partners. The rebels, who called themselves Nationalists, revolted two days after the Republican government arrested Gil-Robles on 12 July. The subsequent civil war would last nearly three years, devastate the country and become a training and weapons proving ground for Italy, Germany and Soviet Union.[13]

General Francisco Franco commanded Spain's military forces in the Canary Islands, headquartered at Tenerife. He had himself flown to Tetuan, a Spanish enclave connected with the port of Ceuta in Morocco. On 19 July, he sent his subordinate Luis Bolin to Rome to ask Mussolini for bomber and fighter warplanes. Mussolini sent twelve Savoia-Marchetta SM.81 Pipistrello (Bat) three-engine bombers to Tetuan, of which nine made it, one crashed into the sea and the other two landed in French Morocco where the authorities arrested the pilots.

Franco turned to Hitler, sending a request for transports that reached him on 23 July. Hitler assembled his military advisors to discuss the request. They decided to fly him twenty Junkers Ju 52 transport planes and ship him six Heinkel He 51 fighter planes and anti-aircraft guns. To mask that blatant act of Berlin aiding a rebel group, they established the cover company *Hispano-Marroqui de Transportes Sociedad Anomina*.

That air force let Franco fly his troops to Seville and soon take over south-west Spain. Meanwhile, in the north-west, Mola defeated Republican forces and secured much of that region. Franco and Mola eventually joined forces then advanced toward Madrid. Meanwhile, Franco's forces took over Majorca island. Ten thousand Republican troops invaded Majorca on 16 August 1936. Mussolini sent Major Arconovaldo Bonaccorsi with 250 Italian troops to bolster the Falangist force. With Bonaccorsi's advice, the Nationalists contained the Republican beachhead and finally forced the enemy to withdraw to the mainland.

Meanwhile, a gathering of generals at Salamanca voted to make Franco their leader with the title 'generalissimo' on 21 September 1936. Franco's National Movement would win the civil war on 31 March 1939. Meanwhile, he united the Fascist Falange and Catholic Carlists into the National Movement with himself its leader on 17 April 1937. He would remain Spain's dictator until his death on 20 November 1975.[14]

Spain's civil war pitted the Republican coalition of liberals, socialists and communists against the Nationalist coalition of monarchists, conservatives and Falangists (Fascists).[15] Rich and middle class Spaniards mostly backed the Nationalists while workers and peasants mostly backed the Republicans. The army split between them. Generals and officers like Franco who had served in Spain's colonial empire won promotions by merit, were naturally more aggressive and tended to be Nationalists. Generals and officers who stayed in Spain and advanced through seniority tended to be Republicans. Common soldiers usually obeyed their commanders.

Spain's civil war was merciless. Republicans and Nationalists committed mass murder, torture and robbery. Communists committed the most atrocities. Red Brigades slaughtered the Catholic clergy, murdering 13 bishops, 4,148 priests, 2,365 monks and 283 nuns. They looted then blew up hundreds of churches and other religious buildings. They forced women to exchange their crucifix necklaces for necklaces adorned with a picture of female Communist leader Dolores Ibarutu, 'La Pasionaria'.[16]

Mussolini and Hitler secretly agreed to cooperate in aiding Franco's rebellion on 28 August. Atop what Berlin already sent, the Germans dispatched twenty-six Junker Ju 52 bombers, fifteen Heinkel He-51 fighters, twenty anti-aircraft guns, fifty machine guns and 8,000 rifles. Rome sent an additional twenty-seven fighter planes, five tanks and forty machine guns.[17] The key respective liaisons for German and Italian cooperation in aiding Franco were military intelligence chiefs Admiral Wilhelm Canaris and General Mario Roatta.

The international community split over Spain's civil war. Italy, Germany and the Vatican recognized Franco's Nationalist movement as Spain's legitimate government. The Soviet Union and Mexico backed the Republican government in Madrid. The British, French, German, Italian and Soviet governments recognized the potential for war to erupt among them if they aided either side. From 3 to 23 August 1936, they negotiated a Non-Intervention Agreement whereby each promised not to send military aid to Spain and to prevent others from doing so. They formed the Non-Intervention Committee in London on 8 September. It included 105 observers along the Spanish-French frontier and a pool of 330 observers of 17 nationalities from which merchant ships sailing for Spain could take aboard two representatives to ensure they were in compliance with international law and documented any attacks and damage against them. That programme became operational on 25 August 1937. During the first six weeks, 323 participating ships entered Spanish waters along with another 415 ships from non-participating countries, while Britain, France, Italy and Germany deployed fifty-two warships around Spain's coasts to inspect those vessels and ensure they carried no war supplies. At times, those warships fired on belligerents. For instance, the German heavy cruiser *Deutschland* retaliated against a shelling attack by a Republican shore battery by bombarding Almeria with 275 shells that destroyed much of the town and killed or wounded 72 people on 31 May.[18]

The United States did not join the Non-Intervention Committee. Typically, Washington followed a parallel course to that of the international community. President Franklin Roosevelt's administration announced a 'moral embargo' of arms to Spain on 11 August 1936. American corporations had around $80 million invested in Spain, with the largest shares held by International Telegraph and Telephone (ITT), Ford and General Motors.[19] Communist worker takeovers and fighting threatened those investments.

Of course, what one does publicly in politics often differs from what does secretly. France, Italy, Germany and the Soviet Union not so covertly sent massive amounts of advisors, arms and supplies to one side or the other. For instance, France's government then resembled Spain's Republicans with its Popular Front coalition of liberals and socialists. France sent Spain's Republicans twenty-five Potez 54 bombers and 20,000 bombs, the first of a stream of weapons, vehicles and equipment.

The Soviet Union funnelled military supplies, weapons and advisors to the Republicans mostly via the Communist International (Comintern) headquartered at the Kremlin and devoted to fomenting revolution around the world.[20] That aid included 363 T-26 and BT-5 tanks, 806 warplanes and 1,895 guns.[21] The Comintern formed 'brigades' of volunteers by nationality to fight for the Republicans. The International Brigades totalled 32,000 fighters, of which the largest contingents were France's 10,000 and Austria's 5,000. The Italian Garibaldi Brigade numbered 3,354 troops and fought with the slogan 'Today in Spain; tomorrow in Italy'. The American Abraham Lincoln Brigade numbered 3,000 fighters of which 681 died from combat, disease or accidents.

Germany was the Nationalists' second largest foreign backer.[22] General Hugo Sperle commanded the German Condor Legion that included an air force with 117 warplanes including thirty-six Ju 52 bombers, twenty-seven He 51 fighters and the rest transport and reconnaissance aircraft.[23] The Condor Legion's most notorious attack was bombing Guernica, the Basque region's capital and killing or wounding 153 civilians on 26 April 1937.

Italy's military intervention was the largest.[24] Mussolini called for army and militia recruits to fight in Spain in the newly created Voluntary Troop Corps (*Corpo Truppo Voluntario*, CTV). By 18 February 1937, the Voluntary Troop Corps sent to Spain a ground force of 48,823 army and militia troops commanded by six generals; an air force of 227 pilots, 702 ground personnel and 248 warplanes including bombers, fighters, transports and reconnaissance; and 542 guns, 105,000 rifles, 2,000,000 grenades, 1,000,000 artillery shells, 140,000,000 rounds of ammunition and 4,000 vehicles conveyed by 62 ships. Over three years, Mussolini supplied Franco's army with 157 tanks, 1,800 guns, 759 warplanes and 320,000,000 rounds of ammunition.[25]

The Italian Voluntary Troop Corps launched a campaign toward Guadalajara on 8 March 1937. The Republican army, including the Italian Communist Garibaldi Battalion, fought off a series of Italian attacks that finally forced them to withdraw on 20 March. An enraged Mussolini reacted by pledging that 'there is no way that I shall withdraw any men from Spain until both the military and the political failure of Guadalajara is avenged'.[26] He ordered the executions of all Italians fighting for the Republicans.

General Ettore Bastico revitalized the Italian troops after the Guadalajara defeat. Thereafter the Italian Corps racked up a series of victorious campaigns at Santander in August 1937, Aragon from March to April 1938, Valencia in July 1938 and Catalonia from December 1938 to February 1939. Italian artillery and warplanes helped the Nationalists blunt Republican offensives at Teruel from December 1937 to February 1938 and at the Ebro River from July to November 1938.

Mussolini sent Roberto Farinacci to meet Franco and assess him and his campaign in March 1937. Farinacci found Franco 'timid' and 'lacking the qualities of a real *condottierro* [military leader]' with 'no precise idea of what the Spain of tomorrow should be like. He is interested only in winning the war and then for a long period after in how to impose an authoritarian or better, dictatorial government to purge the nation of all those who have had any contact, direct or indirect, with the reds'.[27] Mussolini sent Franco a suggestion list that included consolidating his regime into a single state, party and military while conducting policies that bettered the lives of peasants and workers.

The Anti-Comintern Pact, signed by the German and Japanese foreign ministers on 25 November 1936, was the first formal Fascist alliance. The treaty established a defensive military, diplomatic and intelligence pact against operations of the Communist International (Comintern) controlled by the Soviet Union and dedicated to instigating communist revolutions around the world. A year later on 6 November 1937, Mussolini joined Italy to that alliance which he dubbed the 'Axis'.

Hitler and Mussolini invited Franco to join the Anti-Comintern Pact. Franco thanked them but said he wanted to win the civil war before he committed himself. As Franco's victory appeared imminent in early 1939, the *Führer* and *Duce* invited him again. Ciano reported on 21 February 1939 that 'Franco has decided to adhere to the anti-Comintern Pact . . . but it is to remain a secret until complete victory . . . The *Duce* is very pleased about Franco's decision.'[28] Franco signed the Anti-Comintern Pact on 27 March 1939, the day before his army captured Madrid and effectively won the civil war.

Relations between Mussolini and Hitler strengthened steadily atop their common ideological and geopolitical interests. During a meeting with Hitler on 24 October 1936, Ciano explained how each nation should assist the other in identifying and expanding its spheres of influence: 'The Mediterranean is an Italian sea. Any future modification of the balance there must tilt in favour of Italy. So Germany should have freedom of action to the East and the Baltic. By orienting our mutual dynamism in exactly opposed directions, we shall avoid any conflict of interests between Italy and Germany.'[29]

Edda Mussolini Ciano was among those who met Hitler during the visit and later vividly recalled the experience:

> Hitler was no longer the timid, awkward man who had visited Venice two years earlier, wearing a shapeless hat and a too large raincoat reaching to his ankles. In 1936, he was dressed with a certain elegance; he was more self-assured and behaved like an amiable and cultivated man of the world. His blue eyes were charming, although I did not sense the hypnotic power they were said to possess. His voice was low and agreeable, less warm than my father's and . . . could be listened to with pleasure. He spoke calmly, listened attentively and had a pleasant sense of humour. Even his Chaplinesque moustache, which had once seemed so amusing, now fitted his face and gave it a personality.[30]

Mussolini made his first official visit to Germany from 25 to 29 September 1937. During that time, he and Hitler met daily, mostly for the *Duce* to endure the *Führer*'s harangues that lasted two or more hours. On 28 September, the two leaders appeared before 800,000 people. Hitler introduced Mussolini with this accolade: 'Here is one of those rare men . . . who are not made by history but by whom history is made'. Mussolini then made a speech in German, during which he lauded the Fascist and Nazi regimes as 'the greatest and most authentic democracies existing in the present day world'.[31]

Souring the relationship for Mussolini was Germany's increasingly superior hard and soft power, rendering him Hitler's junior partner. Germany's 80 million people were nearly twice as numerous as Italy's 45 million and its economy was nearly four times larger. Germany's rapidly growing military surpassed Italy's military in numbers. Franco's forces appreciated any military aid, but lauded Germany's machines and weapons as more durable and deadly than Italy's.

One symbol of the flipflop in power and influence between the two tyrants was Mussolini's adoption of the German 'goose-step' for the Italian army on 1 February 1938. He explained that 'it is a step which the sedentary, the fat, the stupid and the so-called shorties . . . will never be able to manage. We like it because of that. Our adversaries state that this parade-step is an authentic militarism. We are happy about that.'[32]

Hitler announced on 4 February 1938 that he was assuming personal command of the military. Mussolini envied Hitler's freedom to assert that. By law, Italy's king clearly held that power. Mussolini did what he could to muddy that legal clarity and assert military command. On 30 March, he declared before the Senate: 'In Italy war will be waged by one man alone, the man who is addressing you'. The decree that implemented Mussolini's latest new power read: 'Article I: The Rank of First Marshal of the Empire is hereby created. Article II: This rank is hereby conferred on His Majesty the King and Emperor and on Benito Mussolini, *Duce* of Fascism.'[33] In other words, the King and *Duce* would legally share command although Mussolini ensured that he would dominate it.

Mussolini had the Chamber of Deputies vote to abolish itself on 14 December 1938, to be replaced as a rubber-stamp legislature by the Chamber of Fascists and Corporations (*Camera dei Fasci e delle Corporazioni*). That transformation officially took place on 14 January 1939. He retained the Senate whose members the king appointed. He ensured that Victor Emmanuel tapped only trusted Fascist Party members. The Senate had no fixed number of seats and by 1939 had 455 members. The Fascist Party counted 21,606,468 members or half the population in the Party or its auxiliaries in December 1939.[34]

The next Versailles Treaty restriction that Hitler violated was that Germany could not annex Austria (*Auschluss*). On 7 February 1938, Hitler summoned Austrian Chancellor Kurt von Schuschnigg to his

Obersalzberg villa at Berchtesgaden and tried to bully him into agreeing to annexation and making Austrian Nazi Party leader Arthur Seyss-Inquart the Interior Minister. Schuschnigg promised to present Hitler's demands to Austrian President Wilhelm Miklas. After returning to Vienna, he announced that Austria would hold a referendum on whether to be annexed by Germany on 9 March. Fearing most Austrians would reject that, Hitler demanded on 11 March that Schuschnigg postpone the referendum and resign as chancellor to be replaced by Seyss-Inquart. Schuschnigg announced that he and all the cabinet members would resign except Seyss-Inquart. On 12 March, a German army entered Austria unopposed and greeted by joyous people lining the roads. On 13 March, Hitler announced that Germany had annexed Austria.

Still glowing from that triumph, Hitler made his second trip to Italy to meet with Mussolini, this time at Florence on 8 May, 1938. Hitler was more interested in discussing art than geopolitics. He insisted that they visit the Pitti Palace and Uffizi art museums, something that bored Mussolini. The *Duce* confessed to Ciano that he 'does not like works of art and above all detests that period of history during which the greatest masterpieces were produced . . . he felt a sense of annoyance and physical fatigue unusual in him on the day he was obliged to accompany Hitler on a detailed visit of inspection to the Pitti Palace and to the Uffizi'.[35] Hitler also complicated relations between the King and *Duce*. At public events, he urged Mussolini to stand beside him at the podium in violation of protocol whereby the prime minister stood behind the monarch. Hitler's most important goal was to get Mussolini to back his plan for his latest conquest.

Czechoslovakia was a multinational state whose 1930 population included 7,447,000 Czechs, 3,218,000 Germans, 2,309,000 Slovaks, 720,000 Magyars (Hungarians), 569,000 Ruthenes, 100,000 Poles and 266,000 others.[36] In early September 1938, Hitler issued demands that Czechoslovakian President Edvard Beneš let Germany annex the Sudetenland with its German-speaking majority. Beneš refused. Hitler encouraged Konrad Henlein, who headed the Czech-German Nazi Party, to stage demonstrations and riots. When Beneš remained adamant, Hitler threatened war.[37]

British Prime Minister Neville Chamberlain hoped to prevent that war by meeting with Hitler and trying to find a compromise. What he ultimately did was 'appease' Hitler by conceding him everything he wanted without demanding anything in return. Although ever since, Chamberlain has rightfully been condemned for his 'appeasement policy' that actually made war more likely, what he committed was a more outrageous version of what the British and French governments had been doing ever since the Japanese conquered Manchuria half a dozen years earlier.[38]

On 15 September, Chamberlain journeyed to Berchtesgaden where Hitler harangued him for hours and insisted that the German army would invade and conquer Czechoslovakia if he did not receive the Sudetenland before 1 October. Chamberlain returned to London to consult with his cabinet and French Prime Minister Edouard Daladier. He then met Hitler again, this time at Godesburg on 22 September, with the same results. Chamberlain revealed his utter geopolitical naivete and ignorance when he wistfully declared in a broadcast on 27 September how 'horrible, fantastic, incredible . . . that we should be digging trenches and trying on gas masks because of a quarrel in a faraway country between people of whom we know nothing'.[39]

Chamberlain asked Mussolini and Daladier to join him in meeting Hitler at Munich on 29 September. Chamberlain's request to Mussolini read: 'I have sent a final appeal to Hitler today asking him to refrain from using force for the solution of the Sudetenland problem . . . I have offered to go myself to Berlin at once . . . I hope Your Excellency will be good enough to inform the German Chancellor that you are willing to be represented.'[40] Over the previous 14 years during various diplomatic encounters Chamberlain had fallen deeply and bizarrely under Mussolini's influence. In one official report when he was Foreign Secretary, Chamberlain wrote: 'I thought Mussolini a strong man of singular charm and I suspected not a little tenderness and loneliness of heart . . . I believe him to be accused of crimes in which he had no share and I suspect him to have connived unwillingly at other outrages which he would have prevented if he could.' In another official report, he gushed: 'The more one knows the Italian prime minister, the more one appreciates and loves him.'[41]

The four met at Munich on 29 September and swiftly agreed that Czechoslovakia must transfer the Sudetenland to Germany. They signed that agreement and presented it to Beneš to sign. Beneš reluctantly did so. Chamberlain flew back to London and at the airport, announced to the press corps that he had won 'peace in our time'. That time would be very short.

German troops swiftly occupied the Sudetenland. Ciano was among countless people stunned by Czechoslovakia's brutal dismemberment. He reflected that:

> In my past, my ignorance made me think that to change the borders of a European state was a very serious thing, one that could not be carried

> out without a war. Now I have seen that . . . one can cut slices of territory from one and assign them to another without any great power moving and without disturbing international public opinion.[42]

Chamberlain arrived in Rome on 31 January 1939, for a bumbling, weak-kneed attempt to pull Mussolini from his growing alliance with Hitler. For that, he provoked contempt, not respect from Mussolini and his advisors. Ciano could not believe, 'How far apart we are from these people! It is another world'. Mussolini exclaimed: 'These men are not made of the same stuff . . . as the Francis Drakes and the other magnificent adventurers who created the empire. These, after all, are the tired sons of a long line of rich men and they will lose their empire.'[43]

Hitler ordered the German army to invade the rest of Czechoslovakia on 16 March 1939 and take the German-speaking port city of Memel from Lithuania on the 23rd. The Third Reich annexed both under fire only from protests, not armed resistance.

Hitler's blatant violation of the Munich treaty and easy conquest of those territories prompted Chamberlain's latest attempt to entice Mussolini. The letter dated 23 March that Mussolini received from the prime minister only deepened his contempt for him. In the most milk-toast words Chamberlain described Hitler's violation of the Munich deal and worried that war was inevitable if his conquests persist. But he did 'not seek to interfere with the Rome-Berlin Axis' and simply requested that Mussolini 'take such action in these anxious days as may allay present tension and do something to restore the confidence that has been shattered'.[44] Chamberlain expressed dismay not outraged condemnation, let alone threats. Ciano recorded that: 'Mussolini will answer after striking at Albania. This letter strengthens his decision to act because in it he finds another proof of the inertia of the democracies.'[45]

Some foreign leaders harboured their own ill feeling toward Mussolini. André François-Poncet was France's ambassador to Germany from 1931 to 1938 and to Italy from 1938 to 1940. Ciano learned from Uruguay's foreign minister that François-Poncet believed that Mussolini 'has begun to show signs of mental decay' and in a letter intercepted by Italian intelligence François-Poncet wrote: 'In Germany I had to deal with real gentlemen; here, instead, I have to deal with servants who have become masters.'[46] Foreign Minister Anthony Eden expressed this loathing and warning: 'Mussolini is, I fear, the complete gangster and his pledged word means nothing. It would be most unfortunate to take any action at this moment which gave Mussolini the appearance of a diplomatic triumph.'[47]

The Japanese proposed transforming the Anti-Comintern Pact into a defensive alliance between Japan, Italy and Germany in July 1938.[48] Rounds of bilateral and trilateral talks unfolded over the next ten months. Mussolini and Ciano debated whether that alliance would serve Italian national interests: 'The *Duce* declared himself decidedly in favour of the alliance. I expressed my misgivings, because the alliance will not be popular in Italy and also because I fear that Germany will take advantage of it to push ahead its policy of political expansion in Central Europe.'[49] Ciano was prescient on both fears.

Victor Emmanuel III held mixed views about allying with Germany. Ciano recalled the king's initial reaction to the pending alliance: 'He does not like the Germans, but he detests and despises the French. However, he considers them capable of a sudden attack against us and therefore looks with satisfaction upon a German obligation to come to the military aid of Italy.' The more he thought about the alliance, the more he opposed it. Two months later Ciano recorded that: 'The King is more than ever anti-German. He alluded to German insolence and duplicity and at the same time praised the straightforwardness of the British. In speaking with the *Duce*, he went so far as to call the Germans rascals and beggars.'[50]

Actually, Mussolini also harboured doubts, but, like all his geopolitical views, they were rooted in stereotypes rather than hard knowledge. For instance, as the diplomacy toward an alliance developed in early 1939, he uttered this quip about his erstwhile ally: 'The Germans are a military people, not a warrior people. Give the Germans a great deal of sausage, butter, beer and a cheap car and they never will want to risk their skins.' Hitler and the German people would soon disabuse Mussolini of that stereotype while the Italian military would continually live up to the worst stereotypes about itself.[51]

Mussolini did not want to ally with Japan. Ciano reported that: 'He is of the opinion that an alliance between Germany and Italy should be concluded without Japan. He observes such an alliance would in itself be sufficient to counterbalance existing Anglo-French forces and at the same time would not appear to be anti-British or anti-American.'[52] In that, Mussolini revealed that he did not want to wage war against Britain and France, only deter them from opposing Italian and German imperial ambitions. Had he shared Hitler's vision of eventually conquering those countries then embracing Japan in the alliance would have been crucial to its success. Obviously, Japan would be an enormous asset as an ally because its vast fleet and army could menace, tie down and even conquer British and French colonies in the Far East. Just that threat diverted and spread global-thin British and French economic and military power.

Racism also partly animated Mussolini's reluctance to ally with Japan. Later, after Japan's stunning series of crushing victories against the Americans, British and Dutch across the Pacific Ocean, he expressed very mixed feelings: 'It is all very well for the Japanese to win, because they are our allies, but after all they belong to the yellow race and their successes are gained at the expense of the white race.'[53]

The Japanese themselves worried that with Hitler and Mussolini seizing so many countries a war was increasingly likely with France, Britain and perhaps the Soviet Union. If so, that might drag Japan into a world war that it was not yet ready to fight. Ciano reported that Tokyo would join with two reservations: '(1) to make known in London, Paris and Washington that in the mind of the Japanese the Alliance is directed against Moscow; and (2) . . . that, in case of a European war, Japanese aid would be limited.'[54]

Hitler and Mussolini decided to exclude Japan for now but leave open the possibility for future membership. With Hitler presiding, Ciano and Ribbentrop signed the Pact of Friendship and Alliance, dubbed the Pact of Steel, at the Chancellery Building in Berlin on 22 May 1939. Article III was the key clause: 'If it should happen . . . that one of them becomes involved militarily with another Power or other Powers, the other Contracting Pary will immediately step to its side as an ally and will support it with all military might on land, at sea and in the air.'

After signing, Ciano's words to the German and Italian delegations could not have been more deluded and unwittingly ironic:

> The two great nations, reborn and strengthened by the genius and will of the *Führer* and of the *Duce*, have placed themselves at the vanguard of the history of Europe to preserve the foundations of their age-old civilization and to assure the principles of order and justice . . . two nations with their 150 million workers, citizens and soldiers will march together in the future, anxious to preserve the peace, which remains their highest objective.[55]

The Pact of Steel deeply satisfied *Der Führer*. Ciano noted that: 'I found Hitler very well, quite serene, less aggressive. His eyes are more deeply wrinkled. He sleeps very little. And he spends a great part of the night surrounded by colleagues and friends . . . It is always Hitler who talks! He can be *Führer* as much as he likes, but he always repeats himself and bores his guests.'[56] As for attitudes toward the alliance,

Ciano observed that 'the Pact is better liked in Germany than Italy. Here we are convinced of its usefulness and hence accept it as a matter of course. The Germans . . . put into it a warmth of feelings which we lack. We must recognize that hatred for France has not yet been successful in rousing love for Germany.'[57]

The Pact of Steel was literally and figuratively a death pact. Signatories had to devote all their military forces to the ally if it 'becomes involved militarily with another Power or other Powers'. That open-ended and absolute commitment would ruin both Germany and Italy as each joined the other in disastrous wars.

In Spain, the Nationalists steadily captured more territory from the Republicans in a twosteps forward, one back pattern from their revolt in July 1936 until finally they overran the entire country in 1939, capturing Barcelona on 22 February, Madrid on 28 March and the last Republican strongholds on 31 March 1939. That victory came at an enormous human cost. The civil war devastated Spain with perhaps as many as 450,000 people killed by combat, execution, disease and starvation, hundreds of thousands of homeless and half a million refugees in other countries, mostly France.[58]

Word of Franco's triumph inspired jubilation in Rome and Berlin. Ciano reported that: 'Madrid has fallen and with the capital all the other cities of Red Spain. The war is over. It is a new formidable victory for Fascism, perhaps the greatest one so far.'[59]

The Italian Voluntary Corps steamed for home on 31 May 1939. Over two and a half years, Mussolini sent over 70,000 troops to Spain, of whom 3,819 died and over 12,000 were wounded, and 157 light tanks, 759 warplanes, 6,791 trucks and 3,426 machine guns were destroyed, captured or abandoned. The Germans committed far fewer troops to their Condor Legion, just 14,000, of whom around 300 were killed; financially, Spain cost Berlin 288.7 million reichsmarks. As in Ethiopia, Italy's loss of life in Spain was relatively light but the financial costs were exorbitant – 14 billion lire over three years and two-thirds of the military budget.[60] But with the elation of victory, few people knew about let alone protested that soaring addition to Italy's national debt.

At first Franco followed the Fascist playbook. He joined Spain with the Anti-Comintern Pact on 27 March and withdrew Spain from the League of Nations on 8 May 1939. He called himself *El Caudillo*, the equivalent of Hiter's *Der Führer* and Mussolini's *Il Duce*. He embraced the Fascist agenda of authoritarianism, nationalism and corporatism, but not militarism and imperialism. Instead, to the fury of Mussolini and Hitler whose aid was likely decisive in his winning power, he did not join his fellow Fascist leaders in the Second World War, but instead kept Spain neutral.[61]

Mussolini delivered on 2 February 1939, what he called his 'March to the Sea' speech. His message was that the Mediterranean basin was naturally Italy's sphere of influence but instead an array of other countries hemmed in Italy. Italy thus had the right to break free of those restraints and dominate the Mediterranean. He intended to transform the lands that imprisoned Italy into the Italian empire:

> The bars of this prison are Corsica, Tunisia, Malta, Cyprus; the sentinels are Gibraltar and Suez. Corsica is a pistol pointed at the heart of Italy. Tunisia at Sicily; while Malta and Cyprus constitute a threat to our entire position in the Central and Western Mediterranean. Greece, Turkey and Egypt are always ready to range themselves with Britain to complete absolutely the political and military encirclement of Italy . . . The goal of Italian policy . . . is . . . first . . . to break the bars of the prison . . . Having broken the bars, Italian policy cannot but have one watchword, to march to the Ocean.[62]

Mussolini convened the Grand Council to forge a consensus for the German alliance and pending Italian takeover of Albania on 20 March 1939. Ciano recorded that: 'The *Duce* talked about the necessity of adopting a policy of uncompromising loyalty to the Axis. He made a marvellous speech which was argumentative, logical, cold and heroic.'[63]

Italy had an acquisitive attitude and behaviour toward Albania, its eastern neighbour across the Adriatic Sea. The government occupied Albania and declared it a protectorate in 1917. The League of Nations pressured Italy to restore Albania's independence in 1920. Italy and Albania signed a defensive alliance in 1926. A secret 1937 treaty between Italy and Yugoslavia recognized Albania as an Italian sphere of influence.

King Zog I ruled Albania. His birth name was Ahmed Muktar Zogolli. He fought for Albania's independence in 1912 and 1913, fought with the Austro-Hungarian army against Serbia during the First World War, during which he rose to general, was Shkoder Province's governor from 1920 to 1921, interior minister from 1921 to 1922, prime minister from 1922 to 1924 and president from 1924 to 1928. On 1 September 1928, he declared himself King Zog I and Albania's field marshal.

Mussolini recognized Zog I and tried to solidify Italian-Albanian ties by finding an Italian duchess for him to marry. The new king insisted on having one of Victor Emmanuel's daughters. Victor Emmanuel shuddered at the thought of one of his daughters marrying a Muslim and a brigand. Mussolini aided Albania's development by having a highway constructed that linked the port of Durres (Durazzo) with the capital Tirana in 1938. Italian businesses invested in Albania and Italians settled there.

The idea of conquering Albania originated with Galeazzo Ciano. Mussolini enthusiastically embraced the idea. With Spain's civil war ended and Italian volunteers returning home, Mussolini mobilized 100,000 troops commanded by General Alfredo Guzzoni to invade Albania. Mussolini issued King Zog an ultimatum to accept an Italian protectorate or else on 24 March 1939.

Although Albania's army numbered only 15,000 ill-trained troops, Zog refused. Mussolini ordered Guzzoni to proceed. Ciano noted Mussolini's disposition on the eve of invading Albania: 'He is calm, frightfully calm and more than ever convinced that no one will want to interfere in our affair with Albania. However, he has decided to march and he will march even though all the world may be pitted against him.' Much of *Il Duce*'s tranquil confidence was undoubtedly due to his enjoying Hitler's backing for the aggression. Ciano informed Mussolini that 'Berlin looks upon action at Tirana with sympathy since any Italian victory represents a strengthening of the power of the Axis'.[64]

As Italy's military prepared to invade Albania, King Victor Emmanuel became increasingly alarmed and opposed, although he was too fearful to tell Mussolini that directly. He first tried to butter up *Il Duce*. On 24 March, he sent Duke Pietro Acquarone, who headed the King's Household, to Ciano with word that he intended to give Mussolini a royal reward for his services, likely by making him a noble. Mussolini adamantly opposed that gesture: 'Make me a prince? I would be the first to laugh at the idea; imagine people calling me Prince Mussolini! As for Chancellor of the Empire, all right, but what does it mean? . . . No, nothing doing. Tell Acquarone to thank the King for me and the only thing I want from him is continued cooperation.'[65]

A couple of days later, the king summoned Mussolini and expressed his differences with him on several key issues. Ciano recorded that:

> The *Duce* was very angry with the King this morning, when the King found an opportunity of telling him three distasteful things: (1) he was not in agreement with the policy on Albania since he did not see the point of risking such a venture . . . (2) that the offer made by Acquarone to give the *Duce* some honorary title on the tenth anniversary of Fascism was decided in order to 'forestall any repetition of by the Fascists of the humiliation inflicted upon the King when without his knowledge

> the *Duce* was given the title of Marshal of the Empire – a humiliation which the King still resents'; (3) that Conrad of Bavaria had told him that Mussolini is called 'the Gauleiter of Italy'.

The third point undoubtedly enraged and humiliated Mussolini since a *Gauleiter* was a governor hand-picked and appointed by Hitler. 'The *Duce* commented bitterly on the King's words. He said, "If Hitler had to deal with a nincompoop of a King he would never have been able to take Austria and Czechoslovakia".'[66]

The invasion proceeded. Flotillas disembarked a division each against light resistance at Albania's two major ports, Durazzo and Valora on 7 April. The Italian troops then spread out to occupy key cities across the country. A group of Albanian leaders proposed having Amedeo, the duke of Aosta, as their king. Victor Emmanuel demanded the throne for himself. The Albanians reluctantly agreed. Albania's parliament voted to depose Zog and transfer the crown to Victor Emmanuel on 12 April. Zog fled with his family to exile in Greece.

Albania's official transfer to Italy occurred in Rome on 16 April 1939. Ciano observed:

> The ceremony of offering the Albanian crown to the King of Italy takes place at the Royal Palace. The Albanians, who seem to be lost in the great halls of the Quirinal, have a depressed air . . . The King answers in an uncertain and trembling voice; he is certainly not an orator who makes any impression on an audience and these Albanians, who are a warrior mountain people, look with amazement and timidity on the little man who is seated on a great gilt chair beside which stands a huge statue of Mussolini. They cannot understand what all this is about.[67]

Victor Emmanuel presented a constitution to Albania's delegation on 3 June 1939. Typically, he was petulant at a triumphant moment. In an aside to Ciano, he

> asks who drafted the document and observes in a sarcastic tone that there is no heraldic symbol of the dynasty on the Albanian flag . . . I report this to the *Duce*, who seizes the occasion to deliver an attack on the monarchy . . . The *Duce* declares that he is sick and tired of dragging behind him 'empty baggage cars, which, moreover, very often have their brakes on', that the King 'is a small man, grumpy and untrustworthy, who at this time is concerned with embroidery on the flag and does not feel any pride in seeing the national territory increased by 30,000 square kilometres' and that, in conclusion, 'it is the monarchy which, by its idiotic chatter, prevents the army from becoming Fascist'.[68]

Ciano expressed the quiet official astonishment at how easy Italy's peaceful conquest of Albania had been: 'The operation of emasculating Albania without making the patient scream – the annexation – is now practically completed.'[69] He boasted that: 'There is no question that the mass of people is now won over by Italy. The Albanian people are grateful to us for having taught them to eat twice a day, for this rarely happened before. Even in the physical appearance of the people greater well-being can be noted.'[70]

The truth of Ciano's statement is open to question. What is unquestionable is that, like most colonies, Albania cost the conqueror far more than it was worth. Rome invested in improving or creating roads, railways, ports, schools, hospitals and electricity, water and sewage systems, yet reaped relatively few revenues from Albania to pay for all that. As in other colonies, Italian carpetbaggers made fortunes by corrupting officials for privileges. One justification for the takeover was to exploit Albania's petroleum reserves. Alas, after the first wells were drilled, geologists pronounced the oil too sulphurous to refine. Even worse, Mussolini chose to make Albania the military staging area for what he insisted would be neighbouring Greece's easy conquest. Instead, the Greeks inflicted on Italy a humiliating, devastating defeat until Hitler sent the Wehrmacht to the rescue.

Jews had lived in Italy for over two millennia yet were a sliver of the nation's 44,000,000 population, just 45,410 citizens on 1 January 1932 or about one per cent. The Fascist Party counted 4,819 Jews among its members in 1933.[71]

Mussolini was not an anti-Semite for most of his life.[72] Indeed, he respected Jews for their enterprise, creativity and education and wished other Italians could emulate them. He certainly understood that Jews created wealth many times greater than their numbers compared to non-Jews. He had no desire to kill those geese that laid so many golden eggs for Italy. He counted many Jews among his enthusiastic followers and valued Aldo Fini and Guido Jung among his inner governing circle. Probably his most beloved mistress was Margherita Sarfatti, an intellectual, journalist, art critic and Jew, who enhanced his appreciation for painting, literature and music. For Mussolini, anti-Semitism largely resulted from the attitudes and behaviour of a minority that discredited the majority by provoking non-Jews against them.

Robert Farinacci explained the Fascist attitude toward Jews in an editorial for the newspaper *Il Regime Fascista* on 12 September 1936:

> We must admit that in Italy, the Jews, who are a very small minority, while they have intrigued in a thousand ways to capture positions in finance, business and . . . schools, have not opposed our revolution. We must admit that they have always paid their dues and done their duty even in war. But, unfortunately, theirs is a passive attitude which arouses some suspicion because they have never said a convincing word to persuade the Italian people that they do their duty out of conviction rather than fear or cowardice. There is no tangible evidence that they intend to separate themselves from all the Jews of the world whose only aim is to assure the triumph of international Jewry . . . They will have to prove conclusively that they are Fascists first and Jews second.[73]

At Farinacci's urging, Mussolini expressed his own views on Jews in an unsigned editorial for *Il Populo d'Italia* on 31 December 1936: '[A]nti-Semitism is inevitable wherever Semitism becomes too obstructive, too aggressive and therefore too powerful. Too much Jewishness generates anti-Jewishness . . . The forerunner and justifier of anti-Semitism is always and everywhere the same: the Jew who exaggerates, as he so often does.'[74] Ciano revealed Mussolini's nuanced policy toward Jews in a 1938 diary entry: 'We have also spoken with the *Duce* about the Jewish problem. I expressed myself in favour of a solution that will not create a problem that fortunately does not exist among us. The *Duce* is of the same opinion. He will pour on the fire but he will be careful not to smother it.'[75] In other words, Mussolini wanted to wield mild anti-Semitism to divert public scrutiny and blame for his own regime's failures and setbacks without actually robbing, imprisoning or murdering Jews like Hitler's regime.

Mussolini at once scolded and reassured Italy's Jews that they need not fear the future with this declaration on 16 February 1937:

> The Jews are flooding me with insulting anonymous letters, accusing me of having promised Hitler to persecute them. False. The Germans have never mentioned this subject to us. Nor do I believe that we ought to unleash an anti-Semitic campaign in Italy. The problem for us does not exist. There are not many Jews and, with some exceptions, there is no harm in them . . . And perhaps in small doses Jews are necessary to society, just as yeast is to bread.[76]

Mussolini eventually succumbed to pressure from Berlin and extreme Italian Fascists to adopt Nazi measures against Jews. He emulated Hitler on 14 July 1938, when his regime published a ten-point 'Manifesto of Racial Scientists'. The three key points were: The population of Italy is of Aryan origin, . . . There now exists a pure Italian race . . . The

Jews do not belong to the Italian race.'[77] In September 1938, he decreed that Jews could not marry non-Jews; be employed in the military, bureaucracy, education, banking, law, journalism and insurance; not join any Fascist Party institution; not own or manage businesses with more than a hundred employees; and not own more than 50 hectares of land. Jewish students were segregated in separate schools and could not attend universities. Foreign Jews who had settled in Italy after 1 January 1919 were expelled. The regime's worsening anti-Semitic polices forced around 6,000 Jews to flee and 4,000 to convert to Christianity. By October 1941, 39,444 Italian Jews and 3,474 foreign Jews remained in Italy.[78]

Hitler informed Mussolini that he intended to conquer Poland and needed Italy's military support as required by the Pact of Steel. That appeal stunned Mussolini. He had committed himself to the Pact of Steel because he believed it would at once strengthen both countries, cow rival great powers like Britain, France and the Soviet Union, and force small countries to yield to any Axis demands. Now, the reality of that commitment struck Mussolini. He told Hitler that his military advisors warned him that Italy was unready for war with a great power or powers and would remain so at least until 1942. That in turn stunned Hitler, who urged Mussolini to accelerate his military buildup so that Italy could join Germany in glorious wars that vanquished their enemies. Mussolini promised Hitler that he would do what he could.

When Mussolini expressed to Ciano his despair at being called to fulfil the Pact of Steel, his Foreign Minister urged him to: 'Tear up the Pact. Throw it in Hitler's face and Europe will recognize in you the natural leader of the anti-German crusade. Do you want me to go to Salzburg? Very well, I shall go and shall speak to the Germans as they should be spoken to.'[79]

Mussolini had Ciano join Hitler and Foreign Minister Joachim von Ribbentrop at Salzburg from 11 to 13 August. His mission was 'to inform the Germans that we must avoid a conflict with Poland since it would be impossible to localize it and a general war would be disastrous for everyone. Never has the *Duce* spoken of the need for peace so unreservedly and with so much warmth.' During three days of talks, Ciano failed to convince Hitler to delay his conquest of Poland. He became 'aware of how little we are worth in the opinion of the Germans'. Nonetheless, he found

> Hitler very cordial, but . . . impassive and implacable in his decision. He speaks in the large drawing-room of his house, standing in front

> of a table on which some maps are spread out. He exhibits a truly profound military knowledge. He speaks with a great deal of calm . . . I realize . . . that there is no longer anything that can be done. He has decided to strike and he will . . . He utters words of praise for the *Duce*, but he listens with a far away and impersonal interest to what I tell him about the bad effects a war would have on the Italian people.[80]

That conference stripped Ciano of any lingering admiration he held for Hitler and his Third Reich: 'I return to Rome completely disgusted with the Germans, with their leader, with their way of doing things. They have betrayed us and lied to us. Now they are dragging us into an adventure which we do not want and which may compromise the regime and the country as a whole.' Ciano's report evoked mixed feelings in Mussolini: 'The *Duce*'s reactions are varied. At first he agrees with me. Then he says that honour compels him to march with Germany. Finally, he states that he wants his part of the booty in Croatia and Dalmatia.' The next morning Ciano found 'Mussolini worried. I do not hesitate to arouse in him every possible anti-German feeling by every means in my power. I speak to him of his diminished prestige and of his playing the none-too-brilliant role of second fiddle.'[81] Ciano finally convinced Mussolini the third day after his return:

> The *Duce*, who at first had refused to act independently of the Germans . . . is convinced that we must not march blindly with the Germans. However, he makes one reservation: he wants time to prepare the break with Germany . . . He is of the opinion that it may still be possible, though perhaps difficult, for the democracies to give in, in which case it would not be profitable for us to break with the Germans, since we, too, must have our part of the booty.[82]

To his dismay, Ciano found that Mussolini had changed his mind again by 20 August: 'The *Duce* in my absence, made an about-face. He wants to support Germany at any cost.' He instructed Ciano to tell Berlin that he was firmly committed but before going to war the Italian military needed a long list of economic and military resources including 18,153,000 tons of mostly coal along with oil, iron ore, nickel, tungsten, molybdenum and other minerals, 17,000 vehicles and 150 anti-aircraft batteries that only Germany could supply. Ribbentrop replied that they could immediately send a small stock of iron, coal and timber and several anti-aircraft batteries.[83]

Hitler thereafter was generous to his junior partner. Mussolini recalled that 'Germany's effective contribution of the raw materials in

1940, 1941, 1942 and the first six months of 1943 . . . was imposing: coal, 40,000,000 tons; metals, 2,250,000 tons; synthetic rubber, 22,000 tons; aviation spirit, 220,000 tons; petrol, 421,000 tons. It is unnecessary to quote the minor contributions of vital metals such as nickel.'[84] Just as vitally, Hitler dispatched Wehrmacht forces to rescue Mussolini from the disasters his army suffered in France, Greece and North Africa.

Ciano observed the demoralizing impact on Mussolini of confronting the unbridgeable gap between his imperial ambitions and his actual power: 'The *Duce* was really out of his wits. His military instinct and his sense of honour was leading him to war. Reason has now stopped him. But this hurts him very much. In the military field he was badly served by his advisors who . . . have fostered dangerous illusions in him.'[85]

Hitler and Stalin committed a diplomatic revolution when they shelved their respective ideologies that made them mortal enemies to ally with each other. On 24 August, German Foreign Minister Ribbentrop and Soviet Foreign Minister Vyacheslav Molotov signed the Treaty of Non-Aggression with secret clauses to split Poland and the Baltic States between them, with Germany taking two-thirds of western Poland and Lithuania, while the Soviet Union took Poland's eastern third, Latvia and Estonia; later Hitler ceded Lithuania to Stalin.

Led by seven panzer divisions, German armies numbering two million troops and sixty-six divisions invaded Poland from Germany westward, Czechoslovakia south and German East Prussia north-east on 1 September and swiftly demolished Poland's million-man army split among thirty-nine divisions.[86] London and Paris declared war against Germany on 3 September, but France's million-man army and Britain's growing army in northern France did not attack the thinly spread Wehrmacht forces in western Germany. The Soviet Red Army invaded eastern Poland on 17 September. The Germans captured Warsaw, Poland's capital, on 27 September and destroyed the last stronghold on 6 October. The Wehrmacht had conquered Poland and inflicted 875,000 casualties, with nine out of ten being prisoners, while suffering 59,000 casualties. The Soviets paid just 5,000 casualties to seize their designated territory.

The dazzling victory of Hitler's Wehrmacht at once thrilled and depressed Mussolini. He dreamed of Italy's military soon performing similar feats, but only after several years of a steady buildup of forces, weapons and supplies. He felt trapped by his Pact of Steel duty to join Germany in war against Britain and France, exacerbated by the expectations of the Italian people:

> The Italians . . . after having heard my warlike propaganda for eighteen years cannot not understand how I can become the herald of peace, now that Europe is in flames. There is no explanation except the military unpreparedness of the country, but even for this I am made responsible – me, mind you, who have always proclaimed the importance of our military forces.[87]

He informed the king that he was going to invoke the Pact of Steel and ally openly with Germany against France and Britain. That potentially disastrous act alarmed Victor Emmanuel III so much that he made one of the few decisive acts of his long reign. He told Mussolini that he opposed Italy joining Germany. *Il Duce*'s military advisors repeated their chorus that Italy needed several more years before it would be ready for war. That forced Mussolini to announce Italy's 'non-belligerence'.

Hitler kept up his pressure on Mussolini to join the war. Ciano met *Der Führer* at Salzburg on 1 October and found him 'absolutely sure of himself . . . Hitler spoke for almost two hours and cited figure after figure without referring to a single note . . . What most impressed me was his confidence in ultimate victory. Either he is bewitched or he really is a genius.'[88]

One chronic issue darkened the relationship: Italy's mostly German-speaking region of Alto Adige with 300,000 inhabitants remained contentious between Rome and Berlin. Mussolini feared that Hitler would demand that the region join Germany. Hitler worried that Mussolini would expel the German-speakers. On 21 October 1939, they agreed that the German-speakers would be given a choice of becoming Italianized or moving to Germany. Eventually 185,000 reluctantly agreed to abandon their homes and move to Germany while 82,000 wanted to stay. Only 130,000 South Tyrolians actually emigrated.

The seven months that followed Poland's conquest was dubbed the 'Phoney War' because neither the Germans nor the French and British budged from its territory to attack the other. During the 1930s, the French had constructed along the German frontier an elaborate system of mostly underground defences devised by War Minister André Maginot. Most of the French army hunkered down within or behind the vaunted 'impregnable' Maginot Line.

During that time, Stalin launched a horrifically real war. After imposing ruthless communist dictatorships over Estonia, Latvia, Lithuania and eastern Poland, Stalin turned his guns toward Finland. On 30 November, the Red Army invaded its neighbour but the Finnish army blunted those attacks over the next four months despite being outnumbered ten to one. Eventually, Stalin massed enough troops and supplies to defeat the Finnish army. On 12 March, the Finnish government agreed to a treaty whereby the Soviet Union took two regions, Karelia in the south-east and Salla on the central eastern border.

The United States was the wild card of international diplomacy during the interwar era. Most Americans had enthusiastically embraced President Woodrow Wilson's submission of a declaration of war to Congress and the subsequent overwhelming votes of the Senate and House of Representatives for it in April 1917. The subsequent number of dead and mutilated Americans along with soaring prices and national debt turned ever more Americans against the war and for isolation from geopolitics. After the war, the Senate rejected ratification of the Versailles Treaty that Wilson submitted because of the clauses that would create a League of Nations committed to collective global security. Yet, during the 1920s, the United States played a constructive role in international relations by sponsoring the Washington Conference that resulted in one naval arms control and two non-aggression treaties in February 1922 and the 1924 Dawes Plan and the 1929 Young Plan that resolved pending global financial crises when Berlin halted its reparations payments by lending Germany money, reducing the reparations amount and interest rate and stretching out payments. Then America's economy plunged into depression with the unregulated New York Stock Market's collapse in October 1929 and Congress globalized the Great Depression with the Smoot-Hawley Act that raised import tariffs 50 per cent; world trade collapsed when other countries raised their own tariffs.

Franklin Roosevelt's victory in the 1932 election and his inauguration as president in March 1933 led to the New Deal policies that revived America's economy and international trade. Congress, however, imposed 'Neutrality Laws' in 1936, 1936, 1937 and 1939 that limited the president's ability to aid victims of international aggression. Roosevelt wished he had the power to join the British and French in trying to deter Japanese, German and Italian aggression but those isolationist laws and Congress reflected and shaping prevailing public opinion. He did what he could to encourage Britain and France to stand strong and discourage Japan, Germany and Italy from more aggression.[89]

Roosevelt sent Undersecretary of State Sumner Welles to Rome on 26 February 1940, with the mission to convince Mussolini to stay neutral. Ciano recalled that: 'Unfortunately, the conference with the

Duce . . . took place in a rather icy atmosphere. Mussolini stresses the note of aloofness that he is now showing openly in his relations with the Anglo-Saxons. Sumner Welles left the Mappamondo room more depressed than when he entered it.'[90] Welles found Mussolini's appearance shocking: 'He seemed fifteen years older than his actual age of fifty-six. He was ponderous and static rather than vital. He moved with an elephantine motion; every step appeared an effort. He was heavy for his height and his face in repose fell in rolls of flesh. His close-cropped hair was snow white.'[91] *Il Duce* later commented sarcastically on the interview: 'Between us and the Americans any kind of understanding is impossible because they judge problems on the surface while we go deeply into them.'[92]

Mussolini and Hitler literally summited at the 6,600ft high Brenner Pass between Italy and Austria on 18 March 1940. Ciano vividly described the scene;

> It is snowing at the Brenner Pass. Mussolini is waiting for his guest with anxious elation. Recently he has felt more and more the fascination of the *Führer*. His military successes – the only successes that Mussolini really values and desires – are the cause of this . . . The Hitler meeting is very cordial on both sides. The conference . . . is more a monologue than anything else. Hitler talks all the time, but is less agitated than usual. He makes few gestures and speaks in a quiet tone. He looks physically fit. Mussolini listens to him with interest and with deference. He speaks little and confirms his intention to move with Germany. He reserves to himself only the right moment.

Silently, Mussolini 'resented the fact that Hitler did all the talking; he had in mind to tell him many things and instead had to keep quiet most of the time, a thing which, as dictator . . . he's not in the habit of doing.'[93]

After initial reluctance, Mussolini sooner or later succumbed to backing Hitler's plans. In September 1939, he had refused to join Hitler in war against France and Britain, arguing that Italy would not be ready for war until 1942. He resisted Hitler's pressure for Italy to join Germany in attacking France in May 1940. But as the Wehrmacht's blitzkrieg demolished the French army and their allied British, Belgian and Dutch armies, Mussolini once again flipflopped, with catastrophic results.

Chapter 7

THE MILITARY AND ECONOMIC POWER

> Five generals are prisoners and one is dead. This is the ratio of Italians who have military qualities and those who have none.
>
> (Benito Mussolini)

Italy was economically and militarily unready for war in 1940, embarrassingly deficient in both 'hard' physical and 'soft' psychological power.[1] As for total national power, Italy was trapped in a vicious cycle that included dismal military commanders, officers and soldiers; an economy with relatively low levels of production, productivity, innovation, invention, quality control and entrepreneurship that failed to provide the military with first-rate weapons or adequate supplies; and a culture that tolerated and even encouraged high degrees of corruption, incompetence, favouritism, inefficiency and lassitude.

Astonishingly, after 18 years in power, Mussolini did not organize a High Command until 29 May 1940.[2] For that, he tapped Generals Pietro Badoglio, the chief of staff, Rodolfo Graziani and Franciso Pricolo and Admiral Domenico Cavagnari. The High Command presided over the four separate military organizations, Army, Navy, Air Force and Voluntary Militia for National Security, and was organized in three departments, the First confusedly included operations, training, press and propaganda, the Second supply; and the Third personnel and headquarters.

7.1 Italian Chiefs of Staff, May 1925 to May 1945

Pietro Badoglio	4 May 1925	4 December 1940
Ugo Cavallero	4 December 1940	1 February 1943
Vittorio Ambrosia	1 February 1943	18 November 1943
Giovanni Messe	18 November 1943	1 May 1945

One chronic problem that Mussolini finally resolved as Italy went to war was who should be the military's commander-in-chief. The constitution clearly designated the king in that role, and Victor Emmanuel III had zealously insisted on retaining that title. On 10 June 1940, they cut a deal whereby the king retained the title while Mussolini actually commanded. The trouble was, in stark contrast to President Franklin Roosevelt, Mussolini was incapable of forging a dynamic team among the High Command's leaders that carefully analysed military and economic reports, debated rationally what strategies best advanced their nation's interests, then ensured that appropriate, competent subordinates implemented them. Instead, Mussolini's High Command was never more than a mélange of rival mediocrities who endlessly bickered and undercut each other as Italy's army and navy suffered one disastrous defeat after another.

Italy's High Command learned no lessons from the First World War and subsequent interwar military developments. The sole visionaries were Generals Giulio Douhet and Amedeo Mecozzi, but their colleagues treated them as Casandras. Douhet initiated and Mecozzi continued to advocate the development of land and sea-based warplanes as decisive military weapons for future wars.[3]

Italy failed to produce a single first-rate general or admiral during the war. Indeed, the army field commanders Pietro Badoglio, Italo Balbo Rodolfo Graziani, Ubaldo Soddu, Italo Gariboldi, Mario Roatta, Alberto Pariani, Giuseppe Valle, Alfredo Guzzoni and Vittorio Ambrosio displayed varying ineptness. Perhaps only two generals rose above mediocrity, Ettore Bastico for his campaigns in Spain and Giovanni Messe for his campaigns in the Balkans and North Africa.

The Italian army was top-heavy with officers. In 1940, the army's 56,500 officers outnumbered its 41,200 non-commissioned officers. Italian and German corps had respectively 150 and 66 staff officers.[4] Seniority, rather than merit, determined who received glacial promotions. Italian culture values congeniality and conformity above competence, initiative and innovation. A German staff officer who worked with the Italian army on the Russian front observed that:

> The command apparatus is . . . pedantic and slow. The absence of sufficient communications equipment render the links in the subordinate units precarious. The consequence is that the leadership is poorly informed about the friendly situation and has no capacity to redeploy quickly. The working style of the staff is schematic, static and in some cases lacking in precision.

General Carlo Geloso ruefully observed in Albania of his officers that: 'Some did not show sufficient strength of character, physical robustness, professional competence and initiative together with love of responsibility. Too many have presumably arrived at high rank by virtue of enduring decades of administrative drudgery and without having well understood the meaning of the leadership of men and the active employment of units on the battlefield.'[5]

A key dimension of power is intelligence or getting, understanding and applying information essential to overcoming challenges. The Military Information Service (*Servizio Informazioni Militare*, SIM) was Italy's most important intelligence agency and probably the most successful institution in its national security system. Field agents were adept at intelligence gatherings' 'three Bs', 'Bribery, Blackmail and Burglary'. For instance, one night in 1935, a team got inside the British embassy, cracked the safe, photographed its contents including code books, and got away undetected. Mathematical geniuses deciphered the naval code enabling them to read messages between the Admiralty and the fleets. A team stole the transcripts of a telephone conversation between Foreign Secretary Anthony Eden and Greek King Constantine II in 1937.[6] One Italian hard-power strategy was the pre-war secret bribing of pending enemy generals and politicians to discourage their resistance. SIM agents distributed millions of lire in Ethiopia, Albania and Greece to greedy, cynical military and civilian leaders.[7] How much those bribes and the secrets and inactivity they bought affected the subsequent outcomes of the military campaigns is impossible to determine, and bribery could not be effectively wielded against Britain and soon the Soviet Union and United States.

SIM got most information from open sources, especially newspapers. Mussolini read the twice daily SIM summaries of each great power's newspapers. Like any intelligence agency, SIM at times provided inaccurate reports with disastrous results, with the worst underestimating the power of the Greek army and the British army defending Egypt. Mussolini's decisions to invade Greece and Egypt resulted in humiliating routs.[8]

A vast gap existed between the Italian army's paper and actual strength. In 1940, Mussolini's regime claimed the army had seventy-three divisions; in reality; only thirty-seven divisions or half the propaganda number existed with 1,634,950 troops of all ranks split among them or other headquarters, logistical and training units. The existing divisions themselves were two-thirds smaller.[9] Army Chief of Staff Alberto Pariani transformed three-regiment divisions into two-regiment divisions from 1938 to 1940. He did so not just to make the Italian army appear to have a third more divisions but more importantly from the belief that a two-regiment division would tactically be more flexible than a three-regiment one. That failed to happen because Italian tactics remained mostly rigid mass frontal assaults. Likewise, Italy's air force was a paper tiger. The Air Force claimed to have 8,530 warplanes in 1940; the dismal reality was that only 454 bombers and 129 fighters were operational and they were inferior to British bombers and fighters.[10]

Another critical deficiency was that Italy spent much less on the military and even when Mussolini tried to spend more, failed to keep pace with the other Great Powers. Italian military spending did rise from 8.13 billion lira in 1924–6 to 43 billion lira in 1938 to 1940, yet that was 79.5 per cent and 97 per cent of the respective military spending of Britain and France. Italian military spending as a share of the economy was only 8 per cent in 1939 then rose to peak at 23 per cent in 1941 before dipping slightly to 21 per cent in 1943. Four other Great Powers mobilized a far greater proportion of their economies for war in 1939 and 1943, Germany 23 per cent and 70 per cent, Japan 22 per cent and 43 per cent, Britain 15 per cent and 55 per cent and the Soviet Union 17 per cent in 1940 and 61 per cent in 1943. Although the United States devoted only 1 per cent of its economy on the military in 1939 that rose to 42 per cent in 1943.[11]

7.2 Italy's Economy and Military Spending, 1938–1943[12]

	Military Spending Share of Economy	State Spending Share of Economy	Economy Index Compared to 1938	Military Spending as Share in Lira
1938	31.1	20.8	100.0	10.0
1939	32.8	19.4	107.0	8.0
1940	45.4	22.8	100.4	12.0
1941	64.2	35.6	102.5	23.0
1942	56.4	37.8	103.0	22.0
1943	57.2	41.0	97.5	21.0

7.3 Comparison of Military Spending as Share of Economy, 1939–1944[13]

	1939	1940	1941	1942	1943	1944
Italy	8	12	23	22	21	n.a.
Germany	23	40	52	64	70	n.a.
Japan	22	22	27	33	43	76
Britain	15	44	53	52	55	53
USSR	n.a.	17	28	61	61	53
America	1	2	11	31	42	42

Ironically, the Allied capture of Italy's colonies and devastation of the air force let the High Command shift more money to the army. In 1933, the army took 33 per cent of the defence budget while the navy took 14.8 per cent, the air force 19.1 per cent and the mixed military forces in the colonies 23.1 per cent. In 1943, the army took 60.6 per cent, the navy 15.6 per cent, the air force 11.9 per cent and the colonies 1.8 per cent.

The High Command poorly armed, equipped, clothed, trained, motivated, fed, housed and healed its manpower. Italian military expert Brian Sullivan found one key reason for these deficiencies: 'Italian enlisted-officer relations were stunted by the kind of distance and formality that characterized the British army in the nineteenth century.' In other words, officers cared little for their troops' well-being.[14] Wretched conditions and worsening defeats caused ever more young Italian men to dodge the draft with 85,000 in 1930–40 soaring to 168,000 in 1942–3. For those who did appear at draft boards, one in four were physically unfit and half were shorter than five foot five inches.[15]

Junior officer training was deficient. Sullivan describes officers as 'well educated' but 'suffered from insufficient combat training. All spent two years in a military academy, then one more year in a school of application, if they were in the infantry or cavalry or two years if they were in the artillery or engineers. But the Italian army was notably deficient in regular officers.' Retention was a huge problem: 'In 1940, only a small minority of reserve officers had fought in Ethiopia or Spain. The majority had no combat experience, even in the First World War.'[16]

Sullivan characterized Italian infantry training as mostly

> close-order drill, calisthenics and rigorous marching with full pack. Life-fire practice was minimal since the army could not afford the expenditure of much ammunition. The limited combat training the men

> actually received was directed by ill-educated junior reserve officers with little understanding of effective techniques and even less of current tactical doctrine. Combined arms exercises for the infantry were virtually unknown, but those few that occurred were confined to infantry-artillery co-operation. Most infantry went into combat in 1940–1 without ever having seen a tank, let alone trained with one.[17]

Tough, adaptive, brave non-commissioned officers (NCOs) are any good army's backbone. Here too the Italian army suffered severe weaknesses. Sullivan explained that:

> Shortages of NCOs and the inexperience of the inadequate numbers the army actually possessed also retarded both enlisted and NCO training. Junior NCOs were chosen from each year's intake of conscripts and were rapidly and superficially instructed. They served a year or so, then were released from active duty with their fellow conscripts. Few chose to make the army a career because of low pay, poor benefits and lack of government-guaranteed employment after retirement . . . The contrast with the American army . . . was striking. In June 1940, the ratio of NCOs to privates was 1:33. In the U.S. army the ratio was 1:2.[18]

The standard firearm was the Mannlicher-Carcano model 1891 6mm bolt-action rifle, excellent for the late nineteenth century but obsolete by the 1930s. The 1938 version was 7.55mm but still bolt-action, outgunned by semi-automatic rifles like America's superb M-1 Garand. The Breda 6.5mm machine gun had a low fire rate with twenty-bullet clips to replace. The FIAT 8mm heavy machine gun soon overheated and jammed and also had low fire rates. Grenades and 81mm heavy mortar shells were unreliable with high ratios of duds, small explosions and chunky fragmentation.

To varying degrees every Italian tank was poorly designed and made, with weak engines prone to breakdowns, weak firepower, limited range and thin armour.[19] Perhaps the best thing about Italian tanks were their designations that noted the tonnage and year they were introduced. So the L3/1935 Light Tank was three tons and rolled out in 1935. The worst failure was to produce a medium tank with a 75mm gun and rugged and versatile enough to square off with Soviet T-34 and American Sherman tanks. Of 4,152 armoured vehicles produced from 1940 to 1943, only 535 mounted 75mm or larger guns. Just machine gun bullets could riddle the L3/1935 Light Tank's thin steel shell. The M11/1939 Medium Tank's 37mm gun was mounted in the hull, not a revolving turret. Tanks lacked radios until

1941 and never received long-distance radios that operated when the tank moved. Astonishingly one person at Ansaldo designed all those wretched tanks from 1933 to 1943.[20]

As for artillery, Italy's models were mostly those used in the First World War, while since then its allies and enemies had developed more sophisticated models. Of 7,970 Italian army guns in 1940, only 246 were produced after 1930. Britain's standard field gun and howitzer outshot Italy's 105.18 field cannon and 100.17 howitzer by 8,700m and 3,000m respectively.[21] Ansaldo produced first-rate guns but in miniscule numbers including 114 75mm field guns, 76 74mm anti-aircraft guns, 40 149mm heavy guns and 24 210mm howitzers. Instead, the Italian army depended on around 10,000 First World War-vintage artillery pieces, many Austrian captures. British guns shot heavier shells much further than their nearest Italian equivalents:

> [T]he British 25-pounder gun/howitzer could send its high explosive shell 13,400 yards, the Italian 100/17 howitzer could send its 29 pound shell a maximum of 10,000 yards. The British 4.5 inch gun could fire its 55 pound projectile to a range of 20,500 yards; the Italian 105/28 could shoot its 35 pound shell a maximum of 14,800 yards; the Italian 149/13 howitzer could fire its 94 pound high explosive round only 9,600 yards.[22]

In contrast, two relatively deadly Italian weapons were the 20mm dual-purpose anti-tank and anti-aircraft gun and the 47mm anti-tank gun.

Italian warplanes were just as awful, easily downed by mechanical failures or enemy fire. They included the trimotor Savoia-Marchetti SM.79 and bimotor SM.84 medium bombers and four-engine Piaggio P108 heavy bomber. Air Marshal General Francesco Pricolo actually rejected a good fighter plane, the Reggiane Re.2000, because it required high-octane fuel that Italy could not adequately produce. Italy's medium and heavy bombers lacked good bombsights, stabilizing gyroscopes and crew intercoms. As for bombs, poor-quality fuses and casings caused countless duds and sometimes premature explosions in the bomber. None of its warplanes had night-fighting, instrument flying or blind flying capacities. Those deployed in North Africa did not receive engine filters until 1941, with hundreds downed or grounded from sand before then. Unlike its allies and enemies, Italy's military lacked an air defence system with coordinated radar, anti-aircraft guns and fighter planes. Pilots in fighter squadrons actually communicated with hand signals.

FIAT and Ansaldo jointly manufactured tanks, other armoured vehicles and warplanes. Their tanks included the two-man L3/1935 light tanks with twin 8mm machine guns, the M11/1939 medium tank with a hull mounted 37mm gun and the M13/1940, M14/1941 and M15/1942 medium tanks with revolving turrets with 47mm guns, each mechanically little better than those before it. There were a dozen or so other tanks, assault guns and armoured cars but produced in limited numbers. Of 1,500 tanks the Italian army deployed in 1940, 1,300 were L3/35 Lights.[23]

Fiat-Ansaldo's warplanes included the CR.42 biplane, the open-cockpit G.30, the Breda Ba.65, the Ba.88 ground attack and the SM.85 dive-bomber, all of which may have endangered their crews more than the enemy. Astonishingly, Italy manufactured over 2,000 of the slow-flying biplanes even though enemy fighter pilots and anti-aircraft easily shot them down.[24] Alfa-Romeo was just as inept at designing and producing its war weapons including the Macchi MC.02 fighter plane with its underpowered engine. Eventually, Italy improved its warplanes from third-rate to second-rate with the MC.205, Re.2005 and FIAT G55 fighters. The three-engine Savoia-Marchetti SM.79 was a good medium bomber.

The Italian army was locked in a vicious cycle of bad leadership, training, equipment, weapons, tactics, supplies and morale. Virtually all the infantry and armoured divisions were second or third rate. Only the *Bersaglieri* and airborne divisions were first rate, animated by volunteers intensely trained in technical skills and the 'Lightning' (*Folgore*) spirit. The Ariete armoured division was also considered a first-rate unit.

As for tactics, Sullivan found that:

> Pre-war infantry combat doctrine and training emphasized fire at the expense of manoeuvre, as well as subordination to the original plan instead of initiative. Offensive tactics stressed attack along a single pre-selected axis of advance, backed by heavy crew-served weapons and artillery. If a unit faltered, it would be replaced by another unit, rather than ordered to attack in a different direction. This doctrine ignored the possibility of infiltration tactics and virtually assured plodding advances accompanied by heavy casualties. The result was brittle defences prone to collapse when ammunition ran low. This proved especially true because the Italian army lacked sufficient artillery and motor transport.[25] General Ettore Bastico exemplified that anachronistic Italian army mindset: 'The tank is a powerful tool but let us not idolize it; let us reserve our reverence for the infantryman and the mule.'[26] That attitude was probably the most vital link in the vicious cycle of related reasons for the Italian army's disastrous record.

Mussolini at age 14.

Mussolini as a young man.

Mussolini speaking before a crowd.

Mussolini and family.

Mussolini after nose wounding by Violet Gibson.

Mussolini as Blackshirt speaker.

Mussolini in Libya, 1937.

Mussolini swimming.

Mussolini at his desk.

Mussolini with Neville Chamberlain.

Mussolini with Hitler.

Galeazzo Ciano and Edda Mussolini.

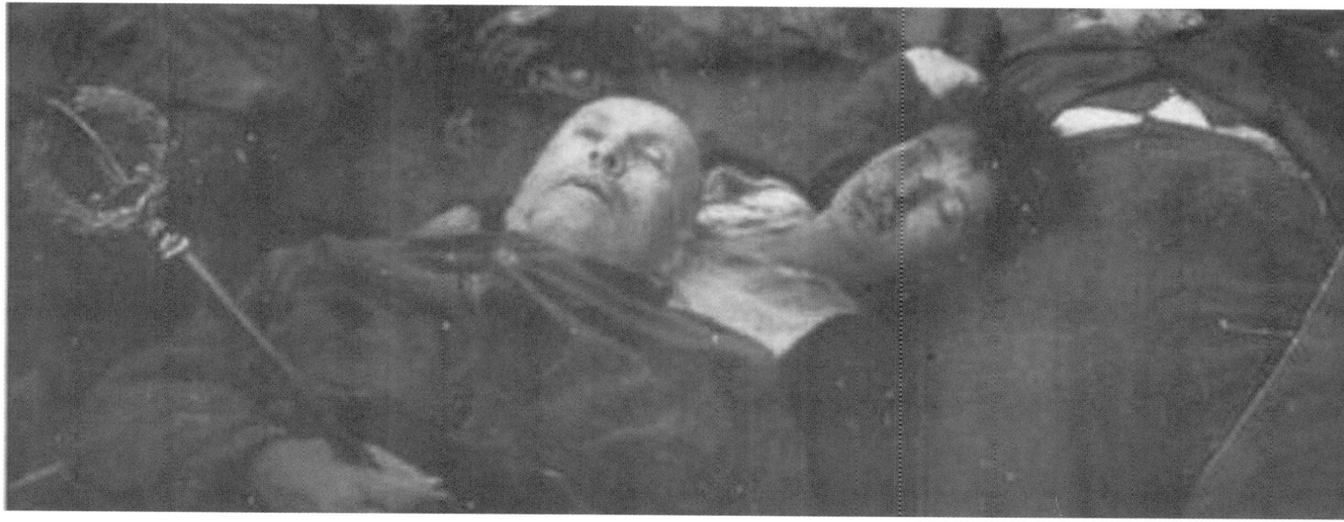

Mussolini and Carla Petacci's corpses, Milan, 29 April 1944.

The Mussolini crypt at Predappio.

Italian mass attack tactics were easily defeated by enemy manoeuvres and massed firepower. A British intelligence officer gave this description: 'The principle characteristic of Italian tactics in both theatres, Libya and East Africa, has been rigidity. They have remained attached to one principle, the concentration of the greatest possible mass for every task that faces them. In the attack they deploy this mass in line and rely solely on weight of numbers to clear the way.'[27]

Alone among the great powers, Italy's army was incapable of Blitzkrieg or Lightning War. The reason was simple. The army was only partly mechanized and so moved only as fast as most men trudged carrying heavy packs and weapons, at most ten miles a day in good weather and level terrain. Indeed, mules drew most supply wagons and field guns. Only four of the seventy combat divisions that Italy raised during the war were armoured – the 131st Ariete, 132nd Ariete, 133rd Littorio and 133rd Ariete.

The motor vehicle to soldier ratio was 1 to 21 in 1940 and 1 to 19 in 1942. In stark contrast, Rommel's Afrika Korps enjoyed a 1 to 3.6 ratio. Just as glaring were the differences between standard Italian and British divisions that fielded respectively 7,000 and 17,300 personnel, 142 and 1,999 trucks, 147 and 1,064 motorcycles, 72 and 136 anti-aircraft guns, 60 and 72 field guns, 146 and 819 automatic rifles and 72 and 444 anti-tank guns, while in addition the British fielded 162 light mortars, 256 tracked ammunition carriers, 197 trailers and six armoured cars that the Italians completely lacked. Italian and British armoured divisions respectively numbered 8,600 and 13,235 personnel, 189 and 280 tanks, 40 and 60 armoured cars, 504 and 956 motorcycles, 918 and 1,415 trucks and 205 and 374 other vehicles.[28]

By June 1940, Italy's army had plenty of veterans from campaigns in Ethiopia, Spain and Greece. Yet that experience failed to translate into prowess. Italy's military suffered one disastrous defeat after another, with soldiers who surrendered often many times more than their dead or wounded comrades. For that, Mussolini could only impotently rage. In December 1940, after getting word of the latest debacle in North Africa, he quipped: 'Five generals are prisoners and one is dead. This is the ratio of Italians who have military qualities and those who have none.'[29]

The navy's problems were as serious as the army's.[30] The command was just as bloated and top-heavy. Warships lacked radar and night-fighting abilities. Commanders had virtually no amphibious, convoy and air reconnaissance abilities. Like the army, the navy's paper strength exceeded its actual strength. The navy boasted having recently built seaworthy *Littorio* class battleships, nineteen *Zara* class and *Bolzano* class cruisers and fifty-nine destroyers, yet land and carrier-based bombers rendered those warships obsolete. Italian light cruisers and destroyers were barely seaworthy with poor designs and weak engines. Italy's navy had no aircraft carriers because its naval command, led by chiefs of staff Admirals Ernesto Burzagli from 1927 to 1931, Gino Ducci to 1934, then Domenico Cavagnari, was the most conservative of the great powers and rejected all proposals to build them.

The navy had 118 submarines in 1940, but they sank only 13 warships and 21 merchant ships, while suffering 88 losses during the war. That compares to the 1,131 German submarines that sank 175 warships and 2,925 merchant ships while losing 632.[31] Tactics were the most vital reason for that vast performance gap. Italy's submarine fleet never emulated Germany's wolf pack, night attack and manoeuvre tactics but simply waited in sea lanes for daylight torpedo launches. Atop that, German submarines could stay submerged three times longer, cruise further and faster underwater and on the surface and had periscopes that rose twice as high. During the war British air and naval superiority combined with severe oil shortages confined Italy's warships mostly to port. Italy's navy steadily expanded from 168,614 officers and sailors on 30 June 1940 to 259,082 on 1 August 1943, volunteers composed most of those personnel.[32]

7.4 Military Spending Service Shares, 1938–1943[33]

	Army	Navy	Air Force	Colonies
1938	33.0	14.8	19.1	23.1
1939	40.3	16.5	19.8	23.4
1940	52.3	11.6	17.3	19.0
1941	63.9	12.0	15.2	9.2
1942	61.7	14.2	10.7	2.0
1943	60.6	15.6	11.9	1.8

A devastating defeat forced a shift in naval policy. On 11 November 1941, a British aircraft carrier launched twenty-one slow-flying biplane torpedo bombers toward the Italian fleet anchored at Taranto and they severely damaged three battleships, a heavy cruiser and two destroyers. The attack came as a complete surprise because the Italian navy lacked radar to detect their approach. Mussolini replaced Cavagnari with

Arturo Ricardi on 11 December 1940, with building an aircraft carrier and developing radar topping his to-do list.

The few times that Italian warships engaged in naval battles, their guns suffered from poor rangefinders, loading mechanisms, firing systems, shell fuses and shell propellent charges. For instance, during the Battle of Matapan from 27 to 29 March 1941, the Italian battleship *Vittorio Veneto* and its escorts fired 636 rounds without a single hit on the British light cruiser flotilla.[34]

Italy's greatest naval victory in the Second World War came on 19 December 1941, inflicted not by warships or warplanes but by commando teams with 'human torpedoes'. The commandos zipped into Alexandria's harbour and sank the battleships HMS *Valiant* and *Queen Elizabeth* with the warheads of 'slow torpedoes' nickname 'hogs' (*maiale*). Elsewhere commandos in explosive speedboats sank the cruiser HMS *York* in March 1940, while frogmen with limpet mines penetrated harbours and sank lesser warships in Algiers and Gibraltar. Submarines bore those commandos and their speedboats to short distances from their targets.

Historian James Burgwyn gave the Italian navy high marks for its supply operations for North Africa:

> The much-maligned Italian navy actually made a substantial contribution in upholding the African maritime supply-line. Convoy protection, to which the heaviest warships were also assigned, became the Italian navy's principal function as time went by . . . Between June 1940 and January 1943, the shipments that reached Africa safely amounted to 80 per cent of vehicles, 88 per cent of weapons and equipment, 81 per cent of other dry cargo and 82 per cent of the fuel . . . Troops were mostly carried over by air.[35]

Military failures were grounded in the nation's political culture impervious to two decades of Mussolini's periodic orders to his High Command to remedy them. For instance, nothing could be done to diminish a soft power weakness that Italians actually celebrate. '*Bella Figura*' values style over substance, of looking good to cover up underlying weaknesses. Yet another military soft power deficiency was the prevailing cultural value of the 'good life' (*Bella Vita*) of family and friends sharing laughter, food and wine and helping each other through difficulties. The common view of the state, even at the local level, was as a corrupt, inept adversary to be milked for any favours. Localism was another dimension of Italian culture that undermined the military. Two decades of Fascism atop two generations of a unified country had poorly diminished traditional Italian identity grounded within family and village or neighbourhood. *Campanilismo* is the Italian word for one's sense of self tethered to the village church steeple. A large share of people still spoke one of a myriad of mutually incomprehensible dialects with standard Italian at best a secondary language; one of five Italians spoke only dialect in 1931.[36] Of course, those traditional identities were strongest among illiterate peasants in the countryside. Urban dwellers tended to be more literate, speak standard Italian as a first language and identity as Italian.

Historian MacGregor Knox characterized Italy's military-industrial complex including 'fighting machine design, metallurgy, assembly-line technique, machine tool production, precision instrumentation, communications electronics and radar and sonar . . . in a condition of stubborn and parochial backwardness. Research and quality control in vital areas such as armour was primitive or non-existent'.[37] For many reasons, Italy's military went to war grossly deficient in weapons, equipment and supplies in 1940. The most critical was that Italy lacked the money and production to make up for the 39 billion lira and 8 billion lira devoured respectively by the Ethiopian and Spanish wars.[38]

Italian industrial production lagged far behind its allies and enemies. In 1938, Italy produced 2.3 million tons of steel to France's 6.1 million tons, Britain's 10.6 million tons and Germany's 22.7 million tons. That same year, Italy produced 15.54 million kilowatt-hours of electrical energy to France's 22.10 million, Britain's 35.81 million and Germany's 61.38 million. From 1940 to 1943, Italy, Germany and America respectively produced 4,211, 18,600 and 57,585 armoured vehicles and 10,238, 62,239 and 157,000 warplanes. Related to Italy's dismal production was its dismal productivity. Although Japan's industrial production was half the size of Italy's, it produced first-rate fighters like the Zero in vast numbers. In 1939, Italy produced 2.4 million tons of steel to Britain's 13.4 million tons and Germany's 22.5 million tons.[39] An audit by Foreign Minister Galeazzo Ciano in 1939 found a vast discrepancy between official and actual numbers of weapons and between their alleged and genuine quality: 'The ammunition depots are short of ammunition. The artillery is outmoded. There has been a good deal of bluffing in the military sphere and even the *Duce* himself has been deceived . . . Valle states there are 3,006 first-line aircraft, while the Navy information service says there are only 982. A gross discrepancy!'[40]

A hard power deficit partly explains Italy's manufacturing backwardness. Italy suffered a relative shortage of skilled engineers and technicians who repair, innovate and invent. In the school year of 1939–40, only 13.6 per cent of 85,535 university students studied engineering. The number of university students majoring in engineering, science and mathematics actually dropped from 17,690 of 53,670 total students in 1919–20 to 11,648 of 85,535 in 1939–40. Driving skills were a much simpler yet important skill. In 1939, there were 469,000 motor vehicles in Italy compared to 1,990,000 in Germany, 2,225,000 in France and 2,242,000 in Britain or 11 vehicles for every 1,000 people in Italy, 25 in Germany, 54 in France, 51 in Britain and 227 in America. Few vehicles demanded fewer mechanics. That affected the military. In November 1940, 2,000 of Italy's 5,146 military vehicles in Libya were broken down for want of mechanics and spare parts.[41]

Astonishingly, Italy's military industrial complex was actually more productive in the First World War than in the Second, despite or more likely due to two decades of Fascist corporatism. Agostino Rocca headed the financial division of the Institute for Industrial Reconstruction (*Instituto Ricostruzione Industriale,* IRS) that partnered with and partly funded key manufacturing firms. On 2 April 1943, he sent Mussolini a report revealing a stark example of that productivity gap:

> During the first thirty-nine months of war (July 1940–January 1943) our works have manufactured 5,049 pieces of artillery. In the first thirty-one months of the last war (June 1915–December 1917) the famous Giovanni Ansaldo works manufactured 3,699. The attached diagram shows that 15 million working hours were needed to make those 5,049 guns, whereas, in the last war, six million hours were needed for those 3,699 guns.[42]

Rocca spotlighted the greater production and ignored the worse productivity. Indeed, he attributed that higher output to *Il Duce*'s policies: 'All that proves that the programme of productive exploitation of the industrial potential approved by you in 1939–40 and carried by the I.R.I. concerns has enabled us to meet the needs of the armed forces liberally.'[43] That one of Italy's leading officials was oblivious to the dismal productivity of a critical company that he oversaw is revealing. Rocca had an impeccable resume. He studied at military school, fought bravely in the First World War, studied engineering after the war at Milan's Polytechnic Institute and in 1922, joined IRI where his brilliance steadily advanced him up the ranks.

7.5 Great Power Gross Domestic Product, 1938–1945 (1990 dollars in billions)[44]

Allies	1938	1939	1940	1941	1942	1943	1944	1945
America	800	869	943	1,094	1,235	1,399	1,499	1,475
Britain	284	287	316	344	353	361	346	331
France	186	199	82	–	–	–	–	101
Italy	–	–	–	–	–	–	177	92
Soviet Union	359	366	417	359	318	464	495	396
Total	1,629	1,721	1,758	1,787	1,906	2,224	2,457	2,394
Axis								
Germany	351	384	387	412	417	426	437	310
Austria	24	27	27	29	27	28	29	12
Italy	141	151	147	144	145	137	–	–
Japan	169	184	192	196	197	194	189	144
France	–	–	82	130	116	110	93	–
Total	685	746	835	911	902	895	748	466
Ratio								
Ally/Axis	2.4	2.3	2.1	2.0	2.1	2.5	3.3	5.1
Soviet/German	1.0	1.0	1.1	0.9	0.8	1.1	1.1	1.3

What Mussolini's war effort needed was the Italian equivalent of Albert Speer as War Production Minister whose reforms caused German production to soar. *Il Duce* had to make do with much less. He recognized that his General Commissariat for War Production was less efficient than the Ministry of Arms and Munitions from 1915 to 1918, but did not transform it into the Ministry for War Production with enhanced powers of economic intervention until February 1943. He sacked General Ugo Cavallero as chief of staff and replaced him with General Vittorio Ambrosia, but he was just as inept.

Italy's economy and military suffered worsening labour shortages. The draft mopped up hundreds of thousands of workers and peasants and the military defeats led to the deaths and maimings of tens of thousands of men and capture of hundreds of thousands more. Mussolini contributed to the manpower shortage by mobilizing and dispatching 'guest workers' for German industries, including 229,000 in 1941 and 81,000 in 1942.[45] They received pay, food and housing and many remitted part of their stipends to their families back in Italy. German authorities disdained Italian workers for their low productivity and sloppy work. A report reached Mussolini 'on the treatment of our labourers in Germany. In certain camps, in addition to beatings, large watchdogs are used which are trained to bite the legs of those workers who are guilty of even slight misdemeanours.' Enraged, Mussolini declared that: 'These things are bound to produce a lasting hatred in my heart. I can even wait many years, but in the end I shall square this account. I will not permit the sons of a race which has given to humanity Caesar, Dante and Michaelangelo to be devoured by the bloodhounds of the Huns.'[46]

Yet another economic weakness was Italy's dependence on imports for nearly all its natural resources. Italy imported 99 per cent of its petroleum. In 1938, Italy dug 1 million metric tons of coal from its own mines and imported 12.1 million tons, while France produced 47.6 million tons and Germany 186.2 million tons. Most imported coal came from Germany, including 12 million tons in 1940–1, 11 million tons in 1941–2 and 12 million tons in 1942–3. Hydroelectricity accounted for 40 per cent of steel production in 1942 and rose from 15 million kilowatt hours in 1938 to 20 million in 1942. Energy consumption was around the same level from 1938 to 1943, before bombings and cutoffs of foreign supply caused energy production to plummet by 75 per cent in 1943. Atop all those vulnerabilities, 80 per cent of Italy's raw material imports passed through Britain's choke-points of Suez and Gibraltar. Astonishingly, Mussolini's regime did not stockpile raw materials as war became more likely. In September 1940, Italy had 14 days' worth of steel, 20 days of nickel and six months of iron ore.[47]

Italian political culture undermined its economy as much as it did its military. To greatly varying degrees, countries at war experience price gouging, shoddy goods and services, tax evasion and outright theft. The relative strength of rule of law and morality shaped by national culture determines those differences. Italy's political culture encouraged those abuses perhaps much more than the other great powers during the Second World War. Italy's civic culture of identity, participation, contribution and even, if need be, sacrifice for the greater good of the nation was relatively weak. Instead, most people avoided or minimized paying taxes, took or gave bribes and extended favouritism toward patrons, friends and relatives, all celebrated as being 'clever' (*furbo*). On the job behaviours included showing up late, going home early, long coffee and cigarette breaks, a leisurely, inattentive work pace and pocketing 'extras'. Mussolini hated those characteristics. That reached a crisis level in June 1942, when Ciano observed as he 'inveighs violently against the merchants, of whom one hundred and thirty-two thousand have already been denounced. He accuses them of constituting another army which stabs in the back while it is engaged in a very hard war. There will be new and tougher penalties added to those already set down.'[48]

Count Dino Grandi was both President of the Chamber of Fasces and Corporations and Minister of Grace and Justice. With Mussolini's approval, he tried to get the Fascist Grand Council to approve a law that raised taxes and the penalties for non-compliance on 6 June 1942. Ciano explained the political and cultural dilemma he and the regime faced in doing that:

> This meant that for the first time in the history of our tax system they are thinking of imprisoning tax evaders. This might do in countries educated in fiscal matters, but not with us, where everyone would take false oaths. If we closed our eyes to this, we would become ridiculous or, if we enforced the law, we would have to enlarge our prisons to the point where half of the budget would go for the maintenance of prisoners.[49]

Grandi's measure failed.

One key power source that Mussolini had achieved was enlisting most Italians in a web of Fascist organizations that promoted nationalism, duty and sacrifice. By 1 October 1942, 27,000,000 of 45,000,000 Italians were members.[50] Membership, however, was not enough to guarantee the endurance of Fascist values against news of an unrelenting series of military defeats that spread to Italy itself, amid worsening inflation, food shortages and deprivations.

Mussolini fumed at Italy's cultural features that undermined its military. Yet, ultimately, *Il Duce* himself was Italy's worst military deficiency.[51] He was an awful leader. He rejected fact-based advice that conflicted with his visions. He believed that his commands were sufficient and did not bother to ensure that his underlings realized them. Many of his orders were impossible to achieve, merely wishful thinking.

Ciano explained Mussolini's view of the military: 'He believes strongly that a smart soldier is a good soldier' and 'that the rigid Prussian military training has made Prussian soldiers invincible. Very often he accuses the King of having diminished the physical prestige of our Army in order to harmonize it with his own "unhappy physique".'[52] Mussolini was livid after the king complained about his decision to have the Italian imitate the German goose-step in January 1938: 'It is not my fault if the king is physically a runt. Naturally he can't do the parade step for the same reason he has always hated horses; he needs a ladder to climb on one. But a physical defect in a sovereign is not a good reason for stunting, as he has done, the army of a great country.'[53]

Chapter 8

THE ROADS TO HUMILIATING DEFEATS

> We go into the field against the plutocratic and reactionary democracies of the West who have repeatedly blocked the march and even threatened the existence of the Italian people . . . [T]his giant struggle is only a phase in the logical development of our revolution; it is the struggle of a poor people against those who wish to starve us with their retention of all the riches and gold of the earth . . . It is the struggle of two centuries and two ideas.
>
> (Benito Mussolini)

> Defeat is one thing; disgrace is another.
>
> (Winston Churchill)

The 'Phoney War' ended in April 1940 when Adolf Hitler and Winston Churchill, First Lord of the Admiralty, decided around the same time to invade Norway. German industries depended on iron ore dug from mines in northern Sweden then transported by train to Norway's northern port of Narvik and then conveyed by ship to German ports. Churchill reasoned that if the British took and held Narvik and northern Norway, they would inflict a major economic blow on Germany. For that reason, Hitler was himself determined to conquer Norway along with Denmark. On 9 April, the Wehrmacht invaded Denmark over land while over the next week task forces landed troops to capture Kristiansand, Oslo, Bergen, Trondheim and Narvik. British task forces landed troops to fight the Germans at Andalsnes, Namsos and Narvik. The German eventually repelled British forces and completed their conquest of Norway by 10 June.

Meanwhile, Hitler launched a massive invasion of France and the Low Countries on 10 May.[1] He had massed 141 divisions in four army groups against 135 French, British, Belgium and Dutch divisions. The key attack was led by seven armoured divisions through the lightly defended Ardennes Forest of eastern Belgium. Ten days later the advanced panzer division reached the English Channel near Abbeville, then punched north against the British army and a French army that fell back to Dunkirk. Behind that spearhead other armies followed to curl south, one that dashed south-east to cut off a million troops manning the Maginot Line, while another pushed south to rumble into undefended Paris on 14 June then further to the Loire River Valley. A third army pushed south-east along the English Channel then split up with divisions overrunning Normandy, Brittanny and the lower Loire valley. Other armies conquered the Netherlands and Belgians whose government surrendered respectively on 15 May and 28 May.

Prime Minister Neville Chamberlain resigned on 10 May and King George V appointed Winston Churchill to take his place. The French government led by Prime Minister Paul Reynaud fled to Bordeaux on 10 June. Churchill tried to coordinate a defence with Reynaud but he, his advisors and the French army were too demoralized to stand and fight. Churchill mobilized a flotilla of navy and civilian vessels to evacuate over 338,000 troops, 198,000 British and 140,000 French and Belgian, from Dunkirk with the last embarking on 4 June. Reynaud resigned as prime minister on 14 June and Marshal Philippe Pétain replaced him.

Word of the German blitzkrieg's stunning advances and rout of enemy forces dazzled Mussolini. Just three days after the German offensive began, he excitedly told his advisors that: 'Some months ago I told you that the Allies had lost the victory. Today I tell you that they have lost the war. We Italians are already dishonoured. Any delay is inconceivable. We have no time to lose. Within a month I shall declare war.'[2] To Ciano, he argued: 'What can you say to someone who doesn't dare risk a single soldier while his ally is winning a crushing victory and that victory can give Italy back the remainder of its national territory and establish its supremacy in the Mediterranean? Is it a pipe-dream? We'll see if it is.'[3]

Churchill was determined to prevent Mussolini from joining the war. On 16 May, he sent *Il Duce* this heartfelt appeal:

> I look back to our meetings in Rome and feel a desire to speak words of goodwill to you as Chief of the Italian nation across what seems to be a

> swift-widening gulf. Is it too late to stop a river of blood from flowing between the British and Italian peoples? . . . I have never been the enemy of Italian greatness . . . It is idle to predict the course of the great battles now raging in Europe, but I am sure that whatever may happen on the Continent, England will go on to the end . . . and . . . we shall be aided in increasing measure by the United States . . . I beg you to believe that it is in no spirit of weakness . . . that I make this solemn appeal . . . Down the ages . . . comes the cry that the joint heirs of Latin and Christian civilization must not be ranged against each other.

To that, Mussolini replied:

> I remind you of the initiative taken by your Government to organize at Geneva sanctions against Italy, engaged in securing for herself a small space of the African sun without causing the slightest injury to your interests and territories or those of others . . . the Italian-German Treaty guides Italian policy today and tomorrow in the face of any event whatsoever.[4]

Mussolini summoned Chief of Staff Pietro Badoglio and Marshal Italo Balbo on 26 May for an announcement that stunned them. Badoglio recalled:

> He was standing behind his writing table, his hands on his hips, looking intensively serious . . . He did not speak at once but silently transfixed us with his penetrating glare . . . Finally . . . he announced: 'I wish to tell you that yesterday I sent a messenger to Hitler with my written declaration that . . . after 5 June I am ready to declare war on Britain'. We were dumfounded and seemed to have lost the power of speech . . . When I was able to speak, I said: 'Your excellency, you know perfectly well that we are absolutely unprepared – you have received complete reports every week'. . . . Feeling absolutely desperate, I added, 'It is suicide'. Mussolini did not answer for a few minutes and then said quite calmly: . . . 'It is evident that today you are too excited to judge the situation correctly. I assure you the war will be over in September and I need a few thousand dead so as to be able to attend the peace conference as a belligerent.'[5]

Mussolini convened the military commanders and Ciano on 29 May and told them to prepare to attack France on 5 June. The military chiefs tersely explained that the deadline was too soon and they pleaded for more time. Mussolini agreed to postpone the attack to 10 June. Ciano warned Mussolini that 'I consider it rather inglorious to fall upon a defeated army and I find it morally dangerous also. Armistice is at the door and if our Army should not overcome resistance during the first assault, our campaign would end with a howling failure.'[6] Ciano was prescient on all counts.

To Mussolini's surprise, Hitler was cool when he informed him that he would soon fight alongside him. Hitler saw clearly that Mussolini, jackal-like, was cynically trying to gorge on a dying victim that the Wehrmacht alone had devastated.

Mussolini appeared at his Palazzo Venezia balcony to justify why Italy was going to war to the tens of thousands of people packing the square on 10 June. The reason was at once simple and profound: 'We go into the field against the plutocratic and reactionary democracies of the West who have repeatedly blocked the march and even threatened the existence of the Italian people' and their 'honour, self-interest and the future . . . [T]his giant struggle is only a phase in the logical development of our revolution; it is the struggle of a poor people against those who wish to starve us with their retention of all the riches and gold of the earth. It is a struggle of the fecund and young peoples against barren peoples slipping to their sunset. It is the struggle of two centuries and two ideas.' The immediate threat was in Italy's geopolitical front yard, the Mediterranean basin: 'we seek to break the territorial and military chains that suffocate us in our sea, for a people of forty-five million souls cannot be truly free unless it has free access to the oceans'.[7]

The first attacks came from the air. Italian bombers struck Malta after dawn on 11 June, but caused little damage. That afternoon, French and British bombers hit factories in Turin and Genoa and also left the targets intact while killing fourteen people and wounding thirty.[8]

Six divisions with 85,000 troops defended France's mountainous south-east frontier. Against them, Mussolini massed 300,000 troops in eighteen regular and four Alpine divisions. The Italians attacked repeatedly from 12 June to the armistice on 25 June, but gained little ground. In all, the Italian inflicted merely 460 casualties on the French while suffering 6,038 casualties, including 650 dead, 2,631 wounded, 2,151 with severe frostbite and 616 missing.[9]

Beyond the Italian front, France's military collapsed. Prime Minister Paul Reynaud stepped down on 17 June and Marshal Pétain replaced him. Pétain sent word to Hitler that he wanted to negotiate an armistice. Hitler arranged the armistice to be signed in the same railway carriage at the same place near Compiègne, France where Germany was forced to sign the armistice that ended the First World War on 11 November 1918. Hitler, Pétain and their respective entourages entered that railway car on 22 June. Under the armistice, France ceded the provinces of Alsace and Lorraine to Germany;

German troops would indefinitely occupy northern and western France; France was reduced to a rump state with its capital at Vichy; the French army would number only 100,000 troops; the navy would be demobilized to skeleton crews aboard warships confined to port; France would pay Germany's occupation costs; and the two million French prisoners would remain in camps until the Vichy government fulfilled all its treaty obligations.

Meanwhile, Mussolini met Hitler at Munich on 18 and 19 June. To Ciano, Mussolini admitted that he 'is very much embarrassed. He feels that his role is secondary . . . in truth, the *Duce* fears that the hour of peace is growing near and sees the unattainable dream of his life, glory on the field of battle, fading once again.'[10]

Mussolini accepted a French request for armistice negotiations. A French delegation arrived in Rome on 23 June. Mussolini had Ciano draft a list of spoils from France that included Italy's takeover of the French fleet, south-east France to the Rhone River and Corsica, Tunisia and Djibouti. The French rejected all these demands and agreed only that the Italian army could occupy what little ground it had taken. In the armistice agreement signed on 24 June, Italy 'won' the small area its army occupied and French forces withdrew 30 miles, leaving a demilitarized zone behind them.

Churchill contemptuously viewed Italy's attack on defeated France as akin to a vulture preying off a corpse. He singled out Mussolini as the arch-villain and absolved the Italy's monarchy and people: 'One man and one man alone, against the crown and Royal Family of Italy, against the Pope and all the authority of the Vatican, against the wishes of the Italian people'.[11]

A deeply symbolic tragic loss happened on 28 June when nervous anti-aircraft gunners at Tobruk shot down the plane carrying General Italo Balbo. All of Mussolini's offensives during the war would literally and figuratively backfire.

Hitler was powerless to follow up his decisive victory on the continent into Britain's conquest. To successfully invade Britain, the Germans had to win control over the skies above.[12] The decisive phase of the Battle of Britain lasted from the first major German bombing attack on 10 July until Hitler paused the offensive on 31 October 1940. During that time, Royal Air Force Hurricane and Spitfire pilots and anti-aircraft guns shot down 1,733 warplanes, mostly bombers, while suffering 915 warplanes destroyed in the air or on the ground, while German bombs killed around 23,000 civilians, wounded 32,000 and drove tens of thousands from their homes.[13]

Hitler's decisive defeat forced him to abandon his dream of vanquishing Britain. Instead, he looked eastward to the Soviet Union for his next major conquest. And for that, he needed all the military allies he could muster. Yet, ironically, Hitler's alliance with Stalin rendered the Anti-Comintern Pact moot. Hitler's dazzling conquests emboldened Japan's government, now led by Prime Minister Hideki Tojo, to transform the Anti-Comintern Pact into a broad Tripartite Pact with Germany and Italy. Hitler enthusiastically agreed and sent Ribbentrop to Rome on 19 September, to talk Mussolini into the Pact. Mussolini approved. Ribbentrop, Galeazzo Ciano and Saburu Kurusu signed the Tripartite Pact forming a defensive alliance among them at Berlin on 27 September 1940. The Pact was designed to activate against the United States, the only great power that fit the description 'attacked by a power at present not involved in the European War or in the Sino-Japanese conflict'. The three invited other states to join them, Hungary did on 20 November, Romania on 23 November, Slovakia on 27 November 1940, Bulgaria on 1 March and Yugoslavia on 25 March 1941.

Mussolini and Hitler followed that up with another Brenner Pass summit on 4 October. Ciano recorded that:

> Rarely have I seen the *Duce* in such good humour and good shape . . . The meeting was cordial and the conversations were certainly the most interesting of all that have taken place so far. Hitler put at least some of his cards on the table and talked about his plans for the future . . . (1) there is no longer any talk about a landing in the British Isles . . . (2) it is hoped to attract France in the orbit of the anti-British coalition . . . (3) greater importance is given to the Mediterranean sector, which is good for us.[14]

Meanwhile, Italy and Britain fought a naval war in the central Mediterranean.[15] Two enemy flotillas escorting supply ships crossed paths 35 miles east of Punta Stilo, Calabria on 9 July 1940. Admiral Inigo Campioni's flotilla included two battleships, six heavy cruisers, sixteen destroyers and ships packed with 2,100 troops, seventy-two Fiat M11/39 tanks, provisions, munitions and fuel bound from Naples to Benghazi. Admiral Andrew Cunningham's flotilla included one aircraft carrier, three battleships, five light cruisers, sixteen destroyers and ships packed with supplies from Alexandria bound for Malta. During the battle twenty-two land-based Italian bombers attacked the British flotilla and a bomb damaged a battleship. Italian gunfire also damaged a light cruiser and two destroyers. The British damaged a battleship, a heavy cruiser and a destroyer. The flotillas then broke off the action and proceeded to their destinations.

A deadlier battle with far fewer warships took place off Cape Spada, Crete on 19 July. Admiral John Collins with one light cruiser and five destroyers squared off against Admiral Ferdinando Casari with two light cruisers. The British sank a light cruiser and killed 121 sailors and captured 555 more. An Italian shell hit the British light cruiser, causing little damage and wounding a sailor.

That year's most important naval battle took place on 11 November after a flotilla of one aircraft carrier, two heavy cruisers, two light cruiser and four destroyers led by Admiral Cunningham got within flying range of Taranto. An Italian fleet of six battleships, seven heavy cruisers, seven light cruisers and thirteen destroyers led by Admiral Inigo Campioni were anchored in Taranto harbour. Twenty-one slow-flying Fairley Swordfish biplane torpedo bombers achieved surprise to disable three battleships and damage a heavy cruiser and two destroyers.

Italy's easy takeover of Albania in 1939 convinced Mussolini that conquering Greece would be just as easy.[16] Visions dazzled *Il Duce* of exploiting Greece's chrome, iron ore, pyrite, nickel, manganese and bauxite mines. Atop those riches would be the glory of asserting Italy's latest imperial expansion. For all that, he grasped any excuse for an invasion.

For instance, Mussolini summoned the Greek ambassador for a blistering on 17 January 1939. Ciano explained why: 'From a report coming from Bucharest it appeared that the Greek military attaché had made insulting remarks about our Army in a conversation with a Hungarian colleague. The poor Greek minister trembled like a leaf when Mussolini, with a face as hard as metal, told him that if, within three days, full satisfaction was not given us, there would be serious consequences.'[17] Mussolini was willing to go to war against Greece for such a silly reason as a cutting quip about Italy by one foreign diplomat to another. In Mussolini's duellist mindset, the honour of Italy and thus himself as *Il Duce* must be avenged on the field of battle. Athens issued an innocuous, vague 'regret' statement that fig-leafed Mussolini's 'honour'. Ironically, when Mussolini did launch a war against Greece, the Italian army proved to be worthy of the attaché's derision.

Mussolini was deadset to match Hitler's conquests by December 1940 with Italy's conquest of Greece. In May 1940, he sent Ciano to Albania with the mission to secretly have General Carlo Geloso prepare to invade Greece with his five divisions. A stunned Geloso replied that he needed at least twenty-five divisions to conquer Greece.[18] Over the summer, Mussolini did send more troops and supplies to him, but then, astonishingly, on 1 October, Mussolini demobilized 600,000 troops or half of the 1,200,000 troops deployed in Italy to aid peasants in the harvest.

What mostly concerned Mussolini was not the imbalance of military power but an excuse for Italy's army to invade Greece. When he could not find a genuine excuse, he made one up. On 14 June, Greek police killed Daut Hoxha, the leader of a gang of cattle rustlers and extortionists who murdered rivals and those who resisted his crimes. On 11 August, Mussolini had Italian Radio announce that the Greeks had assassinated the Albanian 'patriot' Hoxha and cut off his head for display in Athens.

Word that Mussolini intended to invade Greece angered Hitler who had Foreign Minister Ribbentrop tersely insist that he delay the attack indefinitely. Mussolini grudgingly agreed. Then Hitler ordered his army to march into Romania to secure its Ploesti oil field and refinery on 12 October. Infuriated, Mussolini declared: 'Hitler always faces me with a fait accompli. This time I am going to pay him back in his own coin. He will find out from the papers that I have occupied Greece. In this way the equilibrium will be reestablished.'[19]

The worst obstacle was Italy's High Command, usually bitterly divided on most issues but united in insisting that the Italian army in Albania was unprepared to invade Greece and needed massive reinforcements and supplies for even a chance of victory. Mussolini summoned Marshal Pietro Badoglio, Generals Ubaldo Soddu, Mario Roatta and Sebastiano Prasca and Foreign Minister Ciano on 15 October. Mussolini tried to cow the pessimists by angrily declaring that 'if anyone makes difficulties about beating the Greeks, I shall resign from being an Italian'. Ciano backed Mussolini's dream of conquering Greece, sharing his delusion that 'the military operation will be useful and easy'.[20] Before he dismissed them, Mussolini declared: 'I advise you not to pay too much attention to whatever losses you may suffer. I am telling you this because sometimes a commander halts as a result of heavy losses.'[21] Although the campaign was even more disastrous than the pessimists anticipated, Mussolini grimly clung to power.

Supply should have been relatively easy with ships making the approximately eight-hour voyage across the Adriatic from Bari to Durazzo for the Yugoslav front or from Brindisi to Valona for the Greece front. But in Albania, the Italians failed to mass enough trucks and fuel to transport all those supplies and troops across mostly mountainous landscapes to distant fronts. Albania's border with Greece runs 90 rugged miles from the sea to Yugoslavia. Defending Greece's border was General Alessandro Papagos's 120,000 troops in bunkers and forts. The Italian army numbered 150,000 troops led by General Sebastiano Prasca. Ioannis Metaxas was Greece's dictator, having taken power in a coup in 1936. On 28 October, Mussolini sent Metaxas an ultimatum to let the Italian army occupy unspecified strategic places in Greece or else war would result. When Metaxas rejected the demand, Mussolini authorized Prasca to attack.[22]

The attack immediately bogged down, literally because of heavy rain and figuratively because of formidable Greek defences and tactical skills. On 8 November, Mussolini replaced Prasca with Ubaldo Soddu but the new commander was just as inept. Papagos counter-attacked on 14 November and his troops drove the Italians back into Albania and captured the crossroads towns of Pogradec and Port Edda, named after Mussolini's daughter. On 14 December, Papagos launched an offensive aimed at capturing Valona. The Italians blunted that advance.

What explains the Italian army's dismal performance? Soddu revealed how overconfidence by Italy's generals who believed their regime's propaganda was self-defeating: 'The war against Greece was begun in the conviction, common to all, that the enemy was devoid of serious military qualities: this atmosphere of "military promenade", resulted in disorientation as soon as we realized that the enemy, sufficiently well organized and enjoying numerical superiority, was reacting in a manner that had not been foreseen.'[23] Ciano thought the reasons for Italy's humiliating defeats in Greece and North Africa lay more on the front line than in the High Command: 'Our soldiers have fought but little and badly. This is the real, fundamental cause of all that has happened'.[24] Ciano was certainly correct in lamenting the poor quality of Italian soldiers, yet they reflected the command structure of non-commissioned officers, officers and High Command; the economy's relatively poor levels of entrepreneurship, innovation and productivity that supplied the military with inferior and inadequate weapons, munitions, provisions and equipment; and the culture's embrace of appearances (*Bella Figura*) over substance, corruption, favouritism and cynicism. Badoglio expressed the view of most generals when he confided to Popular Culture Minister Alessandro Pavolini that: 'All the fault lies with the leadership of *Il Duce*. He has no business exercising command; he ought to let us handle it.'[25] Of course, all these reasons are right.

Mussolini made Marshal Badoglio the defeat's scapegoat by forcing him to resign on 27 November and replaced him with General Ugo

Cavallero as chief of staff on 6 December. He withdrew Soddu 'for consultations' on 29 December 1940; Soddu resigned for 'health reasons' in January. Mussolini replaced him with Cavallero as commander on the Greek front. He singled out for praise General Giovanni Messe who 'had given an excellent account of himself as commander in Albania, where he had succeeded in blocking the Greek thrust in the most dangerous direction of Valona'.[26]

Cavallero barely managed to prevent an Italian collapse. In early January, Greek offensives threatened to capture Berat and Klisura. Cavallero scraped up enough reserves to blunt both attacks. On 9 January, Cavallero threw the newly arrived Wolf Division into a counter-attack around Klisura but the Greeks repulsed it then circled and decimated it, killing, wounding and capturing all but 160 of its 4,000 troops. Meanwhile, the Greeks pushed toward Valona, the key Italian supply port. Cavallero rushed a mélange of rear-echelon troops to Tepelina 30 miles south-east on the road from Valona and they repulsed the Greek assault.

Italy's army in the Balkans was literally and figuratively starving to death. General Roatta had a team investigate just what was missing:

> Equipment for thirty divisional and twenty corps artillery battalions, 8,000 trucks, 750 ambulances and maintenance vehicles, 1,600 small anti-aircraft cannon, 900 900 88-mm guns (complete with searchlights, rangefinders and sights), 800 medium tanks, 300 armoured cars, 675 anti-tank guns, 9,000 mules, 300 long- and medium-range radio sets, 20,000 rolls of concertina wire, 500,000 engineer stakes, 10,000,000 sandbags and various minor items.[27]

Preceding, accompanying and following Italy's war against Greece was its war against Britain forces in north-east Africa.[28] Mussolini reinforced the existing Tenth Army on Libya's frontier with Egypt and formed a reserve army in western Libya. He grandiosely envisioned two successive campaigns. In the first, Tenth Army would steamroll Britain's XIII Corps in western Egypt to capture Alexandria and the Suez Canal, then in the second phase would advance across the Middle East to capture Iraq's oil fields. The Reserve Army would capture Cairo then advance up the Nile River valley to recapture Ethiopia and eventually East Africa. Britain's XIII Corps soon revealed Mussolini's plans as utter fantasies. Word of catastrophic losses in Libya compounded the dismal morale permeating Mussolini's regime from the ongoing Greek debacle.

General Rodolfo Graziani commanded an Army Group in Libya with Tenth Army guarding the eastern frontier facing Egypt and Fifth Army the Western Frontier facing Tunisia. Tenth Army's 167,000 troops were split among twelve Italian divisions, with three Blackshirt and two Libyan divisions and one Italian armoured brigade and fielded 339 L3 light tanks, 70 M11/39 medium tanks with 37mm guns, 2,506 trucks and around 300 fighters and bombers without sand filters.[29]

Facing Graziani were just 36,000 British and Commonwealth troops of XIII Corps led by General Richard O'Connor with General Archibald Wavell commanding the North Africa and Middle East theatre. It was a classic David and Goliath square off where British strategy, tactics, leadership, troops, tanks and warplanes would prove vastly superior to Italian equivalents. For tanks alone, British Matildas and Cruisers had superior armour, engines, guns and crews to the Italians'.

O'Connor launched an offensive on 9 December, that that in four phases over ten weeks nearly destroyed Graziani's entire army. In each phase, armoured divisions arced south and then west around the Italian line to cave in the rear. During the first phase on the Egyptian-Libyan frontier, O'Connell sent most of his 275 tanks and 30,000 infantry in a wide sweep around the 80,000-man Italian army's southern flank, then crushed them from the rear. British forces captured over 40,000 men and 400 guns and routed the rest. Graziani rallied his corps along a north-south line anchored at the small port of Bardia. O'Connor's troops overran the enemy defences and bagged 40,000 more prisoners, 117 light tanks, 13 medium tanks, 400 guns, 650 trucks and Bardia. Graziani's next line was at Tobruk. After resupplying his army, O'Connor attacked on 21 January. His latest hook around to the Italian army's rear took Tobruk along with 25,000 troops, 258 guns and 87 tanks at the price of 400 casualties.

Graziani ordered his army's remnants to withdraw from Cyrenaica, then flew to safety in Tripoli, leaving his chief of staff General Giuseppe Tellera in command. O'Connor launched his fourth envelopment on 5 February and again devastated Tenth Army and captured Benghazi. Over ten weeks, O'Connor's corps overran 130,000 Italian troops, 400 tanks and 845 guns and advanced 500 miles at the cost of 476 men killed and 1,225 wounded.[30]

Not just Italian soldiers suffered. The Italian army's rout exposed Italian settlers to pent up hatreds that permeated the Arab population. Alan Moorhead, a reporter for the *London Daily Express*, explained the source of those hatreds and the horrendous results: '[T]he Senussi tribes had waged bitter war with the Italians and they were unforgiving'. After the Senussis' defeat and surrender tens of thousands of Arabs were 'dispossessed of their lands or thrown off the communal holdings to make way for Italian settlers'. Security for the settlers disappeared with the Italian army: 'The Arabs had turned at last on the Italian settlers left defenceless . . . In the gap before the arrival of the British they had cut loose to pillage and burn and loot and destroy. With tears the Italian settlers implored us everywhere to stay and guard them. Even their women were not safe.'[31]

Just when O'Connell was preparing XIII Corps for the knockout blow against the Italian army, he received orders to stand down and sent two divisions and most of his air force to Greece. Prime Minister Churchill had received word that Germany would soon join Italy in trying to conquer Greece and was determined to prevent that. In doing so, Churchill swapped the likely British conquest of Libya for what became a humiliating defeat and withdrawal in Greece.

Although Mussolini ensured that Italian newspapers masked or downplayed the catastrophes in the Balkans and North Africa, genuine accounts filtered back to increasingly disturb the public. A police report captured that darkening mood: 'The successful beginning of warlike activities on our fronts . . . induced the majority of the townspeople to judge with excessive frivolity the prosecution of military operations and therefore the recent painful episodes in Greece and on the Egyptian front have surprised public opinion all the more forcefully, in view of the strength of the illusion of an easy war.'[32]

Surpassing dismal war news to agitate Italians were the skyrocketing prices for all goods, especially food. A police report from Venice revealed that most people 'barely make ends meet, in absolutely miserable conditions, rounding out their budgets with the meagre proceeds of work by the women and, in the end, with various expedients not excluding the more or less concealed prostitution of young girls. When such expedients are not available, conditions become absolutely unbearable.'[33] All those calamitous results with the war less than a year old. Italians would endure another four years of worsening conditions.

Italy's debacles deeply embarrassed Mussolini. *Der Führer* called for a summit but *Il Duce* 'does not want to meet Hitler burdened by these numerous failures until they have been at least in part redressed'. He finally met Hitler at his Obersalzberg villa on 18 January 1941. Ciano recorded that: 'The meeting is cordial . . . There are no hidden condolences in the air – condolences that Mussolini feared . . . Hitler talked for about two hours on his coming intervention in Greece . . . Mussolini is elated.'[34] Intervening in Greece would be the first of several times that Hitler wielded his Wehrmacht to rescue Mussolini from his catastrophic follies.

Numerous faults plagued Victor Emannuel III but he harboured no delusions about Italy's ally. Ciano found him: 'preoccupied and shaken by the situation in Libya . . . He is doubtful about Germany.' When Ciano tried to reassure him about Hitler, the king replied: 'He has treated you courteously only because he had to and could not do otherwise . . . But he is a German like the others and will deal with Italy only on the basis of brutal self-interest.'[35]

Mussolini was determined to score a victory before Hitler could take credit. He ordered General Carlo Geloso to launch an offensive with nine divisions against the six Greek divisions defending the Albanian front. The Italians attacked on 9 March, but once again the Greeks in their bunkers slaughtered them. After just a week, Mussolini wearily authorized Geloso to suspend the offensive on 16 March. The Italians suffered 24,000 casualties, four times the 6,200 they inflicted on the Greeks. That offensive was an utter failure tactically but contributed to a sweeping strategic victory a month later. The Greeks rushed divisions from their border with Bulgaria to bolster the Albanian line. Hitler's Wehrmacht would swiftly punch through the slender defences along the Bulgarian frontier.

Hitler agreed not just to rescue Mussolini from his losing war against Greece, but got Mussolini to divert some of his troops in Albania for a joint attack on Yugoslavia.[36] The excuse for Germany and Italy to conquer Yugoslavia was its government's decision to repudiate a treaty. Yugoslavia was governed by Prince Paul, the regent for then 17-year-old King Peter III and Prime Minister Dragiša Cvetković. After months of pressure by Hitler, Paul and Cvetković signed the Tripartite Pact defensive alliance with Germany, Italy, Japan, Hungary, Romania, Slovakia and Bulgaria on 25 March 1941. That enraged most of the military high command which wanted to stay neutral. On 27 March, General Dušan Simonvić led a coup that ousted Paul, Cvetković and their coterie and declared that Peter III was now fully the king. The new government announced its withdrawal from the Tripartite Alliance. Hitler was dead set to make a vicious example of the turncoat government.

The German blitzkrieg, assisted by Italy, Bulgaria, Hungary, Romania and Slovakia, began on 6 April and ended a mere 15 days later with Yugoslavia's army demolished and the country overrun.[37] Peter III and his entourage fled to foreign exile. Foreign Minister Aleksander Radivoge and General Dmitris Cincar-Marković signed an unconditional surrender armistice treaty on 17 April, effective the next day. Hitler split Yugoslavia among Germany, Italy, Bulgaria and

Hungary and granted Ante Pavelić, the leader of the Fascist Ustaše Party, the puppet state of Croatia.

Hitler was good to his word to rescue Mussolini in Greece.[38] The Wehrmacht and the Italian army invaded Greece on 6 April. Axis forces included 650,000 Germans with 1,200 tanks and 560,000 Italian troops with 163 tanks. Much of the 450,000-man Greek army was massed in north-west Greece along with General Henry Wilson's 62,000-man British army to attack the Italian army in Albania. From Bulgaria, German panzer divisions led three armies that overran the thin Greek defences to capture Thessaloniki, Greece's second largest city and port on 9 April, Ioannina, the supply centre for the north-west frontier on 21 April and rumble unopposed into Athens on 27 April. The Greek army and government collapsed. Prime Minister Alexander Koryzis committed suicide on 18 April. Commanding General Georgios Tsolakoglou signed an armistice with German General Sepp Dietrich on 20 April.

General Wilson conducted Britain's latest Dunkirk, this one from the Greek mainland, begun on 21 April and completed on 29 April 1941, with some divisions shipped to Alexandria and others to Crete. Churchill recalled: 'In all over 11,000 of our troops were lost and 50,662 were safely brought out . . . This figure represented about eighty per cent of the forces originally sent into Greece . . . The Royal Air Force . . . inflicted on the enemy confirmed losses of 231 planes . . . [t]heir own losses of 209 machines'.[39] On 27 April, Churchill tried papering over the British defeat in Greece with a scathing BBC broadcast against Mussolini for being rescued in Greece by Hitler: 'Here surely is the world record in the domain of the ridiculous and the contemptible. This whipped jackal Mussolini, who to save his skin has made the people of Italy a vassal state of Hitler's empire, goes frisking up to the side of the German tiger with yelps.'[40]

The British held Crete with 28,600 troops. The German assault began on 20 May, this one from the sky as regiments of an airborne division parachuted down to the three main airfields and secured them as another division landed by hundreds of transport planes. The Royal Navy completed Crete's evacuation by 29 May.

Hitler's Wehrmacht scored its latest dazzling victory. German casualties were relatively light – 4,834 killed and wounded. The campaign cost Italy over 125,000 casualties, including 13,755 dead, 50,874 wounded, 12,368 frostbites and 25,067 missing and pressured dead. In stark contrast, the Greek army suffered 13,800 dead, 42,000 wounded and 240,000 captured. Between the Greek mainland and Crete, the British lost 903 dead, 1,250 wounded and 13,945 captured.[41]

Hitler divided Greece between Germany, Italy and Bulgaria, although naturally he reserved the largest and most resource rich regions and cities for the Third Reich. Italy's spoils from the Greek war were limited to the islands of Corfu, Zante and Cephalonia.

The Balkans were yet another dead-end for Italy's army. Thirty Italian divisions in three armies were now dispersed across the mountainous region.[42] Second Army occupied Montenegro, Kosovo and parts of Slovenia and the Dalmatian coast that Mussolini claimed for Italy, along with western Croatia in alliance with Croatia. Ninth Army occupied Albania, Kosovo and part of Macedonia that Mussolini claimed for Italy. Eleventh Army was scattered across Greece's mainland and main islands. With time ever more of those divisions fought losing wars against swelling insurgencies with the most virulent underground army in each being the Communist Party. For instance, in Albania, Italy's army numbered 85,536 Italian and 7,760 auxiliary Albanian troops. Of the Italian troops, 41,220 were deployed in garrisons and only 13,428 were committed to hunting and fighting guerrillas.[43] The most powerful Communist army was Yugoslavia's led by Joseph Broz Tito.

In North Africa, Marshal Rodolfo Graziani revealed himself to be an utterly inept general. Despite that, Mussolini 'does not know whether to have him court-martialled or merely ask him to retire . . . The *Duce* accuses Graziani of having been responsible for three serious things: a blow to Italian military prestige, the coming of the Germans into Italy and the loss of the Empire.'[44] Not just Italy's military grip on its Libyan colony slipped. The humiliating rout of Italy's army emboldened Libyans to attack Italian colonists whose numbers plummeted to 8,426 fearful survivors by December 1941.[45]

Mussolini shipped piecemeal divisions of the Sixth Army based in the Po River valley to Libya. Among them were the Ariete (Ram) armoured division and the Trento and Trieste motorized divisions, respectively the army's best tank and mechanized troops. Ariete's tanks initially were L3/35 Light Tanks with twin machine guns. Gradually, it received infusions of M13/40 tanks with revolving turrets mounted with 47mm guns that survived the gauntlet of Royal navy submarines and warplanes based on Malta. Another good unit was the Young Fascist (*Giovanni Fascist*) 3,000-man Blackshirt mechanized reconnaissance brigade. The Young Fascists conducted a series of daring raids behind enemy lines.

Hitler appointed General Erwin Rommel to command newly designated German African Corps (*Deutsches Afrika Korps*, DAK) on 5

February.[46] Rommel arrived by plane at Tripoli on February 11, 1941. The Afrika Korps initially consisted of the 15th Panzer and 21st Light Divisions mostly equipped with Panzer III tanks with 50mm guns.

Mussolini named General Ettore Bastico Libya's governor general and commander-in-chief of Axis forces in North Afrika on 19 July 1941. Officially, that subordinated Rommel to Bastico including getting him to approve his plans and obeying his orders. In practice, Rommel mostly ignored Bastico and had aides send him banal vague reports.

Bastico was a traditional Italian officer obsessed with *Bella Figura* appearances of immaculate uniforms, formal speech and rigid distances between ranks. Even worse he channelled the Italian army's obsession with massed infantry assaults against the enemy's front, with tanks at most supporting, never leading. He complained incessantly not only that Rommel paid him no more than sporadic and fleeting attention but dashed about the front by car and plane from unit to unit rather than staying at headquarters like a proper general. Moreover, Rommel mingled with common soldiers, giving them pep talks and listening to their concerns rather than keeping magisterially aloof.

Eighth Army was a skeleton in March 1941 because of all the troops, warplanes, tanks and supplies diverted to the Greek debacle. Atop that, Field Marshal Archibald Wavell, the theatre commander, replaced brilliant General Richard O'Connor with the mediocrity General Philip Neame as Eighth Army's chief; O'Connor would advise Neame.

Rommel launched the Afrika Korps backed by three Italian divisions in the first of a series of sweeping flanking attacks against Eighth Army on 7 March 1941. The blitzkrieg devastated and routed Eighth Army whose remnants eventually fell back to Solum in eastern Libya. Multiplying the disaster, an advanced German reconnaissance unit captured O'Connor and Neame on 6 April. The only bright spot was the 33,000-strong British garrison that held Tobruk far in the Axis rear.

As Mussolini 'won' one war in Greece, he lost another.[47] General Luigi Amedeo, the Duke of Savoia-Aosta, was Ethiopia's viceroy and army commander in East Africa. Italian forces in East Africa appeared formidable on paper – 47,000 regular troops, 27,000 Fascist militia, 182,000 white-officered native troops, 17,000 paramilitary police or 273,000 altogether.[48] As with Italian forces elsewhere, their paper strength far exceeded the real strength.

Facing that huge Italian army were around 9,000 British and native troops in Sudan and 8,500 in Kenya. Initially, the Italian army was successful. Aosta's army invaded British Somalia on 3 August 1940, captured the port of Berbera on 19 August and Sidi el Barrani on 12 September 1940. That would be the peak for Italy's East Africa empire.

The British swelled two armies with reinforcements, General William Platt's in Sudan and General Alan Cunningham's in Kenya. Cunningham's offensive with 75,000 troops into Italian Somaliland began on 16 January 1941, captured Mogadishu on 25 February, then curled north-west into Ethiopia to capture Jijiga on 17 March. A British force recaptured Berbera, British Somalia's port and capital on 16 March, then joined forces with Cunningham's army. Meanwhile, Platt's offensive with 60,000 troops had begun on 8 February and steadily fought eastward to capture Asmara on 1 April and Massawa on 8 April, then drove south into Ethiopia. Cunningham's army captured Addis Ababa on 6 April 1941 and Emperor Haile Selassie triumphantly retook his throne. Aosta surrendered to the British on 19 May 1941, a mere five years after the Italian army marched triumphantly into Addis Abada on 5 May 1936. Italian forces suffered 6,300 dead and 8,700 wounded regular and Fascist troops, as many as 25,000 dead and 28,000 wounded colonial troops and 230,000 captured. The British suffered 1,650 dead and 74,000 hospitalized, most from disease.[49]

The Royal Navy scored a lopsided victory in the Battle of Matapan from 27 to 29 March 1941, in waters south of Crete. Admiral Andrew Cunningham's flotilla of one aircraft carrier, three battleships, seven light cruisers and seventeen destroyers intercepted Admiral Angelo's Lachino's flotilla of one battleship, six heavy cruisers, two light cruisers and thirteen destroyers. Cunningham attacked with warplanes and gun barrages while Lachino's captains ineffectively fired back. The British sank three heavy cruisers and two destroyers, damaged the battleship and a destroyer, killed 2,303 sailors and plucked 1,411 others from the sea at the cost of one man killed, four light cruisers damaged and one torpedo bomber shot down.[50]

Nine months later, the Royal Italian Navy eventually won a measure of vengeance for Matapan and other defeats. An Italian submarine bore commandos with human torpedoes near the entrance to Alexandria harbour on the dark night of 19 December 1941. The teams entered the harbour and planted warheads that sank the battleships HMS *Valiant* and *Queen Elizabeth.*

Hitler's greatest ambition was to conquer the Soviet Union.[51] He had intended to launch a massive offensive in early May 1941, but had to delay that for seven weeks to rescue Mussolini from his failure to defeat Greece. He diverted half a million troops and over a thousand tanks to conquer Yugoslavia and Greece and kept nearly 100,000 troops to repress and exploit those countries. Had the Wehrmacht juggernaut invaded the Soviet Union on 1 May rather than 22 June, the Germans probably would have captured Leningrad, Moscow and Rostov by mid-autumn. Had that happened Stalin might have cut a deal that yielded territory and other resources to Germany or withdrawn further east to a distant defensive line and fought on.

Nonetheless, Hitler massed 3.8 million German and other Axis troops split among three army groups on the frontier against the Red Army's initial three million troops and 11,000 tanks in the western Soviet Union. To the Axis offensive, Mussolini initially contributed a 62,000-man 'Special Corps in Russia' (*Corpo di Spedizione in Russia*, CSIR) split among two infantry divisions, one partly mechanized divisions and a Blackshirt brigade led by General Giovanni Messe from 13 July. That corps also fielded 5,500 motorized transport vehicles, 4,600 horses and mules, 220 guns, 94 anti-tank guns, 82 warplanes and 60 light tanks. That contribution came from sixty-three Italian divisions, including three armoured and two mechanized divisions in mid-1941. Mussolini intended to raise another twenty-six divisions including three armoured and six mechanized divisions over the next year. He actually mobilized a fraction of that.[52]

The German onslaught was stunningly successful. Each army group's commander conducted brilliant armour-led offensives that broke through key stretches of the enemy lines to encircle and destroy entire armies. Over six months, the Germans inflicted 4.5 million casualties, including around four million prisoners, while suffering a million casualties.

The Germans deployed the Italian Corps in mopping-up operations against Soviet troop remnants behind the front line on the Southern Front. Having believed that the Axis would conquer the Soviet Union within a few months, Mussolini and Chief of Staff Cavallero did not send winter coats, boots and blankets to the Italian Corps. Over the winter, 4,600 troops suffered crippling frostbite with the loss of toes, fingers and other body parts.

Meanwhile, President Franklin Roosevelt was determined to provide Britain and its allies with all the military aid possible to sustain their war against Germany and Italy. His first major contribution came on 2 September 1940, when he and Churchill agreed that the United States would swap fifty destroyers in return for 99-year rights to air and naval bases in Newfoundland, Bermuda, St. Lucia, the Bahamas, Jamaica and Guiana. That bolstered the Royal Navy and let Britain withdraw forces from those bases to reinforce more crucial forces elsewhere.

Roosevelt took a critical step when he convinced majorities in the Senate and House of Representatives to pass the Lend-Lease Bill which he signed into law on 11 March 1941. Under Lend-Lease, the United States eventually gave $50.1 billion in military aid to countries fighting the Axis powers, including $31.4 billion to Britain, $11.3 billion to the Soviet Union, $3.2 billion to France and $1.6 billion to China. The most vital aid was to Moscow, an amount that supplied around 10 per cent of its military needs; without that, the Germans might well have defeated the Soviet Union. Lend-Lease was 17 per cent of America's military budget during the war or nearly one in five dollars spent.

In small flotillas, Roosevelt and Churchill with their respective chiefs of staff traversed long stretches of the Atlantic Ocean infested with German submarines to rendezvous at Argentia, Newfoundland from 9 to 12 August 1941. In their first summit, the two men bonded as friends and allies. They and their staffs discussed the global military situation and what the United States might do if it entered the war.

Roosevelt and Churchill formulated and signed the Atlantic Charter of eight principles that they were dedicated to upholding on 12 August which they released to the world two days later. Those principles included no territorial gains for themselves nor territorial changes for others without the consent of those involved; the right of people to self-government and restoration for those deprived of it; free international trade, freedom of the seas and economic development for all nations; international justice for all peoples; and cooperation of all nations in promoting international peace and security.[53]

Roosevelt and Churchill agreed to split defence of Atlantic Ocean sea lanes between them with America's navy patrolling the western and Britain the eastern sides. Roosevelt gave American naval captains the order to shoot at any German submarines. On 31 October, a German submarine sank the destroyer USS *Reuben James* that was escorting a convoy to Britain, killing 116 of the 160-man crew. Roosevelt did not ask Congress for a declaration of war against Germany, worried that even if a majority was in favour, a large minority opposed would reveal weakness to the enemy.

Then the Japanese navy attacked America's fleet and air force at Pearl Harbor, Hawaii on 7 December 1941. The Japanese fleet included six aircraft carriers whose 353 aircraft made two waves of attacks that sank four battleships, damaged four more, destroyed 188 warplanes, damaged 159 warplanes, killed 2,403 military personnel and wounded 1,178 others. The devastating attack was the first of a half year series of military campaigns whereby Japanese task forces invaded and captured the American colony of the Philippines, the British colonies of Malaya, Singapore and Burma and the Dutch colony of the East Indies or Indonesia. The Japanese gambled that their attacks would be so devastating that the Americans could never muster the hard and soft power that could eventually defeat them.

Roosevelt asked Congress for a declaration of war on 8 December; the Senate approved by 82 to zero and the House of Representatives by 388 to 1. He would have liked to have included Germany in that declaration but could not justify it. To his relief, Hitler and Mussolini announced on 11 December, that they would join Japan in its war against America.

Foreign Minister Ciano recorded the reaction in Berlin and Rome to Pearl Harbor:

> A night telephone call from [Foreign Minister] Ribbentrop; he is joyful over the Japanese attack on the United States. He is so happy, in fact, that I congratulated him even though I am not so sure about the advantages. One thing is now certain: America will enter the conflict and the conflict will be long enough to permit her to put all her potential strength into action. This is what I said to the King this morning, when he too expressed his satisfaction. He ended by admitting that in 'the long run' I might be right.[54]

The reality that Italy would wage war against America did not deeply worry Mussolini. He mostly disdained Americans and their president, viewing them through odious stereotypes. For instance, in May 1939, he offended Ambassador William Philips by asserting that 'America is in the hands of the Jews'. Mussolini detested Roosevelt. His wife Rachele recalled that the president was the only statesman that 'he never liked . . . He thought him a mistaken idealist who was fanning the flames of war and that, like all Americans, he hadn't the slightest notion of European problems. He said to a journalist one day: "You'll see. Once the Americans have set foot in Europe it will not be easy to shift them"'.[55] Typically, he focused on one superficial Roosevelt trait, his lower body's paralysis from polio, and was oblivious to the president's underlying rock-hard character and dazzling political skills. At one point, he ranted that 'never in the course of history has a nation been guided by a paralytic. There have been bald kings, fat kings, handsome and even stupid kings, but never kings who, in order to go to the bathroom and the dinner table, had to be supported by other men.'[56]

Over the next two and a half years, Mussolini and his regime locked themselves into utter delusions about American political, economic, military and culture power. Ciano explained the unbridgeable gap between the ideological correctness that Italians and Germans alike had to parrot and what they secretly believed: 'America is a big bluff. This slogan is repeated by everyone, big and little, in the conference rooms and in the antechambers. In my opinion, the thought of what the Americans can and will do disturbs them all and the Germans shut their eyes to it. But this will not stop them from thinking about what America can do and they feel shivers run down their spines.'[57]

Mussolini's views of America shifted over his 21 years in power and Italy's views subsequently shifted with them. During the 1920s, he expressed his admiration for America's economic dynamism and innovation and welcomed investments in Italy by tycoons like William Randolph Hearst and John Pierpont Morgan. The 1929 Wall Street Crash, caused by unbridled greed, followed by Washington's protectionist policies that caused the global Great Depression soured Mussolini on America. During the 1930s, his contempt for the United States deepened as President Franklin ineffectively and sporadically protested aggression by the Fascist powers, Japan, Italy and Germany. The number of books on America published in Italy reflected that rising interest and anger, with ten books from 1922 to 1929, fifty-one from 1930 to 1940 and seven from 1941 to 1943.[58]

Mussolini envied not just America's hard economic and military power, but more so its soft cultural power. The average American was not just more affluent than people elsewhere but enjoyed an unmatched lifestyle for bettering oneself and having fun. Italians eagerly watched American films and read American novels. America was the first country that most Italians and other emigrants from around the world dreamed of reaching. More importantly, somehow that liberal republic had forged among most of its citizens a profound sense of national pride and identity that Mussolini struggled to impose on Italians through Fascism. The *Encyclopedia Italiana* defined Americanism as 'the admiration, whether naïve or reasoned, but mostly excessive, for American . . . ideas or things, an admiration which at times even becomes a fashion, in contrast to European cultural traditions'.[59] Privately, Mussolini ruefully admitted his admiration for 'this singular America in which every American always owes something to his countrymen, to his city, to the State, to the nation as both a civic and social sense . . . as solidarity, as an obvious fact, as a moral duty. I love that wholly American sense of the majority which decides and which everyone . . . must follow.'[60]

Churchill journeyed with his joint chiefs of staff to Washington where, from 22 December to 14 January 1942, they met with Roosevelt and his joint chiefs of staff. Their first decision was to create the Allied Combined Chiefs of Staff which would officially be headquartered in Washington, although most British service chiefs returned to London, leaving subordinate liaisons behind.

Roosevelt and Churchill called their alliance the United Nations, dedicated to fulfilling the Atlantic Charter's principles. They organized a signing at the White House of the Declaration of the United Nations by envoys of the then twenty-six Allied countries on 1 January 1942. The Big Four were America, Britain, China and the Soviet Union. Once the Soviet Union survived the initial German onslaught and the United States was forced into the global war by Japan's attack, the destruction of the Axis powers was inevitable. The only question was when and how?

Roosevelt, Churchill and the Combined Chiefs debated grand strategy. They swiftly forged a consensus that the priority was to defeat Germany and Italy first then Japan. They failed to agree on a strategy against Germany and Italy. Roosevelt and his staff favoured an invasion of north-west France in late 1942. Churchill and his staff argued for an American invasion of French North Africa and then push eastward to crush the Afrika Korps between Eighth Army pushing westward. The British argued that an invasion of France would fail for lack of enough troops and supplies. An invasion of French North Africa would likely succeed because the French troops were demoralized and divided after the catastrophic 1940 defeat and thus would soon surrender. The green American troops would gain valuable combat experience against second-rate French troops rather than battle-hardened German troops. The Americans and British agreed to disagree for now.

Mussolini's bitterness worsened over his alliance with Hitler and Italian debacles. By March 1942, his disillusion was overwhelming: 'This war is not for the Italian people. The Italian people are not mature or consistent enough for so grave and decisive a test. This war is for the Germans and Japanese, not for us.'[61] Of course, what Mussolini could never admit was that his own decisions ultimately decided Italy's fate.

During each summit with Hitler, Mussolini shrivelled deeper into his feelings of inadequacy and failure. Ciano recalled their April 1942 meeting at Salzburg as typical: 'Hitler talks, talks, talks. Mussolini suffers – he, who is in the habit of talking himself and who instead, has to remain practically silent . . . Mussolini . . . pretended he was listening in ecstasy, continually nodding his head in approval.'[62]

Chronic pain compounded Mussolini's chronic stress of commanding Italy in a war where the nation suffered one shameful, devastating defeat after another, mostly because of his own inept leadership. He was constantly tense, irritable and distracted. His peptic ulcer gnawed away at him. His diet was mostly an array of medicines and liquid foods. He lost 20kg in weight. He moved, recalled and thought sluggishly. Without his daily head shavings, people would see that his receding hair had turned white.

Compounding Mussolini's emotional and physical woes was the crushing news that his son Bruno, an air force pilot, died along with two crew members during a test-flight of a bomber near Pisa on 7 August, 1941. Mussolini vented his grief in letters to his dead son that several months later were published as the book *Parlo con Bruno* (*I Speak with Bruno*). Fears for his children extended to Vittorio, also a pilot and Edda, a nurse who served in Albania then for three months at Stalino, Ukraine on the Russian Front. In March 1941, Edda survived her hospital ship's sinking by British bombers in the Adriatic Sea. She recuperated from the horrors she had experienced by holing up at the casino on Capri and losing lots of money.

The war in North Africa continued strategically to seesaw.[63] British forces in North Africa received two new commanders in 1941, Claude Auchinleck replaced Archibald Wavell as theatre chief in July and General Alan Cunningham became XIII Corps' chief in August. Churchill ordered Cunningham to expand XIII Corps into the Eighth Army on 29 September. For three months, Cunnigham massed reinforcements and supplies until the Eighth Army numbered 118,000 troops and 730 tanks in two corps to Rommel's 119,000 troops and 500 tanks. Cunningham launched a flank attack on 18 November, but lost over 500 tanks over the next four days. Auchinleck replaced Cunnigham with General Neil Ritchie on 25 November. Eighth Army relieved Tobruk on 27 November. With his supplies exhausted, Rommel withdrew his army to Gazala on 7 December, then, as the Eighth Army approached, to El Agheila on 15 December where the Afrika Korps dug in.

Although popularly called the Afrika Korps, Berlin officially renamed *Panzergruppe Afrika*, *Panzerarmee Afrika* on 22 January 1942. It included three Italian corps, XX with the Ariete armoured and Trieste mechanized divisions, XXI with the Pavia, Trento and Sabratha infantry divisions and X with the Bologna and Brescia infantry divisions.

Rommel launched an offensive on 21 January, that drove Eighth Army back to Gazala and captured Benghazi with its huge supply depot on 29 January. Churchill generously acknowledged Rommel's military brilliance during a speech before the House of Commons in January 1942: 'We have a very daring and skilful opponent against us and, may I say across the havoc of war, a great general.'[64]

Rommel outflanked and routed Eighth Army at Gazala on 26 May and in the pursuit over the next month drove the British all the way to El Alamein in Egypt just 70 miles from Alexandria. The greatest victory was capturing Tobruk with 33,000 defenders on 21 June. Overall, Rommel's troops inflicted over 50,000 casualties and destroyed or captured 1,188 armoured vehicles while suffering 3,600 German and 3,000 Italian casualties and 400 German and 125 Italian tanks. Auchinleck, the Theatre Commander, sacked Ritchie and assumed command of Eighth Army on 25 June.

Churchill was with Roosevelt in the White House when they learned that Rommel had captured Tobruk. Churchill recalled that:

> This was one of the heaviest blows . . . during the war. Not only were its military effects grievous, but it effected the reputation of the British armies. At Singapore 85,000 men had surrendered to inferior numbers of Japanese. Now a garrison of . . . 33,000 . . . seasoned soldiers had laid down their arms to perhaps one-half their number . . . Defeat is one thing; disgrace is another.[65]

Roosevelt consoled Churchill by agreeing to his call for an American army to land in French Morocco and Algeria in late autumn then fight eastward to crush Axis force against Britain's Eighth Army fighting westward. Roosevelt had his Joint Chiefs of Staff begin planning that invasion, codenamed Operation Torch, with General Dwight Eisenhower as its commander.

Mussolini visited Libya for three weeks from 29 June to 20 July 1942. He spent most of his time with General Bastico who scapegoated Rommel for the Italian military's failures. Although, of course, the Italian command was responsible for its own defeats, German arrogance exacerbated their humiliation. *Il Duce* was angered that Rommel 'did not pay him a visit during the three weeks and more that Mussolini spent there. The attitude of the soldiers is also insolent. German motor vehicles do not yield the right of way to anyone, even to our generals and at the slightest opportunity of acquiring a little booty take everything.'[66]

Rommel launched a series of attacks on the British position at El Alamein from 1 to 27 July, but they failed to break through. The

150,000 British troops actually outnumbered the 56,000 German and 40,000 Italian troops. The Axis forces inflicted 13,250 casualties while suffering around 10,000 killed and wounded and 7,000 captured.

Critical to the North Africa campaign was the British-held island of Malta, an unsinkable aircraft carrier mid-way between Sicily and Tunisia. The German and Italian air forces bombed Malta to rubble, but the British borrowed deeper underground. In between attacks, the British emerged to clear the rubble and wreckage from their airfields and fly retaliatory strikes.

Cavallero wanted to mass Axis forces to capture Malta led by Italian and German airborne divisions. Italy's contribution would be the Folgore Airborne and La Spezia divisions. Hitler was leery of an airborne invasion of Malta. German airborne divisions had suffered devastating casualties while capturing Crete in May 1941. He feared similar losses in Malta with the good chance the Allies might hold out and capture the entire force if it could not be reinforced. With the Malta operation blocked, Mussolini sent the Folgore and La Spezia divisions to Libya.

Mussolini wrangled a concession from Hitler that typically undermined their alliance. On 18 September, *Panzerarmee Afrika* under Rommel was renamed Italo-German Panzer Army (*Armata Corazzata Italo-Tedesca,* ACIT) under control of Italy's Supreme Command (*Commando Supremo,* CS) or Chief of Staff. From now, the Supreme Command approved Rommel's plans.

Atop that bureaucratic entanglement, the Afrika Korps suffered a devastating loss when the Royal Navy and Air Force sank three submarines and supply ships carrying 730 tons of fuel oil bound for Libya on 27 and 28 August and 3 September. Britain's 'Ultra' codebreaking programme led to those crucial victories at sea.

Churchill replaced Auchinleck with Harold Alexander as theatre commander on 8 August. He assigned General William Gott to command Eighth Army, but his plane was shot down on 7 August. Churchill named second choice General Bernard Montgomery Eighth Army's commander on 8 August.[67]

Montgomery massed 230,000 troops against Rommel's 90,000 troops (40,000 German and 50,000 Italian) or nearly a three to one advantage, 1,029 to 547 tanks, 750 to 350 warplanes, 435 to 192 armoured cars, 908 to 552 artillery pieces and 1,451 to 499 anti-tank guns. The Americans contributed to Montgomery's buildup by sending ships packed with 300 Sherman tanks and 100 self-propelled guns to Alexandria.

Montgomery launched his campaign with a devastating artillery and bombing barrage on 23 October, followed by a massive infantry and tank assault. He continued his attacks until Eighth Army finally crushed and routed the enemy on 11 November. In all, British forces killed at least 2,000, wounded 4,000 and captured 35,000 Axis troops and destroyed over 500 tanks while suffering 13,560 casualties and 390 destroyed tanks. Rommel withdrew his surviving forces ever westward as Montgomery's Eighth Army slowly followed.

General Dwight Eisenhower commanded the American invasion of French Morocco and Algeria, codenamed Operation Torch.[68] The plan was for three corps-sized task forces to land at widely separate places, General George Patton's Western at Fedala near Casablanca, Safi and Mehdia in Morocco, General Lloyd Fredendall's Central at beaches on either side of Oran, Algeria and General Charles Ryder's Eastern at beaches on either side of Algiers, Algeria. Each task force numbered around 32,000 troops with Americans composing Western and Central while Eastern was American and British.

Eisenhower and the Combined Chiefs had debated not invading Morocco and instead invading Tunisia much closer to the Afrika Korps battling Eighth Army in Libya. That idea was rejected for fear the Tunisian invasion would be too vulnerable to Axis warplane attacks from Sicily air bases and beyond air support from British held Gibraltar. Tragically, Eisenhower placed America's most aggressive general, Patton, the furthest from the Afrika Korps and two untested generals much closer. Among the war's what-ifs is Patton's task force landing in lightly defended Tunisia instead of Morocco. That might well have bagged Axis forces in North Africa in December 1942 rather than half a year later in May 1943. And that in turn would have advanced the timetables of subsequent campaigns along with the war's end in Europe.

The task forces landed on 8 November and within days each had subdued the French forces before them. By chance, Admiral Jean Darlan, Vichy's commander-in-chief, was visiting his sick son, a soldier in Algeria. He agreed to sign an armistice on 10 November, in return for being named High Commissioner for French North Africa.

Word of the Allied invasion of Morocco and Algeria stunned Mussolini, Hitler and their High Commands. Hitler wrote to Mussolini that to 'give up Africa means to give up the Mediterranean' and that 'would mean not only the ruin of revolutions, but also the ruin of our people's futures'.[69] Mussolini concurred, calling 'the landing of the American army in the Mediterranean . . . an event of major strategic significance, destined to modify if not reverse the balance of power in a sector where Italy had always considered of the greatest importance'.[70]

Hitler talked Mussolini into accepting Marshal Albert Kesselring as his deputy commander on 10 November 1942. Kesselring established his headquarters near Frascati, 20 miles south of Rome. In return for that, Hitler agreed that Rommel, who officially was already under General's Bastico's command, must start following his orders. Mussolini dispatched Chief of Staff Ugo Cavallero to Tripoli with orders to General Bastico to defend Libya to the last soldier. On 13 November, Cavallero flew to Benghazi, Rommel's current headquarters. Fearing a confrontation or, worse, conversion, Cavallero did not meet Rommel, but instead sent him an order strictly subordinating him to Bastico's command. Rommel continued to ignore orders from Cavallero and Bastico because they were now under Kesselring's command, with whom the Desert Fox consulted for key strategic choices.

Rommel's first choice under the new command structure was to withdrew the Afrika Korps' remnants from Benghazi on 19 November and deploy it at Agedabia, 600 miles west of Alamein. Kesselring arranged a meeting among Rommel, Cavallero and Bastico at the Arco dei Fileni or victory arch at the border between Tripolitania and Cyrenaica on 24 November. The next day they received Mussolini's order to standfast at the Marsa Brega Line at El Agheila Pass. Rommel flew back to Berlin to meet Hitler, who promised to send three divisions to Tripoli. He then flew with Hermann Göring to meet Mussolini and Cavallero in Rome.

Eighth Army advanced on the Marsa Brega Line. Facing obliteration from Eighth Army's overwhelming forces, Rommel disobeyed orders and withdrew westward. He abandoned Tripoli without a fight and did not stop until he reached the 40-mile Mareth Line in Tunisia stretching between the sea 50 miles south of Gabes and the rugged Matmata Hills.

Meanwhile, Torch's easternmost task force at Algiers was 500 miles from Tunis. Eisenhower consolidated the Allied forces in Algeria into the British First Army commanded by General Kenneth Anderson and ordered it to advance eastward. First Army eventually included the British IX Corps, the French V Corps and the American II Corps. With no opposition, First Army rumbled swiftly forward and reached north-eastern Tunisia in mid-November.

Hitler and Mussolini rushed troops to Bizerte and Tunis to form what became the German LXXXX Corps led by General Walther Nehring. As units arrived, Nehring deployed them in two semicircles a score or so miles from Bizerte and Tunis. By mid-November, just 16,000 German and 9,000 Italian troops defended those lines.

Anderson's First Army launched a three-pronged offensive on 21 November, that punched through those defences and advanced as far as Jefna, Chouigui and Djedeida until Axis troops stopped them. With reinforcements, Nehring counter-attacked on 1 December and Axis troops drove First Army back to a north-south line in central northern Tunisia along the Grand Dorsal Mountain Range, with the Axis controlling the passes. Over the next four months, that front remained largely stagnant except for a successful German offensive and then successful American counteroffensive. Hitler replaced Nehring with General Hans-Jurgen von Arnim on 8 December and with reinforcements expand the German corps into the Fifth Panzer Army.

Roosevelt, Churchill and the Combined Chiefs of Staff met at Casablanca, Morocco, from 14 to 24 January 1943. Planning strategy was the key reason for their meeting. Capturing the Axis army in Tunisia was a matter of months. The key question was where next to invade. Roosevelt and his staff wanted to ship most American and British troops to Britain from which in May 1944, they would invade Normandy the same time that another Allied army invaded the French Riviera with the two eventually joining forces in eastern France. Churchill, backed by his staff, insisted on his 'soft underbelly' strategy of attacking eastward across the Mediterranean basin, first Sicily followed by the Italian peninsula, Balkans and Greece. His winning argument was that the Allies should always fight the Axis somewhere. Why shelve half a million or so troops in Britain for a year when they could instead liberate nearby Sicily?[71] Roosevelt agreed with Churchill and got his reluctant staff to go along. For the invasion, they agreed that Marshal Harold Alexander would command the Army Group that included Generals George Patton and Bernard Montgomery respectively heading the American Seventh and British Eighth Armies.

The fate of Mussolini and Italy now rested in the hands of Roosevelt, Churchill and the Combined Chiefs of Staff. A key question was whether Mussolini could somehow be enticed to change sides. Italy had suffered a series of humiliating defeats. Surely, Mussolini would recognize that winning the war was impossible now that America, the Soviet Union and Britain were united against the Axis. To avoid his regime's inevitable destruction, he might grasp a Allied offer to stay in power in return for joining ranks with them.

Secretary of State Cordell Hull revealed that:

> President Roosevelt and I believed almost from the time of Mussolini's declaration of war against the United States, four days after Pearl Harbor, that we should draw a distinction between the Italians on the one hand and the Germans and Japanese on the other . . . [that] it might be possible to withdraw Italy from the war before the surrender of Germany and Japan and that this withdrawal would in fact hasten their surrender. Italy's retirement . . . would be accelerated if we were to adopt an attitude toward the Italians different from that toward the Germans and Japanese.[72]

Analysts of America's Office of Strategic Services (OSS) concluded that Mussolini's commitment to his alliance with Hitler was probably unbreakable. Yet every military disaster alienated more Italians, including those within his regime. Perhaps the dissidents could be encouraged to overthrow him. In November 1942 an American proposal to do that circulated through the High Commands in Washington and London.

The British rejected that notion:

> There is nothing to be gained by making any direct or indirect appeal to both sentiment and history or holding out any inducement to the Italian people or armed forces to overthrow the Fascist regime and abandon the Germans. A policy of appeals and promises could only be really effective when there was a question of building up some dissident movement or leader which could challenge established government. At present there is no such movement or leader in Italy nor are there any potential leaders outside Italy of sufficient calibre.[73]

On the last day of the Casablanca conference, Roosevelt announced to the press corps that:

> The elimination of German, Japanese and Italian war power means the unconditional surrender by Germany, Italy and Japan. That means a reasonable assurance of future world peace. It does not mean the destruction of the population of Germany, Italy or Japan, but it does mean the destruction of the philosophies in those countries which are based on conquest and the subjection of other people.[74]

Although Roosevelt and Churchill had agreed on that policy, the prime minister wanted to keep it secret for fear that if the Fascist leaders knew the Allies would destroy them and their regimes, they would fight to the death. Churchill had favoured omitting Italy from that policy to encourage a break between Mussolini and Hitler. He yielded not just to Roosevelt but also his own staff that unconditional surrender would include Italy. Now with the secret revealed, Churchill could only mumble his concurrence to avoid any show of disunity between them.[75]

Half a year later on 25 July, Italian King Victor Emmanuel would dismiss Mussolini, have him arrested and replace him with Marshal Pietro Badoglio. But rather than immediately declare neutrality and soon switch sides, the king and prime minister assured Hitler that they remained faithful Axis allies. It took them six weeks to muster the backbone to negotiate first an armistice then an alliance with America and Britain.

How much, if at all, the Allied unconditional surrender policy made the new government hesitate is unclear. After all, within days of purging Mussolini they outlawed the Fascist Party. That certainly appeared to accord with the Allied policy of eliminating the Fascist 'philosophy' of 'conquest and subjection'. They could have reassured the Allies that they intended eventually to restore Italy's constitutional monarchy with a freely elected parliament and full civil and human rights for Italians. Churchill did not believe the unconditional surrender policy affected the king and prime minister but attributed their timidity to their weak characters.[76]

As for the future military occupation of Italy, Churchill advised Roosevelt in June 1943 that:

> It seems wise to make [newly conquered regions] run themselves as much as possible. Malignant or prominent Fascists must be removed and we should be prepared to replace them with trustworthy administrators to the extent that these can be found from the local population. I am sure that it would be a mistake to flood all these places with hundreds of British and American gauleiters [proconsuls], however well-meaning and well trained they may be.[77]

Foreign Secretary Anthony Eden explained this potential dilemma:

> The limited objective of converting Italy into a definite liability to Germany may be from the military point of view of even greater value than the bigger objective of actually bringing Italy out of the war, since a neutral or even an Italy fighting on the Allied side could easily develop into a liability for the Allies . . . In the event of an internal collapse, the Germans would have the choice either of abandoning Italy to her fate and making a frontier on the Brenner [Pass] or of sending troops to Italy to restore and possibly maintain the situation . . . A German occupation of Italy would be intensely distasteful to the Italian people, would greatly increase unrest in the country and should predispose the population and thus facilitate any military operations on our own part against Italy.[78]

Meanwhile, on the Eastern Front, Mussolini committed ever more divisions to the Italian Eighth Army led by General Italo Gariboldi throughout the first nine months of 1942. By September, Eighth Army peaked at 229,000 troops in nine divisions split equally among three corps and fielded 16,700 motorized vehicles, 1,150 guns, 19 self-propelled guns, 55 light tanks, 380 45mm anti-tank guns and 25,000 horses and mules.[79] The Germans deployed Eighth Army on the Don River front north of General Paulus's Six Army fighting at Stalingrad. Eighth Army included

Reports about the Eastern Front's horrors including the mass murders and destruction, reached Rome. Ciano summarized a May 1942 report:

> The brutality of the Germans, which has now reached the proportions of a continuous crime . . . leaves no doubt of its truthfulness. Massacres of entire populations, raping, killing of children – all these are matters of daily occurrence. Against his there is the cold Bolshevik decision to resist and fight to the end, certain of victory. On the other hand, the morale of the Germans is lower than might be imagined.[80]

The Soviet counter-attack against the German Sixth Army at Stalingrad began on 19 November 1942 with pincer movements that eventually surrounded the city. The Germans ordered the armies in the region including Gariboldi's Eighth Army to rescue Sixth Army but the Soviet blunted those attacks. General Friedrich Paulus surrendered on 31 January 1943. The Soviets then turned their guns against adjacent Axis armies including Eighth Army. In March, the Red Army routed Eighth Army which 'lost ninety-seven per cent of its artillery, eighty per cent of the horse and mules and seventy per cent of vehicles'. The army suffered 84,830 dead and 27,600 wounded or disabled from frostbite. The Soviets relentlessly destroyed Eighth Army front and rear. The Italians ran a gauntlet of partisans behind the lines who killed 4,000 troops and captured 7,000 during the ten-day retreat. By the summer of 1943, Eighth Army had virtually ceased to exist with 114,520 officials deaths and 95,000 captured. Most prisoners died in captivity.[81]

Mussolini renamed the Axis forces in North Africa the Italian First Army on 30 January 1943. First Army's peak strength was 113,000 troops, 70,000 Italians and 43,000 German split among XX Corps with Italian Giovanni Fascisti and Trieste Divisions and the German 90th Light Division; XXI Corps with the Italian La Spezia and Pistoia Divisions and the German 164th Light Divisions; and the autonomous German 15th

Panzer and Italian Centauro Armoured Divisions. German armoured divisions now included Panzer IVs with long 75mm guns and Mark VI Tigers with thicker armour and 88mm guns. Each of those tanks was superior to the American Sherman with its short 75mm gun and the British Crusaders with 57mm guns. The Italian navy performed admirably convoying supply ships to Tunisia. From 1 December 1942 to 8 May 1943, 157,000 troops, 8,500 vehicles, 400 tanks and armoured cars reached Tunisia; 306,500 tons of 433,169 tons of supplies and 94,000 tons of 133,000 tons of fuel oil were unloaded.[82] Nonetheless, the Germans were caustic about their Italian allies. Kesselring loved the sensuality of Italian culture but deplored its negative military effects: 'The Italian is easily contented. He actually has three fashionable passions: coffee, cigarettes and women . . . The Italian soldier is not a soldier from within . . . Combat value of the almost totally untried Italian units is the great question.'[83]

Montgomery's Eighth Army entered Tripoli unopposed on 23 January 1943, three to four months and 1,117 miles from the beginning of the El Alamein campaign. Montgomery's army deployed before the Mareth Line on 15 February 1943, three months and 1,300 miles after Alamein.

Eisenhower gave British General Harold Alexander command of the Army Group of the First and Eighth British Armies. The Axis and Allied defences along either side of the Dorsal front in central Tunisia and the southern Mareth Line appeared formidable, but Rommel spotted a weakness. There was a hundred-mile gap between the southern end Anderson's First Army and Montgomery's Eighth. First Army's north-south line included the British IX Corps northward, the French V Corps central and the American II Corps southward. Intelligence reports revealed that II Corps was poorly deployed, organized, supplied and led by General Lloyd Fredendall, who cowered with his staff in a bombproof underground bunker 75 miles from the front.

Rommel launched a pincer attack by Fifth Army's 10th Panzer and First Army's 21st Panzer divisions on 14 February that over the next week drove II Corps back 50 miles. That engagement became known as the Battle of Kasserine Pass for its key position that the Germans overran. Eisenhower replaced Fredendall with Patton on 7 March. Patton rebuilt II Corps' ranks, supplies, discipline and morale.

Meanwhile, Hitler withdrew Rommel for an extended sick leave on 9 March. He accepted Mussolini's choice to replace him with General Giovanni Messe, who had proficiently led Italy's Eighth Army on the Eastern Front. Mussolini lauded Messe as a general and soldier, whose 'military past may be brilliant. In the First World War he held various commands, even of shock troops toward the end and as an "*ardito*" [Commando] he was known and respected among ex-servicemen. From the Fascist political point of view he was generally considered one of the safest of the generals who were more or less complacent recipients of the Party ticket'. Mussolini described Messe as 'below the average in height, his face is broad and open – he has a clear eye which looks you straight in the face and his speech is blunt; on seeing him you would conclude that he is a gentleman, that is he is a man sincere and loyal'.[84]

Then came the series of defeats that the Allies inflicted on Messe's army in Tunisia culminating with the Axis surrender in May 1943. For Mussolini, those defeats were not inevitable given the overwhelming Allied forces arrayed against them, but revealed that behind his earlier admirable record and stately façade lurked 'one of the most typical and loathsome traitors . . . and for me represented one of my most disagreeable surprises'.[85] Messe's Tunisia defeats had many causes, but treason was not among them.

Messe's first defeat began with simultaneous attacks by Montgomery's Eighth Army and Patton's II Corps on 16 March. Montgomery outflanked the Mareth Line by sending two corps in a long loop around the Matamata Hills that smashed through the Tebaga Pass on 27 March and threatened to cut off First Army. Patton launched II Corps in a two-pronged attack that routed Axis forces and by 25 March, captured the Maknassy and Sened passes leading respectively to the ports of Sfax and Gabes, approximately 40 miles distant.

That forced Messe to withdraw north to a new line. Patton asked Alexander for permission to punch eastward and cut off Messe's retreat. Alexander ordered him to stay put because Montgomery was supposed to do that. Montgomery, however, failed to push forward to the sea in time and Messe escaped with most of his army. The Axis armies now formed a 140-mile defence line that began a score or so miles west of Bizerte and arched to end a score or so miles south of Tunis.

Amidst the unfolding disaster in Tunisia, Benito Mussolini made scapegoats of several key advisors including Dino Grandi, Minister of Grace and Justice and President of Fasces and Corporations; Education Minister Giuseppe Bottai; and even Foreign Minister Galeazzo Ciano, his son-in-law. Ciano recalled that fateful late afternoon when 'the *Duce* calls me. The moment I enter the room I perceive that he is very much embarrassed. I grasp what he is trying to tell me . . . then adds in a low voice that he is changing his entire cabinet.' As compensation, he offers

Ciano the viceroyalty of Albania. That Ciano adamantly rejected. He had no intention of 'going as the executioner and hangman of those people to whom I promised brotherhood'.[86] He settled for being Italy's ambassador to the Vatican, a plunge in status and power but at least safe and close to home.

Chief of Staff General Vittorio Ambrosio sent a wish list to Berlin in February 1943, that included 750 tanks, 7,400 trucks, 750,000 anti-tank mines, 500 aircraft, 326 radar systems, 40 sonar systems, 30 minesweepers, eight frigates and twelve motor torpedo boats. Nonplussed, Ambrosio followed that up in April with a list that included 1,250 tanks, 372 cannons, 1,350 anti-tank guns, 7,400 trucks, 500 aircraft and aviation fuel.[87] Italy received a fraction of those requests.

By late April 1943, Allied forces in Tunisia numbered over 500,000 troops and 1,400 tanks split among the twenty divisions of First and Eighth Armies. Axis forces numbered around 250,000 troops including 157,000 Germans and 87,000 Italians split between the German Fifth Panzer Army and Italian First Army. The Allies enjoyed plentiful food, munitions and other vital supplies, along with overwhelming air, tank and naval power, while Axis forces lacked all that. Messe sent this dire message to Mussolini on 22 April:

> Owing to the very serious exhaustion of the troops, the inadequacy of artillery and ammunition and the almost complete lack of armoured vehicles compared with the enemy's crushing superiority in material, the situation is growing steadily greyer. Our air force – and our ally's as well – may be called non-existent compared with the really overwhelming and intensively active enemy air force. In spite of all, you may be sure that the order to resist to the last will be faithfully carried out.[88]

The Allied armies launched a joint offensive on 22 April that punched through the Axis lines in a score of places. By 7 May, Allied forces were fighting their way into Bizerte and Tunis. Arnim agreed to surrender on 8 May. The Allies captured a quarter of a million Axis troops at the cost of 70,000 casualties over the past half year, starting with the Alamein and Torch campaigns. The Tunisia campaign was among the war's most decisive turning points, ranking with Midway, Stalingrad and Normandy. Just where the Allies pivoted after Tunisia, was controversial then and since. But what is unquestionable is that it led to the overthrow of Benito Mussolini and his Fascist regime, at least briefly.

Chapter 9

THE OVERTHROW

> I am certainly the most intensely disliked or, rather, loathed man in Italy, which is only natural on the part of the ignorant, suffering, victimized, under-nourished masses subject to the terrible physical and moral burden… Political and military circles aim their sharpest criticisms at those who bear the responsibility for the military conduct of the war. (Benito Mussolini)

During the Casablanca Conference in January 1943, the Allied leaders agreed that Sicily would be the next objective after vanquishing the Axis in North Africa. Two armies, George Patton's Seventh and Bernard Montgomery's Eighth, would invade the island on 8 July. The successful landing of those armies led to Benito Mussolini's overthrow.

Pantelleria is a tiny island between Sicily and Tunisia. Mussolini issued orders to transform that island with 10,000 civilians into a fortress to buffer Sicily from any enemy threat launched from Tunisia. He described that effort:

> Some thousands of workmen were sent out there. In the course of a year or two we had to improve the harbour basin so as to make it suitable for ships and other craft of medium tonnage, construct an airfield and a two-storey underground aerodrome, install anti-aircraft and shore batteries, concentrate ample reserves of supplies and munitions, improve the network of communications and mine the short stretches of coast where the possibility of a landing existed… [T]he island contained forty batteries, several squadrons of fighter planes and a garrison of about twelve thousand men.[1]

In March 1943, Mussolini appointed Admiral Gino Pavesi to command the 11,420-man garrison.

What Mussolini sought in Pantelleria was an Italian version of Britain's impregnable Malta. What he got instead was his latest humiliating capitulation. Malta's defenders had endured months of Axis bombing and invasion threats. Starting on 8 May, Pantelleria's defenders endured a month of air and naval bombardment that devastated the towns and fortifications alike, although only 56 people were killed and 116 wounded. On 11 June, Pavesi asked for and received Mussolini's permission to surrender. Mussolini reasoned that: 'To order him to resist to the last seemed to be a useless gesture . . . Pavesi's telegram painted the situation as absolutely untenable.'[2]

General Alfredo Guzzoni commanded Axis forces on Sicily. He had only held that command since 1 June, when Mussolini appointed him to replace the lacklustre General Ezio Rosi. Headquarters was at the plateau-top walled city of Enna in eastern central Sicily. Mussolini detailed Sicily's defenders on 1 July as including:

> 230,000 soldiers of the Army and Fascist Militia (including 10,000 officers) incorporated in six coastal divisions and four mobile divisions (the Napoli, Livorno, Assietta and Aosta), three German divisions, one armoured, plus the air and naval forces. All told, no less than 300,000 men, along with a fairly deep system of strongpoints. There were no fewer than 1,500 pieces of artillery of all calibres and thousands of machine guns.[3]

The Allied invasion of Sicily began on 10 July. Montgomery's Eighth Army landed along a 32-mile stretch of south-east coast between the large port of Syracuse and Pachino. Patton's Seventh Army landed along a 40-mile stretch of southern coast between the small fishing ports of Scoglitti and Licata. Airborne divisions preceded each landing by parachuting to secure positions that diverted the enemy and protected the beaches. After securing their beachheads, the plan was for Montgomery to push north to capture Messina, the port at Sicily's north-east corner and cut off the Axis retreat to the mainland while Patton protected his flank. Instead, Montgomery's advance bogged down before Axis defences from Cantania westward while Patton's divisions spread out to punch through the Axis forces before them and overrun Sicily's western half and capture Palermo on the north coast on 22 July. Patton then turned his army east to fight toward Messina.

Meanwhile, after experiencing the first Allied air bombardment, Guzzoni and his staff fled Enna for various remote rural locations until they ended up in Messina and then a ferry across to the peninsula. In doing so, Guzzoni mostly lost communications and thus command over his army. Without direction from above, division commanders acted autonomously as best they could but often at odds with each other. An Italian journalist explained:

> The effects of which on the unity of our troops and the organization of war services have certainly been deleterious . . . [T]here were plain signs of the formations crumbling up . . . of marines and airmen straggling back to Messina to re-embark and get back to the mainland . . . the case of certain divisions which melted away without fighting . . . The conduct of the Bersaglieri and the Gela coastal division was spoken of. On the other hand, the case of the air and naval formations which dissolved instantly at the mere sight of the enemy forces had a devastating effect.[4]

Guzzoni scapegoated his soldiers for his own inept, cowardly command. He condemned: 'the shameful phenomena of disintegration that has afflicted some units and services of all the armed forces located in Sicily – with no exceptions – which casts deep discredit on the Italian soldier, especially in comparison with the Allied armed forces'. German Colonel Wilhelm Schmaltz identified that disintegration's source: '[T]he lack of fighting spirit among the Italians in Sicily came from the fact that the will to fight originates with commanders and these commanders had lost control of the situation.'[5]

Mussolini's purge of Grandi, Bottai and Ciano from his inner circle earlier in February 1943 did not intimidate his critics and rivals, but enraged and united them. The Allied capture of Tunisia and invasion of Sicily emboldened them to overthrow him. Three groups dedicated to overthrowing Mussolini developed. The key was convincing the timid king to assert his dormant constitutional power and dismiss Mussolini as prime minister.

Former prime minister Ivanoe Bonomi organized a secret coalition among six political parties, from right to left – the Liberal, Labour Democratic, Christian Democratic, Action, Socialists of Proletariat Unity and Communist Parties – that called themselves the United Freedom Front on 27 April 1943. Bonomi intended the United Freedom Front to be the centre-left counter to the Italian Popular Union dominated by the Communist Party, even though he accepted the Communist Party among United Freedom Front's members.

The first direct appeal by Mussolini's opponents to talk the king into dismissing Mussolini took place on 3 July, when Grandi secured an audience with him. Victor Emmanuel offered this guarded but encouraging reply: 'The time will come and I know I can count on you. Let your king choose the right moment and in the meantime help us to find constitutional means.'[6] Meanwhile, Marshals Pietro Badoglio and Enrico Caviglia, Generals Vittorio Ambrosio and Giuseppe Castellano, Duke Pietro Acquarone, the royal household minister, and Bonomi discussed arresting *Il Duce* and other high-ranking Fascists after which the king would have the plotters from a government. Victor Emmanuel rejected that plan when they presented it to him on 15 July. That same day, Grandi, Bottai, Ciano, Roberto Farinacci and Carlo Scorza met at Fascist Party headquarters to discuss Grandi's proposed resolution for the Grand Council to approve for the king to assume supreme executive powers. They enlisted other Grand Council members to make nineteen altogether and on 16 July, asked Mussolini to convene the Grand Council. Mussolini angrily rejected the request.

Hitler sent Mussolini an urgent message requesting a summit. They met at a villa near Feltre, a resort town backed by the Dolomite Mountains in north-east Italy on 19 July. As usual, Hitler dominated the meeting, speaking nearly nonstop as Mussolini occasionally muttered agreement. Mussolini recalled:

> He began his speech with a clear and systematic resume of the raw material situation and the necessity for defending the territories where they were to be found. He went on to speak of the air force, its employment and its present and future possibilities. Passing to the battle now being fought in Sicily, he promised the dispatch of fresh reinforcements, particularly artillery and troops. Suddenly, an aide rushed into the room and whispered, 'At this moment Rome is undergoing a violent enemy air bombardment'. This news, which I . . . conveyed aloud to the *Führer* and bystanders, made a deep and painful impression.

Hitler resumed his harangue as 'news of the attack on Rome continued to come in. Then a talk took place between myself and the *Führer* in which I stressed the necessity of sending further aid to Italy. This talk continued on the return journey in the car and train. On parting from Hitler, I said to him: "Ours is a common cause, *Führer*".'[7]

Mussolini hurried back to Rome, met Victor Emmanuel and explained his talks with Hitler. He 'found the King frowning and nervous. "A tense situation", he said. "It can't go on much longer. Sicily has gone west now. The Germans will double-cross us. The discipline of the troops has broken down. The airmen at Ciampino [Rome's airport] fled as far as Velletri during the attack. They call it "dispersing".' [8]

Over several days, Victor Emmanuel and Duke Pietro d'Acquarone, his confident and Royal Household chief, debated what to do. Finally, the king decided to act decisively. On 22 July, he had d'Acquarone inform Generals Castellano and Ambrosio that within a week he would dismiss Mussolini and ask Badoglio to form a government dedicated to withdrawing Italy from the war.

Mussolini also made a crucial decision. Confident he could rally a majority against the dissidents, he summoned the Fascist Grand

Council to convene at five o'clock on the afternoon of 24 July. Rachele was upset when he told her that he was going to meet his 'comrades'. 'I burst out, "Comrades? Is that what you call that bunch of traitors who are deceiving you? . . . Have them all arrested, Benito. Do that before you even start".'[9]

Mussolini later rued not taking her advice. He opened the session with these remarks: 'The war . . . has reached an extremely critical stage. What seemed impossible . . . even after the entry of the United States in the Mediterranean, has come to pass – the invasion of our home territory.' As a result, he admitted that 'I am certainly the most intensely disliked or, rather, loathed man in Italy, which is only natural on the part of the ignorant, suffering, victimized, under-nourished masses subject to the terrible physical and moral burden . . . Political and military circles aim their sharpest criticisms at those who bear the responsibility for the military conduct of the war.'[10]

Following his speech, Mussolini angrily recalled: 'Grandi began to speak. His speech was a violent philippic: the speech of a man who was at last giving vent to a long-cherished rancour. He bitterly criticized the activity of the Party' and concluded that "It is high time for the King to emerge from obscurity and an assume his responsibilities".'[11] The essence of Grandi's resolution declared:

> [T]he immediate restoration is necessary of all State functions, allotting to the King, the Grand Council, the Government, Parliament and Corporations the tasks and responsibilities laid down by our statutory and constitutional laws. It invites the Head of Government to request His Majesty the King . . . to assume, together with the effective command of the Armed Forces . . . that supreme initiative of decision which our institutions attribute to him.[12]

Then, over nine and a half hours, the members mostly debated Grandi's resolution:

> The discussion was orderly and civilized. It never got out of hand. In fact, every time the speakers flattered me, I interrupted them and asked them not to labour the point. The position of each member of the Grand Council could be discerned even before the voting; there was a group who had negotiated with the Crown, a group of accomplices and a group . . . who probably did not realize the seriousness of the vote.[13]

The Grand Council voted in favour 19 to 8, with one abstention at 2.40 on the morning of 25 July. Enraged, Mussolini rose and declared: '"You have provoked a crisis of the Regime. The session is closed". The Party

Secretary was going to give the "Salute to the *Duce*", when I checked him with a gesture saying, "No, you are excused". They all went away in silence.'[14]

Victor Emmanuel summoned Mussolini to his Villa Savoia Palace residence late on the afternoon of 25 July. Mussolini vividly recalled:

> Everywhere within . . . were reinforcements of Carabinieri . . . The King, in Marshal's uniform, stood in the doorway of the villa. Two officers were stationed in the hall inside. When we had entered the drawing-room, the King, in a state of abnormal agitation and with his features distorted, said, clipping his words: 'My dear *Duce*, it's no longer any good. Italy has gone to bits. Army morale is at rock bottom. The soldiers don't want to fight any more . . . .The Grand Council's vote is terrible . . . At this minute you are the most hated man in Italy'.

He avoided directly saying that he was dismissing Mussolini, but instead said that Marshal Emilio Badoglio would 'form a government'. Mussolini replied that 'I realise the people's hatred . . . One can't govern for such a long time and impose so many sacrifices without provoking resentments . . . I wish good luck to the man who takes the situation in hand.'[15]

What then happened surprised Mussolini:

> [T]he king accompanied me to the door. His face was livid and he looked smaller than ever, almost dwarfish. He shook my hand and went in again. I descended the few steps and went towards my car. Suddenly, a Carabinieri captain stopped me and said: 'His Majesty has charged me with the protection of your person'. I was continuing to my car when the captain said to me, pointing to a motor-ambulance standing nearby, 'No, We must get in there'. I got into the ambulance, together with my secretary . . . A lieutenant, three Carabinieri and two police agents got in as well as the captain and placed them by the door armed with machine guns. When the door was closed, the ambulance drove off at top speed. I still thought that all this was being done, as the King said, to protect my person.[16]

That was partly true, The king had ordered Mussolini's arrest. That evening Italian Radio broadcasted this news: 'His Majesty the King and Emperor has accepted the resignation of His Excellency Cavaliere and Marshal of Italy Benito Mussolini from his duties as chief of government, prime minister and secretary of state and has appointed Cavaliere and Marshal of Italy Pietro Badoglio to be chief of government, prime minister and secretary of state.' Then Badoglio's voice sounded with these words that disappointed countless listeners in Italy and the Allies when they learned of them, but were really targeted at Hitler and his advisors: 'The war is continuing. Italy, the jealous guardian of her age-old traditions, remains loyal to the pledged word.'[17]

News of Mussolini's overthrow inspired mass jubilation and attacks the next day against his discredited regime. Mussolini ruefully admitted that: 'The crowd destroyed the headquarters of all the Fascist organizations, pulled down Lictor symbols, assaulted people and, with a stupid and brutal iconoclasm, wiped out everything that might remind them of Mussolini or Fascism. While thousands of portraits and busts of myself were hurled out of the window, pictures of Victor of Savoy and Pietro Badoglio were hung out everywhere.' Prime Minister Badoglio followed up those popular attacks against Mussolini's defunct regime by issuing orders for 'destroying everything in the sphere of ideas, institutions or anything else created in the twenty years of Fascism'.[18]

Badoglio explained why the overthrow of Mussolini and his Fascist regime was so swift and easy. The Fascist leaders were

> completely out of touch . . . with public opinion . . . They behaved as if they were completely deaf and were consequently cut off from all contact with the people. The King struck one resolute blow at their leader and without any resistance or violence the whole Fascist structure collapse . . . Fascism fell, as was fitting, like a rotten pear.[19]

Mussolini absurdly attributed Victor Emmanuel's decision to these motives:

> The King was behind this plot because he had reason to believe that a victory won or snatched from defeat by Fascism would make him more insignificant than ever. For twenty years he had been awaiting a good opportunity. He was waiting until a certain emotional national frame of mind had been reached, a popular and universal emotion which at a given moment would flare up at a word'.[20]

Of course, the king dismissed Mussolini because Italy's devastating defeat was inevitable if not imminent, not a glorious Fascist victory. Indeed, Victor Emmanuel recognized that the core Fascist value of imperialism was ultimately self-destructive as it provoked an overwhelming enemy alliance to rise against and destroy it.

Over the next few weeks, the police first took Mussolini to a barracks outside Rome followed by the island of Ponza on 28 July, the island of Maddelena on 8 August and finally, on 28 August, Hotel Campo Imperatore at Gran Sasso in the Apennine Mountains, a hundred mostly rugged road miles from Rome.

Meanwhile, for 45 days, nearly seven weeks, Victor Emmanuel III and Badoglio squandered a chance to save mainland Italy from becoming a battlefield with hundreds of thousands of dead, wounded and homeless and hundreds of shattered cities and towns. They failed immediately to send a secret message asking for talks with the Allies. Instead, they diligently performed their duties as a faithful German ally.[21]

Hitler and his High Command naturally were appalled to learn that the Fascist Grand Council and King Victor Emmanuel III had overthrown Mussolini and replaced him with Badoglio as prime minister. Hitler had Ambassador Hans Georg von Mackensen ask the king about the status of the alliance and permission to visit Mussolini. Victor Emmanuel had Badoglio assure Mackensen that 'Italy remained a faithful ally and that [w]hile confirming the excellent care enjoyed by H.E. Mussolini and his complete satisfaction with the treatment accorded him, Marshal Badoglio regrets that he is unable . . . to consent to the proposed visit.'[22]

Fearing that Badoglio's government would soon announce Italy's neutrality or, far worse, join the Allies, Hitler ordered seven divisions to reinforce the five divisions already in the country. By early August those German divisions were deployed alongside Italian divisions around Italy and their commanders instructed to prepare plans to immediately disarm them when the order arrived.

The king and prime minister issued decrees that abolished the Fascist Party, the Fascist Grand Council, the Chamber of Fasces and Corporations and the Supreme Tribunal for the Defence of the State, integrated the Fascist militia within the army on 28 July. Badoglio named General Mario Roatta the military Chief of Staff and General Giacomo Carboni the national police chief. The King established a Commission of Judges under the President of the Court of Causation to investigate allegations of massive corruption by Fascist leaders and retrieve any money, property and other benefits that had been illegally taken.

The Allies rejoiced at news of Mussolini's overthrow. Churchill expressed the fervent hope of all of them 'that Italy, free from Mussolini's dictatorship, might fight on our side, which she did for several years of the [last] war with lasting beneficial results to the state of Europe'.[23] However, no official in Washington or London publicly called for that. The Allied leaders assumed that the new government would announce its neutrality as a first possible step to alliance and that itself might trigger a German invasion. Hitler had the Wehrmacht invade his puppet Vichy French regime led by Pétain after the Allies invaded French North Africa; Hitler eliminated Vichy's autonomy and subordinated it totally to the Third Reich. The Allies did not want inadvertently to provoke that fate for the new Italian government.

Instead, two days after Mussolini's overthrow, Churchill declared before the House of Commons that:

> We do not know what is going to happen in Italy and now that Mussolini has gone and once the Fascist power is certainly and irremediably broken . . . [i]t would be a grave mistake when Italian affairs are in this flexible, fluid, formative condition, for the Rescuing Powers, Britain and the United States . . . to act to break down the whole structure and expression of the Italian state. We certainly do not seek to reduce Italian life to a condition of chaos and anarchy and to find ourselves without any authorities with whom to deal.[24]

Two days later, Eisenhower reinforced Churchill's message with these words:

> We commend the Italian people and the House of Savoy on ridding themselves of Mussolini, the man who involved them in wars as the tool of Hitler and brought them to the verge of disaster . . . You want peace. You can have peace immediately and peace under honourable conditions which our Governments have already offered you. We are coming as liberators. Your part is to cease immediately any assistance to the German military forces in your country. If you do this, we will rid you of the Germans and the horrors of war. As you have seen in Sicily, our occupation will be mild and beneficent . . . The ancient liberties and traditions of your country will be restored.[25]

Those back-to-back messages should have reassured Italy's king and prime minister that the Allies would accept their government and not try to impose any significant changes or punishments. But instead they kept dithering. Finally, on 31 July, they decided to send two envoys to elicit specific conditions for an armistice, but without the power to negotiate. Diplomats Blasco Lanza d'Ajeta and Alberto Berio respectively flew to Lisbon and Tangiers. Allied representatives presented them this statement: 'The Italian government should place themselves in the hands of the Allies' Governments, who will then state their terms.' The king and prime minister refused to do so and passed another two weeks hoping for better conditions. On 3 August, Bonomi met Badoglio and on behalf of the United Freedom Front asked him to denounce the alliance with Germany and withdraw Italy from the war. Badoglio tersely informed Bonomi that 'the war goes on'.[26]

Victor Emmanuel and Badoglio sent General Giuseppe Castano to Madrid on 15 August, to meet British Ambassador Samuel Hoare and express their desire to open negotiations. Hoare informed Churchill who was summiting with the president at Quebec. Churchill and Roosevelt immediately agreed to a meeting but in more accessible and neutral Lisbon rather than Fascist Francisco Franco's capital, Madrid. They had Eisenhower oversee the talks. Eisenhower dispatched Generals Walter Bedell Smith, his chief of staff and Kenneth Strong, his intelligence chief to Lisbon where, accompanied by British ambassador Ronald Campbell and American charge d'affaires George Kennan, they met Castano on 19 August.[27] The Allied envoys informed Castellano that a truce depended on Italy's unconditional surrender.

While the Italians objected to unconditional surrender, Eisenhower learned a much more vital reason stalled them:

> The Italians wanted to surrender. However they wanted to so only with the assurance that such a powerful Allied force would land on the mainland simultaneously with their surrender that the government itself and their cities would enjoy complete protection from the German forces. Consequently they tried to obtain every detail of our plans. These we would not reveal because the possibility of treachery could never be excluded. Moreover, to invade Italy with the strength the Italians themselves believed necessary was a complete impossibility for the very simple that we did not have the troops in the area nor the ships to transport them.[28]

The Allied envoys explained that to Castellano who flew with that message and a radio transmitter back to Rome.

The Allies completed their conquest of Sicily on 16 August, when Patton's Seventh Army captured Messina. The Italians suffered around 5,000 dead and 117,000 prisoners, while 95,000 troops, including wounded, escaped to the mainland. Around 35,000 Italian troops, mostly native Sicilians, deserted during the campaign. The Germans suffered around 10,000 dead and captured but withdrew around 40,000 troops to the mainland. Of Allied forces, Seventh Army and Eighth Army respectively suffered around 8,800 and 12,800 casualties, a relatively light cost for capturing a strategic island and inflicting so many enemy casualties.[29]

Churchill talked Roosevelt into invading the Italian peninsula.[30] He argued that Victor Emmanuel and Badoglio would soon denounce the Axis and embrace the Allies, partly pressured by demands from Italy's elite and long-suffering masses of people: 'The fury of the Italian population will now be turned against the German intruders who have . . . brought these miseries upon Italy . . . We should stimulate this process in order that the new liberated anti-Fascist Italy shall afford us at the earliest moment a safe and friendly area on which we can base the whole forward air attack upon South and Central Germany.'[31] Of course, those same bombers could reach the same targets from bases in Sardinia or Corsica at a tiny fraction of the cost in blood and treasure of invading and fighting north up Italy's mountainous peninsula, but, tragically, that was not discussed.

Churchill's insistence on invading Italy was part of his stepping-stone strategy east across the Mediterranean basin to the Balkans and Greek Islands rather than east from Normandy France toward Berlin. He did propose that an army land near Trieste in the northern Adriatic Sea then fight its way north-east across the Alps via the Ljubljana Gap toward Vienna 300 miles away. The Germans would have defended that route as easily as they did the Italian peninsula. Regardless, North Africa, Pantelleria and Sicily were the first steps in that advance. Churchill insisted that his strategy would tear out the innards of the Third Reich's 'soft underbelly'. Besides, the planned invasion of France was nine months away. Allied forces should attack nearby Italy rather than sit idle. And negotiations were unfolding for Italy's government to switch sides. With Italy as an ally, the American and British armies would advance north under showers of applause, flowers and kisses from liberated Italians rather than showers of Axis bullets and bombs.

America's Joint Chiefs of Staff argued that invading the mountainous Italian peninsula would literally and figuratively be a dead-end and diversion of crucial military power away from the invasion of France in spring 1944. The Allies could only destroy the Third Reich by battling their way to its capital by the shortest and swiftest route and that began on Normandy's beaches. They did favour capturing lightly defended Sardinia and Corsica to provide air bases to bomb all of Italy and southern France and as a staging area for a second Allied invasion of France in spring 1944, this one at the Riviera. Churchill's so-called 'soft underbelly' had a rock-ribbed defence of steep, stoney mountains ideal for defence. The new argument that Italy's government would surrender with an Allied invasion won over Roosevelt and the Joint Chiefs. But the Joint Chiefs did not envision fighting their way up the entire peninsula, just to a defensive line north of the ports of Naples and Bari.[32]

Generals Harold Alexander, Bernard Montgomery and Mark Clark, the respective Army Group, British Eighth Army and mostly American Fifth Army received instructions to prepare to invade the Italian peninsula, part of Eighth Army at the toe on 3 September, then Fifth Army at Salerno and the rest of Eighth Army at Taranto on 9 September. They planned and prepared under the cloud of not knowing whether Italy's army would fight against or with them.

The king and his ministers squandered ten more crucial days nervously debating what to do. Meanwhile, they learned on 25 August of a pending coup by Fascist hardliners. Police Minister Carboni struck first by having arrested and locked up in Novara prison 'Hierarch' leaders Giuseppe Bottai, Achille Starace, General Ubaldo Soddu, Marshal Ugo Cavallero, Raffaello Riccardi and Nicolo De Cesare along with their underlings; police shot and killed Ettore Muti as he tried to escape.

Those Fascist leaders not immediately arrested faced a dilemma. Should they flee the regime to avoid a possible future arrest? If so, where could they go? Berlin would not welcome them as long as Victor Emmanuel and Badoglio remained faithful Axis allies. A neutral country like Switzerland, Spain or Portugal was the best bet. The trouble was that to prevent flights by traitors and other criminals, the regime issued only temporary passports for specific official trips abroad.

Galeazzo Ciano asked the Vatican for political asylum but was rejected. He and Edda then hoped to fly with their three children for refuge in Spain. The king and prime minister rejected Ciano's request for a passport. Edda knew Colonel Eugen Dollman, the SS chief in Rome. She asked him to provide a plane to take them to Spain. After receiving approval from Hitler, Dollman arranged to have them flown there on 27 August. That flight, however, ended in Munich, not Madrid. Hitler had them held at the heavily-guarded Schloss Hirschberg at Allmannshausen on Lake Starnberg 20 miles south of Munich. Eventually Mussolini's wife Rachele and their two youngest children joined them.

Roosevelt and Churchill issued Eisenhower a 44-clause 'long surrender' document and instructions to invade Italy across the Messina Straits and at Salerno in early September. Under the key clauses Italy's government would 'give the Allies complete control over the Italian armed forces and all the facilities and material resources at their disposal; to ensure the maximum exploitation consistent with international law of the resources of the country for the Allied war effort, both as a base of operations and as a source of consumable conditions and services; and to effect the final destruction of Fascism'.[33]

Victor Emmanuel finally struggled from his stupor on 1 September and decided to surrender Italy unconditionally. Allied headquarters then was at Cassibile, Sicily, ten miles south of Syracuse. He sent Castellano there to accept the Allied terms. Upon Castellano's arrival, Smith presented him with a short armistice version whereby the king would announce Italy's surrender after an Allied army landed on the mainland. Smith did not reveal the exact day of the planned invasion.

The king would receive word just before it happened and shortly thereafter he would broadcast the news of Italy's surrender. Another delay ensued as the king and Badoglio discussed the terms. They asked for an Allied airborne division to land at Rome to fight alongside the few intact Italian divisions. Eisenhower gave his approval. On 3 September, Castellano signed the document and flew back to Rome.

That same day, Montgomery landed two divisions at Reggio Calabria, a port city at Italy's toe just across the Messina Straits from Sicily. Reggio Calabria was 866 miles from the Brenner Pass leading to the Third Reich. Eisenhower sent General Maxwell Taylor, who commanded the 82nd Airborne, and his aide Colonel William Gardiner on a perilous mission. On 7 September, they flew to Gaeta where they were driven to Rome to confer with Badoglio about the airdrop. Badoglio urged Taylor to cancel the airdrop, fearing that the Germans deployed in the region would converge and overwhelm it. He then issued this bombshell declaration that 'it is no longer possible to accept an immediate armistice as this could provoke the occupation of the capital and the violent assumption of the government by the Germans'.[34]

Badoglio's attempt to weasel out of the deal enraged Eisenhower. He did cancel the airborne operation but the Allied landings in Italy would proceed on schedule. Eisenhower warned Badoglio:

> I intend to broadcast the existence of the armistice at the hour originally planned. If you or any part of your armed forces fail to cooperate as previously agreed I will publish to the world the full record of this affair. I do not accept the message of this morning postponing the armistice . . . Failure now on your part to carry out the full obligations of the signed agreement will have the most serious consequences for your country.[35]

When the agreed-upon hour of 6.30 on 8 September came, Eisenhower broadcast this message: 'The Italian government has surrendered its armed forces unconditionally . . . All Italians who now act to help eject the German aggressors from Italian soil will have the assistance and support of the united nations.'[36] An hour and fifteen minutes later, Badoglio broadcasted these words: 'Recognizing the impossibility of continuing an unequal struggle, the Italian government has asked General Eisenhower for an armistice. The request has been granted. All acts of hostility everywhere against the Anglo-American troops on the part of the Italian forces are to cease. The Italian forces will reply, however, to attacks from other sources.'[37] He issued orders for all Italian warships to steam for safety at Allied ports. Although the Germans eventually captured most Italian troops, most warships escaped.

Within half an hour of Badoglio's announcement, Wehrmacht Operations Chief Albert Jodl tersely broadcasted the code word 'Achse' (Axis) and German division commanders across the peninsula ordered nearby Italian division commanders to surrender. As if they were helplessly trapped in a nightmare, Victor Emmanuel and Badoglio fatalistically accepted rather than resisted the German takeover. There were twenty-four Italian divisions in Italy and thirty-five divisions in the Balkans, Greece, France and Russia. Without orders to resist, most Italian division commanders meekly surrendered to the German forces that approached them. Over the next month, the Germans disarmed, transported and interned 615,000 Italians in prison camps and killed or wounded 19,000 among those who resisted. Hundreds of thousands of other Italian troops deserted to their homes. Around 30,000 Italian troops fled to Switzerland whose government interned them for the duration of the war. The only Italian victories were in Sardinia and Corsica, the garrisons of which actually forced the small German contingents to surrender then let Allied forces land.[38]

As soon as Kesselring heard Badoglio's broadcast, he ordered two Germann divisions to occupy Rome. Without a shot fired, the six Italian divisions in and around Rome surrendered. Victor Emmanuel, Badoglio, their families, Chief of Staff General Vittorio Ambrosio, Army Chief of Staff General Mario Roatta and their advisors packed into five cars and drove the steep twisting road across the Apennine Mountains to Pescara where two navy corvettes carried them to Brindisi. They stepped ashore on 10 September. Brindisi would serve as Italy's makeshift capital for the next month.

It was not until the next morning of 11 September that Badoglio broadcasted a message for Italian troops to consider the Germans their enemies and not until 13 September, that he issued an explicit order for the Italian army to resist the Germans. By then, without orders, most Italian commanders had surrendered their troops to the Germans.

Had Badoglio issued that order shortly after Mussolini was arrested seven weeks earlier, the Italy army would eventually have overwhelmed the half-dozen German divisions then deployed on the peninsula. Divisions could have been rushed to plug each Alpine pass against German reinforcements. The Allies would have landed ever more divisions to fight alongside the Italian army and eliminate any remaining German resistance. Within a month or so most of Italy could have been liberated.

One bright spot was the Italian navy's fate. Most of the six battleships, nine heavy cruisers, thirty-two destroyers and forty-eight submarines were anchored at La Spezia. Their captains ordered anchors raised and steamed their warships for Allied ports. Most of those warships reached safety, although the Germans did capture eighteen submarines in port while bombers sank a battleship.[39]

Fifth Army landed at Salerno against fierce German opposition while the remaining divisions of Montgomery's Eighth Army docked unopposed at Taranto on 9 September. Salerno was a terrible choice for a landing as steep mountains rose behind the port. General Heinrich von Vietinghof commanded the Tenth Army responsible for defending the southern Italian peninsula. He posted the 16th Panzer Division at Salerno and rushed three other divisions there after learning of the landing. The fighting raged for ten days before the Americans finally drove off the Germans and pushed inland as two divisions of Montgomery Eighth Army appeared from the south on 19 September. The Allies won the battle for Salerno while suffering 14,000 casualties and inflicting 3,500.

That would be the pattern of war on the mountainous peninsula for the next 20 months. The Allied armies battered themselves against one nearly impregnable German position after another often for weeks or even months. Eventually, the Allies took the position after bombarding it with enough bombs and shells that devastated the defenders. But the survivors simply withdrew to other strongholds. And when the guns finally fell silent after 20 months of incessant warfare, the Allies had advanced no further than the Po River valley.

Meanwhile, two rival rump governments claimed to be Italy's legitimate sovereign, Far behind Allied lines, Victor Emmanuel moved his capital among several southern cities. For the capital of his Fascist Republic, Benito Mussolini selected the small town of Salo overlooking Lake Garda in the north. Foreign armies controlled both governments. Meanwhile, a guerilla war raged behind German lines all the way to the Swiss border as Italian nationalists and communists attacked German and Fascist Italian forces, as they struggling politically to position themselves for taking power in post-war Italy.

Chapter 10

THE SALO REPUBLIC

> I call you again to work and to arms. Our will, our courage, our faith will give back to Italy its future, its possibility of life and its place in the world.
>
> (Benito Mussolini)

> Fascism must die heroically. (Benito Mussolini)

Benito Mussolini's captivity lasted 45 days. He could only dream of rescue. Meanwhile, his humiliating overthrow and captivity deeply depressed him. Flavia Iurato, the Hotel Campo Imperatore manager, described him and his routine:

> There was no longer anything of the well-fed, self-assured dictator about him. Instead, he looked anxiously about him as if he feared some trap, rolling his eyes which stood out in his emaciated face . . . The prisoner took his meals in his room and Police Inspector Gueli and Lt. Faiola of the Carabinieri, who were in charge of him, were always present. At the end of the meal Gueli and Faiola hastened to remove the knives and even the forks . . . to forestall any attempt at suicide.[1]

Mussolini's dream finally came true. He vividly recalled the rescue:

> On September 11th, a strange atmosphere of uncertainty and expectation reigned on the Gran Sasso. It was now known that the Government had fled together with the King . . . In the early hours of the 12th a thick whitish mass of cloud covered the summit of Gran Sasso . . . Toward noon the sun broke through the clouds and the whole sky seemed to shine in the clear September air. It was exactly 2 p.m. and I was sitting by the open window with my arms folded when a glider landed a hundred yards from the building. Four

> or five men in khaki got out, rapidly assembled two machine guns and then came forward. A few seconds later other gliders landed in the immediate vicinity and the men from these carried out the same manoeuvre . . . The alarm was sounded. All the Carabinieri and police rushed out of the Refuge, weapons in hand . . . I remained by the window and saw that another and more numerous group of Germans, having seized the funicular, had come up and were now marching compactly and resolutely from the station square toward the inn. At the head of the group was Skorzeny.[2]

Domenico Antonelli, the hotel manager during the rescue, gave this dramatic account:

> [T]here came a deafening roar of engines. Everybody rushed outside. About ten machines were visible, with gliders in tow. At that very moment the gliders were cast off and began to plane down. Here, all was confusion. No one thought of giving orders. The police left their machine guns without the slightest attempt at firing and took shelter in the hotel . . . The platoon went running down the northern slope. They did not return until the following morning, when all had been quiet for some time. Faiola, too, ran into the hotel and rushed up to the second floor, shouting like a madman, 'Excellency, the Germans!' While this ridiculous and regrettable scene was taking place, the gliders began to land undisturbed. From the first one, which landed about two hundred and fifty yards from the hotel . . . an Italian General of Police, [Fernando] Soleti, emerged, followed by a German officer who was pressing the muzzle of a machine-gun into his ribs. Meanwhile, a German N.C.O. emerged from another glider and calmly began to film the scene. Soleti came towards the hotel, shouting, 'Don't shoot!' . . . A hundred and thirty Germans, commanded by a captain, had come down from the air . . . The Germans surrounded the hotel in case of resistance . . . Mussolini in the meantime had already assumed the manners of a dictator; he moved with more confidence, he spoke with emphasis, he thrust out his jaw.[3]

SS Captain Otto Skorzeny was among the Second World War's most brilliant and daring commandos. Hitler had given the mission to General Kurt Student who commanded the paratroop corps that captured Crete from the British 1940. Student tapped Skorzeny to lead the rescue team.

Mussolini thrilled as:

> Skorzeny's men, after taking possession of the machine guns at each side of the Refuge gate, came to my room in a body. Skorzeny, sweating and much moved, stood to attention and said: 'The *Führer*, who night after night, ever since your capture, has been thinking how to set you free, gave me this task'. I replied: 'I was certain from the beginning that the *Führer* would afford me this proof of his friendship. Thank him and I thank you, Captain Skorzeny'.

Ironically, the ineptness and timidity of Italy's armed forces that contributed to Mussolini's overthrow also contributed to his rescue. Without firing a shot, Skorzeny's commandos had intimidated the Carabinieri and police into surrender. A Storch reconnaissance plane landed on the meadow. Skorzeny and Mussolini squeezed in and the pilot raced the plane toward the meadow's edge where the mountain descended steeply to the valley below. The Storch dropped heavily through the thin air before propelling forward. They landed at the small Practica di Mare Airfield 16 miles south of Rome. There Mussolini and Skorzeny got into a waiting three-engine Junkers Ju 52 for Vienna where they stayed at the Hotel Continental. The next day they flew to Munich where Mussolini's family awaited him.

Mussolini was flown to Rastenburg to meet Hitler at his Wolf' Lair headquarters on 14 September. *Der Führer* told *Il Duce* that he would reestablish him in power in Italy, but in a small northern town rather than in Rome, Milan or another city that would be bombed.[4] Clearly, Mussolini was to be Hitler's puppet dictator of a rump pseudo-state, but he reasoned that status and refuge was better than foreign exile. But Hitler's first order of state business for Mussolini appalled him.

Hitler told Mussolini that:

> I don't doubt that you will agree with me that one of the first acts of the new government will have to be to sentence to death the traitors of the Grand Council. I judge Count Ciano four times a traitor: traitor to his country, traitor to fascism, traitor to the alliance with Germany, traitor to his family. If I were in your place perhaps nothing would have stopped me from rendering justice with my own hands. But I advise you: It is preferable that the death sentence be carried out in Italy.

Mussolini heatedly protested: 'But you're talking of the husband of the daughter whom I adore, the father of my grandchildren.' Hitler was unmoved: 'All the more reason Count Ciano merits punishment in that not only has he failed in fidelity to the country, but in fidelity to his family.' When Mussolini suggested that the price was too much, Hitler warned that if he spurned the state he offered, 'Northern Italy will have to envy the fate of Poland if you don't accept. In such a case, Count Ciano will naturally not be handed over, he will be hanged here in Germany.'[5]

Mussolini's second Fascist regime began on 15 September 1943, with two broadcasts by anonymous Italian voices from Radio Munich. The first was that 'Mussolini has resumed the leadership of Fascism in

Italy'. Then came Mussolini's quoted words to his 'loyal comrades in all Italy, as from today . . . I resume the supreme leadership of Fascism in Italy'.

Mussolini explained in his own words why he had replaced the monarchy with a republic in a 18 September broadcast: 'It is not the regime that has betrayed the monarchy, it is the monarchy that has betrayed the regime. When a monarchy fails in its duties, it loses every reason for being. The state we want to establish will be national and social in the highest sense of the word, that it will be Fascist, thus returning to our origins.' Four principles would guide Mussolini's Fascist Republic: alliance with Germany and Japan; reorganization of the military so that Fascist militia dominated; death for all nineteen Grand Council members who voted against Mussolini on 25 July; and the purge of 'parasitical plutocrats'. He ended with these words: 'I call you again to work and to arms. Our will, our courage, our faith will give back to Italy its future, is possibility of life and its place in the world.'[6]

He announced the official founding of what he initially called the National Republican State of Italy (*Stato Nazionale Repubblicana d'Italia*) on 23 September, but renamed it the succinct Italian Social Republic (*Repubblicana Sociale Italiana*, RSI) in December. He appointed Alessandro Pavolini secretary general of what he now called the Fascist Republican Party (*Partito Fascista Repubblicano*, PFR).

Mussolini's first stop on his journey back to Italy was Forli's airport then a car to his summer residence Rocca delle Caminate near his boyhood home at Predappio on 25 September. Over the next few weeks he considered that and several other small towns for his capital before finally selecting Salo on Lake Garda's western shore. Safety rather than convenience was the primary concern that led him to his 'Salo Republic'. Hopefully the Allies would not bother dispatching bombers or commandos to that remote site.

He initially housed his government at Villa Feltrinelli where he lived with his family, then moved it to the Villa delle Orsoline in nearby Gargnano. His government's key officials were Pavolini as Fascist Party Secretary, Rodolfo Graziani as Defence Minister, Guido Buffarini-Guidi as interior minister commanding the national police force and Renato Ricci commanding the Republican National Guard (*Guarda Nazionale Republicana*, GNR) or Black Brigades (*Brigate Neri*). The Italian army absorbed the National Guard in August 1944.

Mussolini's Salo Republic looked impressive on paper. Officially, his Fascist Republican Party numbered 487,000 members, his Italian Fascist Republic's military 400,000 troops and his police 140,000.[7]

The real numbers were fractions of those. He renamed his Blackshirt Voluntary Militia for National Security (*Milizia Voluntaria per la Sicurezza Nationale*, MVSN), founded in January 1923, the Republican National Guard (*Guardia Nazionale Repubblicana*, GNR). Eventually the Berlin and Salo regimes organized four Italian divisions that fought with the Germans on the Italian front, San Marco, Monterossa, Littorio and Italia. They were all understrength and plagued with bad morale and desertions.

Mussolini's key decision during his seven-month Salo Republic sojourn was to convene a Fascist Party conference at the Castello Vecchio in Verona on 14 November 1943, although he did not attend. The delegates had two key issues to decide. First, they debated and approved the eighteen-point Verona Manifesto mostly composed by Mussolini. This acknowledged that Fascism had stifled debate and exacerbated corruption and promised a more democratic Fascism of open, frank discussions of problems and possible solutions; promotions based on merit rather than bribes or connections; the end to the arrest and imprisonment of regime critics; and a constituent assembly to form a social democratic constitution with an independent judiciary. Mussolini never tried to realize any of those promises. The delegates also voted to condemn to death for treason all nineteen members of the Fascist Grand Council that voted to oust Mussolini.

Mussolini's regime was nothing more than Hitler's puppet to exploit for its manpower and production. General Rudolf Rahn, the plenipotentiary, and SS General Karl Wolff actually controlled the Salo Republic. Spies and listening devices shadowed Mussolini and all his top officials. The Germans transferred the Bank of Italy's 95 tons of gold reserves from Rome to Berlin for 'safe keeping'. They dismantled the machinery and assembly lines of Italy's most productive factories and sent them, often with the workers, for reassembly in Germany.[8] The Salo Republic's conscription for 1944 should have received 180,000 draftees between 18 and 20 years old. Of the 87,000 rounded up, half ended up as labourers in German factories and mines. Of the leftover conscripts, Mussolini placed 25,000 in the Republican National Guard and used the rest to flesh out the four Fascist Italian army divisions. Meanwhile, Mussolini's rump state steadily diminished as Allied forces ground their way north up the peninsula, while Hitler annexed to the Third Reich eight northern Italian provinces and Croatian Fascist dictator Ante Pavelić seized Italian Dalmatia, Istria and eastern Venezia Giulia. Only eight countries recognized Mussolini's regime, Germany, Japan and other Axis allies and puppet states. Mussolini fumed that

Francesco Franco, Spain's Fascist dictator, did not acknowledge his regime despite their common ideology and all the troops, weapons and supplies that he sent him that helped him take power in the civil war from 1936 to 1939.

The last summit between Hitler and Mussolini could not have been more ironic. On 15 July 1944, Mussolini journeyed to Germany to inspect four Italian divisions training there at various bases. That done, on 20 July, he flew to Hitler's Wolf's Lair (*Wolfsschanze*) headquarters near Rastenburg in East Prussia. That same day, a conspiracy to assassinate Hitler and overthrow his regime nearly succeeded.

Spearheading the plot was Colonel Klaus Graf von Stauffenberg. He would leave a briefcase bomb under the table at the packed staff conference headed by Hitler. He would then fly back to Berlin where the conspirators would declare a new government as soon as they learned that Hitler was dead. A thick table leg protected Hitler from the full blast that killed four and wounded twenty others; Hitler escaped with bruises and ringing ears. He ordered the Gestapo to arrest and summarily execute all suspects. Eventually, the Gestapo arrested over 7,000 suspects and executed 4,980 of them, including Stauffenberg. The investigation discovered that Rommel was aware of the plot although he did not join the conspirators; he was ordered to take cyanide.

Mussolini recalled that Hitler greeted him with an embrace and calmly explained: '*Duce*, a short time ago I was the target of a bomb. What happened today is an omen of destiny.' Mussolini replied: 'After this miracle it is impossible that our cause should know defeat.' Hitler gave Mussolini a tour of the blast site and then he typically talked at him for hours before escorting him to the station. As Mussolini was about to board the train, Hitler took his arm and said: 'I know that I can count on you and I beg you to believe me when I say that I consider you my best friend and perhaps my only friend in world.'[9]

Mussolini took a short trip from Gargano in August 1944, to inspect a stretch of the nearby Gothic defence line that had blunted the Allied advance for months, but more importantly, to visit his son Bruno's grave in the family cemetery near Predappio. After returning to Gargnano, Rachele recorded in her diary his outrage at news of a German atrocity in Milan: 'The Germans have had fifteen hostages executed in a public square to avenge the death of some German soldiers killed by partisans . . . He poured out his feelings to me: "The Germans have no sense of fairness at all. Why humiliate a city like Milan with such an exhibition of summary justice".'[10]

Mussolini, like Napoleon after the Allies and French Senate forced his first abdication as emperor, had received as compensation a minor realm to rule. And much like Napoleon on Elba, Mussolini had little to do. He did not govern the Salo Republic, he presided over it. Workaholism was the only positive trait that Mussolini shared with Napoleon. Mussolini was accustomed to 14-hour days making critical decisions, chairing an array of policy committees and receiving generals, ministers, ambassadors, corporate chiefs and delegations of workers, peasants and mothers. Now he was miserable with all that time to fill. Instead, the results of a myriad of bad choices and might-have-beens extending back through his life swirled through his mind, haunting him.

Nonetheless at Salo, Mussolini kept a daily routine. He entered his office at 8.45 each morning and stayed there until 2.30, took a half-hour rest then returned until around 9.00 in the evening. He performed the pantomime of governance, reading reports, signing decrees, talking with advisors, receiving visitors. He spent much of his working time writing nineteen anonymous articles for the Milan based newspaper *Corriere della Sera* that justified his 23 years ruling Italy, taking credit for what little went right and blaming others for all that went wrong. For that, his articles were mostly mixes of lies, exaggerations, avoidances and myths, His editor was Carlo Silvestri, a socialist journalist. The articles were later published as a pamphlet with 300,000 copies distributed. After the war, those articles were gathered, edited and published as *Mussolini's Memoirs*.[11]

Rachele and their two youngest children joined Mussolini at Villa Feltrinelli on 3 November 1943, followed eventually by their son Vittorio and his family, their daughter Edda and her children and over 200 other relatives of theirs found cramped housing in the area. Villa Feltrinelli was not a happy home. Mussolini complained to his secretary Giovanni Dolfin that:

> I cannot live here any more. The domestic area has become suffocating. Every day troubles, anger, scenes. My human ability to support this has touched the extreme limit . . . My wife, who doesn't give me peace . . . is now carrying out real investigations and interrogating even the household staff . . . She tries to make me look ridiculous.[12]

Rachele's wrath was provoked by learning that her husband had housed his mistress Clara Petacci at Villa Fiordaliso in Gardone Riviera just six miles from Villa delle Orsoline that housed his government.

Mussolini first met Clara at a beach near Ostia on 24,April 1932. She was from a wealthy family whose father was a Fascist Party member.[13] She had a crush on Mussolini from her early teen years and wrote him love letters and poetry. She was driving the sportscar her parents gave her for her eighteenth birthday with some family members when she spotted Mussolini who was out for a drive with an aide. She waved and shouted at him to stop and he did. He was as smitten with her as he was with him. He got her phone number and three days later called her home and talked her mother into letting her visit him at Palazzo Venezia. She was then 24 years old and 28 years younger than Mussolini. When they became lovers is unclear. She actually married army officer Riccardo Federici on 27 June 1934. Mussolini had him sent as a military attaché to Tokyo where he stayed until 1945. Meanwhile, he installed her in a suite at Palazzo Venezia in October 1936. Her family enriched themselves from Clara's relationship with Mussolini from government contracts and status that garnered business deals.

Clara did what she could to relieve and distract Mussolini. His German doctor Georg Zacharie, obviously a connoisseur, recalled why Mussolini was so attracted to Clara:

> She was an intelligent woman, simple and transparent . . . She loved to dress well and had many jewels given her by the *Duce* . . . She possessed charm in exceptional measure. It happened not just to me but many others to be completely conquered by the fascination she emanated. She was for the *Duce* the only suitable woman. She could give him courage and reanimate him. When he was with her his humour was always excellent and his mind serene.[14]

Clara genuinely loved Mussolini and would join him even when she knew partisans would likely capture and kill them both.

Rachele's outrage at Clara's presence swelled until she erupted on 24 October 1944. With some friends and Interior Minister Guido Buffarini-Guidi, she barged past the bodyguards at Clara's villa and demanded that she stop seeing her husband. When Clara demurred, Rachele called Mussolini and insisted that he send away his mistress. Ashamed and embarrassed, he meekly agreed that Clara should leave and apologized to Rachele for betraying her.[15]

Meanwhile, the American Fifth and British Eighth armies ground their way up the Italian peninsula. Eighth Army drove unopposed into Bari on 11 September and Foggia on 27 September 1943 and soon exploited their respective deep port for supplies and reinforcements and large airfield for long-range and short-range bombers and fighter planes.

Fifth Army captured Naples on 1 October, but engineers did not clear all the sunken ships and mines from the harbour to reopen the port to shipping until 22 October. General Harold Alexander established his Supreme Allied Commander Mediterranean (SACMED) headquarters at the Royal Palace (*Reggia di Caserta*) at Caserta, 20 miles north-east of Naples.

The Germans held four separate defence lines that ran from sea to sea across the peninsula below Rome from September 1943 to June 1944. The most famous was the third line called Gustav that included the mountaintop monastery at Cassino. The Allied armies eventually breached each and advanced a dozen or so miles before they collided with the next. A German air raid on Bari harbour on 2 December sank twenty-nine ships, including a munitions ship that exploded, killed around a thousand military personnel and a thousand civilians, destroyed 38,000 tons of cargo and crimped Eighth Army operations for over two months before engineers cleared most of the harbour.

Astonishingly, Alexander and Clark did not consider outflanking the Gustav Line with a landing behind it. Prime Minister Winston Churchill conceived the strategy and urged them to implement it. Initially, Alexander and Clark were willing to commit just one division to the landing. That appalled Churchill who argued that German reserves would soon overwhelm that solitary division. He insisted that they commit a least a corps to the landing. On 22 December, Alexander grudgingly agreed and instructed Clark to plan the operation with VI Corps. Tragically, VI Corps' commander was General John Lucas, who was utterly inept and timid.

Navy landing craft carried 36,000 troops and 3,000 vehicles ashore along an eight-mile stretch of beach straddling the neighbouring resort towns of Anzio and Nettuno on 21 January 1944; they pushed at most a mile inland and formed a defensive perimeter. That same day, Fifth Army launched its latest series of blood-soaked assaults on the Gustav Line, including the Monte Cassino monastery, which the Germans repeatedly repulsed over the next several months. From his headquarters at Frascati 40 miles away, Kesselring rushed reserve divisions to Anzio.

Anzio is 40 miles south of Rome and just 10 miles south-west of north-south Highway 7, the best route to get there. Lucas did not send his divisions in either direction. Instead, for the next four weeks until he was relieved of command, he simply hunkered down with his corps as reinforcements and supplies massed along the perimeter while eventually eleven German divisions hemmed in, shelled and bombed the beachhead. From 16 to 20 February, the Germans launched an assault that nearly overwhelmed VI Corps. On 22 February, Clark finally replaced Lucas with General Lucian Truscott, a brilliant leader, strategist and tactician. Of the Anzio campaign, Churchill mournfully remarked: 'We hoped to land a wildcat that would tear out the bowels of the Boche. Instead, we have stranded a vast whale with its tail flopping about in the water.'[16]

The Allies eventually won their latest campaign of attrition on both the Gustav Line and at Anzio.[17] Fifth and Eighth Army, now commanded by British General Oliver Leese, finally pulverized and punched through the Gustav Line after sustained artillery barrages, bombing and infantry assaults from 11 to 23 May. Truscott launched an offensive against the German perimeter at Anzio on 23 May that broke through two days later. With the Germans on the run, Clark made a crucial mistake. Rather than curl Fifth Army around and cut off the German army's remnants retreating east of Rome, he instead pushed north toward Rome, entering the undefended city on 4 June. Thus did Clark sacrifice the chance to capture much of the German army on the glorious altar of liberating Rome and beating Eighth Army commander Leese to that prize. Kesselring withdrew his forces to a series of lines north of Rome, with the Gothic the best known, that he defended over the next 11 months.

The escape of Italy's government from imminent German capture immensely relieved the Allied leaders. Churchill had worried nearly as much that the opposition parties would topple the monarchy and declare a republic. He wrote: 'I was sure that King Victor Emmanuel and Badoglio would be able to do more for what had now become the common cause than any Italian government formed from the exiles or opponents of the Fascist regime. The surrender of the Italian fleet was solid proof of their authority.'[18]

Roosevelt and Churchill issued their first direct instructions to Prime Minister Badoglio on 10 September, urging him 'to win peace and freedom for the Italian people and to win back for Italy an honourable place in the civilization Europe'. Badoglio replied: 'I can assure you that the Italian people, under their King, ardently desire at the cost of any sacrifice to obtain liberty and a just peace . . . We will march with you our American and English friends.'[19]

The Allied leaders had Eisenhower boost the Italian government's legitimacy by giving the king autonomy over the peninsula's foot, a realm informally called the Kingdom of South Italy. On 23 September, they instructed Eisenhower to get Italy's government publicly to declare war against Germany and promise future free elections for the Italian people.

Allied representatives signed with Badoglio the 44-article 'long armistice' on 29 September. The key article was number 30 whereby 'the Italian government will carry out all directives which the United Nations may call for, including the abolition of Fascist institutions, the dismissal and internment of Fascist personnel, the control of Fascist funds, the suppression of Fascist ideologies and teaching'.

The next obvious step was for Italy belatedly to join the Allies. Indeed, Badoglio recognized how vital declaring war against Germany was:

> Everywhere the German troops were committing horrible outrages against our troops and the civilian population. It was imperative to declare war on Germany so that our men who fell into the hands of the Germans should not be treated as *francs-tireurs* and shot. But another reason appeared to me as being of even greater importance: how could we prove to the British and Americans that we were really their allies and determined to fight alongside them if we did not declare war on the common enemy?[20]

How indeed? Yet, despite everything, Victor Emmanuel and Badoglio kept dithering while their country literally burned and their fellow Italians died. They moved their government to Salerno. Badoglio replaced General Mario Roatta with General Giovanni Messe as Chief of Staff. What Badoglio was holding out for was a written Allied guarantee that let him remain prime minster. The Allied preferred to keep their options open over the composition of Italy's government. The Allies finally agreed to sign a six-point deal with the line: 'The Government of Marshal Badoglio must continue in office.'[21] That done, Victor Emmanuel and Badoglio finally co-signed a declaration of war against Germany on 13 October, nearly two and a half months after Mussolini's arrest. The Allies welcomed Italy as a 'co-belligerent' rather than an equal.

The formal Allied occupation of Italy began on 10 November 1943, with establishment of the Allied Control Commission (ACC), later renamed the Allied Commission (AC).[22] The initial political and military commissioners were Americans Robert Murphy and General Kenyon Joyce and British Harold Macmillan and General Noel Mason-MacFarlane. Eventually the Allied Commission numbered over 1,500 personnel split among twenty-six committees with different duties. The Allied Commission worked far behind the front line and coordinated effort with the Allied Military Government (AMG) that administered territory directly behind the lines. As the front line ground sporadically north, the Allied Commission took over territory from the Military Government. A Combined Chief of Staff directive articulated the essence of occupation policy for Italy but were universally applicable to any occupied enemy country:

> The administration shall be benevolent with respect to the civilian population so far as consistent with strict military requirements. The civilian population is tired of war, resentful of German overlordship and demoralized by the Fascist regime and will therefore be responsive to a just and efficient administration. It should be made clear to the local population that military occupation is intended: (1) to deliver the people from the Fascist regime which led them to into the war; and (2) to restore Italy as a free nation.[23]

The immediate crucial task was feeding the Italian people who faced mass starvation. An Allied report ominously warned that: 'Conditions in Southern Italy and Sicily are such that unless reasonable quantities of food are supplied very promptly we will experience sabotage, unrest and a complete cessation of those activities necessary to our advance.'[24]

The six-party United Freedom Front that Ivanoe Bonomi organized on 3 August 1943 both politically opposed the Kingdom of South Italy and militarily fought the Germans and Mussolini's Salo Republic.[25] Five of the six parties were dedicated to liberal democracy for Italy either as a republic or a constitutional monarchy where parliament held most power. The Communist Party, distantly led by Palmiro Togliatti in the Kremlin, followed the Popular Front strategy as a short-term expedient to amass power for a future communist revolution. By accepting a totalitarian party in a democratic coalition, Bonomi hoped to harness and transform it.

Bonomi began his political career in the Socialist Party but was expelled in 1912 for his reformist views. He established the centre-left Reform Socialist Party and was rewarded with several ministries including War and the Treasury. He retired from politics after Mussolini took power only to reemerge amidst Italy's devastating defeats and Mussolini's collapsing support. He founded the Labour Democratic Party in early 1943 and recruited among workers in Rome and southern Italy.

Like Bonomi, Alcide De Gasperi headed several ministries in various cabinets before Mussolini. He founded the Christian Democratic Party in Milan in September 1942, as the indirect heir to Luigi Sturzo's Italian Popular Party that lasted from 1919 to 1926 and upheld traditional

Catholic values and a constitutional monarchy. The Action Party established by Ferruccio Parri in January 1943 was inspired by Carlo Rosselli's Justice and Liberty group in Paris that mingled republicanism and socialism. Action Party received critical financial support from Fiat, Olivetti and Milan Commercial Banks. Action Party's leadership was in flux as the Gestapo arrested many of its chiefs. The Socialist Party of Proletarian Unity, the latest Socialist Party version, was also split among factions with Gaetano Salvemini and Pietro Nenni the most prominent leaders. The Liberal Party was a conservative party inspired by Count Camillo Cavour's pragmatism and nationalism. The Republican Party was not a full member but aligned with the United Freedom Front.

The United Freedom Front renamed itself the National Liberation Committee (*Comitato de Liberazione Nationale*, CLN) inspired by the French Resistance model, on 9 September. The Committee's first key act was to condemn the flight of the king and prime minister and to declare themselves Italy's legitimate government. But Bonomi's provisional government itself had to flee for safety behind Allied lines on 10 September, as German troops entered Rome. The National Liberation Committee called for a 'Second Resurgence' (*Risorgimento Secondo*) of Armed Resistance (*Armata Resistenza*) and organized regional underground Committees of National Liberation that launched hit and run attacks by partisans or guerillas (*partigiani*) against German and Fascist forces.

The Allies' paramilitary and intelligence organizations, America's Office of Strategic Services (OSS) and Britain's Special Operations Executive (SOE), parachuted commandos, arms, munitions, radios and other supplies to resistance groups behind German lines.[26] The Allies dropped 6,400 tons of supplies to the partisans by May 1945, with 68 per cent from American planes.[27] Commandos received these instructions:

> You will have no political authority whatsoever and you will not give official recognition to . . . power by any party or group of parties. You will inform the Committee of National Liberation that the Rome government has the full support of the Allies and that the Regional and Local authorities should not question its authority. You should give your moral support to all groups and parties which constitute a potential source of law and order and you should withhold it from all extremist movements, whether political or military.[28]

That last directive imposed a frustrating dilemma for the commandos.

The most powerful resistance group was the Committee of National Liberation of Upper Italy (CLNAI) that formed in Milan on 31 January

1944. Not surprisingly, most CLNAI partisans were communists. The Communist Party was perfectly positioned to launch and dominate Italian resistance against the Germans and Mussolini's Salo Republic. Mussolini had outlawed the Communist Party in 1923, forcing its members either to burrow politically underground within Italy or flee to a friendly country. Those that remained formed a secret organization linked to the Communist International (Comintern) headquartered in the Kremlin. Palmiro Togliatti was the Italian Communist Party's general secretary, but he stayed in Moscow. Communist Party membership steadily expanded to reach 100,000 by the end of the war. The Communists masked themselves with Italian nationalism by calling their military units Patriotic Action Groups (*Gruppi di Azione Pattriotica*, GAP) with numbered Garibaldi Brigades, but they fooled few people. Envoys of the Supreme Allied Commander got the Committee of National Liberation of Upper Italy to agree to hand over all authority and arms to the Allied Military Government as soon as it established control.

Stalih wanted to impose communist regimes in every country. That goal was easy in countries that the Red Army overran. Elsewhere communist takeovers depended on the Communist Party's military wing defeating the Germans and their allies while the Communist Party's political wing established control over local and regional governments and all workplaces. The strongest communist-dominated resistance movements were in France, Yugoslavia and Italy. In July 1944, the Italian Communist Party ordered its cadres to implement this 'Popular Front' strategy:

> Only the participation of all the people in the insurrection will guarantee victory . . . The re-education of the Italian people, the radical elimination of Fascism and its economic roots, these will only be possible if all kinds of employees, not only workers, actively intervene in political life . . . as conscious creators of the new democracy . . . .The assumption of power before the arrival of the Allied forces is essential for the political direction and future development of the Italian people.[29]

Of course, 'new democracy' was a euphemism for communist dictatorship.

Fortunately for Italy, Togliatti was not a hardcore, ruthless Stalinist, but a pragmatist who sought to forge constructive relations with Italy's liberal parties and the American and British occupiers. Togliatti criticized Communist cadres who 'have made damaging references to the Allies whom they branded as enemies of a new socially reconstructed Italy. Against this they pour praises on the Russians whom they recognize as the true friends of future Italy.'[30]

The democratic parties feared that the Communist Party and Socialist Party were massing money, weapons and supplies for a violent post-war revolution. An Allied report detailed that fear:

> Representatives of the Right and Centre parties state, privately if not in public, that the Socialist-Communist bloc aims at creating a one-party State, the hallmark of dictatorship. To permit the Left to come to power would be equivalent to signing their own death warrants. Consequently the political activities of right and centre are directed primarily towards preventing the Left from extending its control.[31]

Of the parties dedicated to democracy, only one fielded large numbers of partisans, the Action Party that accounted for about one in four. Overall, two-thirds of partisans were affiliated either with the Communist Party or Action Party. Each of the other political parties had partisans with their numbers, distribution and acts varying greatly. The Committee of National Liberation tried to forge a coalition among the democratic partisan groups by announcing the creation of the Volunteer Corps for Freedom (*Corpo Voluntari della Liberata*, CVL) on 9 January 1944, but it did not become operational until 9 June 1944.

The number of partisans and their attacks steadily rose. In May 1944, General Alexander revealed to *The Times* that partisans were holding down six of the twenty-five German divisions in Italy. An intelligence report by Mussolini's regime in mid-summer 1944 estimated that the partisans totalled 82,000 rebels with 25,000 in Piedmont, 17,000 in Emilia and northern Tuscany, 14,000 in Liguria, 16,000 in Venezia Guilia and 5,000 in Lombardy. By the war's end, the partisans numbered around 250,000, including 35,000 women, although most were poorly armed. Eventually they were organized in 43 military zones with 104 divisions usually numbering from 800 to 1,500 fighters and 52 autonomous mountain brigades. The fighting was merciless. The Nazis tortured and executed captured partisans and shot ten Italians for every German soldier killed. The partisans suffered at least 35,828 dead and 21,158 wounded along with 9,980 civilians killed and 412 wounded.[32]

Three mass murders surpassed all others. In Rome, partisans detonated a bomb that killed thirty-two German soldiers on 23 March 1944. The Nazis retaliated by rounding up 335 political prisoners, trucking them to the Ardeatine Cave on the Appian Way south of Rome and shooting them on 25 March. The Nazis rounded up and murdered 212 men, women and children in Civitelli on 29 June 1944 after partisans killed two German soldiers. The worst was the Nazi murder of at least 770 men, women and children at Marzabotto from 28 to 30 September 1944, in reprisal for partisan attacks from their stronghold on nearby Monte Sole. The deadliest partisan attack came on 20 December 1943, when a mined bridge just south of Rome blew up a train carrying troops, munitions and fuel to the front; around 500 German soldiers died and hundreds more were wounded.

The Allied command was Janus-minded about the Italian resistance. For the war's duration, they certainly welcomed its military help in diverting, delaying and destroying German troops and supplies. Partisan revolts preceded and aided the Allied liberation of Naples, Florence, Livorno, Ravenna and Bologna along with countless towns. General Alexander, the theatre commander, broadcasted on 19, 20 and 27 June 1944 the rather puzzling appeal for partisans to 'kill the Germans from behind in order to prevent their retaliation and thus kill even more'.[33] But the Allies worried that the Communists had hijacked the resistance as the prelude to a post-war revolution. On 25 June 1944, the Allies tried to assert some control over the resistance by naming General Rafaele Cardona to head the Volunteer Corps for Liberty that the Committee of National Liberation had ineffectively founded half a year earlier. They parachuted Cardona in northern Italy where he painstakingly tried to unite the fragmented democratic groups.

Fascist Republican Party Secretary Alessandro Pavolini ordered the arrest, trial and execution of the nineteen Fascist Grand Council members who had voted to depose Mussolini and set up a tribunal for their trial on 13 October. The secret police eventually rounded up six for trial. The Gestapo had kept Galeazzo Ciano under house arrest at Schloss Hirschberg near Allmannshausen on Lake Starnberg 20 miles south of Munich since his arrival with his family on 27 August; they eventually sent Edda and her three children to join Mussolini at his Salo Republic. On 19 October, the Gestapo flew Ciano to Verona where he was imprisoned in Castello Vecchio. The most distinguished of those eventually imprisoned with him was Emilio De Bono, among Mussolini's earliest Fascist comrades, one of the *Quadrumviri* who led the March on Rome and had since then served numerous leadership posts in the regime. The others included Luciano Gottardi, the Fascist Confederation of Industrial Workers' president; Carlo Pareschi, the Agriculture and Forests minister; Giovanni Marinelli, the Postal and Telegraph Service undersecretary; and Tullio Cianetti, a former Corporations minister.

After the war, Edda explained how her relationship with Ciano had changed from their first heady days when he was a diplomat in China: 'In Shanghai I was very much in love with Galeazzo. I was also very jealous of him . . . Afterward there remained much affection between us, but little by little love ended.'[34] Yet Edda stood by her man after his arrest. She was allowed to visit him in prison on 22 October and 27 November. In one of his last diary entries, Ciano described Edda as his 'wife, who in my many hours of sorrow has revealed herself as a strong, sure and faithful companion'.[35]

Ciano's arrest imposed a terrible dilemma for Edda. She 'had always loved and admired my father more than anyone else in the world'. But her husband's arrest enraged her and on 18 December she begged her father to amnesty him. He lamely replied that:

> I can do nothing for Galeazzo . . . I have not been involved, I am not involved and I will not get involved in the proceeding . . . Justice must follow its regular course . . . Many of those who are asking for Ciano's head have nothing against him; they ask it instead because they want to see me in a decisive test, to see if I will have the courage to say that I will accept the sentence, whatever it is.

He later said, 'To me, Ciano is already dead . . . He could not go about in Italy, be seen, have a name . . . Those who voted for the Grandi resolution will be condemned.'[36] Edda recalled that: 'When he told me that he could do nothing for my husband and that justice must follow its course, my reaction resembled that of one of the ancient furies. Beating the table with my fists, I threw at my father all I thought of him, his attitude, his German allies . . . and . . . my contempt and disgust.'[37] Mussolini complained that 'it is my singular destiny to be betrayed by everyone including my own daughter'.[38]

The Tribunal officially began on 1 December 1943. The charges against the nineteen were treason for aiding the enemy by deposing Mussolini. The treason charge enraged Ciano who declared:

> The stuff of madmen! That I should be accuse of treason and helping the enemy! I was perhaps the only one in the Grand Council who argued for continuing the war until the end and I exhorted Mussolini very strongly to demand from the Germans much greater help than they seemed to give us . . . And now the tremendous accusation of treason is made against me . . . Let them shoot me immediately . . . but not call me a traitor![39]

The trial was held in Verona's fortress, the Castello Vecchio, on 8 January 1944. Colonel Aldo Vecchi was the court's president, who presided over the seven-judge panel and prosecutor Andrea Fortunato. The judges would decide treason charges for the six defendants before them and the other thirteen *in absentia*. The judges unanimously found all nineteen guilty of treason. Of them, Cianetti received a 30-year sentence for extenuating circumstances while the others were condemned to be shot in the back by a firing squad. On the morning of 11 January 1944, the five were taken to the shooting range of Fort Procolo outside Verona, tied in chairs facing away from the 25-man firing squad, all militia volunteers, who opened fire at the command.

In his memoir of the war, Winston Churchill issued his own judgement of the trial's meaning:

> Mussolini agreed to let loose a wave of calculated vengeance. All those leaders of the old Fascist regime who had voted against him in July 1943 and could be caught in German-occupied Italy were brought to trial . . . Without exception they received the death sentence . . . The trial of Ciano was in keeping with all the elements of Renaissance tragedy. Mussolini's submission to Hitler's vengeful demands brought him only shame and the miserable neo-Fascist republic dragged on by Lake Garda – a relic of the broken axis.[40]

The National Liberation Committee organized an 'Anti-Fascist Congress' with around ninety delegates at Bari on 28 and 29 January 1944. The Congress not only condemned Mussolini and Fascism, but also the monarchy. In his keynote address, Senator Benedetto Croce declared: 'As long as the present King remains head of the State, we feel that Fascism is not finished, that it remains attached to us, that it continues to corrode us and to weaken us, that it will resurge more or less camouflaged and to sum up, we cannot breathe and live'.[41] The Congress called on Victor Emmanuel to abdicate. The delegates split over how to govern Italy after the abdication. Some would have Victor Emmanuel's son become Umberto II. Others wanted to abolish the monarchy and make Italy a republic. Many leaned toward letting the people decide between a constitutional monarchy and a dominant parliament or a republic in a national plebiscite after the war ended.

Victor Emmanuel III announced on 12 April 1944, that he would retire but not abdicate and let his son take over his daily duties as soon as the Allies liberated Rome. That encouraged five of the six parties in the Committee of National Liberation to join Badoglio's government and swear allegiance to the king; only the Action Party abstained.

After American troops liberated Rome on 4 June, Victor Emmanuel had Badoglio resign as prime minister and asked the opposition parties to form a government. After several days of haggling, the leaders agreed on 8 June that Ivanoe Bonomi would be prime minister with a cabinet that prominently included Christian Democrat Alcide De Gasperi, Communist Palmiro Togliatti, Socialist Giuseppe Saragat, Action Party Guido de Ruggiero, Liberal Benedetto Croce and Marcello Soleri and Admiral Raffaele De Courten. Victor Emmanuel named Crown Prince Umberto the 'Lieutenant-General of the Realm', with the authority to perform royal duties in his father's place. On 25 June, Bonomi shifted power to himself and his cabinet by getting the king to sign a decree that empowered them to issue decrees in the lieutenant-general's name rather than his own. Yet Victor Emmanuel remained king largely because Prime Minister Churchill rejected President Roosevelt's preference that Italy become a republic; the differences between them naturally reflected those between Britain's constitutional monarchy and America's republic that each respectively represented.

The Allies recognized that any war crimes and crimes against humanity that Italy's Fascist regime may have committed were miniscule compared to the horrors inflicted by the Nazi regime. The Allied priority was stabilizing occupied Italy by ensuring that needy people were fed, sheltered and doctored. As for war crimes, the Allies let the Italian government conduct its own purge (*epurazione*) of Fascism and Fascists from Italy.

Naturally, anti-Fascists wanted to prosecute Fascists for their crimes. The question was just what crimes were the Fascists guilty of committing? After all, the Fascist Party had won seats in a national election and the king had appointed Mussolini the prime minister. Thereafter, Mussolini, with the king's either eager or grudging approval, got Parliamentary votes in favour or issued decrees that systematically transformed Italy into a dictatorship. Superficially, those measures were constitutional. If Mussolini was guilty of crimes was not Victor Emmanuel also guilty for approving his authoritarian decrees or issuing his own?

Badoglio issued the first tentative purge order on 4 November 1943, with instructions to the prefects of Brindisi, Taranto, Lecce and Bari in the liberated region of Puglia to dismiss Fascists who had committed crimes from public positions. The trouble was that those prefects, like others across Italy, were Fascists and either had themselves engaged in corruption and other crimes or tolerated colleagues who had.

Governor General Charles Poletti took the first step against Fascists in Rome on 26 June 1944, with an order to purge Fascists from the municipal government. Italy's government formed a 'High Commission for Sanctions against Fascism' of twelve members with two from each party and headed by Carlo Sforza on 27 July. Sforza established four sections, with two that respectively investigated and indicted illegal Fascist seizures of property and money, a third that prosecuted those indicted and a fourth that purged Fascists from all public offices including government, schools and corporatist organizations.

The High Commission formed lower commissions to investigate and act at local levels in liberated Italy. By 30 November 1944, 112 of 157 lower commissions had been created and had examined 28,399 cases of which 6,859 were serious enough for higher review and of them 495 were expelled from public office. Of higher officials, 3,210 were examined with 1,355 acquitted, 1,316 received fines and 539 were expelled. Similar results came from other regions northward liberated by the Allies. By May 1946, 143,781 of 277,701 officials elsewhere were investigated, of which 13,737 were formally tried and 1,476 were expelled.[42]

The first prominent Fascists put on trial were Pietro Caruso, Rome's secret police chief, and his deputy Roberto Occhetto, who collaborated with Gestapo chief Herbert Kappel to round up, torture and execute hundreds of real and alleged partisans, including the massacre of 335 Italian political prisoners at Ardeatine cave on 24 March 1944. A lynch mob surged into Regina Coeli Prison to kill Caruso but killed another inmate instead before the authorities drove them off. Caruso was found guilty on 21 September and executed the next day; Occhetto received a 30-year prison term. Amid months of rising criticism that he was inept, Sforza resigned as High Commissioner on 27 December. Bonomi replaced him as High Commissioner.

Throughout his Salo Republic days, Mussolini was a ghost of himself, corpulent, lethargic, morose and wallowing in self-pity. He resided at the Villa Feltrinelli with his squabbling, noisy, demanding immediate and extended family. He was generous in giving money to needy relatives from his dwindling sources like his newspaper *Il Populo d'Italia* and book sales. He got so desperate that he sold his beloved *Populo* for 75 million lire to Milan industrialist Gian Cella.[43]

Rachele recalled that:

> As the days passed he became more thoughtful than ever. I could tell by the way that he talked from time to time that the deadly struggle between Italians behind the lines was a constant torment to him. Even at meals he sat gloomy and distraught . . . His temper was better at the beginning of the day when our grandchildren . . . came down to say good morning in their happy, carefree way and accompany him to the Villa Feltrinelli . . . From my window I often saw him, lost in thought, in a garden chair by the clear waters.[44]

Foreign Ministry official Luigi Bolla insightfully described Mussolini as

> a prisoner of the myths created by him to his design, a prisoner of his past . . . of having destroyed and not created, of not having formulated any message that could survive him. He knew the game was up . . . In the squalid corner of the Villa Feltrinelli, almost hallucinogenic . . . he followed in slow motion the false routine of the old times . . . almost the parody of himself'.[45]

Doctor Zacharia observed *Il Duce*'s steady decay in body and spirit then plummet: 'In the days preceding the collapse . . . he . . . had a serious nervous attack, a true breakdown. He became apathetic and showed an absolute lack of energy and intelligence.'[46]

Not surprisingly, Mussolini became increasingly obsessed with his mortality as Allied armies advanced up the peninsula toward his lair and elsewhere crushed Hitler's regime between the American and British armies from the west and the Soviet Red Army from the east. He granted two interviews to journalists in March 1945. In the first, he claimed that 'Death has become a friend. It does not frighten me any more'. In the second, he said 'I have no illusions about my destiny. They will not give me a trial . . . they'll probably kill me and say that I committed suicide, a victim of remorse.'[47]

Mussolini told General Rodolfo Graziani that 'Fascism must die heroically'.[48] He fantasized about dying with his Blackshirts in a last stand in Valtellina Valley with the Alps and Swiss border behind them. Fascism's demise aside, its *Duce* did not die heroically.

SS General Karl Wolff, the German military governor of Northern Italy, visited him on 14 April 1945 and told him that he was conducting secret negotiations with Allen Dulles, the OSS station chief in Switzerland, for an armistice and urged Mussolini to back his effort. Mussolini agreed and thereafter sought to cut his own cease-fire deal with the Committee on National Liberation.

Mussolini journeyed with officials and guards packed in five cars from Salo to Milan on 18 April; he had ten more days to live.[49] They stayed at the prefecture building. He had Carlo Silvestri contact the partisan underground for a non-punitive surrender deal. As he awaited a response, the Committee of National Liberation for North Italy publicly issued this decree: 'Members of the Fascist government and the *gerarchi* [elite] of fascism who are guilty of suppressing the constitutional guarantees, destroying popular liberties, creating the Fascist regime, compromising and betraying the fate of the country and leading it to the present catastrophe are to be punished with the penalty of death and in less serious instances life imprisonment.'[50]

That decree obviously targeted for death Benito Mussolini who had led that Fascist revolution. Despite that, he agreed to meet a delegation from the North Italian Committee of National Liberation that included General Cardona, Christian Democratic leader Achille Marazza and Action Party leader Ricardo Lombardi on 25 April, with Milan's Cardinal Ildefonso Schuster, Milan's Metropolitan, acting as the go-between at his palace. Mussolini and his delegation arrived early. After greeting him, Cardinal Schuster urged him to surrender immediately for history's sake. Mussolini angrily replied: 'History? Do you talk to me about history? All I believe in is ancient history. History written without passion and long after the event.'[51] After the partisan leaders appeared, Cardona informed Mussolini that they would accept only unconditional surrender but promised him a fair trial for his crimes. Mussolini refused and strode angrily out with his entourage. Later that day, the Committee of National Liberation issued an order for Mussolini to be summarily executed if he were captured.

That evening, Mussolini and his entourage packed into ten cars and headed north to Como where they hoped to find a way to exile in Switzerland. That night they stayed at the guarded prefecture building. There Mussolini may have written his last letter to Rachele: 'We may never see each other again . . . I ask your forgiveness for all the harm I have unwittingly done you. But you know that you have always been the only woman I have really loved . . . Kisses to you and the children. Your Benito.'[52] The original letter does not exist and most historians believe that Rachele concocted it to, as Ray Moseley explained, 'salve her injured pride. It was apparently more than she could bear that her husband's mistress had followed him to the end, died with him and trumped her in the accompanying publicity.'[53]

Early on 26 April, Mussolini and his entourage headed for the Swiss border through rain and fog, fearful that partisans infesting the region might block their way. They spent the night at the tiny village of Menaggio. There they were joined by Carla Petacci, her brother Marchello, his wife and their two children. The next morning, 28 April, a German convoy of twenty-eight trucks bound for Switzerland entered the town. Mussolini got the convoy's commander, Lieutenant Schallmayer, to join their forces, give him a helmet and greatcoat as a disguise and let him ride in one of the trucks like a common soldier.

Urbano Lazzaro commanded the partisan company of the 52nd Garibaldi Brigade that blocked the road heading north to Switzerland. As Mussolini's column approached the roadblock, the Germans and partisans briefly exchanged gunfire before Schallmayer surrendered. The partisans searched each truck, first recognized Barracu, then Mussolini. Although Mussolini carried a pistol he gave up without a fight. One of Lazzaro's men jubilantly shouted, 'We're got big head!' Lazzaro recalled that: 'His face was like wax and his stare glassy, but somehow blind. I read there utter exhaustion but not fear . . . Mussolini seemed completely lacking in will, spiritually dead.' Lazzaro declared to *Il Duce*, 'I arrest you in the name of the Italian people'.[54]

The partisans took the prisoners to the nearby town of Dongo and imprisoned them in the barracks. Lazzaro sent word up the chain of command what to do with Mussolini. Headquarters at Milan sent back word to execute him and bring his body to Milan. There are different versions of what then happened.[55] Most likely on the morning of 28 April, the partisans extracted Mussolini and Carla, drove them to the nearby hamlet of San Guilino di Mezzegra, stood them against a wall and machine-gunned them. Then they trucked the bullet-riddled corpses to Milan's Piazzale Loreto. There *Il Duce* and his mistress were hung upside down alongside sixteen other executed Fascist leaders.

Two days later, Adolf Hitler and his newlywed wife, Eva Braun, committed suicide at *Der Führer*'s command bunker in Berlin as Soviet troops battled German defenders a few hundred yards away. Eva bit a cyanide capsule while Hitler placed a pistol to his right temple and pulled the trigger.

The war did not immediately end with the deaths of the two Fascist tyrants. For two preceding months, secret talks unfolded over the possible surrender of Axis forces in Italy. General Karl Wolff initiated those talks after accepting the reality that the Allies would soon crush Germany. He was determined to end the war as soon as possible to avoid further death and destruction. In late February 1945, he sent an Italian intermediary to Allen Dulles, the OSS station chief in Berne, Switzerland, asking to meet to discuss surrender terms. Dulles agreed and they arranged a time and place via go-betweens. They finally met at a safe house in Zurich on 5 March. Wolff convinced Dulles of his sincerity and power to arrange a surrender. Dulles informed Washington and after days of debate that included President Roosevelt, Prime Minister Churchill and the Combined Chiefs of Staff, a consensus emerged. Dulles received approval to proceed.

What followed was another six weeks of secret meetings and negotiations before a breakthrough. The key steps came on 25 and 26 April, when Wolff convinced first Marshal Rodolpho Graziani, the Fascist Republic commander, then Field Marshal Heinrich von Vietinghoff, the German army commander, to agree to the surrender. They then sent two envoys to Allied headquarters at Caserta on 29 April. Colonel Victor von Schweinitz signed the armistice agreement for Vietinghoff, Major Eugen Wenner for Wolff and Graziani and General William Morgan for General Harold Alexander, the Allied theatre commander. The cease-fire took take place on 2 May.

Hitler bequeathed the leadership of the Third Reich to Admiral Karl Dönitz, who was then at Flensburg in northern Germany near the Danish border. Dönitz authorized the surrender of Axis forces in Italy, then General Hans-Georg von Fredeborg's forces in north-west Germany, Holland and Denmark on 4 May and finally sent General Alfred Jodl to General Dwight Eisenhower's headquarters at Rheims, France to sign the surrender for all remaining German forces on 5 May, with the cease-fire effective on 8 May 1945.

Tragically, the war continued against Japan in the Pacific and East Asia for another three months. Japan's tyrannical control over the population far exceeded that of the Nazi and Italian regimes. During the Second World War, Japan's soldiers nearly all fought to the death rather than surrender, something German soldiers rarely and Italian soldiers almost never did. Atop that, Japan's government armed civilians with spears and grenades and indoctrinated them to sacrifice themselves against American troops; on the island of Saipan, mothers held their children's hands and jumped off cliffs and schoolgirls held grenades to their breasts and pulled the pins rather than suffer the disgrace of surrender.

The Americans captured the Okinawan island chain south-west of Japan on 22 June, after two months and three weeks of fighting that inflicted 50,000 American casualties, including 12,500 dead and 110,000 Japanese casualties, including 95,000 dead. The next campaign would be the invasion of Kyushu Island on 1 November 1945 and Honshu Island on 1 February 1946. The Joint Chiefs of Staff estimated that Japan's final defeat would take years and a least a million American casualties and millions of Japanese who would rather die fighting or by suicide for their semi-divine emperor rather than surrender. Japan's military could not defend against the atomic bombs that obliterated Hiroshima on 6 August and Nagasaki on 9 August. Even then, Japan's six-man War Council presided over by the emperor split evenly over rather to surrender or keep fighting. The emperor decided in favour of surrender. He broadcast that decision on 14 August and Japan's government formally surrendered aboard the battleship USS *Missouri* amidst a fleet of over 250 Allied warships in Tokyo Bay on 2 September 1945, finally ending the Second World War.

Chapter 11

THE LEGACY

> I am convinced that your historic March on Rome created a turning point in the history of the world.
>
> (Adolf Hitler)

> As Goethe said his greatest misfortune was the birth of Napoleon, who obfuscated his glory, so Mussolini can say that his greatest misfortune was the birth of Hitler.
>
> (Galeazzo Ciano)

> I challenged the world and it proved too strong for me; I despised other men and they are taking their revenge.
>
> (Benito Mussolini)

> The madness of the Leader had become the religion of his followers.
>
> (Galeazzo Ciano)

> I have ruined Italy! I have ruined Italy! (Benito Mussolini)

What is Benito Mussolini's place in history?

Il Duce once admitted, 'I work and I try, yet that all is but farce'.[1] On the surface, Mussolini was a cartoonist's dream, pompous, vain and blustering. Yet the results of his tyranny were mass death and destruction for Italians and every country he ordered Italy's military to invade. As Adolf Hitler's puppet in the so-called Salo Republic, Mussolini ruefully admitted that 'I challenged the world and it proved too strong for me; I despised other men and they are taking their revenge'.[2] That was a good if incomplete summary. What Mussolini admitted to was hubris, of being so deluded that his ambitions far exceeded his power to realize them with the result that he destroyed himself and all others entangled with him.

Mussolini's performance as commander-in-chief fell short what his predecessors had accomplished. Most vitally, Mussolini chose to join the side that ultimately lost the Second World War, while in the First World War, Italy's leadership chose the winning side. During that war, the government actually mobilized more troops and suffered worse losses than Mussolini's regime did during the Second World War. From 23 May 1915 to 11 November 1918, 5,903,140 men served in the military from 34,671,377 Italians in 1915, with 578,000 killed, 947,000 wounded including 463,000 permanently disabled and 520,000 captured for 2,058,000 total casualties. From 10 June 1940 to 8 September 1943: 2,500,000 men served in the military of 44,467,000 Italians in 1940. Italy suffered 444,523 dead during the Second World War. Of those deaths, 92,767 soldiers and 25,499 civilians officially died and 106,228 were listed as missing and presumed dead. Italy suffered another 187,522 dead, 67,462 combatants and 120,060 civilians, from September 1943 to May 1945; the combatants included 44,720 partisans who died fighting and 9,980 partisans killed in reprisals. In all, Italy's military suffered around 355,000 dead from combat or mortal wounds along with disease, frostbite and starvation, including 100,000 among prisoners of the Soviets and 33,000 among prisoners of the Germans. Over 640,000 Italians either volunteered or were conscripted to work in Germany. Around 64,000 Italian civilians died from bombings compared to 60,000 in Britain and 700,000 in Germany.[3]

Mussolini's military was less strict than Italy's military in the First World War. From June 1940 to September 1943, the military found guilty and executed around 150 men for various crimes, mostly desertion. From May 1915 to November 1918, the military charged 350,000 soldiers for various crimes, issued 4,028 death sentences and actually conducted 750 executions. In stunning contrast to Italy's military in both wars, Hitler's Wehrmacht condemned 35,000 soldiers to death and executed 22,000 of them.[4]

Italy's Jewish population suffered horrendous losses, although the portion of dead was lower than in most other Nazi-occupied countries.[5] Of 44,500 Italian Jews in September 1945, the Nazis murdered 173 in Italy and shipped 7,495 to concentration camps where only 610 survived. Around 5,000 Jews escaped to Switzerland and as many as 3,000 fought as partisans. The Nazis and Fascists robbed Italian Jews of enormous wealth. By June 1944, confiscations included 75,089,047 lire of bank deposits, 36,396,831 lire of state-owned company stocks, 731,442,219 lire of private business stocks, 855,348,608 lire of home furnishings and 198,300,003 lire of factory equipment. Thereafter this tapered off because so little Jewish wealth remained.[6]

Blackshirted thugs viciously murdered hundreds of political enemies, mostly communists, from 1919 to 1943. Mussolini was well aware of those murders and not just tolerated but condoned them. The most notorious victim was Giacomo Matteotti, the United Socialist Party chief and outspoken parliamentary critic of Mussolini and Fascism. On 10 June 1924, five Fascists led by Amerigo Dumini, a hitman with at least a dozen other murder victims, kidnapped Matteotti on a Rome street, pushed him into a car, and when he resisted, stabbed him to death. They dumped his body in a ravine outside of Rome,

Plausible deniability is an American presidential term but is as venerable as political authority itself. How complicit Mussolini was for Matteotti's murder is unknowable. Quite likely he looked hit team leader Amerigo Dumini in the eye and uttered something resembling Henry II's words to four devoted knights about Thomas Becket, 'Will no one rid me of this turbulent priest?'

Mussolini ultimately was among the dead inflicted by the wars he unleashed. He dreamed of a glorious Thermopylae-like death with 50,000 Fascist zealots in Valtellina Valley in north Italy with their backs to the Alps against overwhelming masses of enemy troops. Instead he was machine-gunned beside his mistress by Italian partisans devoted to destroying his regime, carted to a Milan square where his naked corpse was battered by the enraged crowd then strung up feet-first for all to jeer.

As for the Italian Empire, Mussolini did not begin Italian imperialism, he expanded it. What was the legacy of Italy's empire for the natives? Italian conquests cost altogether the lives of hundreds of thousands of natives who died fighting the invaders or from starvation and disease exacerbated by war. For instance, Libya's population dropped from 1.400,000 in 1907 to 825,000 in 1931.[7] Once the Italians repressed the population, they did build modern roads, railways, ports, hospitals, schools and electrical, water and sewage systems that benefited natives with access to them. The Italians abolished slavery. Small but growing classes of educated wealthy natives emerged in each colony, while most natives remained poverty-stricken, illiterate and perhaps poorer because of inflation. Nonetheless, better hygiene and diets, access to medicine and suppression of long-standing feuds among groups led to steep population increases in each colony. For instance, Eritrea's population soared from 274,944 in 1905 to 614,353 in 1939.[8] Catholic orders ran most schools and required all students to learn Catholic theology regardless of their own faith. Psychologically, natives bore the stigma of being considered morally, intellectually and culturally inferior to Italians and other Europeans. The Italians may have reconciled some ethnic or religious groups with historic animosities toward each other and exacerbated others. They provoked national feelings that may have previously been muted or non-existent.

Mussolini was not responsible for all the death and destruction that Italy suffered during the Second World War. The Allied Italian campaign was controversial then and has remained so ever since. British military historian J.F.C. Fuller succinctly expressed the dominant critical view of the 608-day battle up the peninsula as: 'tactically the most absurd and strategically the most senseless campaign of the whole war'.[9] Italy was literally and figuratively a dead-end for Allied forces. The Allies expended enormous military, economic and moral power for a prolonged blood-soaked stalemate broken by a series of sporadic Allied advances that got no further than the southern Po River valley when the war ended. Although the number of divisions on each side varied, generally the Germans tied down twice as many Allied divisions. In contrast to nearly all other fronts, the peninsula was mostly a stagnant, meatgrinder of trench and fortification combat similar to the First World War. Artillery, not small arms, inflicted most of the 312,000 and 435,000 casualties the Allies and Germans respectively suffered from September 1943 to May 1945. About half the German casualties were prisoners taken during the Wehrmacht's last demoralized weeks. At the war's end, Axis forces in Italy numbered 459,224 German troops and 160,180 Italians including four regular divisions and the Republican National Guard. Those troops tied down 1,550,000 Allied troops, nearly a one to three ratio.[10]

No one was more responsible for the Allied invasion of the Italian peninsula than Winston Churchill. He argued that after landing in Italy's foot the Allied armies would swiftly drive north, eventually to Germany itself. The blood-soaked stalemate revealed his beliefs to have been nothing more than wishful thinking. Whether he ever admitted that to himself is unknown. All along he insisted that the Italian campaign was strategically vital despite all contrary evidence. During a visit to Rome in August 1944, he projected his mingled rage and despair on the Italians: 'Italy has done us great damage and must be punished and ground down. Now let the Italians stew in their own juices.'[11] In other words, he wanted to double down on the Italian campaign rather than invest those precious military chips elsewhere, like France.

Churchill opposed the Normandy landings scheduled for early June 1944, virtually until the last minute. He insisted that the result would be a catastrophic defeat. When the campaign proved to be a success he then opposed the Riviera landing scheduled for mid-August 1944, again warning that calamity would result. His major objection was that seven divisions were diverted from the Italian campaign for the southern France campaign. He clung to the Italian campaign despite the glacial advance. He insisted that the Allies land in Yugoslavia, Greece and even the island of Rhodes in the far eastern Mediterranean, anywhere but France. That such a brilliant mind could host such delusions is most puzzling about Churchill.

An alternative Mediterranean strategy would have ended the war sooner with far fewer losses in blood and treasure. In July 1943, the Allies would have bypassed Sicily and invaded lightly defended Sardinia and Corsica. That would have given them a central position for bombers to pound enemy positions on Sicily, the Italian peninsula and southern France. It also would have been the perfect jumping-off point for invading the French Rivera simultaneously with the invasion of Normandy in early May, not early June 1944. Not knowing where the next Mediterranean landing would take place, the Germans would have had to spread their forces thin around Sicily, Italy's peninsula and southern France. Part of the Allied forces invading the Riviera would seize and defend the Maritime Alps on the Franco-Italian frontier. That would have forced the Germans in Italy into a bloody stalemate as they launched attack after fruitless attack on that line, just as the Allies actually did against the Germans up the Italian peninsula over 20 months.

Reinforced with all the troops, supplies, arms, munitions, warplanes and landing craft that were actually squandered in Sicily and the Italian peninsula, the twin invasions of France would have pulverized German forces and united in Burgundy probably in late June, reached the Rhine in late July and quite likely Berlin and beyond in late August 1944. Not only would that have saved countless Allied lives, it would have saved countless Germans and Eastern Europeans from Communism imposed by the conquering Soviet Union. Italy's destruction and death would have been a fraction of the historic devastation.

There were no Allied war crime trials for Italy's Fascist and military leaders.[12] Two reasons were critical. First, the scale of Italian war atrocities was miniscule compared to the deliberate mass death inflicted on millions of victims by the Germans and the Japanese. Second, King Victor Emmanuel and a group of conspirators deposed

Mussolini, outlawed the Fascist Party, then conducted their own trials, purges from public offices and summary executions of Fascists across the country.

Purges of Fascists persisted for years, some legal, others not. For instance, in January and February 1946, the government examined 394,041 officials, reprimanded 8,803 and expelled 1,580; of those penalized, 728 were high officials.[13] Political violence in Italy did not end with the Fascist regime. Antifascist murders persisted long after the war ended. Partisans and mobs murdered thousands of Fascists from 25 July 1945 through the late 1940s. In May 1945 alone, the Communists may have executed more than 20,000 Fascist Party members or collaborators in regions and cities they controlled.[14] Despite those trials, purges and assaults, animosities between Italy's Fascist resisters and collaborators never reached the expanse, acrimony and time between those in France.

Italy's government issued an amnesty on 22 June 1946. All sentences of five years or less were suspended and the criminals released. All other prison terms were halved. All death sentences were reduced to 30 years in prison. Before then, of thirty-six Fascists who received death sentences, only two were executed.[15]

During the post-war era Italy, like Germany and Japan, transformed politically from Fascism to democracy and economically from devastation and mass poverty into mass prosperity. The difference was that the Americans imposed and tutored democracy during their military occupations of Germany (1945–9) and Japan (1945–52), while the Italians largely established a democracy by themselves, assisted with American economic aid and advice.

Victor Emmanuel finally abdicated in favour of his son Umberto on 9 May 1946, a year after the war in Europe ended. Italy held two critical national elections on 2 June 1946. One election was to choose delegates to a Constituent Assembly that would draft a constitution. The top three party winners were Alcide De Gasperi's Christian Democrats with 35.21 per cent and 207 seats, Pietro Nenni's Socialists with 20.68 per cent and 115 seats and Palmiro Togliatti's Communists with 18.93 per cent and 104 seats. The other election was to decide whether Italy should remain a constitutional monarchy or become a republic. Voters favoured a republic by 54.69 per cent to 45.31 per cent. Italy's republican constitution was ratified on 22 December 1947 and the republic was formally inaugurated on 1 January 1948.

Italy's first election as a republic took place on 18 April 1948. The three top party winners were Alcide De Gasperi's Christian Democrats with 48.5 per cent for 305 deputies and 131 senators, Palmiro Togliatti's Communists with 31.09 per cent for 183 deputies and 72 senators and Giuseppe Saragat's Socialists with 7.1 per cent for 33 deputies and 10 senators. That distribution of power became the pattern throughout the Cold War until 1991. Christian Democrats dominated by winning pluralities then forming coalitions with minor parties that let them form and lead every government. That political stability both shaped and reflected the steady expansion of Italy's economy with high growth to 1973, then slower growth when the Organization for Petroleum Exporting Countries (OPEC) quadrupled oil prices that year and doubled them again over the next decade. Italy was among the founding members of the North Atlantic Treaty Organization (NATO) in 1949, the European Coal and Steel Community (ECSC) in 1952, the European Economic Community (EEC) in 1967 and the European Union (EU) in 1993.

In all, Italy's leaders admirably transformed the political system from Fascism to liberal democracy during and after the war and nurtured economic growth and political stability through the present.

Like the Sorcerer's hubristic Apprentice, Benito Mussolini dreamed of creating a better world. He justified his dictatorship and aggression by promising prosperity, prestige and peace for Italians and their conquests. His wife Rachele spoke for countless admirers in Italy and around the world: 'I have never looked for forgiveness for Mussolini because I do not recognize that he did anything wrong. He made war, but was he the only head of government whoever did this? His only crime was to have lost.'[16]

Even at the height of Mussolini's power in the late 1930s before the catastrophic defeats began, many people, especially those who best knew him, had mixed views of him. In his post-war memoir, Giovanni Giuriati, a high Fascist official explained that outlook:

> I am one of Mussolini's ministers, I told myself. I am standing beside a great figure in history, an authentic history-maker. I loved this enchanting man so much and undoubtedly still love him . . . Mussolini . . . talks like a genius, but slips into puerile banality; he sets off with determination and plays around like a spoiled, capricious child; he preaches like a great convert and leaves people confounded with a cynical expression; he imposes a frightening workload on himself for the people's sake and shows off his contempt for men in general; he invokes God, but delights in heretical pronouncements. Despite all of this he is still a great man to whom you willingly offer the best part of yourself.[17]

None of Mussolini's advisors knew him more intimately than Galeazzo Ciano, his son-in-law and Foreign Minister from June 1936 to March 1943. Ciano was among the nineteen of twenty-eight Fascist Grand Council members who voted to oust Mussolini on 25 July 1943. Eventually the Germans arrested Ciano and turned him over to Mussolini's Salo Republic. In December 1943, as he awaited trial for treason, he had his visiting wife Edda smuggle out a farewell letter that he had written King Victor Emmanuel. After apologizing for his own failures, he states: 'One man, one man alone, Mussolini, through unscrupulous personal ambitions, "out of thirst for military glory" (to use his own actual words) had deliberately led the nation into the bottomless pit.'[18]

Mussolini's greatest talent was showmanship. He promoted himself as a mythic, all-powerful, all-knowing leader who would transform Italy into a prosperous, prestigious empire and he would steamroll anyone or anything in his way. For a while, that became a self-fulfilling prophesy as he beguiled ever more of Italy's elite, most importantly the king and the masses of people into zealously believing that. They cheered as he amassed more power until he transformed Italy's democracy into a dictatorship.

Mussolini's speeches electrified crowds although transcripts revealed that their style far surpassed their substance. The messages are mostly banal cliches, promises and critiques melodramatically delivered with his deep voice mingling seduction, defiance, mockery, indignation and hope. Although only five foot five inches tall, he seemed like a giant to most viewers with his huge bald head, jutting jaw, stocky body, wide-stance and chopping gestures. Countless men fantasized about being like Mussolini while countless women fantasized about him carrying them to bed.

That zeal lasted only as long as Mussolini appeared genuinely to develop Italy's economy, culture and colonies. Most Italians adored him until the series of military disasters began. Then his popularity steadily eroded and eventually transformed into worsening hatred. That drastic seesaw of mass emotions puzzled an American army interrogator at an internment camp on Ischia island in Naples Bay where Mussolini's wife Rachele spent several months after the war. She recalled the interrogator circling back to the same question: 'Can you explain, Excellency, why millions of Italians who worshipped Mussolini for twenty years should have made a complete turnaround in this way?' Rachele was very bright, wise and perceptive, but also fiercely proud: 'I couldn't admit to this officer, who had been the enemy, that the Fascist regime had destroyed itself; that some officials had weakened through fear of the future or through ambition.'[19]

Mussolini self-destructed like countless other dictators throughout history. If Mussolini's showmanship propelled him to the heights of power, hubris melted his wings and plummeted him into the abyss. He believed his own mythology and sought conquests impossible for Italy to win. The result was the destruction of his regime and himself and the devastation of Italy and other countries victimized by his imperialism. Mussolini was like the Wizard in the Land of Oz who terrified and manipulated people who believed he was God-like. Yet that belief deflated with each defeat, the equivalent of the curtain being raised and increasingly revealed him as a pompous, deluded buffoon.

Biographer Denis Mack Smith explained that vicious cycle:

> Until almost the last moment he continued to believe that propaganda was the main weapon required and that his job as leader was, first, to establish and maintain the myth of his own infallibility and then to clothe in plausibly realistic garments all the many other illusions he had thought it expedient to create . . . It was an absolutely unserious world, where prestige, propaganda and public statements were what counted; and it's hard to avoid the conclusion that the central message and the real soft core at the heart of Italian fascism.[20]

Effective propaganda is believable even if it consists mostly of exaggerations, omissions and lies. Like countless tyrants, Mussolini violated the art of propaganda in two ultimately self-defeating ways.[21] First, the propaganda preparing Italians for war promoted Italy's invincible military as inevitably victorious over its effete French, British and Greek enemies. Instead, the French, British and Greeks inflicted devastating defeats on Italy's military. That ruined Mussolini's credibility. People increasingly dismissed any propaganda emitting from his regime. Second, Mussolini believed and acted on his own propaganda. Time after time, he ordered military campaigns with disastrous results, despite pleas by his generals and admirals that the army and navy were unprepared. As a war leader, Churchill was Mussolini's opposite. Churchill brilliantly constructed his speeches to at once give the British people a realistic understanding of the daunting challenges they faced and a vivid explanation of just how they would eventually vanquish their enemies.

Mack Smith explained the dynamic between Mussolini and Fascism: 'Italian Fascism was more than just Mussolini. But the quirks of character in this one man were a crucial factor in both its successes and failures.'[22] Fascism itself conveyed a literally and figuratively fatal flaw. Mussolini made central to Fascism the Social Darwinian view that violent struggle among groups was not just natural but by vanquishing the weak, the strong improved humanity. He bristled that Italians had a reputation for being reluctant and bad soldiers. He was dead set to transform Italians into a version of Prussians, stoical, disciplined, obedient and patriotic. He was deluded to believe that war would be that transformation's crucible. Instead, the series of disastrous military campaigns turned ever more Italians against Mussolini, Fascism and war.

Imperialism, the conquest and colonization of one people by another, was central to the ideology and policies of Fascism and Nazism. Mussolini and Hitler launched a series of wars to win respectively 'vital space' (*spazio vitale*) and 'living space' (*lebensraum*). Eventually they straitjacketed their regimes with dreams of conquests but their alliance proved to be a mutual suicide pact. Each unwittingly dragged down the other as an ally and defeated himself because his ambitions far exceeded his power to realize them. Mussolini lost wars against France, Greece and Britain, until Hitler rescued him with German armies. Hitler launched his Wehrmacht against the Soviet Union and for six months German armies encircled and destroyed Russian armies, inflicting more than 3.5 million casualties. Then the Soviets rallied, thanks to massive American military and economic aid, and over the next three and a half years punched steadily westward until May 1945, when they captured Berlin with Hitler dead from a self-inflicted pistol shot in its ruins.

Yet, the Germans might have defeated the Soviets had Hitler and Mussolini not made another catastrophic mistake. With hubris mingled with alliance duties to Tokyo, Mussolini and Hitler declared war on the United States on 11 December 1941, four days after Japan's devastating attack at Pearl Harbor. Each suffered the delusion that America was a flabby giant whose troops would be easily crushed in combat. America's economic and military might was invincible once President Roosevelt mobilized it for global war. Washington supplied Moscow with $11 billion worth of military aid, enough to prevent its collapse then propel its steamroller advance to the heart of Germany.

Mussolini preceded Hitler as a dictator by a decade and inspired Hitler to model his National Socialist movement on *Il Duce*'s Fascist movement. Although during the war Hitler poorly disguised his contempt for Italy's military, he never lost his appreciation for Mussolini's extraordinary political feats. On the twentieth anniversary of Mussolini's takeover of Italy, Hitler gushed: 'I am convinced that your historic March on

Rome created a turning point in the history of the world. When you were leading the Fascist Revolution to victory, I was still battling against fortune's reverses and my struggle ended in a serious defeat and for myself, personally, imprisonment for more than a year.'[23]

As tyrants and Fascists, Mussolini and Hitler changed places, as Mussolini morphed from being Hitler's lodestar into his shadow. Mussolini's decision to ally Fascist Italy with Nazi Germany and war against the other great powers eventually led to the destruction of both regimes along with most of the rest of Europe and the violent deaths of both tyrants. Galeazzo Ciano found a beguiling analogy: 'As Goethe said his greatest misfortune was the birth of Napoleon, who obfuscated his glory, so Mussolini can say that his greatest misfortune was the birth of Hitler'.[24] Had Hitler never existed, Mussolini would likely be recalled as a relatively benevolent tyrant who developed the economy and conquered Abyssinia.

Ciano expressed the swelling rage of Mussolini and the Fascist elite that 'the policy of Berlin toward Italy was nothing but a network of lies, intrigues and deceit. We were never treated like partners, but always as slaves. Every move took place without our knowledge; even the most fundamental decisions were communicated to us after they had been put into execution. Only the base cowardice of Mussolini could tolerate this without protest and pretend not to see it.'[25]

As a concept, Mussolini popularized 'totalitarianism' although his own Fascist regime, like similar regimes in Germany and Japan, fell short of amassing and asserting all political, economic and social power in its hands. For Mussolini, totalitarianism was more about intended than physical power: 'We want the Italians to make a choice . . . we will pursue our fierce totalitarian will . . . We want to make the nation Fascist so that tomorrow Italians and Fascists . . . will be the same thing.'[26] Mussolini's notion of totalitarianism was succinctly conveyed by the slogan, 'All would be for the state, nothing against the state, no one outside the state'.[27]

Totalitarian and authoritarian regimes must be distinguished.[28] Historically, the only totalitarian regimes were Communist because Communism strives to control all political, economic, social and cultural relationships. Fascist regimes were authoritarian that only partly controlled most political, economic, social and cultural relationships. The clearest difference between totalitarian and authoritarian regimes is their respective economies. Communist regimes nationalize all property and determine all production, prices and pay. Fascist regimes allow private enterprise and property to persist but manage them to develop the economy.

Authoritarian regimes vary greatly in their actual respective powers. Historian Georg Mosse compared Nazi Germany and Fascist Italy during prolonged research in each during 1936. Profound political and cultural differences between them lurked behind their similar authoritarian facades best symbolized by an experience Mosse had on an Italian train:

> [E]very train had a carabiniere with a machine-gun. The people in my compartment were telling anti-Mussolini jokes. The carabiniere of course walked up and down the train corridor and I, coming from a German ambience, was terrified. But what happened in the end was that the carabiniere came into the compartment, not to arrest us, but to tell other Mussolini jokes . . . Such an episode could never have happened in Germany.[29]

Historian A.J.P. Taylor asserted this damning assessment:

> Fascism never possessed the ruthless drive, let alone the material strength, of National Socialism. Morally it was just as corrupting – or perhaps more so from its very dishonesty. Everything about Fascism was a fraud. The social peril from which it saved Italy was a fraud; the revolution by which it seized power was a fraud; the ability and policy of Mussolini were fraudulent. Fascist rule was corrupt, incompetent, empty; Mussolini himself was a vain, blundering boaster without either ideas or aims.[30]

In May 1940, Mussolini fretted about sitting on the sidelines while Hitler's Wehrmacht routed the Allied armies and rapidly overran the Low Countries and northern France. His generals warned him that Italy's military was unready for war. Indeed, it suffered severe, intertwined 'hard' physical and 'soft' psychological power deficiencies that throughout the war led it to suffer one devastating and humiliating defeat after another. A snide quip by Italy's battlefield allies and enemies alike captured the military failures: 'An Italian tank has four gears, one to drive forward and three to drive backward.' That, of course, figuratively referred to the Italian army's notorious reputation for being plagued by deficient hard power like weapons, equipment and logistics and soft power like leadership, motivation, morale and bravery.

Benito Mussolini's enduring legacy is that while his Fascist regime was destroyed, his Fascist ideology persisted and increasingly flourishes politically and culturally.[31]

What is Fascism? Fascism is more than 'a generic phenomenon characteristic of those of whom one disapproves', historian MacGregor Knox's tongue-in-cheek definition.[32] Fascism has clear characteristics whose details and degrees vary among regimes and they include authoritarianism, nationalism, corporatism, populism, vigilantism, imperialism and a charismatic dictator. A Fascist regime should have at least six of these traits, a proto- or neo-fascist regime has three to five.

A leader or political party can call their system or creed whatever they like, but if it has six or more Fascist characteristics it is Fascist. For instance, Hitler's National Socialist regime was Fascist to its core, although Hitler's version emphasized the so-called 'superior Aryan race', a hazy notion that nonetheless to fully realize resulted in the mass murder of six million 'non-Aryans'. Likewise, Japan's political system was clearly Fascist from around 1925 to 1945, with its authoritarianism, nationalism, corporatism, populism, vigilantism and imperialism. A charismatic dictator was the only missing ingredient; Japan's Fascist leadership was collective while its semi-divine emperor held merely symbolic power.

Fascist movements, parties or factions took over Italy led by Benito Mussolini from 1922, Turkey by Mustafa Kemal Ataturk from 1923, Spain by Miquel Primo de Rivera from 1923, Poland by Jozef Pilsudski from 1926, Japan by a cabal of zealots from 1926, Yugoslavia by King Alexander I from 1929, Germany by Adolf Hitler from 1933, Greece by Ioannis Metaxas from 1936, Spain by Franciso Franco from 1939, Croatia by Ante Pavelić from 1941, Hungary by Ferenc Szalasi from 1944 and Argentina by Juan Peron from 1944, to name those most prominent during the twentieth century's first half.

The Allied destruction of the Fascist regimes of Germany, Japan and Italy during the Second World War made that creed unpopular. Instead, for five subsequent decades of the Cold War, Communism threatened to engulf countries around the world. The United States organized groups of states into alliances to contain and at times directly war against that threat.

Over the long term, Communism was doomed, infected with a self-destructive political virus. Historically, Communism has surpassed all other political systems in its ability to control and exploit masses of people, but is the worst for economic development. The reason is simple. Communism asserts total control over all political, economic and social relationships. The state owns all production and property and determines what is produced, what jobs are needed and what prices are paid for goods and labour. That system churned out masses of poorly-made products made by exploited workers. By eliminating human enterprise, invention, innovation, markets, private property and incentives for individuals to realize their respective dreams, Communist economies stagnated and fell further behind liberal economic and political systems. Atop Communism's economic catastrophes were concentration camps and mass murder committed by Joseph Stalin's Soviet Union, Mao Zedong's China, Kim Jong-il's North Korea and Pol Pot's Cambodia, while to varying degrees all other Communist regimes in Eastern Europe, Cuba, Vietnam and Laos each imprisoned and murdered thousands of people, of whom many were the most intelligent, entrepreneurial and creative.

Communism's catastrophic self-inflicted crimes and failures led to Fascism's revival. China led the way when Deng Xiaoping abandoned Communism as literally and figuratively a mass human dead end and embraced Fascism in 1978, although he never called it that but insisted that he was fulfilling Communism. Chinese Fascism has been as successful as Chinese Communism was an utter disaster in developing the economy. China today has an economy only slightly less large, productive, enterprising and innovative than that of the United States. Although most Chinese remain poor, the middle class is steadily expanding and may become the majority within a decade.

Liberal and nationalist revolutions from 1989 to 1991 destroyed the Soviet Union, its subjected eastern European states and the Communist creed that had throttled them beginning in 1917. The Soviet Union broke up into fifteen independent countries with Communism abandoned in each. For a decade, Russian President Boris Yeltsin tried to develop liberal democracy and a liberal economy but failed. His designated successor in 2001, Vladimir Putin, abandoned liberalism for Fascism, although he does not call it that. Putin's regime is authoritarian, nationalist, populist, corporatist, vigilantist and imperialist and as dictator he excludes a quiet but powerful charisma and has created a personality cult with hundreds of millions of disciples in Russia and around the world, including across America.

In western Europe, neo-Fascist political parties emerged in several countries but only one took power, Viktor Orban's Fidesz Party in Hungary from 1998 through the present. Elsewhere the strongest neo-Fascist parties are the Alternative for Germany in Germany and the National Front, renamed the National Rally in 2018, in France. All three parties espouse leaving the European Union and North Atlantic Treaty Organization and forming close ties with Putin's Russia.

Elsewhere prominent recent neo-Fascist tyrants include Hugo Chavez and Franciso Madero of Venezuela, Rodrigo Duterte of the Philippines and Daniel Ortega of Nicaragua.

Fascism and other tyrannical creeds endure because human nature endures.[33] Indeed, social scientists have identified an 'authoritarian personality' borne by countless people that is driven to control and be controlled by others.[34]

Fascism appeals to deep human yearnings. Each individual, of course, can be located on a spectrum for his or her natural affinity for being free or led, open-minded or close-minded, attracted by hard facts or soothing myths and scornful or adoring of demagogues. While most people claim to love freedom, most of them seem to prefer the security, identity, meaning, status and sometimes wealth provided by a beloved group like a family, crime gang, sports team, fraternity, business, religion, race or nation, to name a few. For that they will conform to the group's values, aspirations, traditions, myths and even dictates. Historically, various types of authoritarian regimes that subject individuals have prevailed. Democratic systems with limited government power and expansive individual liberties are modern phenomena that may eventually become extinct; the ancient Athenian and Roman republics had minorities of free men with political rights and representation amidst populations of subjected slaves, peasants, labourers and women.

Foreign Minister Galeazzo Ciano was speaking of Adolf Hitler and his Third Reich when he observed: 'The madness of the Leader had become the religion of his followers.'[35] Charismatic leaders exude confidence, power and vision. They appeal to people's hopes, fears and hates. Most people adore charismatic leaders and live vicariously through their triumphs. Historically, most people seem to prefer leaders who appear strong and promote comforting fantasies to leaders who appear weak and promote hard truths. No creed has a monopoly on charismatic leaders. They emerge from or create Liberal, Fascist, Communist, Christian, Muslim and other political or religious regimes.

What does differ among different creeds is the relative propensity for promoting truths or myths. For instance, Liberalism is a knowledge-grounded ideology. The Liberal or Humanistic assumption is that each individual is born a unique bundle of potentialities, mostly positive, some negative. Our moral and practical duty as humans is to nurture one another to fulfil each's greatest potentials and sublimate anything negative into something positive within a liberal community.

Knowledge, the interpretation of related facts or truths and their application to solving problems, is critical to human development.

Truth and knowledge is not essential to most other creeds and indeed may be disparaged. Religious creeds are rooted in supernatural claims that cannot be proven, only believed. Communists and Fascists justify their respective totalitarian and authoritarian systems with 'Big Lies' about enemies that can only be defeated if individuals are subjected to the collective will for the collective good.

Communist and Fascist regimes impose political cultures on populations that destroy the natural will of most people for personal freedom and instead socialize them to obey without question their superiors. Those repressive and exploitative political cultures endure. For instance, East Germany experienced a Communist regime from 1945 to 1991, when a liberal revolution demolished it and that country was unified with West Germany. Yet, while Germany is politically unified, the country remains deeply split between the liberal west and authoritarian east. The neo-Fascist Alternative for Germany Party is strongest in eastern Germany whose population was brainwashed to believe in Communism for half a century and those attitudes seep into the minds of those born since then.

Fascist demagogues trumpet a bundle of related themes. The nation is in crisis because of foreign and domestic enemies. We, the people, are victims of those enemies that must be violently destroyed. Only the supreme leader with overwhelming power can make the nation great again. One must rule or be ruled, kill or be killed. The nation must dominate or outright takeover all other nations with their inferior, dangerous peoples.

Two recent mass media phenomena have made Fascism and other authoritarian ideologies like Islamism more prolific and appealing than ever. One was the rise of what adherents called 'talk' radio and critics called 'hate' or 'rant' radio in America during the 1980s, personified by demagogue Rush Limbaugh, which then proliferated on cable television and the internet during the 1990s. The second phenomena was the rise of social media via the internet and smartphones during the twenty-first century's first decades. Inflammatory messages and lies metastasize through those medias. The number of Americans who read professional fact-based journalism through newspapers, magazines, journals and books diminished steadily. Those American 'hate/rant media' vehicles rapidly spread worldwide to undermine every democracy. Vladimir Putin's Fascist regime has mastered the art of spreading propaganda through social media, most notoriously in America's 2016 election that Donald Trump won and Britain's 2016 referendum on European Union membership that isolationists won.[36]

Exacerbating that authoritarian mass media revolution is the failure of America's school system and undoubtedly those of countless other countries, to nurture students in rational, creative, critical thinking skills and historical and scientific knowledge. Ignorant people are dupes for the 'big lies' of demagogues that feed their fears, hates and hopes.

Even the most seemingly deep-rooted democracies are susceptible to being ripped up and replaced by Fascism. The United States provides a disturbing example with the rise to power of Donald Trump and his Trumpian or 'Make America Great Again' (MAGA) movement. Trump's former chief of staff General John Kelly and Joint Chiefs chair General Mark Milley both declared that Trump was a 'fascist' that Kelly defined as 'a far right authoritarian ultranationalist political ideology and movement characterized by a dictatorial leader, centralized autocracy, militarism, forcible oppression of opposition, belief in a natural social hierarchy'.[37] Robert Paxton, Fascism's leading historian, wrote that after the 6 January 2020 insurrection when over 2,000 Trumpians stormed and sacked the Capitol on his behalf, calling Trump a fascist 'now seems not just acceptable, but necessary'.[38]

With all due respect to the generals and professor, Trump is not a Fascist. The Fascist check-list includes seven ingredients – authoritarianism, corporatism, populism, vigilantism, nationalism, imperialism and a charismatic dictator. Trump scores high as a charismatic (developing) dictator, a qualified populist and an unabashed vigilantist, but falls short in the other categories.

Trump's charisma and apparent populism is astounding. In what has been called Trump Derangement Syndrome, he won half the votes in the 2024 election despite or more likely because he was a convicted 34-count felon; had three other felony trials pending or suspended against him; provoked an insurrection that trashed the Capitol; swore he would be a dictator on day one in office; threatened vengeance against all those who opposed him; had failed as a businessman with six bankruptcies; and had numerous civil suits against him for fraud, defamation, sexual assault and other crimes. Yet, Trump is half a populist because America is split evenly between those who adore and those who abhor him. Genuine populists try to unite nearly everyone in a common cause, often by pitting them against some hated foreign or domestic enemy. Most Americans support Trump on only one issue, illegal immigration.

Trump does score high as a vigilantist. Militant groups like the Proud Boys and Oath Keepers spearheaded the 6 January insurrection, beating police defending the Capitol. When Trump condemns someone, bullies troll that target with emailed, telephoned and face-to-face threats of violence. Trump shamelessly uses his presidential powers to reward his allies and punish his foes. He has intimidated virtually all Republicans to praise and parrot everything he does and says, no matter how outrageous or destructive. Trump pardoned all 1,600 or so indicted 6 January rioters, greenlighting them and countless other thugs to commit more vicious atrocities on his behalf with impunity.

Like Mussolini, Trump was indicted for an array of crimes. Mussolini served several prison stints. Trump got away with his crimes without spending a day in jail. Congress twice impeached Trump for various 'high crimes and misdemeanours' but each time the Senate votes fell short of the two-thirds conviction threshold. In 2024, four separate jurisdictions had together filed ninety-one felony criminal charges against him; one trial resulted in thirty-four felony convictions while Trump lawyers and six Supreme Court Justices prevented the others from coming to trial. In addition, Trump has been sued in civil court on numerous charges including sexual assault and fraud, but has merely paid fines rather than served jail time. Where Mussolini and Trump differ is the scale and type of their crimes. Although Trump has repeatedly committed serious felonies, none are known to include having hitmen murder his enemies.

Authoritarianism and corporatism are related. An authoritarian state has a dedicated professional civil service of technocrats that dominates a nation's key political, economic, social and cultural groups and relationships. Under corporatism, private property and business enterprises persist but the state manages markets by organizing industries into cartels that expand production, innovation, profit, wages and benefits for owners and employees alike. With Elon Musk, the world's richest person, as his hatchet man, Trump is eviscerating the federal government by firing its professional, expert civil servants and either leaving the posts empty or filling them with ideologues and sycophants; indeed, first to be axed were the inspector generals who root out fraud, corruption and incompetence. A corporatist state uses trade barriers selectively to protect and nurture vital infant industries and technologies, a sniper rifle not a shotgun approach. Trump's imposition of indiscriminate cross-the-board tariff jumps of 10 per cent and 25 per cent ricochet back at America's economy with worsening investor uncertainty, inflation and joblessness damaging the economy. Authoritarians try to protect the people from health, safety and environmental threats; Trump is destroying federal health, safety and environmental laws and regulations.

As for nationalism, Trump belies his 'Make America Great Again' mantra with policies that systematically demolish American democracy, power, wealth and prestige. True nationalists know that creating and leading military and economic alliances enhances the power of all members against common foes; strengthening weaker members strengthens all. Trump is making enemies of America's allies and making an ally of one of America's most implacable foes. Trump has essentially sold out to Russian President Vladimir Putin by denigrating NATO; cutting off military and intelligence aid to Ukraine; bullying President Volodymyr Zelensky to yield to Putin; purging America's intelligence and scientific communities; provoking self-destructive trade wars; and destroying American democracy. Nationalists genuinely love their country. Trump was a draft dodger who openly disdains those who risk their lives for their country as 'losers and suckers'. General Kelly, who lost a son in combat in Iraq, revealed that Trump viewed selflessly serving ones' country as 'something he just didn't understand. What's in it for them?'[39]

Imperialism clearly parts Mussolini and Trump. *Il Duce* blundered Italy into a series of disastrous wars in Ethiopia, Greece and North Africa either to expand or defend the Italian empire. Although Trump declared his intention to take over Greenland, the Panama Canal, Gaza and Canada, ambition is not enough; he will be an imperialist only if he actually illegally seizes foreign territory and annexes it to the United States.

Although Trump is not a fully-fledged Fascist, he certainly fits the classic 'authoritarian personality' profile. Mussolini and Trump share the psychological diagnosis of being 'malignant narcissists'. A full page public letter by 225 mental health professionals in the *New York Times* on 24 October 2024, warned that Trump posed 'an existential threat to democracy' by bearing 'symptoms of severe, untreatable personality disorder – malignant narcissism' that 'makes him deceitful, destructive, deluded and dangerous. He is unfit for leadership . . . Because of their sadism, malignant narcissists often derive joy from inflicting suffering on others.'[40] Trump admires and models himself after tyrants like Putin who he lauds as a 'genius', 'brilliant man' Xi Jinping of China, 'very honourable' Kim Jong-un of North Korea and even Adolf Hitler.[41] Like Mussolini, Trump created a personality cult of himself as an all-knowing, all-powerful demi-god who would solve all his nation's problems and achieve 'greatness'.

People are pathological when they repeatedly commit legal or moral crimes without remorse. Mendacity is a felony under oath but otherwise a moral crime. Trump far exceeds Mussolini in at least one pathology, mendacity. Although Mussolini at times lied, he actually prided himself on being able to cite facts. Mussolini did not invent but joined an existing far right chorus in propagating the 'mutilated peace' myth whereby America, Britain and France cheated Italy of its rightful conquests after the First World War. In contrast, no one in American history has uttered a sliver of Trump's lies. Critical to Trump's rise to the White House was propagating Big Lies or myths for masses of ignorant, gullible, angry, fearful people to believe and act upon. The *Washington Post* fact-checked all his spoken and written words during his first four years as president and revealed 30,574 'false or misleading statements'.[42] During his 2024 presidential campaign, Trump's 'untruths' averaged sixty-four per speech compared to six for his Democratic Party opponent Kamala Harris. Trump's most destructive lies were that he won the 2020 presidential election but the Democrats stole it through fake votes; that the 6 January insurrection was a peaceful protest against Congress for validating that stolen election; and that Ukraine started the war with Russia. Of them the most consequential was that he won the 2020 election but the Democratic Party's massive voting fraud sent rival Joe Biden to the White House; one in three Americans (33 per cent) and two in three Republicans (66 per cent) believed that lie.

What explains Trump's popularity despite all the harm he has inflicted on America and countless Americans? Bullying certainly is a moral crime and in certain contexts can be illegal. Trump perfectly illustrates the bully and his appeal. In any schoolyard, kids will gather to watch a bully pick on a vulnerable child. Most kids hate the bully but fear prevents them from resisting him; a handful might be brave and moral enough to protest or even protect the victim. Meanwhile, nearly as many kids egg on the bully, identify with his physical power and warped charisma and become his devoted followers. Throughout his public life, especially after announcing his presidential election campaign in 2015 through today, Trump's bullying of an array of designated scapegoat countries, ethnicities, groups and individuals has been virtually non-stop. With Trump back in the White House, he is once again the Bully-in-Chief. Here again, Trump surpasses Mussolini whose speeches rarely singled out individuals to insult and mock.

Like Mussolini for Italy, Trump is gutting America's illiberal democracy, however not into a Fascist regime but in many ways its opposite. Kleptocracy is government of the thieves, by the thieves and for the thieves. Trump is not a Fascist, but a Kleptocrat who is transforming America's democratic system into a spoils system where he, his billionaire cronies and all his other corporate sponsors can loot government for all they can get away with. The results are levels of corruption and incompetence not seen since America's late nineteenth century's Gilded Age.

Differences between Mussolini and Trump do not end with ideology. Intelligence starkly splits them. Mussolini was actually very bright if ill-educated. He wrote not only his own speeches but also two novels, three plays and hundreds of essays. He carefully read and understood philosophical tomes and enjoyed classic novels of Western literature. Trump may be America's dimmest president, incapable of understanding the basic facts of virtually any subject, at war against science and history, intellectually, culturally and morally a barren desert.

Despite that, Trump surpasses Mussolini as a tyrant. Mussolini ultimately failed while Trump ultimately triumphed in taking and keeping power for the foreseeable future.

Mussolini did not rest permanently in peace after his brutal execution, pummelling by a mob and then hoisting upside down in a public square. Initially, he was buried in an unmarked grave at Musocco Cemetery in north Milan. A young Fascist named Domenico Leccisi and two comrades dug him up and carried away his body on 23 April 1946. Over the next 16 weeks they hid the decayed corpse in various places until finally they convinced monks at Certosa di Pavia monastery to accept it. Police detectives finally caught the thieves and retrieved the corpse which was then hidden in a vault at the Cerro Maggiore Capuchin Monastery in Milan for 11 years. Meanwhile, Leccisi served 21 months of a six-year sentence for various crimes. Mussolini's descendants received government permission to bury what was left of *Il Duce* in the family vault at Predappio on 31 August 957. And since then, a procession of the devout and curious visit to stare and reflect. Someone set off a bomb at the vault's entrance on Christmas night, 1971, but the explosion did not destroy his tomb within. Rachele joined her husband in the vault after she died at age 89 on 30 October 1979, appropriately 57 years from the day the King Emmanuel Victor III named him prime minister.[43]

Italy's Fascist movement never died, but did go underground for a while then reemerged in a nearly unrecognizable form. Arturo Michelini and Giorgio Almirante founded the neo-Fascist Italian Social Movement (*Movimento Sociale Italiana*, MSI) on 26 December 1946. Although they espoused nationalism and corporatism, they accepted the democratic political system and rejected authoritarianism and imperialism. Wags jested that the acronym MSI actually stood for 'Mussolini Always Immortal' (*Mussolini Sempre Immortale*). From the late 1940s to the early 1990s, the Italian Social Movement averaged around 5 per cent of election votes and that share of seats in the Chamber of Deputies.

When Almirante died in 1988, Gianfranco Fini took his place. Seeking to transform the party's image, Fini renamed it the National Alliance (*Alleanza Nazionale*) in January 1994 and declared that the National Alliance was now post-fascist and no longer nostalgically celebrated Mussolini. In the March 1994 election, The National Alliance won 13.4 per cent of the votes and 107 deputies, making it the third largest party. Silvio Berlusconi's Forza Italia Party won a plurality of votes and formed a coalition government that included the National Alliance with four ministries, although Fini did not take one.

The National Alliance morphed into the People of Freedom in 2009 and the Brothers of Italy (*Fratelli d'Italia*) in 2014. Under Giorgia Meloni's leadership, the Brothers of Italy won 43.8 per cent of the vote in the September 2022 election and she became prime minister. By then, the Brothers of Italy had scrubbed any Fascist residue from the party and its politicians and was essentially a conservative party.

At times, an insight can briefly illuminate even the most deluded mind. During *Il Duce*'s last months at Salo, as he slumped or shambled around his villa, he often muttered, 'I have ruined Italy! I have ruined Italy!'[44] Benito Mussolini may never have uttered a greater truth.

NOTES

Abbreviations

Klibansky, *Mussolini Memoir* = Raymond Klibansky, ed., *Benito Mussolini's Memoirs, 1942-1943, with Documents Relating to the Period* (New York: Howard Fertig, 1947).

Muggeridge, *Ciano's Diary* = Malcolm Muggeridge, ed., *Ciano's Diary, 1939-1943* (London: William Heinemann, 1947).

Introduction

1 For leading biographies, see: Christopher Hibbert, *Benito Mussolini* (London: Longmans, 1962); Ivone Kirkpatrick, *Mussolini: The Study of a Demagogue* (London: Odhams Books, 1966); Laura Fermi, *Mussolini* (Chicago: University of Chicago Press, 1966); Richard Collier, *Duce!: The Rise and Fall of Benito Mussolini* (London: Collins, 1971); Denis Mack Smith, *Mussolini* (New York: Alfred Knopf, 1982); Jasper Ridley, *Mussolini: A Biography* (New York: St. Martin's Press, 1998); R.J.B. Bosworth, *Mussolini* (London: Arnold, 2002); Nicolas Ferrell, *Mussolini: A New Life* (New York: Phoenix Press, 2005).

For the leading Italian Mussolini biographer and Fascist expert, see: Renzo De Felice, *Mussolini il Fascista*, 2 vols (Turin: Einaudi, 1966, 1968); Renzo De Felice, *Mussolini il Duce*, 2 vols (Turin: Einaudi, 1974, 1981); Renzo De Felice, *Le Interpretazioni del Fascismo* (Bari: Laterza, 1983).

For critical biographies while he was in power, see: George Seldes, *Sawdust Caesar: The Untold History of Mussolini and Fascism* (New York: Harper and Brother's, 1935); David Darrah, *Hail Caesar!* (Boston: Hale, Cushman and Flint, 1936).

For Mussolini's memoirs, see: Benito Mussolini, *Memoirs: 1942-1943 with Documents Relating to the Period* (New York: Howard Fertig, 1975); Max Ascoli, ed., *Benito Mussolini: My Rise and Fall* (New York: Da Capo, 1998).

2 Bosworth, *Mussolini*, 162.

3 Charles Maier, *In Search of Stability: Explorations in Historical Political Economy* (Cambridge: Cambridge University Press, 1988), 91; Roland Sarti, ed., *The Ax Within: Italian Fascism in Action* (New York: New Viewpoints, 1973), 159.

4 Mack Smith, *Mussolini*, 110.

5 Muggeridge, *Ciano's Diary*, 99.

6 Bosworth, *Mussolini*, 171.

7 Ibid., 123.

8 Ibid., 243.

9 Mack Smith, *Mussolini*, 127.

10 Rachele Mussolini, *The Real Mussolini by Rachele Mussolini as Told to Abert Zarca* (Farnborough: Saxon House, 1973), 204.
11 Mack Smith, *Mussolini*, xiv.
12 For Mussolini's relations with women, see: Vittorio Mussolini, *Mussolini: The Tragic Women in His Life* (London: NEL, 1973).
13 Edda Mussolini Ciano, *My Truth as Told to Albert Zarca* (New York: William Morrow and Company, 1977), 112.
14 Ridley, *Mussolini*, 179.
15 R.J.B. Bosworth, *Mussolini's Italy: Life Under the Fascist Dictatorship, 1915-1945* (New York: Penguin, 2007), 342.
16 Bosworth, *Mussolini*, 91–2.
17 Rachele Mussolini, *The Real Mussolini*, 11–12.
18 Mack Smith, *Mussolini*, 126.
19 Bosworth, *Mussolini*, xvii.
20 Mack Smith, *Mussolini*, 148.
21 Muggeridge, *Ciano's Diary*, x.
22 Sarti, ed., *Ax Within*, 25.
23 Bosworth, *Mussolini*, 70.
24 Mack Smith, *Mussolini*, 140.
25 Michael Alpert, *A New International History of the Spanish Civil War* (New York: St. Martin's Press, 1994), 8.
26 Bosworth, *Mussolini*, 163.
27 Ernst Nolte, *Three Faces of Fascism: Action Francaise, Italian Fascism, National Socialism* (New York: Holt, Rinehart, Winston, 1966); James Gregor, *The Ideology of Fascism: The Rationale of Totalitarianism* (New York: Free Press, 1969); S.J. Woolf, ed., *The Nature of Fascism* (London: Weidenfeld and Nicolson, 1968); Charles Delzell, *Mediterranean Fascism, 1919-1945* (New York: Harper and Row, 1970); Michael Ledeen, *Universal Fascism: The Theory and Practice of the Fascist International* (New York: Howard Fertig, 1972); Heinz Lubasz, ed., *Fascism: Three Major Regimes* (New York: John Wiley, 1972); Paul Hayes, *Fascism* (London: George Allen and Unwin, 1973); James Gregor, *Interpretations of Fascism* (Morristown, N.J.: General Learning Press, 1974); Henry Turner, ed., *Reappraisals of Fascism* (New York: New Viewpoints, 1975); Martin Kitchen, *Fascism* (London: Macmillan, 1976); Mihaly Vaida, *Fascism as a Mass Movement* (London: Allison and Busby, 1976); Walter Laqueur, ed., *Fascism: A Reader's Guide* (New York: Penguin, 1979); S.J. Woolf, ed., *Fascism in Europe* (London: Methuen, 1981); Francis Carsten, *The Rise of Fascism* (Berkeley: University of California Press, 1982); Stanley Payne, *Fascism: Comparison and Definition* (Madison: University of Wisconsin Press, 1987); Roger Griffin, *The Nature of Fascism* (New York: Routledge, 1993); Roger Eatwell, *Fascism: A History* (London: Chatto and Windus, 1995); Roger Griffin, ed., *Fascism* (New York: Oxford University Press, 1995); Stanley Payne, *A History of Fascism, 1914-1945* (Madison: University of Wisconsin Press, 1995); George Blum, *The Rise of Fascism in Europe* (Westport, Conn.: Greenwood Press, 1998); George Mosse, *The Fascist Revolution: Toward a General Theory of Fascism* (New York: Howard Fertig, 1999); George Mosse, *International Fascism, 1920-1945: New Thoughts and New Approaches* (New York: Harper Collins, 2000); Philip Morgan, *Fascism in Europe, 1919-1945* (New York: Routledge, 2003); Robert Paxton, *The Anatomy of Fascism* (New York: Vintage, 2004); R.J.B. Bosworth, ed., *The Oxford Handbook of Fascism* (New York: Oxford University Press, 2010); Patrick Zander, ed., *The Rise of Fascism: History, Documents and Key Questions* (New York: Bloomsbury, 2016).

28 Abbott Gleason, *Totalitarianism: The Inner History of the Cold War* (New York: Oxford University Press, 2001), 32.
29 Ibid., 147.
30 Ibid., 19.
31 Bosworth, *Mussolini*, 156.
32 Ibid., 327.
33 Ibid., 289.
34 Mabel Berezin, *Making the Fascist Self: The Political Culture of Interwar Italy* (Ithaca, N.Y.: Cornell University Press 1997), 58.
35 Shlomo Ben-Ami, *Fascism From Above: The Dictatorship of Miguel Primo de Rivera in Spain, 1923-1930* (New York: Oxford University Press, 1983), 131–2.
36 Bosworth, *Mussolini*, 324.
37 For comparisons of Fascism, Nazism and their founders, see: Alexander De Grand, *Fascist Italy and Nazi Germany: The Fascist 'Style' of Rule* (New York: Routledge, 1995); Timothy Mason, *Nazism, Fascism and the Working Class* (New York: Cambridge University Press, 1995); Richard Bessell, ed., *Fascist Italy and Nazi Germany: Comparisons and Contrasts* (New York: Cambridge University Press, 1996); Aristotle Kallis, *Fascist Ideology: Territory and Expansionism in Italy and Germany, 1922-1945* (New York: Routledge, 2000); MacGregor Knox, *Common Destiny: Dictatorship, Foreign Policy and War in Fascist Italy and Germany* (New York: Cambridge University Press, 2000); Robert Paxton, *The Anatomy of Fascism* (New York: Vintage, 2004).
38 For an interesting comparison of tyrants before they took power, see: Brandon Gauthier, *Before Evil: Young Lenin, Hitler, Stalin, Mussolini, Mao and Kim* (New York: Tortoise Books, 2022).
39 F.W. Deakin, *The Brutal Friendship: Mussolini, Hitler and the Fall of Italian Fascism* (New York: Phoenix Books, 2000).
40 Adolf Hitler, *Mein Kampf*, translated by Ralph Manheim (Boston: Houghton Mifflin, 1971), 681.
41 Bosworth, *Mussolini*, 222–3.
42 Ibid., xv, 1–2.
43 Paul Preston, *Franco: A Biography* (New York: Fontana Press, 2011), 275.

Chapter 1: The Upbringing

1 Bosworth, *Mussolini*, 43.
2 Rachele Mussolini, *The Real Mussolini*, 12.
3 Bosworth, *Mussolini*, 50–1.
4 Max Ascoli, ed., *My Rise and Fall by Benito Mussolini* (New York: Da Capo, 1998), 5.
5 Max Gallo, *Mussolini's Italy: Twenty Years of the Fascist Era* (New York: Macmillan, 1973), 6.
6 Mack Smith, *Mussolini*, 3.
7 Quoted in ibid., 4.
8 Bosworth, *Mussolini*, 42.
9 Quoted in Mack Smith, *Mussolini*, 5.
10 Martin Collier, *Italian Unification, 1820-1871* (New York: Heinemann, 2002); Derek Beales and Eugenio Biagini, *The History of the Unification of Italy* (New York: Routledge, 2002).
11 Denis Mack Smith, *Italy and Its Monarchy* (New Haven, Conn.: Yale University Press, 1989).

12 Christopher Seton-Watson, *Italy from Liberalism to Fascism, 1870-1925* (London: Methuen, 1967); John Gooch, *Army, State and Society in Italy, 1870-1915* (New York: Macmillan, 1989); Denis Mack Smith, *Modern Italy: A Political History* (Ann Arbor: University of Michigan Press, 1997).
13 Robert Goldstein, *Political Repression in Nineteenth Century Europe* (New York: Routledge, 2009), 4.
14 R.J.B. Bosworth, *Italy and the Wider World, 1860-1960* (New York: Routledge, 1996), 114–36.
15 Vera Zamagni, *The Economic History of Italy,1860-1990* (Oxford: Clarendon, 1993).
16 Spencer Di Scala, *Italy from Revolution to Republic, 1700 to the Present* (Boulder, Colo.: Westview Press, 1995), 166.
17 Paul Kennedy, *The Rise and Fall of the Great Powers* (New York: Vintage, 1989), 199–202.
18 William Hilton-Young, *The Italian Left: A Short History of Political Socialism in Italy* (Westport, Conn.: Greenwood, 1975); Richard Hostetter, *The Italian Socialist Movement: Origins, 1860-1882* (New York: Literary Licensing, 2012).
19 R.J.B. Bosworth, *Italy, the Least of the Great Powers: Italian Foreign Policy before the First World War* (Cambridge: Cambridge University Press, 1980); R.J.B. Bosworth, *Italy and the Wider World, 1860-1960* (New York: Routledge, 1996).
20 Giuseppe Finaldi, *A History of Italian Colonialism, 1860-1907: Europe's Last Empire* (New York: Routledge, 2016).
21 Tekeste Negash, *Italian Colonialism in Eritrea, 1882-1941: Policies, Praxis and Impact* (Stockholm: Almquist & Wiksell International, 1987).
22 Ibid., 3.
23 Richard Caulk, *'Between the Jaws of Hyenas': A Diplomatic History of Ethiopia* (Wiesbaden, Germany: Otto Harrassowitz Verlag, 2002), 563, 566–7. See also: Raymond Jonas, *The Battle of Adwa: An African Victory in the Age of Empire* (Cambridge, Mass.: Havard University Press, 2015).

Chapter 2: The Radical

1 Bosworth, *Mussolini*, 51.
2 Spencer Di Scala, *Mussolini, 1883-1915: Triumph and Transformation of a Revolutionary Socialist* (New York: Palgrave Macmillan, 2016).
3 Angelica Balabanoff, *My Life as a Rebel* (New York: Harper and Brothers, 1938), 60.
4 Mack Smith, *Mussolini*, 11.
5 Ascoli, ed., *My Rise and Fall by Benito Mussolini*, 16.
6 Gallo, *Mussolini's Italy*, 17.
7 With ghostwriters, Rachele expressed herself through two insightful and mostly true memoirs: Rachele Mussolini, *My Life with Mussolini in Collaboration with Michael Chinigo* (London: Robert Hale, 1959); Rachele Mussolini, *The Real Mussolini by Rachele Mussolini as Told to Albert Zarca* (Farnborough: Saxon House, 1973).
8 Rachele Mussolini, *The Real Mussolini*, 15–17.
9 Rachele Mussolini, *My Life with Mussolini*, 21, 22.
10 Rachele Mussolini, *The Real Mussolini*, 18.
11 Ibid., 26.
12 John Cook and Chris Paxton, *European Political Facts, 1900-1996* (New York: Palgrave Macmillan, 1998), 163.
13 Emilo Gentile, *The Struggle for Modernity: Nationalism, Futurism and Fascism* (Westport, Conn.: Praeger, 2003), 52.

14 Ibid.
15 Gunter Berghaus, *Futurism and Politics: Between Anarchist Rebellion and Fascist Reaction* (Providence, R.I. Berghahn, 1996); Emilo Gentile, *The Struggle for Modernity: Nationalism, Futurism and Fascism* (Westport, Conn.: Praeger, 2003); Christine Poggi, *Inventing Futurism: The Art and Politics of Artificial Optimism* (Princeton, N.J.: Princeton University Press, 2008).
16 Gentile, *The Struggle for Modernity*, 49, 50.
17 Ibid., 41, 49–50.
18 Claudio Segre, *The Fourth Shore: The Italian Colonization of Libya* (Chicago: University of Chicago Press, 1975).
19 Gallo, *Mussolini's Italy*, 26.
20 Philip Cannistraro and Brian Sullivan, *Il Duce's Mussolini's Other Woman: The Untold Story of Margherita Sarfatti, Benito Mussolini's Mistress and How She Helped Him Come to Power* (New York: William Morrow, 1993).
21 Bosworth, *Mussolini*, 171.
22 Margherita Sarfatti, *The Life of Benito Mussolini* (London: Thorton Butterworth, 1926).
23 Dieter Nohlen and Philip Stover, eds, *Elections in Europe: A Data Handbook* (New York: Nomos, 2010), 1047.
24 William Nester, *Land of War: A History of European Warfare from Achilles to Putin* (New York: Stackpole Books, 2023).
25 Paul Kennedy, *The Rise and Fall of the Great Powers* (New York: Vintage, 1989), 256; Niall Ferguson, *The Pity of War: Understanding World War I* (New York: Basic Books, 1999), 110.
26 Ferguson, *Pity of War*, 106.
27 Mack Smith, *Mussolini*, 22.
28 Bosworth, *Mussolini*, 104.
29 Ibid.
30 Ibid., 105.

Chapter 3: The Fascist Movement

1 Emilo Gentile, *The Struggle for Modernity: Nationalism, Futurism and Fascism* (Westport, Conn.: Praeger, 2003), 59.
2 Ibid.
3 James Gregor, *Young Mussolini and the Intellectual Origins of Fascism* (Berkeley: University of California Press, 1979); Alexander De Grand, *Italian Fascism: Its Origins and Development* (Lincoln: University of Nebraska Press, 1982).
4 Gallo, *Mussolini's Italy*, 39–40.
5 Ibid., 39, 37.
6 Ibid., 38.
7 Stuart Hughes, 'Men of Steel: Dueling, Honor and Politics in Liberal Italy', in Pieter Spierenberg, ed., *Men and Violence: Gender, Honor and Rituals in Modern Europe and America* (Columbia: Ohio University Press, 1998).
8 Gallo, *Mussolini's Italy*, 44.
9 Ibid., 4.
10 John Gooch, 'Italy During the First World War', in Allen Millett and Williamson Murray, *Military Effectiveness: The First World War* (Boston: Allen and Unwin, 1988), 161.
11 Ibid., 162–3.
12 Mark Thompson, *The White War: Life and Death on the Italian Front, 1915-1919* (London: Faber and Faber, 2008); John Macdonald and Zeljko Cimpric, *Caporetto*

and the Isonzo Campaign: The Italian Front, 1915-1918 (London: Pen and Sword, 2015).
13 Gallo, *Mussolini's Italy*, 50.
14 Bosworth, *Mussolini's Italy*, 343.
15 Seth Roland, *Caporetto: The Scapegoat Battle* (London: Macdonald, 1965).
16 Ascoli, ed., *My Rise and Fall by Benito Mussolini*, 50, 51.
17 Gallo, *Mussolini's Italy*, 75.
18 Ferguson, *The Pity of War*, 295; Cormac O'Grada, *The Hidden Victims: Civilian Casualties of the Two World Wars* (Princeton, N.J.: Princeton University Press, 2024).
19 Charles Maier, *Recasting Bourgeois Europe: Stabilization in France, Germany and Italy in the Decade after World War I* (Princeton, N.J.: Princeton University Press, 1975); Douglas Forsyth, *The Crisis of Liberal Italy: Monetary and Financial Policy 1914-1922* (Cambridge: Cambridge University Press, 1993).
20 Denis Mack Smith, *Modern Italy: A Political History* (Ann Arbor: University of Michigan Press, 1997), 276; Spencer Di Scala, *Italy from Revolution to Republic, 1700 to the Present* (Boulder, Colo.: Westview Press, 1995), 207; Stephen Broadberry and Mark Harrison, eds, *The Economics of World War I* (New York: Cambridge University Press, 2009).
21 Ferguson, *The Pity of War*, 295.
22 Gallo, *Mussolini's Italy*, 109.
23 Ascoli, ed., *My Rise and Fall by Benito Mussolini*, 55.
24 Ibid., 135.
25 Gallo, *Mussolini's Italy*, 73.
26 Lucy Hughes-Hallett, *The Pike: Gabriele D'Annunzio: Poet, Seducer and Preacher of War* (New York: Alfred Knopf, 2013).
27 Alan Sharp, *The Versailles Settlement: Peacemaking in Paris, 1919* (New York: St. Martin's, 1991): Manfred Boemeke, Gerald Feldman and Elisabeth Glasser, eds, *The Treaty of Versailles: A Reassessment after 75 Years* (New York: Cambridge University Press, 1998); Margaret Macmillan, *The Peacemakers: The Paris Peace Conference and Its Attempt to End War* (New York: Hodder, 2003).
28 James Burgwyn, *The Legend of the Mutilated Victory: Italy, the Great War and the Paris Peace Conference, 1915-1919* (Westport, Conn.: Greenwood Press, 1993).
29 Ascoli, ed., *My Rise and Fall by Benito Mussolini*, 75–6.
30 Michael Ledeen, *The First Duce: D'Annunzio at Fiume* (Baltimore: Johns Hopkins University Press, 1977); Dominique Kirchner Reill, *The Fiume Crisis: Life in the Wake of the Hapsburg Empire* (Cambridge, Mass.: Belknap Press, 2020).
31 Gallo, *Mussolini's Italy*, 85.
32 Bosworth, *Mussolini*, 136.
33 Gallo, *Mussolini's Italy*, 87.
34 Ibid., 88.
35 Ibid., 89.
36 Nohlen and Stover, eds, *Elections in Europe*, 1047.
37 Gallo, *Mussolini's Italy*, 90.
38 Ascoli, ed., *My Rise and Fall by Benito Mussolini*, 124–5.
39 Mack Smith, *Modern Italy*, 287.
40 Di Scala, *Italy*, 207.
41 Bosworth, *Mussolini*, 154; Gallo, *Mussolini's Italy*, 113.
42 Bosworth, *Mussolini*, 152.
43 Bosworth, *Mussolini's Italy*, 109.
44 Alexander De Grand, *The Italian Left in the Twentieth Century: A History of the Socialist and Communist Parties* (Bloomington: University of Indiana Press, 1989);

Silvio Pons, *The Rise and Fall of the Italian Communist Party: A Transnational History* (Palo Alto, Calif.: Stanford University Press, 2024).

45 Joan Barth Urban, *Moscow and the Italian Communist Party: From Togliatti to Berlinguer* (Ithaca, N.Y.: Cornell University Press, 1986).

46 Gallo, *Mussolini's Italy*, 120.

47 Ibid.

48 Nohlen and Stover, eds, *Elections in Europe*, 1047.

49 Gallo, *Mussolini's Italy*, 123.

50 Both quotes from Gallo, *Mussolini's Italy*, 123, 124.

51 Bosworth, *Mussolini's Italy*, 151, 153.

52 Gallo, *Mussolini's Italy*, 133.

53 Mack Smith, *Mussolini*, 51.

54 Ascoli, ed., *My Rise and Fall by Benito Mussolini*, 176–7.

55 Mack Smith, *Modern Italy*, 320.

56 Gallo, *Mussolini's Italy*, 159.

Chapter 4: The Fascist State

1 Klibansky, *Mussolini Memoir*, 151.

2 Dante Germino, *The Italian Fascist Party in Power: A Study in Totalitarian Rule* (Minneapolis: University of Minnesota Press, 1959); Roy MacGregor-Hastie, *The Day of the Lion: The Life and Death of Fascist Italy* (New York: Macdonald, 1963); Samuel Halperin, *Mussolini and Italian Fascism* (New York: Van Nostrand, 1964); Fredrico Chabod, *A History of Italian Fascism* (London: Weidenfeld and Nicolson, 1963); Gaetano Salvemini, *The Fascist Dictatorship in Italy* (New York: Howard Fertig, 1967); Alan Cassels, *Fascist Italy* (London: Routledge, 1969); Elizabeth Wiskemann, *Fascism in Italy* (London: Macmillan, 1969); Edward Tanenbaum, *Fascism in Italy: Society and Culture, 1922-1945* (London: Allen Lane, 1973); Roland Sarti, ed., *The Ax Within: Italian Fascism in Action* (New York: New Viewpoints, 1974); Max Gallo, *Mussolini's Italy: Twenty Years of the Fascist Era* (London: Abelard-Schuman, 1974); Giampero Carocci, *Italian Fascism* (New York: Penguin, 1975); James Gregor, *Italian Fascism and Developmental Dictatorship* (Princeton, N.J.: Princeton University Press, 1979); Philip Cannistraro, ed., *Historical Dictionary of Fascist Italy* (Westport, Conn.: Greenwood, 1982); Adrian Lyttleton, *The Seizure of Power: Fascism in Italy, 1919-1929* (Princeton, N.J.: Princeton University Press, 1987); Philip Morgan, *Italian Fascism, 1919-1945* (London: Macmillan, 1995); John Whittam, *Fascist Italy* (Manchester: Manchester University Press, 1995); R.J.B. Bosworth, *The Italian Dictatorship: Problems and Perspectives in the Interpretation of Mussolini and Fascism* (London: Arnold, 1998); Emilio Gentile, *The Struggle for Modernity: Nationalism, Futurism and Fascism* (Westport, Conn.: Praeger, 2003); Ruth Ben-Ghiat, *Fascist Modernities: Italy, 1922-1945* (Berkeley: University of California Press, 2004); John Pollard, *The Fascist Experiment in Italy* (New York: Routledge, 2005); R.J.B. Bosworth, *Mussolini's Italy: Life under the Fascist Dictatorship, 1915-1945* (New York: Penguin, 2007); Christopher Duggan, *Fascist Voices: An Intimate History of Mussolini's Italy* (New York: Oxford University Press, 2013); Giuseppe Finaldi, ed. *Mussolini and Italian Fascism* (New York: Routledge, 2014).

3 Alexander De Grand, *The Italian Nationalist Association and the Rise of Fascism in Italy* (Lincoln: University of Nebraska Press, 1978).

4 Gallo, *Mussolini's Italy*, 166.

5 Ibid., 167.

6 Sarti, ed., *Ax Within*, 48.

7 Mack Smith, *Mussolini*, 63.
8 Sarti, ed., *Ax Within*, 23, 24–5.
9 Harry Fornari, *Mussolini's Gadfly: Roberto Farinacci* (Nashville: Vanderbilt University Press, 1971).
10 Sarti, ed., *Ax Within*, 96.
11 Claudio Pavone, *A Civil War: A History of the Italian Resistance* (New York: Verso, 2014), 60.
12 Klibansky, *Mussolini Memoir*, 53.
13 Bosworth, *Mussolini*, 192.
14 Nohlen and Stover, eds, *Elections in Europe*, 1047.
15 Gallo, *Mussolini's Italy*, 184.
16 Charles Delzell, *Mussolini's Enemies: The Italian Anti-Fascist Resistance* (Princeton, N.J.: Princeton University Press, 1961), 22–3.
17 Mack Smith, *Mussolini*, 78.
18 Bosworth, *Mussolini*, 196.
19 Ascoli, ed., *My Rise and Fall by Benito Mussolini*, 227–33.
20 Gallo, Mussolini's Italy, 197.
21 Mack Smith, *Mussolini*, 166.
22 Sarti, ed., *Ax Within*, 110.
23 Ibid., 90.
24 Mack Smith, *Mussolini*, 164.
25 Bosworth, *Mussolini*, 218.
26 Ibid., 222–3.
27 Delzell, *Mussolini's Enemies*, 38–41; Gallo, *Mussolini's Italy*, 242.
28 Charles Delzell, *Mussolini's Enemies: The Italian Anti-Fascist Resistance* (Princeton, N.J.: Princeton University Press, 1961); James Gregor, *Italian Fascism and Developmental Dictatorship* (Princeton, N.J.: Princeton University Press, 1979); Larry Ceplair, *Under the Shadow of War: Fascism, Anti-Fascism and Marxists, 1918-1937* (New York: Columbia University Press, 1987).
29 Bosworth, *Mussolini*, 279.
30 'Italy, 4 May, 1929: Fascist Unity List', *Data Base and Search Engine for Direct Democracy*, website.
31 Bosworth, *Mussolini*, 209.
32 Rachele Mussolini, *My Life with Mussolini*, 62.
33 MacGregor Knox, *Hitler's Italian Allies: Royal Armed Forces, Fascist Regime and the War of 1940-1943* (New York: Cambridge University Press, 2000), 23.
34 Christopher Duggan, *Fascism and the Mafia* (New Haven, Conn.: Yale University Press, 1989).
35 Roland Sarti, *Fascism and the Industrial Leadership in Italy, 1919-1940: A Study of Private Power under Fascism* (Berkeley: University of California Press, 1971).
36 Franklin Adler, *Italian Industrialists from Liberalism to Fascism: The Political Development of the Industrial Bourgeoisie* (New York: Cambridge University Press, 1996).
37 David Roberts, *The Syndicalist Tradition and Italian Fascism* (Manchester: Manchester University Press, 1979).
38 Gallo, *Mussolini's Italy*, 199.
39 Victoria De Grazia, *The Culture of Consent: Mass Organization and Leisure in Fascist Italy* (Cambridge: Cambridge University Press, 1981).
40 Gallo, *Mussolini's Italy*, 220.
41 Berezin, *Making the Fascist Self*, 60, 62.
42 Ibid., 61.
43 Bosworth, *Mussolini*, 226.

44 Delzell, *Mussolini's Enemies*, 129.
45 Sarti, ed., *Ax Within*, 146.
46 Ibid.
47 Ibid., 178.
48 Ibid., 171.
49 Ibid., 150–1.
50 Knox, *Hitler's Italian Allies*, 40.
51 Sarti, ed., *Ax Within*, 149, 152–3.
52 Ibid., 156–7.
53 Knox, *Hitler's Italian Allies*, 24.
54 Carl Ipsen, *Dictating Demography: The Problem of Population in Fascist Italy* (New York: Cambridge University Press, 1996).
55 Bosworth, *Mussolini*, 231.
56 Robin Pickering-Iazzi, ed., *Mothers of Invention: Women, Italian Fascism and Culture* (Minneapolis: University of Minnesota Press, 1995); Victoria De Grazia, *How Fascism Ruled Women: Italy, 1922-1945* (Berkeley: University of California Press, 1992).
57 Bosworth, *Mussolini*, 231.
58 Sarti, ed., *Ax Within*, 149; Mack Smith, *Mussolini*, 210.
59 Gentile, *Struggle for Modernity*, 151.
60 Jerre Mangione, *La Storia: Five Centuries of the Italian American Experience* (New York: Harper Perennial, 1992); Maria Lurino, *The Italian Americans: A History* (New York: W.W. Norton, 2014).
61 Gallo, *Mussolini's Italy*, 234.
62 John Diggins, *Mussolini and Fascism: The View from America* (Princeton, N.J.: Princeton University Press, 1972); Howard Smyth, *Secrets of the Fascist Era: How Uncle Sam Obtained Some of the Top-level Documents of Mussolini's Period* (Carbondale: Southern Illinois University Press, 1975); Gaetano Salvemini, *Italian Fascist Activities in the United States* (New York: Centre for Migration Studies, 1977); Diane Ghirado, *Building New Communities: New Deal America and Fascist Italy* (Princeton, N.J.: Princeton University Press, 1989).
63 David Forgacs, ed., *Rethinking Italian Fascism: Capitalism, Populism and Culture* (London: Lawrence and Wishart, 1986); Mabel Berezin, *Making the Fascist Self: The Political Culture of Interwar Italy* (Ithaca, N.Y.: Cornell University Press, 1997); Marla Stone, *The Patron State: Culture and Politics in Fascist Italy* (Princeton, N.J.: Princeton University Press, 1998).
64 Gentile, *Struggle for Modernity*, 84.
65 Victoria De Grazia, *How Fascism Ruled Women: Italy, 1922-1945* (Berkely: University of California Press, 1992); Perry Willson, *The Clockwork Factory: Women and Work in Fascist Italy* (New York: Oxford University Press, 1994); Robin Pickering-Iazzi, ed., *Mothers of Invention: Women, Italian Fascism and Culture* (Minneapolis: University of Minnesota Press, 1995); Barbara Spackman, *Fascist Virilities: Rhetoric, Ideology and Social Fantasy in Italy* (Minneapolis: University of Minnesota Press, 1996).
66 Gentile, *Struggle for Modernity*, 111.
67 Ibid., 78.
68 Berezin, *Making the Fascist Self*, 50.
69 Bosworth, *Mussolini*, 211.
70 Ibid., 294.
71 Simonetta Falasca-Zamponi, *Fascist Spectacle: The Aesthetics of Power in Mussolini's Italy* (Berkeley: University of California Press, 1997).
72 Berezin, *Making the Fascist Self*, 104.

73 Harvey Sachs, *Music in Fascist Italy* (New York: W.W. Norton, 1988); Richard Golsan, ed., *Fascism, Aesthetics and Culture* (Hanover, N.H.: University of New England Press, 1992); Karen Pinkus, *Bodily Regimes: Italian Advertising under Fascism* (Minneapolis: University of Minnesota Press, 1995); Jeffrey Schapp, *Staging Fascism: 18BL and the Theater for Masses* (Stanford: Stanford University Press, 1996).
74 Gentile, *Struggle for Modernity*, 62.
75 Ben-Ghiat, *Fascist Modernities*, 24.
76 Dennis Doordan, *Building Modern Italy: Italian Architecture, 1914-1936* (Princeton, N.J.: Princeton University Press, 1988); Richard Etlin, *Modernism in Italian Architecture. 1890-1940* (Cambridge: Cambridge University Press, 1991).
77 Ben-Ghiat, *Fascist Modernities*, 67–8.
78 H.S. Harris, *The Social Philosophy of Giovanni Gentile* (Urbana: University of Illinois Press, 1960); Adrian Lyttleton, ed., *Italian Fascisms from Pareto to Gentile* (New York: Harper Torchbooks, 1975); James Gregor, ed., *Giovanni Gentile: Origins and Doctrine of Fascism* (New York: Routledge, 2004).
79 Ben-Ghiat, *Fascist Modernities*, 141.
80 Ibid., 71.
81 Ibid., 70.
82 Elaine Mancini, *The Free Years of the Fascist Film Industry, 1930-1935* (Ann Arbor: University of Michigan Press, 1985); Marcia Landy, *Fascism in Film: The Italian Commercial Cinema, 1931-1943* (Princeton, N.J.: Princeton University Press, 1986); James Hay, *Popular Film Culture in Fascist Italy: The Passing of the Rex* (Bloomington: University of Indiana Press, 1987).
83 Tracy Koon, *Believe, Obey, Fight: The Political Socialization of Youth in Fascist Italy, 1922-1943* (Chapel Hill: University of North Carolina Press, 1985).
84 Gallo, *Mussolini's Italy*, 220–1.
85 Mack Smith, *Mussolini*, 150.

Chapter 5: The Roads to Empire

1 Ascoli, ed., *My Rise and Fall by Benito Mussolini*, 131–2.
2 Denis Mack Smith, *Mussolini's Roman Empire* (New York: Penguin, 1977), 32.
3 Luigi Villari, *Italian Foreign Policy under Mussolini* (London: Devin Adair, 1956); Alan Cassels, *Mussolini's Early Diplomacy* (Princeton, N.J.: Princeton University Press, 1970); James Burgwyn, *Italian Foreign Policy in the Interwar Period, 1918-1940* (Westport, Conn.: Praeger, 1997); John Gooch, *Mussolini and His Generals: The Armed Forces and Fascist Foreign Policy, 1922-1940* (New York: Cambridge University Press, 2007).
4 Santi Corvaja, *Hitler and Mussolini: The Secret Meetings* (New York: Enigma Books, 2001); Christian Groeschal, *Mussolini and Hitler: The Forging of an Alliance* (New Haven, Conn.: Yale University Press, 2020).
5 Gallo, *Mussolini's Italy*, 168.
6 Ibid.
7 James Barros, *The Corfu Incident of 1923: Mussolini and the League of Nations* (Princeton, N.J.: Princeton University Press, 2015).
8 Kurt Ludecke, *I Knew Hitler: The Story of a Nazi Who Escaped the Blood Purge* (New York: Charles Scribner's Press, 1937), 67–8.
9 Ibid., 141, 143.
10 Cassels, *Mussolini's Earliest Diplomacy*, 262.
11 Ibid., 150.

12 Claudio Segre, *The Fourth Shore: The Italian Colonization of Libya* (Chicago: University of Chicago Press, 1975).
13 Mack Smith, *Mussolini's Roman Empire*, 32–43.
14 Daniel Binchy, *Church and State in Fascist Italy* (New York: Oxford University Press, 1970); John Pollard, *The Vatican and Italian Fascism, 1929-1932: A Study in Conflict* (Cambridge: Cambridge University Press, 1985).
15 Both quotes from Bosworth, *Mussolini*, 238.
16 Ibid., 251.
17 Rachele Mussolini, *My Life with Mussolini*, 73.
18 Gallo, *Mussolini's Italy*, 201.
19 Ibid., 245–6.
20 Peter Calvocoressi and Guy Wint, *Total War: Causes and Courses of the Second World War* (New York: Penguin, 1980); Anthony Adamthwaite, *The Making of the Second World War* (New York: Routledge, 1989); A.J.P. Taylor, *The Origins of the Second World War* (New York: Simon and Schuster, 1996); Robert Boyce and Joseph Maiolo, eds, *The Origins of World War II: The Debate Continues* (New York: Red Globe, 2003); P.M.H. Bell, *The Origins of the Second World War in Europe* (New York: Pearson Longman, 2007); Richard Overy, *The Origins of the Second World War* (New York: Routledge, 2022).
21 Bosworth, *Mussolini*, 269.
22 Georg Grote, *The History of the South Tyrol Question: From National Rage to Regional State* (Bern: Peter Lang, 2012).
23 Bosworth, *Mussolini*, 275.
24 Ibid., 281.
25 Rachele Mussolini, *The Real Mussolini*, 145–6.
26 Bosworth, *Mussolini*, 281.
27 Harold Marcus, *A History of Ethiopia* (Berkeley: University of California Press, 2002).
28 Richard Caulk, *'Between the Jaws of Hyenas': A Diplomatic History of Ethiopia* (Wiesbaden, Germany: Otto Harrassowitz Verlag, 2002).
29 George Baer, *The Coming of the Italo-Ethiopian War* (Cambridge, Mass.: Harvard University Press, 1967); Frank Hardie, *The Abyssinian Crisis* (London: Batsford, 1974); Esmonde Robertson, *Mussolini as Empire Builder: Europe and Africa, 1932-1936* (London: Macmillan, 1977); George Steer, *Caesar in Abyssinia* (New York: Faber and Faber, 2011); Robert Mallett, *Mussolini in Ethiopia, 1919-1935: Origins of Fascist Italy's African War* (New York: Cambridge University Press, 2018).
30 Bosworth, *Mussolini*, 284–5.
31 Knox, *Mussolini Unleashed*, 34–5.
32 Negash, *Italian Colonialism in Eritrea*, 49, 51.
33 Angelo Del Boca, *The Ethiopian War,1935-1941* (Chicago: University of Chicago Press, 1969); A.J. Barker, *The Civilizing Mission: The Italo-Ethiopian War, 1935-1936* (London: Cassell, 1968); A.J. Barker, *The Rape of Ethiopia, 1936* (New York: Ballantine Books, 1971); Anthony Mockler, *Haile Selassie's War: The Italian-Ethiopian War, 1934-1940* (New York: Random House, 1984); Jeff Pearce, *Prevail: The Inspiring Story of Ethiopia's Victory over Mussolini's Invasion, 1935-1941* (New York: Skyhorse, 2017).
34 George Baer, *Test Case: Italy, Ethiopia and the League of Nations* (Stanford, Calif.: Hoover Institute Press, 1976).
35 Elisebeth Wiskemann, *The Rome-Berlin Axis: A History of the Relations between Hitler and Mussolini* (Oxford: Oxford University Press, 1949), 76.
36 Winston Churchill, *Memoirs of the Second World War: An Abridgement of the Six Volumes of The Second World War* (Boston: Houghton Mifflin, 1987), 287.

37 Bosworth, *Mussolini*, 309.
38 Rachele Mussolini, *My Life with Mussolini*, 85.
39 Rachele Mussolini, *The Real Mussolini*, 1.
40 Knox, *Mussolini Unleashed*, 4.
41 Ibid.
42 Ray Moseley, *Mussolini's Shadow: The Double Life of Count Galeazzo Ciano* (New Haven, Conn.: Yale University Press, 1999), 17–18.
43 Ibid., 18–20.
44 Ben-Ghiat, *Fascist Modernities*, 126; Mack Smith, *Mussolini's Roman Empire*, 76; Charles Stephenson, *Mussolini, Mustard Gas and the Fascist Way of War: Ethiopia, 1935-1941* (London: Pen and Sword, 2024).
45 Ben-Ghiat, *Fascist Modernities*, 126; Charles Stephenson, *Mussolini, Mustard Gas and the Fascist Way of War: Ethiopia, 1935-1941* (London: Pen and Sword, 2024); Mack Smith, *Mussolini's Roman Empire*, 76; Bosworth, *Mussolini's Italy*, 406; Brian Sullivan, 'The Italian Armed Forces, 1918-40', in Allen Millett and Williamson Murray, *Military Effectiveness: The Interwar Period* (Boston: Allen and Unwin, 1988), 171, 190.
46 Alberto Sbacchi, *Ethiopia under Mussolini: Fascism and the Colonial Experience* (London: Zed Books, 1985); Haile Larebo, *The Building of an Empire: Italian Land Policy and Practice in Ethiopia, 1935-1941* (New York: Oxford University Press, 1994).
47 Negash, *Italian Colonialism in Eritrea*, 51–3.
48 Mack Smith, *Mussolini's Roman Empire*, 108.
49 Ben-Ghiat, *Fascist Modernities*, 130.
50 Sarti, ed., *Ax Within*, 194–5.
51 Muggeridge, *Ciano's Diary*, 68.
52 Sarti, ed., *Ax Within*, 189.
53 Ibid., 192.
54 Knox, *Mussolini Unleashed*, 30–1; Mack Smith, *Mussolini's Roman Empire*, 121.

Chapter 6: The Axis Pact of Steel

1 Mack Smith, *Mussolini*, 128.
2 Ray Moseley, *Mussolini's Shadow: The Double Life of Count Galeazzo Ciano* (New Haven, Conn.: Yale University Press, 2000).
3 Edda Mussolini Ciano, *My Truth as Told to Albert Barca* (New York: William Morrow and Company, 1977).
4 Ibid., 93.
5 Ibid., 24.
6 Ibid., 152–3.
7 Hugh Gibson, ed., *The Complete Unabridged Diaries of Count Galeazzo Ciano, 1936-1943* (Garden City, N.Y.: Doubleday, 1946); Malcom Muggeridge, ed., *Ciano's Diary, 1939-1943* (London: William Heinemann, 1947).
8 Muggeridge, *Ciano's Diary*, xiii, xviii.
9 Charles Delzell, *Mussolini's Enemies: The Italian Anti-Fascist Resistance* (Princeton, N.J.: Princeton University Press, 1961); James Gregor, *Italian Fascism and Developmental Dictatorship* (Princeton, N.J.: Princeton University Press, 1979); Larry Ceplair, *Under the Shadow of War: Fascism, Anti-Fascism and Marxists, 1918-1937* (New York: Columbia University Press, 1987).
10 Mosely, *Mussolini's Shadow*, 33–5.
11 Stanley Payne, *Fascism in Spain, 1923-1977* (Madison: University of Wisconsin Press, 1999).

12 Stanley Payne, *The Collapse of the Spanish Republic, 1933-1936* (New Haven, Conn.: Yale University Press, 2006).
13 Michael Alpert, *A New International History of the Spanish Civil War* (New York: Palgrave Macmillan, 1994); Anthony Beevor, *The Spanish Civil War* (New York: Penguin, 2001); Hugh Thomas, *The Spanish Civil War* (New York: Penguin, 2001); Paul Preston, *The Spanish Civil War: Reaction, Revolution and Revenge* (New York: W.W. Norton, 2006); Stanley Payne, *The Spanish Civil War* (New York: Cambridge University Press, 2012).
14 Stanley Payne, *The Franco Regime, 1936-1975* (Madison: University of Wisconsin Press, 2011).
15 Bolloten Burnet, *The Spanish Revolution: The Left and the Struggle for Power during the Civil War* (Chapel Hill: University of North Carolina Press, 1979); Michael Seidman, *The Victorious Counter-Revolution: The Nationalist Effort in the Spanish Civil War* (Madison: University of Wisconsin Press, 2011).
16 Alpert, *New International History*, 127.
17 Ibid., 34, 47.
18 Ibid., 116.
19 Ibid., 109.
20 Dan Richardson, *Comintern Army: The International Brigades and the Spanish Civil War* (Lexington: University of Kentucky Press, 1983); Stanley Payne, *The Spanish Civil War, the Soviet Union and Communism* (New Haven, Conn.: Yale University Press, 2004).
21 Payne, *The Spanish Civil War, the Soviet Union and Communism*, 156.
22 Raymond Proctor, *Hitler's Luftwaffe in the Spanish Civil War* (Westport, Conn.: Praeger, 1983); Robert Whealey, *Hitler and Spain: The Nazi Role in the Spanish Civil War, 1936-1939* (Lexington: University of Kentucky Press, 1989).
23 Alpert, *New International History*, 85.
24 John Coverdale, *Italian Intervention in the Spanish Civil War* (Princeton, N.J.: Princeton University Press, 2016).
25 Alpert, *New International History*, 93; Cloverdale, *Italian Intervention*, 115, 171, 176–7, 393, 417.
26 Bosworth, *Mussolini*, 318.
27 Ibid., 319.
28 Muggeridge, *Ciano's Diary*, 32–3.
29 Bosworth, *Mussolini*, 326.
30 Edda Mussolini Ciano, *My Truth*, 121–2.
31 Max Gallo, *Mussolini's Italy* (New York: Macmillan, 1973), 278; Bosworth, *Mussolini*, 329.
32 Bosworth, *Mussolini*, 333.
33 Gallo, *Mussolini's Italy*, 284.
34 Bosworth, *Mussolini's Italy*, 455.
35 Muggeridge, *Ciano's Diary*, 215.
36 P.M.H. Bell, *The Origins of the Second World War in Europe* (New York: Pearson Longman, 2007), 265.
37 Telford Taylor, *Munich: The Price of Peace* (New York: Doubleday, 1979), Erik Goldstein and Igor Luks, *The Munich Crisis: Prelude to World War II* (London: Routledge, 1999); David Faber, *Munich 1938: Appeasement and World War II* (New York: Simon and Schuster, 2008).
38 Martin Thomas, *Britain, France and Appeasement: Anglo-French Relations in the Popular Front Era* (Oxford: Berg, 1996); Peter Neville, *Hitler and Appeasement: The British Attempt to Present the Second World War* (New York: Bloomsbury, 2006).
39 Neville, *Hitler and Appeasement*, 107.

40 Gallo, *Mussolini's Italy*, 288.
41 Cassels, *Mussolini's Early Diplomacy*, 312–13.
42 Mosely, *Mussolini's Shadow*, 45.
43 Muggeridge, *Ciano's Diary*, 10.
44 Mario Toscano, *The Origins of the Pact of Steel* (Baltimore: Johns Hopkins University Press, 1967), 197.
45 Muggeridge, *Ciano's Diary*, 54.
46 Ibid., 11.
47 Faber, *Munich, 1938*, 77.
48 Elizabeth Wiskemann, *The Rome-Berlin Axis: A Study of the Relations between Hitler and Mussolini* (Oxford: Oxford University Press, 1949); Mario Toscano, *The Origins of the Pact of Steel* (Baltimore: Johns Hopkins University Press, 1967).
49 Muggeridge, *Ciano's Diary*, 47.
50 Ibid., 5, 52.
51 Ibid., 42.
52 Ibid., 25.
53 Ibid., 444.
54 Ibid., 61.
55 Toscano, *Origins of the Pact of Steel*, 368.
56 Muggeridge, *Ciano's Diary*, 90–1.
57 Ibid., 91.
58 Beevor, *Battle for Spain*, 20–2.
59 Muggeridge, *Ciano's Diary*, 57.
60 Alpert, *New International History*, 168, 171; Bosworth, *Mussolini's Italy*, 402; Mack Smith, *Mussolini's Roman Empire*, 105; Brian Sullivan, 'The Italian Armed Forces, 1918-40', in Millett and Murray, *Military Effectiveness: The Interwar Period*, 170.
61 Stanley Payne, *Franco and Hitler: Spain, Germany and World War II* (New Haven, Conn.: Yale University Press, 2008).
62 Bruce Strang, *On the Fiery March: Mussolini Prepares for War* (Westport, Conn.: Praeger, 2003), 213–14.
63 Muggeridge, *Ciano's Diary*, 52–3.
64 Ibid., 64.
65 Ibid., 55.
66 Ibid., 56.
67 Ibid., 70–1.
68 Ibid., 98–9.
69 Ibid., 99.
70 James Burgwyn, *Mussolini Warlord: Failed Dreams of Empire, 1940-1943* (New York: Enigma Books, 2012), 168.
71 Sarti, ed., *Ax Within*, 206; Strang, *On the Fiery March*, 23.
72 Meir Michaelis, *Mussolini and the Jews: German Italian Relations and the Jewish Question in Italy, 1922-1945* (New York: Oxford University Press, 1978); Stuart Hughes, *Prisoners of Hope: The Silver Age of the Italian Jews, 1924-1974* (Cambridge, Mass.: Harvard University Press, 1983); Alexander Stille, *Benevolence and Betrayal: Five Jewish Families under Fascism* (New York: Penguin, 1993).
73 Sarti, ed., *Ax Within*, 198.
74 Ibid., 200.
75 Ibid., 205.
76 Mosely, *Mussolini's Shadow*, 48.
77 Gallo, *Mussolini's Italy*, 287.
78 Alan Cassels, Italy and the Holocaust', in Saul Friedman, ed., *Holocaust Literature: A Handbook of Critical, Historical and Literary Writings* (Westport, Conn.: Praeger, 1993), 385–6; Sarti, ed., *Ax Within*, 206.

79 Muggeridge, *Ciano's Diary*, 130.
80 Ibid., 124.
81 Ibid., 125.
82 Ibid., 126.
83 Ibid., 135.
84 Klibansky, *Mussolini Memoir*, 58.
85 Muggeridge, *Ciano's Diary*, 135–6.
86 Richard Hargreaves, *Blitzkrieg Unleashed: The German Invasion of Poland, 1939* (Mechanicsburg, Penn.: Stackpole Books, 2009); David Williamson, *Poland Betrayed: the Nazi-Soviet Invasion of 1939* (Mechanicsburg, Penn.: Stackpole Books, 2011).
87 Muggeridge, *Ciano's Diary*, 165.
88 Ibid., 162.
89 William Nester, *Franklin D. Roosevelt and the Art of Leadership: Battling the Great Depression and the Axis Powers* (London: Frontline Books, 2024).
90 Muggeridge, *Ciano's Diary*, 212.
91 Sumner Welles, *The Time for Decision* (New York: Harper and Brother's, 1944), 84.
92 Muggeridge, *Ciano's Diary*, 212.
93 Ibid., 223–4, 225.

Chapter 7: The Military and Economic Power

1 For the best works in English on Italy's military before and during the Second World War, see: MacGregor Knox, *Mussolini Unleashed, 1939-1941: Politics and Strategy in Fascist Italy's Last War* (Cambridge: Cambridge University Press, 1982); Victor Madej, ed., *Italian Army Handbook, 1940-1943* (Allentown, Pen.: Game Publishing Company, 1984); John Gooch, 'Italy During the First World War', in Allen Millett and Williamson Murray, *Military Effectiveness: The First World War* (Boston: Allen and Unwin, 1988), 157–89; Brian Sullivan, 'The Italian Armed Forces, 1918-40', in Allen Millett and Williamson Murray, *Military Effectiveness: The Interwar Period* (Boston: Allen and Unwin, 1988), 169–217; MacGregor Knox, 'The Italian Armed Forces, 1940-3' in Allen Millett and Williamson Murray, *Military Effectiveness: The Second World War* (Boston: Allen and Unwin, 1988), 136–79; MacGregor Knox, *Hitler's Italian Allies: Royal Armed Forces, Fascist Regime and the War of 1940-1943* (New York: Cambridge University Press, 2000); Brian Sullivan, 'The Italian Soldier in Combat, June 1940-September 1943: Myths, Realities and Explanations', in Paul Addison and Angus Calder, eds, *Time to Kill: The Soldier's Experience of War in the West, 1939-1945* (New York: Random House, 1997), 177–205.
2 John Gooch, *Mussolini and his Generals: The Armed Forces and Fascist Foreign Policy, 1922-1940* (New York: Cambridge University Press, 2007); John Whittam, 'The Italian General Staff and the Coming of the Second World War', in Adrian Preston, ed., *General Staffs and Diplomacy before the Second World War* (New York: Routledge, 2021).
3 Brian Sullivan, 'The Italian Armed Forces, 1918-1940', in Allan Millet and Williamson Murray, eds, *Military Efficiency in the Interwar Period* (New York: Cambridge University Press, 1996).
4 Knox, *Hitler's Italian Allies*, 57.
5 Both quotes from Knox, 'The Italian Armed Forces, 1940-3', Millett and Murray, *Military Effectiveness*, 152, 171.
6 Knox, *Mussolini Unleashed*, 6.
7 Mack Smith, *Mussolini*, 258.

8 Macgregor Knox, 'Fascist Italy Assesses Its Enemies', in Ernst May, ed., *Knowing One's Enemies: Intelligence Assessment before the Two World Wars* (Princeton, N.J.: Princeton University Press, 1984).
9 Max Gallo, *Mussolini's Italy* (New York: Macmillan, 1973), 303; Knox, *Mussolini Unleashed*, 100.
10 Mack Smith, *Mussolini's Roman Empire*, 177.
11 Sullivan, 'The Italian Armed Forces, 1918-40', in Millett and Murray, *Military Effectiveness*, 171, 172; Knox, *Hitler's Italian Allies*, 26.
12 Knox, *Hitler's Italian Allies*, 26.
13 Ibid., 27.
14 Brian Sullivan, 'The Italian Soldier in Combat, June 1940-September 1943: Myths, Realities and Explanations', in Paul Addison and Angus Calder, eds, *Time to Kill: The Soldier's Experience of War in the West, 1939-1945* (New York: Random House, 1997), 180.
15 Bosworth, *Mussolini's Italy*, 476; Sullivan, 'The Italian Armed Forces, 1918-40', in Millett and Murray, *Military Effectiveness*, 174.
16 Sullivan, 'The Italian Soldier in Combat, June 1940-September 1943: Myths, Realities and Explanations', in Addison and Calder, *Time to Kill*, 182–3.
17 Ibid., 180.
18 Ibid., 182.
19 Ralph Ricci, *Italian Tanks and Fighting Vehicles of World War 2* (London: Pique Publications, 1975).
20 Knox, *Hitler's Italian Allies*, 54; Knox, 'The Italian Armed Forces, 1940-3' in Millett and Murray, *Military Effectiveness*, 154.
21 Knox, *Hitler's Italian Allies*, 54; Knox, 'The Italian Armed Forces, 1940-3' in Millett and Murray, *Military Effectiveness*, 154.
22 Sullivan, 'The Italian Soldier in Combat, June 1940-September 1943: Myths, Realities and Explanations' in Addison and Calder, *Time to Kill*, 184–6.
23 Ibid., 186.
24 Knox, *Hitler's Italian Allies*, 43.
25 Sullivan, 'The Italian Soldier in Combat, June 1940-September 1943: Myths, Realities and Explanations', in Addison and Calder, *Time to Kill*, 180.
26 Burgwyn, *Mussolini Warlord*, 156.
27 Knox, *Hitler's Italian Allies*, 152.
28 Ibid., 124–6.
29 Muggeridge, *Ciano's Diary*, 317.
30 Robert Mallett, *The Italian Navy and Fascist Expansionism, 1935-1940* (New York: Routledge, 1989); James Sadkovitch, *The Italian Navy in World War II* (Westport, Conn.: Greenwood Press, 1994).
31 Erminio Bagnasco, *Submarines of World War Two* (Annapolis, Maryland: Naval Institute Press, 2018); Clay Blair, *Hitler's U-Boat War: The Hunters, 1939-1942* (New York: Random House, 1998); Clay Blair, *Hitler's U-Boat War: The Hunted, 1942-1945* (New York: Random House, 1998).
32 Knox, *Hitler's Italian Allies*, 157.
33 Ibid., 26.
34 Ibid., 63.
35 Burgwyn, *Mussolini Warlord*, 158.
36 Ben-Ghiat, *Fascist Modernities: Italy, 1922-1945*, 138.
37 Knox, *Hitler's Italian Allies*, 42.
38 Sullivan, 'The Italian Armed Forces, 1918-40' in Millett and Murray, *Military Effectiveness*, 191.

39 Knox, *Hitler's Italian Allies*, 49–50; Knox, *Mussolini Unleashed*, 31; Sullivan, 'The Italian Armed Forces, 1918-40' in Millett and Murray, *Military Effectiveness*, 172–3.
40 Mosely, *Mussolini's Shadow*, 65.
41 Knox, *Hitler's Italian Allies*, 30; Sullivan, 'The Italian Armed Forces, 1918-40' in Millett and Murray, *Military Effectiveness*, 173; Knox, 'The Italian Armed Forces, 1940-3' in Millett and Murray, *Military Effectiveness*, 166.
42 Klibansky, *Mussolini Memoir*, 125.
43 Ibid.
44 Mark Harrison, *The Economics of World War II: Six Great Powers in Comparison* (New York: Cambridge University Press, 1998).
45 Bosworth, *Mussolini*, 394–5.
46 Muggeridge, *Ciano's Diary*, 375–6.
47 Knox, *Hitler's Italian Allies*, 47; Gallo, *Mussolini's Italy*, 303; Strang, *On the Fiery March*, 309; Knox, *Mussolini Unleashed*, 69.
48 Muggeridge, *Ciano's Diary*, 478.
49 Ibid., 477–8.
50 Gentile, *The Struggle for Modernity*, 78.
51 Denis Mack Smith, *Mussolini as a Military Leader* (Reading: University of Reading Press, 1974); Anthony Pansini, *The Duce's Dilemma: An Analysis of the Tragic Events Associated with Italy's Part in World War II* (Waco, Texas: Greenvale Press, 1997); James Burgwyn, *Mussolini Warlord: Failed Dreams of Empire, 1940-1943* (New York: Enigma Books, 2012).
52 Muggeridge, *Ciano's Diary*, 18.
53 Gibson, ed., *The Complete Unabridged Diaries of Count Galeazzo Ciano*, 120.

Chapter 8: The Roads to Humiliating Defeats

1 Julian Jackson, *The Fall of France: The Nazi Invasion of 1940* (New York: Oxford University Press, 2004); Alistair Horne, *To Lose a Battle: France 1940* (New York: Penguin, 2007); Karl Heinz Frieser, *The Blitzkrieg Legend: The 1940 Campaign in the West* (Annapolis: Naval Institute Press, 2013).
2 Muggeridge, *Ciano's Diary*, 249.
3 Knox, *Mussolini Unleashed*, 87.
4 Churchill, *Memoirs of the Second World War*, 287–8.
5 Pietro Badoglio, *Italy in the Second World War* (Oxford: Oxford University Press, 1948), 15.
6 Muggeridge, *Ciano's Diary*, 268.
7 Bosworth, *Mussolini*, 369; Knox, *Hitler's Italian Allies*, 17.
8 Knox, *Mussolini Unleashed*, 125.
9 Etienne Plan et Eric Lefevre, *La Bataille des Alps, 10-15, Juin: L'Armee Invaincue* (Paris: G. Lavanzelle, 1982); Emmanuelle Sica, *Mussolini's Army in the French Riviera: Italy's Occupation of France* (Chicago: University of Illinois Press, 2016).
10 Muggeridge, *Ciano's Diary*, 267.
11 David Ellwood, *Italy, 1943-1945* (New York: Holmes and Meier, 1982), 33.
12 James Holland, *The Battle of Britain: Five Months That Changed History, May-October 1940* (New York: St. Martin's Griffin, 2012); Christopher Bergstrom, *The Battle of Britain: An Epic Conflict Revisited* (London: Casemate, 2015); Stephen Bungay, *The Most Dangerous Enemy: A History of the Battle of Britain* (London: Aurum Press, 2015).
13 Basil Liddell Hart, *History of the Second World War* (Old Saybrook, Conn.: Konecky and Konecky, 1970), 108.

14 Muggeridge, *Ciano's Diary*, 296.
15 Vincent O'Hara, *The Struggle for the Middle Sea: The Great Navies at War in the Mediterranean Theater, 1940-1945* (Annapolis, Maryland: Naval Institute Press, 2009); Jack Greene and Alessandro Massignani, *The Naval War in the Mediterranean, 1940-1943* (Annapolis, Maryland: Naval Institute Press, 2011).
16 John Car, *The Defense and Fall of Greece, 1940-1941* (London: Pen and Sword, 2020).
17 Muggeridge, *Ciano's Diary*, 16–17.
18 Mosely, *Mussolini's Shadow*, 114.
19 Muggeridge, *Ciano's Diary*, 297.
20 Ibid., 297.
21 Gallo, *Mussolini's Italy*, 321.
22 Mario Cervi, Mario, *The Hollow Legions: Mussolini's Blunder into Greece, 1940-1941* (London: Chatto and Windus, 1972).
23 Knox, *Mussolini Unleashed*, 221.
24 Muggeridge, *Ciano's Diary*, 311.
25 Gallo, *Mussolini's Italy*, 322.
26 Klibansky, *Mussolini Memoirs*, 5.
27 Knox, *Mussolini Unleashed*, 276.
28 Thomas Jentz, *Tank Warfare in North Africa: The Opening Campaigns* (London: Schiffer Military History, 1998); Alan Moorehead, *The Desert War: The North African Campaign, 1940-1943* (New York: Penguin, 2001).
29 Burgwyn, *Mussolini Warlord*, 33.
30 Ibid., 65.
31 Moorehead, *Desert War*, 101–02.
32 Knox, *Mussolini Unleashed*, 261.
33 Ibid., 262.
34 Muggeridge, *Ciano's Diary*, 324–5, 330.
35 Ibid., 325.
36 Martin Creveld, *Hitler's Strategy, 1940-1941: The Balkan Clue* (Cambridge: Cambridge University Press, 1973).
37 James Burgwyn, *Empire on the Adriatic: Mussolini's Conquest of Yugoslavia, 1941-1943* (New York: Enigma Books, 2005); Steven Pavlowitch, *Hitler's New Disorder: The Second World War in Yugoslavia* (New York: Columbia University Press, 2008).
38 Rodrigo Vaquero, *The Axis Conquers Greece* (London: Helion, 2025).
39 Churchill, *Memoirs of the Second World War*, 432.
40 Burgwyn, *Mussolini Warlord*, 84.
41 Cervi, *Hollow Legions*, 308.
42 Davide Rodogno, *Fascism's European Empire: Italian Occupation during the Second World War* (New York: Cambridge University Press, 2006).
43 Burgwyn, *Mussolini Warlord*, 264.
44 Muggeridge, *Ciano's Diary*, 444.
45 Bosworth, *Mussolini's Italy*, 382.
46 Jack Greene and Allesandro Massignani, *Rommel's North African Campaign, September 1940-November 1942* (New York: Da Capo, 1999); John Bierman and Colin Smith, *War Without Hate: The Desert Campaign of 1940-1943* (New York: Penguin, 2004); Martin Kitchen, *Rommel's Desert War: Waging World War II in North Africa, 1941-1943* (New York: Cambridge University Press, 2009).
47 W.E. Crosskill, *The Two Thousand Mile War* (London: R. Hale, 1980); Michael Glover, *An Improvised War: The Ethiopian Campaign, 1940-1941* (London: Hippocrene, 1987); Ralph Riccio and Massimiliano Afiero, *Birth and Fall of an Empire: The Italian Army in East Africa* (New York: Helion Company, 2024).

48 Sullivan, 'The Italian Soldier in Combat, June 1940-September 1943: Myths, Realities and Explanations', in Addison and Calder, *Time to Kill: The Soldier's Experience of War in the West, 1939-1945* (New York: Random House, 1997), 190.
49 Ibid.
50 Burgwyn, *Mussolini Warlord*, 57.
51 David Stahel, *Operation Barbarossa and Germany's Defeat in the East* (New York: Cambridge University Press, 2009); Frank Ellis, *Barbarossa 1941: Reframing Hitler's Invasion of Stalin's Soviet Empire* (Topeka: University of Kansas Press, 2015).
52 Burgwyn, *Mussolini Warlord*, 118.
53 Churchill, *Memoirs of the Second World War*, 491–2.
54 Muggeridge, *Ciano's Diary*, 407.
55 Rachel Mussolini, *The Real Mussolini by Rachele Mussolini as Told to Abert Zarca* (Farnborough: Saxon House, 1973), 172.
56 Muggeridge, *Ciano's Diary*, 88, 349.
57 Ibid., 462.
58 Gentile, *Struggle for Modernity*, 161.
59 Ibid., 162.
60 Ibid., 163.
61 Muggeridge, *Ciano's Diary*, 443.
62 Ibid., 462–3.
63 James Holland, *Together We Stand: Turning the Tide in the West: North Africa, 1942-1943* (New York: HarperCollins, 2006); Ralph Riccio and Massimiliano Afiero, *The Italian Army in North Africa, 1940-1943* (London: Helion, 2023); Robert Forczyk, *Desert Armour: Tank Warfare in North Africa, 1942-43: From Gazala to Tunisia* (London: Osprey, 2023).
64 Churchill, *Memoirs of the Second World War*, 435.
65 Ibid., 583–4.
66 Muggeridge, *Ciano's Diary*, 489.
67 John Bierman and Colin Smith, *The Battle of Alamein: Turning Point of World War II* (New York: Viking, 2002); Niall Barr, *The Pendulum of War: The Three Battles of El Alamein* (London: Overlook Press, 2006).
68 Rick Atkinson, *An Army at Dawn: The War in North Africa, 1942-1943* (New York: Henry Holt, 2002).
69 Ibid., 164.
70 Klibansky, *Mussolini Memoir*, 1.
71 For a good summary of the American High Command view, see: Dwight Eisenhower, *Crusade in Europe* (New York: Doubleday, 1948), 158–61, 167–9.
72 Ellwood, *Italy, 1943-1945*, 22–3.
73 Ibid., 32.
74 Nester, *Roosevelt*, 143.
75 Churchill, *Second World War*, 670.
76 Ibid., 670, 672–4.
77 Ellwood, *Italy 1943-1945*, 51.
78 Elena Agarossi, *A Nation Collapses: The Italian Surrender of September 1943* (New York: Cambridge University Press, 2000), 17.
79 Burgwyn, *Mussolini Warlord*, 126.
80 Muggeridge, *Ciano's Diary*, 473.
81 Burgwyn, *Mussolini Warlord*, 210, 211, 219.
82 Ibid., 293.
83 Atkinson, *Army at Dawn*, 320–1.
84 Klibansky, *Mussolini Memoir*, 10.

85 Ibid.
86 Muggeridge, *Ciano's Diary*, 554–5.
87 Knox, *Hitler's Italian Allies*, 105–06.
88 Klibansky, *Mussolini Memoir*, 21.

Chapter 9: The Overthrow

1 Klibansky, *Mussolini Memoir*, 9.
2 Ibid., 23.
3 Ibid., 35.
4 Ibid., 44.
5 Both quotes from: Agarossi, *A Nation Collapses*, 45, 46.
6 Gallo, *Mussolini's Italy*, 349.
7 Klibansky, *Mussolini Memoir*, 50–1.
8 Ibid., 52.
9 Rachele Mussolini, *The Real Mussolini*, 242–3.
10 Klibansky, *Mussolini Memoir*, 55–6.
11 Ibid., 61–2.
12 Ibid., 65–6.
13 Ibid., 63–4.
14 Ibid., 64.
15 Ibid., 81.
16 Ibid., 82.
17 Gallo, *Mussolini's Italy*, 362–3.
18 Klibansky, *Mussolini Memoir*, 97–8.
19 Badoglio, *Italy in the Second World War*, 45–6.
20 Klibansky, *Mussolini Memoir*, 47.
21 Edena Agarossi, *A Nation Collapses: The Italian Surrender of September 1943* (New York: Cambridge University Press, 2000).
22 Klibansky, *Mussolini Memoir*, 191.
23 Charles O'Reilly, *Forgotten Battles: Italy's War of Liberation 1943-1945* (New York: Lexington Books, 2001), 54.
24 Ellwood, *Italy, 1943-1945*, 34.
25 Agarossi, *A Nation Collapses*, 69.
26 Gallo, *Mussolini's Italy*, 365.
27 For a good account of the negotiations see: Eisenhower, *Crusade in Europe*, 183–6.
28 Ibid.
29 Sullivan, 'The Italian Soldier in Combat, June 1940-September 1943: Myths, Realities and Explanations', in Addison and Calder, eds, *Time to Kill*, 203; Atkinson, *Day of Battle*, 168, 172.
30 Richard Lamb, *The War in Italy, 1943-1945: A Brutal Story* (London: John Murray, 1993); George Botjer, *Sideshow War: The Italian Campaign, 1943-1945* (College Station: Texas A and M University Press, 1996); Rick Atkinson, *The Day of Battle: The War in Sicily and Italy, 1943-1944* (New York: Henry Holt, 2007); James Holland, *Italy's Sorrow: A Year of War, 1944-1945* (New York: St. Martin's Press, 2008); James Holland, *The Savage Storm: The Battle for Italy, 1943* (New York: Atlantic Monthly Press, 2023).
31 Ray Moseley, *Mussolini: The Last 600 Days of Il Duce* (Guilford, Conn.: Lyon Press, 2021), 19.

32 For a good summary of the American High Command view, see: Eisenhower, *Crusade in Europe*, 158–61, 167–9.
33 Charles Harris, *Allied Administration of Italy, 1943-1945* (London: Her Majesty's Stationery Office, 1957), 106.
34 Agarossi, *A Nation Collapses*, 88.
35 Ibid., 94–5.
36 Atkinson, *Day of Battle*, 195.
37 Gallo, *Mussolini's Italy*, 374.
38 Agarossi, *A Nation Collapses*, 112, 118; Sullivan, 'The Italian Soldier in Combat, June 1940-September 1943: Myths, Realities and Explanations', in Addison and Calder, eds, *Time to Kill*, 204.
39 George Botjer, *Sideshow War: The Italian Campaign, 1943-1945* (College Station: Texas A and M University Press, 1996), 50.

Chapter 10: The Salo Republic

1 Klibansky, *Mussolini Memoir*, 244–5.
2 Ibid., 133–4.
3 Ibid., 250–2.
4 Roman Dombrowski, *Mussolini: Twilight and Fall* (London: Heinemann, 1956); Graham Fisher and Michael MacNair-Wilson, *Blackshirt: The Decline and Fall of a Dictator* (New York: Belmont, 1961); Luisa Quartermaine, *Mussolini's Last Republic: Propaganda and Politics in the Italian Social Republic* (Exeter: Elm Book Publications, 2000); Ray Moseley, *Mussolini: The Last 600 Days of Il Duce* (Guilford, Conn.: Lyon Press, 2021); Philip Morgan, *The Fall of Mussolini: Italy, the Italians and the Second World War* (New York: Oxford University Press, 2009); R.J.B. Bosworth, *Mussolini and the Eclipse of Italian Fascism: From Dictatorship to Populism* (New Haven, Conn.: Yale University Press, 2021).
5 Moseley, *Mussolini's Shadow*, 188.
6 Moseley, *Mussolini: The Last 600 Days of Il Duce*, 16–17.
7 Ben-Ghiat, *Fascist Modernities*, 204.
8 Gallo, *Mussolini's Italy*, 388, 389.
9 Ibid., 407–08.
10 Rachele Mussolini, *My Life with Mussolini*, 163.
11 Raymond Klibansky, *Mussolini's Memoirs, 1942-1945, with Documents Related to the Period* (New York: Howard Fertig, 1975).
12 Moseley, *Mussolini: The Last 600 Days of Il Duce*, 86.
13 R.J.B. Bosworth, *Claretta: Mussolini's Last Lover* (New Haven, Conn.: Yale University Press, 2017).
14 Moseley, *Mussolini: The Last 600 Days of Il Duce*, 158.
15 Rachele Mussolini, *The Real Mussolini*, 81–6.
16 Atkinson, *Day of Battle*, 507.
17 Robert Katz, *The Battle for Rome: The Germans, the Allies, the Partisans and the Pope* (New York: Simon and Schuster, 2003); Victor Failmezger, *Rome—City in Terror: The Nazi Occupation, 1943-1944* (London: Osprey, 2020).
18 Ellwood, *Italy 1943-1945*, 41.
19 Badoglio, *Italy in the Second World War*, 90.
20 Ibid., 96.
21 Ibid., 97.
22 Charles Harris, *Allied Administration of Italy, 1943-1945* (London: Her Majesty's Stationery Office, 1957).

23 Ellwood, *Italy 1943-1945*, 52.
24 Harris, *Allied Administration of Italy*, 89.
25 Luigi Villari, *The Liberation of Italy, 1943-1947* (Appleton, Wisconsin: C.C. Nelson, 1959); David Ellwood, *Italy, 1943-1945* (New York: Holmes and Meier, 1985); Maria Wilhelm, *The Other Italy: Italian Resistance in World War II* (New York: W.W. Norton, 1988); David Ward, *Antifascisms: Cultural Politics in Italy, 1943-1946: Benedetto Croce and the Liberals, Carlo Levi and the 'Actionists'* (Madison, N.J.: Farleigh Dickinson University Press, 1996); Phillp Cooke, ed., *The Italian Resistance: An Anthology* (Manchester: Manchester University Press, 1997); Jane Slaughter, *Women and the Italian Resistance, 1943-1945* (Denver: Arden Press, 1997); Charles O'Reilly, *Forgotten Battles: Italy's War of Liberation 1943-1945* (New York: Lexington Books, 2001); Claudio Pavone, *A Civil War: A History of the Italian Resistance* (New York: Verso, 2014).
26 Max Corvo, *The O.S.S. in Italy, 1942-1945* (New York: Praeger, 1989); R. Absalom, *A Strange Alliance: Aspects of Escape and Survival in Italy, 1943-1945* (Florence, Italy: Leo S. Olshki, 1991); Nicola Cacciatore, *Italian Partisans and British Forces in the Second World War* (New York: Palgrave Macmillan, 2023).
27 Moseley, *Mussolini: The Last 600 Days of Il Duce*, 107.
28 Ellwood, *Italy 1943-1945*, 160–1.
29 Ibid., 159.
30 Ibid., 177.
31 Ibid., 193.
32 Ibid., 157; Botjer, *Sideshow War*, 169; Delzell, *Mussolini's Enemies*, 503, 538.
33 Moseley, *Mussolini: The Last 600 Days of Il Duce*, 132.
34 Mosely, *Mussolini's Shadow*, 132.
35 Muggeridge, *Ciano's Diary*, 560.
36 Mosely, *Mussolini's Shadow*, 201–02.
37 Edda Mussolini Ciano, *My Truth*, 226.
38 Bosworth, *Mussolini*, 17.
39 Mosely, *Mussolini's Shadow*, 204.
40 Churchill, *Memoirs of the Second World War*, 797.
41 Delzell, *Mussolini's Enemies*, 333.
42 Roy Domenico, *Fascists on Trial, 1943-1948* (Chapel Hill: University of North Carolina Press, 1991), 87, 89.
43 Moseley, *Mussolini: The Last 600 Days of Il Duce*, 162.
44 Rachele Mussolini, *My Life with Mussolini*, 163.
45 Moseley, *Mussolini: The Last 600 Days of Il Duce*, 33.
46 Ibid., 173.
47 Dominico, *Italian Fascists on Trial*, 145.
48 Bosworth, *Mussolini*, 27.
49 F.W. Deakin, *The Last Days of Mussolini* (New York: Penguin, 1966).
50 Moseley, *Mussolini: The Last 600 Days of Il Duce*, 238.
51 Gallo, *Mussolini's Italy*, 420.
52 Rachele Mussolini, *The Real Mussolini*, 283.
53 Moseley, *Mussolini: The Last 600 Days of Il Duce*, 251.
54 Bosworth, *Mussolini*, 32.
55 For the most in-depth account of Mussolini's last days and all the versions of what happened, see: Moseley, *Mussolini: The Last 600 Days of Il Duce*, 190–323. See, also: Luciano Garibaldi, *Mussolini: The Secrets of His Death* (New York: Enigma Books, 2004).

Chapter 11: The Legacy

1 Moseley, *Mussolini: The Last 600 Days of Il Duce*, 1.
2 Mack Smith, *Mussolini*, 317.
3 Claudio Pavone, *A Civil War: A History of the Italian Resistance* (New York: Verso, 2014), 495; MacGregor Knox, *Hitler's Italian Allies: Royal Armed Forces, Fascist Regime and the War of 1940-1943* (New York: Cambridge University Press, 2000), 21; Charles Delzell, *Mussolini's Enemies: the Italian Anti-Fascist Resistance* (Princeton, N.J.: Princeton University Press, 1961), 548; Cormac O'Grada, *The Hidden Victims: Civilian Casualties of the Two World Wars* (Princeton, N.J.: Princeton University Press, 2024).
4 Knox, *Hitler's Italian Allies*, 34; MacGregor Knox, 'Expansionist Zeal, Fighting Power and Staying Power in the Italian and German Dictatorships', in Richard Bessel, ed., *Fascist Italy and Nazi Germany: Comparisons and Contrasts* (New York: Cambridge University Press, 1996), 129; Gooch, 'Italy During the First World War', in Allen Millett and Williamson Murray, *Military Effectiveness*, 183.
5 Susan Zuccotti, *The Italians and the Holocaust: Persecution, Rescue and Salvation* (New York: Basic Books, 1987); Ivo Herzer, ed., *The Italian Refuge: The Resue of the Jews During the Holocaust* (Washington D.C.: Catholic University of America Press, 1989); Saul Friedman, ed., *Holocaust Literature: A Handbook of Critical, Historical and Literary Writings* (Westport, Conn.: Praeger, 1993).
6 Moseley, *Mussolini: The Last 600 Days of Il Duce*, 122–3; Bosworth, *Mussolini's Italy*, 472.
7 Bosworth, *Mussolini's Italy*, 381.
8 Negash, *Italian Colonialism in Eritrea*, 149.
9 Atkinson, *Day of Battle*, 583.
10 Richard Holmes, 'The Italian Job: Five Armies in Italy, 1943-1945', in Paul Addison and Angus Calder, eds, *Time to Kill: The Soldier's Experience of War in the West, 1939-1945* (New York: Random House, 1997), 207, 216; Atkinson, *Day of Battle*, 581.
11 Fabio Rizi, *Benedetto Croce and the Birth of the Italian Republic*, 1943-1952 (Toronto: University of Toronto Press, 2019), 91.
12 Roy Domenico, *Fascists on Trial, 1943-1948* (Chapel Hill: University of North Carolina Press, 1991).
13 Ibid., 201.
14 Ellwood, *Italy 1943-1945*, 186.
15 Domenico, *Fascists on Trial*, 213.
16 Rachele Mussolini, *The Real Mussolini*, 11.
17 Gentile, *The Struggle for Modernity*, 140.
18 Knox, *Mussolini Unleashed*, 286.
19 Rachele Mussolini, *The Real Mussolini*, 215.
20 Mack Smith, *Mussolini's Roman Empire*, 252.
21 Vincent Arnold, *The Illusion of Victory: Fascist Propaganda and the Second World War* (New York: Peter Lang, 1998).
22 Mack Smith, *Mussolini: The Last 600 Days of Il Duce*, xiv.
23 Gallo, *Mussolini's Italy*, xi.
24 Mosely, *Mussolini's Shadow*, 110.
25 Muggeridge, *Ciano's Diary*, 558–9.
26 Gleason, *Totalitarianism*, 16.
27 Bosworth, *Mussolini*, 15–16.
28 For pioneering although dated explorations of totalitarianism, see: Friedrich von Hayek, *The Road to Serfdom* (Chicago: University of Chicago Press, 1944); Hannah Arendt, *The Origins of Totalitarianism* (1949) (New York: Harcourt, Brace and Janovich, 1973).

For more recent studies, see: Carl Friedrich and Zbigniew Brzezinski, *Totalitarian Dictatorship and Autocracy* (Cambridge, Mass.: Harvard University Press, 1956); Carl Friedrich, ed., *Totalitarianism in Perspective: Three Views* (New York: Praeger, 1969); Leonard Shapiro, *Totalitarianism* (New York: Praeger, 1972); Ernest Menze, ed., *Totalitarianism Reconsidered* (Port Washington, N.Y.: Kennikat, 1981); Simon Tormey, *Making Sense of Tyranny: Interpretations of Totalitarianism* (Manchester: Manchester University Press, 1995); Abbott Gleason, *Totalitarianism: The Inner History of the Cold War* (New York: Oxford University Press, 2001); Philip Gray, *Totalitarianism: The Basics* (New York: Routledge, 2013); Timothy Synder, *On Tyranny: Twenty Lessons from the Twentieth Century* (New York: Crown, 2017); Paul O'Brien, *Total State: Totalitarianism and How We Can Resist It* (New York: Wordwell, 2023); Flagg Taylor, *The Great Lie: Classic and Recent Appraisals of Ideology and Totalitarianism* (New York: Regnery Gateway, 2023); Simona Forti, *Totalitarianism: A Borderline Idea* (Palo Alto, Calif.: Sanford University Press, 2024).

For comparative studies, see: James Gregor, *Marxism, Fascism and Totalitarianism: Chapters in the Intellectual History of the Twentieth Century* (Palo Alto, Calif.: Stanford University Press, 2008); Michael Geyer and Sheila Fitzpatrick, eds, *Beyond Totalitarianism: Stalinism and Nazism Compared* (New York: Cambridge University Press, 2008); Bruce Pauley, *Hitler, Stalin and Mussolini: Totalitarianism in the Twentieth Century* (New York: Wiley Blackwell, 2014).

For the best overviews of authoritarianism, see: Jeanne Kirkpatrick, *Dictatorships and Double Standards: Rationalism and Reason in Politics* (New York: Simon and Schuster, 1982); Bob Altemeyer, *The Authoritarian Specter* (Cambridge, Mass.: Harvard University Press, 1996); Wendy Brown, Peter Gordon and Max Pensky, *Authoritarianism: Three Inquires in Critical Theory* (Chicago: University of Chicago Press, 2018); Eric Frantz, *Authoritarianism: What Everyone Needs to Know* (New York: Oxford University Press, 2019); Larry Diamond and Marc Plattner, *Authoritarianism Goes Global: The Challenge to Democracy* (Baltimore: Johns Hopkins University Press, 2016); Stevem Levitsky and Daniel Ziblatt, *How Democracies Die* (New York: Broadway Books, 2018); Jerzy Wintr, ed., *The New Authoritarianism: Challenges to Democracy in the 21st Century* (New York: Verlag Barbara Budrich 2019); Timothy Synder, *The Road to Unfreedom: Russia, Europe, America* (New York: Crown, 2019); Anne Applebaum, *The Twilight of Democracy: The Seductive Alure of Authoritarianism* (New York: Knopf Doubleday, 2020); Frank Dikotter, *Dictators* (New York: Bloomsbury, 2020); Ruth Ben-Ghiat, *Strongmen: Mussolini to the Present* (New York: W.W. Norton, 2021); Ben Rhodes, *After the Fall: The Rise of Authoritarianism in the World We've Made* (New York: Random House, 2022).

29 Georg Mosse, *Nazism: A Historical and Comparative Analysis of National Socialism* (New Brunswick, N.J.: Transaction Publications, 1978), 104–05.

30 A.J.P. Taylor, *The Origins of the Second World War* (New York: Simon and Schuster, 1996), 56.

31 Nicholas Doumanis, *Myth and Memory in the Mediterranean: Remembering Fascism's Empire* (London: Macmillan, 1997); R.J.B Bosworth and Patrizia Dogliani, eds, *Italian Fascism: History, Memory and Representation* (New York: Macmillan, 1999); Madeleine Albright, *Fascism: A Warning* (New York: Harper, 2018).

32 Knox, *Hitler's Italian Allies*, 1.

33 Alastair Hamilton, *The Appeal of Fascism: A Study of Intellectuals and Fascism* (London: Anthony Blond, 1971); James Gregor, *The Fascist Persuasion in Radical*

Politics (Princeton, N.J.: Princeton University Press, 1974); George Mosse, *Masses and Man: Nationalist and Fascist Perceptions of Reality* (New York: Transaction Books, 1980); John Milfull, ed., *The Attractions of Fascism: Social Psychology and Aesthetics of the 'Triumph of the Right'* (New York: Berg, 1990); Wilhelm Reich, *The Mass Psychology of Fascism* (New York: Farar, Straus and Giroux, 1980); Jason Stanley, *How Fascism Works: The Politics of Us and Them* (New York: Random House, 2018).

34 For classic studies that explore the authoritarian personality, see: Theodor Adorno, Else Frenkel-Brunswick, Daniel Levinson and Nevitt Stanford, *The Authoritarian Personality* (New York: Harper, 1950); Karen Horney, *New Ways in Psychoanalysis* (New York: W.W. Norton, 1939); Karen Horney, *Our Inner Conflicts* (New York: W.W. Norton, 1945); Karen Horney, *Neurosis and Human Growth* (New York: W.W. Norton, 1950); Eric Fromm, *The Escape from Freedom* (New York: Farrar and Rinehart, 1941); Arthur Schlesinger, *The Vital Center: The Politics of Freedom* (Boston: Houghton Mifflin, 1949), Richard Crossman, ed., *The God That Failed* (New York: Harper Brothers, 1949); Erik Erikson, *Childhood and Society* (New York: W.W. Norton, 1950).

For more recent studies, see: Herbert Kelman and Lee Hamilton, *Crimes of Obedience: Towards of Social Psychology of Authority and Responsibility* (New Haven, Conn.: Yale University Press, 1989); Joost Merloo, *The Rape of the Mind: The Psychology of Thought Control, Menticide and Brainwashing* (New York: Martino Publishing, 2015); Mattias Demmet, *The Psychology of Totalitarianism* (New York: Chelsea Green, 2016); Dean Haycock, *Tyrannical Minds: Psychology, Profiling, Narcissism and Dictatorship* (New York: Pegasus, 2021).

35 Muggeridge, *Ciano's Diary*, 558.

36 William Nester, *Putin's Virtual War: Russia's Subversion and Conversion of America, Europe and the World Beyond* (London: Frontline, 2019).

37 Michael Schmitt, 'Ex-Chief of Staff Says Trump Would Rule Like a Dictator', *New York Times*, October 24, 2024.

38 Robert Paxton, 'I've hesitated to call Donald Trump a Fascist until now', *Newsweek*, 11 January 2024; Elisabeth Zerofsky, 'Robert Paxton, a leading Historian of Fascism, long resisted applying the label to Trumpism. Then he changed his mind. "It's the real thing"', *New York Times Magazine*, October 27, 2024.

39 Michael Schmitt, 'Ex-Chief of Staff Says Trump Would Rule Like a Dictator', *New York Times*, October 24, 2024.

40 'A letter from 225 mental health professionals on Trumps' dangerous psychopathology', *New York Times*, 24 October 2024.

41 Peter Baker, 'Trump Clings to His Image as Strongman', *New York Times*, November 1, 2024.

42 Factcheckers, 'In Four Years Trump Made 30,574 False or Misleading Statements', *Washington Post*, 20 January 2021, website; Peter Baker, 'Torrent of lies Redefines Political Norms', *New York Times*, November 4, 2024.

43 For the best account, see: Moseley, *Mussolini: The Last 600 Days of Il Duce*, 350–9.

44 Ibid., 173.

BIBLIOGRAPHY

Primary

Ascoli, Max, ed., *Benito Mussolini: My Rise and Fall*, New York: Da Capo, 1998.

Badoglio, Pietro, *Italy in the Second World War: Memories and Documents*, New York: Praeger, 1976.

Balabanoff, Angelica, *My Life as a Rebel*, New York: Harper and Brothers, 1938.

Churchill, Winston, *Memoirs of the Second World War: An Abridgment of the Six Volumes of the Second World War*, Boston: Houghton Mifflin, 1987.

Ciano, Edda Mussolini, *My Truth as Told to Albert Barca*, New York: William Morrow and Company, 1977.

Eisenhower, Dwight, *Crusade in Europe*, New York: Doubleday, 1948.

Gibson, Hugh, ed., *The Complete Unabridged Diaries of Count Galeazzo Ciano, 1936-1943*, Garden City, N.Y.: Doubleday, 1946.

Hitler, Adolf, *Mein Kampf*, translated by Ralph Manheim, Boston: Houghton Mifflin, 1971.

Klibansky, Raymond, ed., Benito Mussolini, *Memoirs: 1942-1943 with Documents Relating to the Period*, New York: Howard Fertig, 1977.

Ludecke, Kurt, *I Knew Hitler: The Story of a Nazi Who Escaped the Blood Purge*, New York: Charles Scribner's Press, 1937.

Muggeridge, Malcolm, ed., *Ciano's Diary, 1939-1943*, London: Heinemann, 1947.

Muggeridge, Malcolm, ed., *Ciano's Diplomatic Papers*, London: Odham, 1948.

Mussolini, Rachele, *My Life with Mussolini in Collaboration with Michael Chinigo*, London: Robert Hale, 1959.

Mussolini, Rachele, *The Real Mussolini as told to A. Zarca*, Farnborough, Eng.: Saxon House, 1973.

Mussolini, Vittorio, *Mussolini: The Tragic Women in His Life*, London: NEL, 1973.

Nohlen, Dieter and Philip Stover, eds, *Elections in Europe: A Data Handbook*, New York: Nomos, 2010.

Welles, Sumner, *The Time for Decision*, New York: Harper and Brothers, 1944.

Zander, Patrick, ed., *The Rise of Fascism: History, Documents and Key Questions*, New York: Bloomsbury, 2016.

Secondary

Absalom, R., *A Strange Alliance: Aspects of Escape and Survival in Italy, 1943-1945*, Florence, Italy: Leo S. Olshki, 1991.

Adamthwaite, Anthony, *The Making of the Second World War*, New York: Routledge, 1989.

Addison, Paul and Angus Calder, eds, *Time to Kill: The Soldier's Experience of War in the West, 1939-1945*, New York: Random House, 1997.

Adler, Franklin, *Italian Industrialists from Liberalism to Fascism: The Political Development of the Industrial Bourgeoisie*, New York: Cambridge University Press, 1996.

Adorno, Theodor, Else Frenkel-Brunswick, Daniel Levinson and Nevitt Stanford, *The Authoritarian Personality*, New York: Harper, 1950.

Agarossi, Elena, *A Nation Collapses: The Italian Surrender on September 1943*, New York: Cambridge University Press, 2000.

Albright, Madeleine, *Fascism: A Warning*, New York: Harper, 2018.

Alpert, Michael, *A New International History of the Spanish Civil War*, New York: Palgrave Macmillan, 1994.

Altemeyer, Bob, *The Authoritarian Specter*, Cambridge, Mass.: Harvard University Press, 1996.

Applebaum, Anne, *The Twilight of Democracy: The Seductive Alure of Authoritarianism*, New York: Knopf Doubleday, 2020.

Arendt, Hannah, *The Origins of Totalitarianism* (1949), New York: Harcourt, Brace and Janovich, 1973.

Arnold, Vincent, *The Illusion of Victory: Fascist Propaganda and the Second World War*, New York: Peter Lang, 1998.

Atkinson, Rick, *An Army at Dawn: The War in North Africa, 1942-1943*, New York: Henry Holt, 2002.

Atkinson, Rick, *The Day of Battle: The War in Sicily and Italy, 1943-1944*, New York: Henry Holt, 2007.

Baer, George, *The Coming of the Italo-Ethiopian War*, Cambridge, Mass.: Harvard University Press, 1967.

Baer, George, *Test Case: Italy, Ethiopia and the League of Nations*, Stanford, Calif.: Hoover Institute Press, 1976.

Bagnasco, Erminio, *Submarines of World War Two*, Annapolis, Maryland: Naval Institute Press, 2018.

Barker, A.J., *The Civilizing Mission: The Italo-Ethiopian War, 1935-1936*, London: Cassell, 1968.

Barker, A.J., *The Rape of Ethiopia, 1936*, New York: Ballantine Books, 1971.

Barr, Niall, *The Pendulum of War: The Three Battles of El Alamein*, London: Overlook Press, 2006.

Barros, James, *The Corfu Incident of 1923: Mussolini and the League of Nations*, Princeton, N.J.: Princeton University Press, 2015.

Beales, Derek and Eugenio Biagini, *The History of the Unification of Italy*, New York: Routledge, 2002.

Beevor, Anthony, *The Spanish Civil War*, New York: Penguin, 2001.

Bell, P.M.H., *The Origins of the Second World War in Europe*, New York: Pearson Longman, 2007.

Ben-Ami, Schlomo, *Fascism From Above: The Dictatorship of Miguel Primo de Rivera in Spain, 1923-1930*, New York: Oxford University Press, 1983.

Ben-Ghiat, Ruth, *Fascist Modernities: Italy, 1922-1945*, Berkeley: University of California Press, 2004.

Ben-Ghiat, Ruth, *Strongmen: Mussolini to the Present*, New York: W.W. Norton, 2021.

Berezin, Mable, *Making the Fascist Self: The Political Culture of Interwar Italy*, Ithaca, N.Y.: Cornell University Press, 1997.

Berghaus, Gunter, *Futurism and Politics: Between Anarchist Rebellion and Fascist Reaction*, Providence, R.I. Berghahn, 1996.

Bergstrom, Christopher, *The Battle of Britain: An Epic Conflict Revisited*, London: Casemate, 2015.

Bessell, Richard. ed., *Fascist Italy and Nazi Germany: Comparisons and Contrasts*, New York: Cambridge University Press, 1996.

Bierman, John and Colin Smith, *The Battle of Alamein: Turning Point of World War II*, New York: Viking, 2002.

Bierman, John and Colin Smith, *War Without Hate: The Desert Campaign of 1940-1943*, New York: Penguin, 2004.

Binchy, Daniel, *Church and State in Fascist Italy*, New York: Oxford University Press, 1970.

Blair, Clay, *Hitler's U-Boat War: The Hunters, 1939-1942*, New York: Random House, 1998.

Blair, Clay, *Hitler's U-Boat War: The Hunted, 1942-1945*, New York: Random House, 1998.

Blum, George, *The Rise of Fascism in Europe*, Westport, Conn.: Greenwood Press, 1998.

Boemeke, Manfred, Gerald Feldman and Elisabeth Glasser, eds, *The Treaty of Versailles: A Reassessment after 75 Years*, New York: Cambridge University Press, 1998.

Bosworth, R.J.B., *Italy, the Least of the Great Powers: Italian Foreign Policy before the First World War*, Cambridge: Cambridge University Press, 1980.

Bosworth, R.J.B., *Italy and the Wider World, 1860-1960*, New York: Routledge, 1996.

Bosworth, R.J.B., *The Italian Dictatorship: Problems and Perspectives in the Interpretation of Mussolini and Fascism*, London: Arnold, 1998.

Bosworth, R.J.B., *Mussolini*, London: Arnold, 2002.

Bosworth, R.J.B., *Mussolini's Italy: Life under the Fascist Dictatorship, 1915-1945*, New York: Penguin, 2007.

Bosworth, R.J.B., ed., *The Oxford Handbook of Fascism*, New York: Oxford University Press, 2010.

Bosworth, R.J.B., *Claretta: Mussolini's Last Lover*, New Haven, Conn.: Yale University Press, 2017.

Bosworth, R.J.B., *Mussolini and the Eclipse of Italian Fascism: From Dictatorship to Populism*, New Haven, Conn.: Yale University Press, 2021.

Bosworth, R.J.B. and Patrizia Dogliani, eds, *Italian Fascism: History, Memory and Representation*, New York: Macmillan, 1999.

Botjer, George, *Sideshow War: The Italian Campaign, 1943-1945*, College Station: Texas A and M University Press, 1996.

Boyce, Robert and Joseph Maiolo, eds, *The Origins of World War II: The Debate Continues*, New York: Red Globe, 2003.

Broadberry, Stephen and Mark Harrison, eds, *The Economics of World War I*, New York: Cambridge University Press, 2009.

Brown, Wendy, Peter Gordon and Max Pensky, *Authoritarianism: Three Inquires in Critical Theory*, Chicago: University of Chicago Press, 2018.

Bungay, Stephen, *The Most Dangerous Enemy: A History of the Battle of Britain*, London: Aurum Press, 2015.

Burgwyn, James, *The Legend of the Mutilated Victory: Italy, the Great War and the Paris Peace Conference, 1915-1919*, Westport, Conn.: Greenwood Press, 1993.

Burgwyn, James, *Italian Foreign Policy in the Interwar Period, 1918-1940*, Westport, Conn.: Praeger, 1997.

Burgwyn, James, *Empire on the Adriatic: Mussolini's Conquest of Yugoslavia, 1941-1943*, New York: Enigma Books, 2005.

Burgwyn, James, *Mussolini Warlord: Failed Dreams of Empire, 1940-1943*, New York: Enigma Books, 2012.

Burnet, Bolloten, *The Spanish Revolution: The Left and the Struggle for Power during the Civil War*, Chapel Hill: University of North Carolina Press, 1979.

Cacciatore, Nicola, *Italian Partisans and British Forces in the Second World War*, New York: Palgrave Macmillan, 2023.

Calvocoressi, Peter and Guy Wint, *Total War: Causes and Courses of the Second World War*, New York: Penguin, 1980.

Cannistraro, Philip, ed., *Historical Dictionary of Fascist Italy*, Westport, Conn.: Greenwood, 1982

Cannistraro, Philip and Brian Sullivan, *Il Duce's Other Woman: The Untold Story of Margherita Sarfatti, Benito Mussolini's Jewish Mistress, and How She Helped Him Come to Power*, New York: William Morrow, 1993.

Car, John, *The Defence and Fall of Greece, 1940-1941*, London: Pen and Sword, 2020.

Carocci, Giampero, *Italian Fascism*, New York: Penguin, 1975.

Carsten, Francis, *The Rise of Fascism*, Berkeley: University of California Press, 1982.

Cassels, Alan, *Fascist Italy*, London: Routledge, 1969.

Cassels, Alan, *Mussolini's Early Diplomacy*, Princeton, N.J.: Princeton University Press, 1970.

Caulk, Richard, *'Between the Jaws of Hyenas': A Diplomatic History of Ethiopia*, Wiesbaden, Germany: Otto Harrassowitz Verlag, 2002.

Ceplair, Larry, *Under the Shadow of War: Fascism, Anti-Fascism and Marxists, 1918-1937*, New York: Columbia University Press, 1987.

Cervi, Mario, *The Hollow Legions: Mussolini's Blunder into Greece, 1940-1941*, London: Chatto and Windus, 1972.

Chabod, Fredrico, *A History of Italian Fascism*, London: Weidenfeld and Nicolson, 1963.

Collier, Martin, *Italian Unification, 1820-1871*, New York: Heinemann, 2002.

Collier, Richard, *Duce!: The Rise and Fall of Benito Mussolini*, London: Collins, 1971.

Cook, John and Chris Paxton, *European Political Facts, 1900-1996*, New York: Palgrave Macmillan, 1998.

Cooke, Philip, ed., *The Italian Resistance: An Anthology*, Manchester: Manchester University Press, 1997.

Corvaja, Sanit, *Hitler and Mussolini: The Secret Meetings*, New York: Enigma Books, 2001.

Corvo, Max, *The O.S.S. in Italy, 1942-1945*, New York: Praeger, 1989.

Coverdale, John, *Italian Intervention in the Spanish Civil War*, Princeton, N.J.: Princeton University Press, 2016.

Creveld, Martin, *Hitler's Strategy, 1940-1941: The Balkan Clue*, Cambridge: Cambridge University Press, 1973.

Crosskill, W.E., *The Two Thousand Mile War*, London: R. Hale, 1980.

Crossman, Richard, *The God That Failed*, New York: Harper Brothers, 1949.

Darrah, David, *Hail Caesar!*, Boston: Hale, Cushman and Flint, 1936.

De Felice, Renzo, *Mussolini il Fascista*, 2 vols., Turin: Einaudi, 1966, 1968

De Felice, Renzo, *Mussolini il Duce*, 2 vols., Turin: Einaudi, 1974, 1981.

De Felice, Renzo, *Le Interpretazioni del Fascismo*, Bari: Laterza, 1983.

De Grand, Alexander, *The Italian Nationalist Association and the Rise of Fascism in Italy*, Lincoln: University of Nebraska Press, 1978.

De Grand, Alexander, *Italian Fascism: Its Origins and Development*, Lincoln: University of Nebraska Press, 1982.

De Grand, Alexander, *The Italian Left in the Twentieth Century: A History of the Socialist and Communist Parties*, Bloomington: University of Indiana Press, 1989.

De Grand, Alexander, *Fascist Italy and Nazi Germany: The Fascist 'Style' of Rule*, New York: Routledge, 1995.

De Grazia, Victoria, *The Culture of Consent: Mass Organization and Leisure in Fascist Italy*, Cambridge: Cambridge University Press, 1981.

De Grazia, Victoria, *How Fascism Ruled Women: Italy, 1922-1945*, Berkeley: University of California Press, 1992.

Deakin, F.W., *The Last Days of Mussolini*, New York: Penguin, 1966.

Deakin, F.W., *The Brutal Friendship: Mussolini, Hitler and the Fall of Italian Fascism*, New York: Phoenix Books, 2000.

Del Boca, Angelo, *The Ethiopian War,1935-1941*, Chicago: University of Chicago Press, 1969.

Delzell, Charles, *Mussolini's Enemies: The Italian Anti-Fascist Resistance*, Princeton, N.J.: Princeton University Press, 1961.

Delzell, Charles, *Mediterranean Fascism, 1919-1945*, New York: Harper and Row, 1970.

Demmet, Mattias, *The Psychology of Totalitarianism*, New York: Chelsea Green, 2016.

Di Scala, Spencer, *Italy from Revolution to Republic, 1700 to the Present*, Boulder, Colo.: Westview Press, 1995

Diamond, Larry and Marc Plattner, *Authoritarianism Goes Global: The Challenge to Democracy*, Baltimore: Johns Hopkins University Press, 2016).

Diggins, John, *Mussolini and Fascism: The View from America*, Princeton, N.J.: Princeton University Press, 1972.

Dikotter, Frank, *Dictators*, New York: Bloomsbury, 2020.

Dombrowski, Roman, *Mussolini: Twilight and Fall*, London: Heinemann, 1956.

Domenico, Roy, *Fascists on Trial, 1943-1948*, Chapel Hill: University of North Carolina Press, 1991.

Doordan, Dennis, *Building Modern Italy: Italian Architecture, 1914-1936*, Princeton, N.J.: Princeton University Press, 1988.

Doumanis, Nicholas, *Myth and Memory in the Mediterranean: Remembering Fascism's Empire*, London: Macmillan, 1997.

Duggan, Christopher, *Fascism and the Mafia*, New Haven, Conn.: Yale University Press, 1989.

Duggan, Christopher, *Fascist Voices: An Intimate History of Mussolini's Italy*, New York: Oxford University Press, 2013.

Eatwell, Roger, *Fascism: A History*, London: Chatto and Windus, 1995.

Ellwood, David, *Italy, 1943-1945*, New York: Holmes and Meier, 1985.

Erikson, Erik, *Childhood and Society*, New York: W.W. Norton, 1950.

Etlin, Richard, *Modernism in Italian Architecture. 1890-1940*, Cambridge: Cambridge University Press, 1991.

Faber, David, *Munich 1938: Appeasement and World War II*, New York: Simon and Schuster, 2008.

Falasca-Zamponi, Simonetta, *Fascist Spectacle: The Aesthetics of Power in Mussolini's Italy*, Berkeley: University of California Press, 1997.

Ferguson, Niall, *The Pity of War: Explaining World War I*, New York: Basic Books, 1999.

Fermi, Laura, *Mussolini*, Chicago: University of Chicago Press, 1966.

Ferrell, Nicolas, *Mussolini: A New Life*, New York: Phoenix Press, 2005.

Fisher, Graham and Michael MacNair-Wilson, *Blackshirt: The Decline and Fall of a Dictator*, New York: Belmont, 1961.

Finaldi, Giuseppe ed., *Mussolini and Italian Fascism*, New York: Routledge, 2014.

Finaldi, Giuseppe *A History of Italian Colonialism, 1860-1907: Europe's Last Empire*, New York: Routledge, 2016.

Forczyk, Robert, *Desert Armour: Tank Warfare in North Africa, 1942-43: From Gazala to Tunisia*, London: Osprey, 2023.

Forgacs, David, ed., *Rethinking Italian Fascism: Capitalism, Populism and Culture*, London: Lawrence and Wishart, 1986.

Forgacs, David, *Italian Culture in the Industrial Era, 1880-1980, Cultural Industries, Politics and the Public*, Manchester, Eng.: Manchester University Press, 1990.

Fornari, Harry, *Mussolini's Gadfly: Roberto Farinacci*, Nashville: Vanderbilt University Press, 1971.

Forsyth, Douglas, *The Crisis of Liberal Italy: Monetary and Financial Policy 1914-1922*, Cambridge: Cambridge University Press, 1993.

Forti, Simona, *Totalitarianism: A Borderline Idea*, Palo Alto, Calif.: Sanford University Press, 2024.

Frantz, Eric, *Authoritarianism: What Everyone Needs to Know*, New York: Oxford University Press, 2019.

Friedman, Saul, ed., *Holocaust Literature: A Handbook of Critical, Historical and Literary Writings*, Westport, Conn.: Praeger, 1993.

Friedrich, Carl and Zbigniew Brzezinski, *Totalitarian Dictatorship and Autocracy*, Cambridge, Mass.: Harvard University Press, 1956.

Friedrich, Carl, ed., *Totalitarianism in Perspective: Three Views*, New York: Praeger, 1969.

Frieser, Karl, *The Blitzkrieg Legend: The 1940 Campaign in the West*, Annapolis: Naval Institute Press, 2013.

Fromm, Eric, *The Escape from Freedom*, New York: Farrar and Rinehart, 1941.

Gallo, Max, *Mussolini's Italy: Twenty Years of the Fascist Era*, London: Abelard-Schuman, 1974.

Garibaldi, Luciano, *Mussolini: The Secrets of His Death*, New York: Enigma Books, 2004.

Gauthier, Brandons, *Before Evil: Young Lenin, Hitler, Stalin, Mussolini, Mao and Kim*, New York: Tortoise Books, 2022.

Gentile, Emilio, *The Struggle for Modernity: Nationalism, Futurism and Fascism*, Westport, Conn.: Praeger, 2003.

Germino, Dante, *The Italian Fascist Party in Power: A Study in Totalitarian Rule*, Minneapolis: University of Minnesota Press, 1959.

Geyer, Michale and Sheila Fitzpatrick, eds, *Beyond Totalitarianism: Stalinism and Nazism Compared*, New York: Cambridge University Press, 2008.

Ghirado, Diane, *Building New Communities: New Deal America and Fascist Italy*, Princeton, N.J.: Princeton University Press, 1989.

Ginsborg, Paul, *A History of Contemporary Italy: Society and Politics, 1943-1988*, New York: Palgrave Macmillan, 2003.

Gleason, Abbott, *Totalitarianism: The Inner History of the Cold War*, New York: Oxford University Press, 2001.

Glover, Michael, *An Improvised War: The Ethiopian Campaign, 1940-1941*, London: Hippocrene, 1987.

Goldstein, Erik and Igor Luks, *The Munich Crisis: Prelude to World War II*, London: Routledge, 1999.

Goldstein, Robert, *Political Repression in Nineteenth Century Europe*, New York: Routledge, 2009.

Golsan, Richard, ed., *Fascism, Aesthetics and Culture*, Hanover, N.H.: University of New England Press, 1992.

Gooch, John, *Army, State and Society in Italy, 1870-1915*, New York: Macmillan, 1989.

Gooch, John, *Mussolini and his Generals: The Armed Forces and Fascist Foreign Policy, 1922-1940*, New York: Cambridge University Press, 2007.

Gray, Philip, *Totalitarianism: The Basics*, New York: Routledge, 2013.

Greene, Jack and Allesandro Massignani, *Rommel's North African Campaign, September 1940-November 1942*, New York: Da Capo, 1999.

Greene, Jack and Alessandro Massignani, *The Naval War in the Mediterranean, 1940-1943*, Annapolis, Maryland: Naval Institute Press, 2011.

Gregor, James, *The Ideology of Fascism: The Rationale of Totalitarianism*, New York: Free Press, 1969.

Gregor, James, *The Fascist Persuasion in Radical Politics*, Princeton, N.J.: Princeton University Press, 1974.

Gregor, James, *Interpretations of Fascism*, Morristown, N.J.: General Learning Press, 1974.

Gregor, James, *Italian Fascism and Developmental Dictatorship*, Princeton, N.J.: Princeton University Press, 1979.

Gregor, James, *Young Mussolini and the Intellectual Origins of Fascism*, Berkeley: University of California Press, 1979.

Gregor, James, ed., *Giovanni Gentile: Origins and Doctrine of Fascism*, New York: Routledge, 2004.

Gregor, James, *Marxism, Fascism and Totalitarianism: Chapters in the Intellectual History of the Twentieth Century*, Palo Alto, Calif.: Stanford University Press, 2008.

Griffin, Roger, *The Nature of Fascism*, New York: Routledge, 1993.

Griffin, Roger, ed., *Fascism*, New York: Oxford University Press, 1995.

Groeschal, Christian, *Mussolini and Hitler: The Forging of an Alliance*, New Haven, Conn.: Yale University Press, 2020.

Grote, Georg, *The History of the South Tyrol Question: From National Rage to Regional State*, Bern: Peter Lang, 2012.

Halperin, Samuel, *Mussolini and Italian Fascism*, New York: Van Nostrand, 1964.

Hamilton, Alastair, *The Appeal of Fascism: A Study of Intellectuals and Fascism*, London: Anthony Blond, 1971.

Hardie, Frank, *The Abyssinian Crisis*, London: Batsford, 1974.

Hargreaves, Richard, *Blitzkrieg Unleashed: The German Invasion of Poland, 1939*, Mechanicsburg, Penn.: Stackpole Books, 2009.

Harris, Charles *Allied Administration of Italy, 1943-1945*, London: Her Majesty's Stationery Office, 1957.

Harris, H.S., *The Social Philosophy of Giovanni Gentile*, Urbana: University of Illinois Press, 1960.

Hay, James, *Popular Film Culture in Fascist Italy: The Passing of the Rex*, Bloomington: University of Indiana Press, 198

Haycock, Dean, *Tyrannical Minds: Psychology, Profiling, Narcissism and Dictatorship*, New York: Pegasus, 2021.

Hayek, Friedrich von, *The Road to Serfdom*, Chicago: University of Chicago Press, 1944.

Hayes, Paul, *Fascism*, London: George Allen and Unwin, 1973.

Herzer, Ivo, ed., *The Italian Refuge: The Rescue of the Jews During the Holocaust*, Washington D.C.: Catholic University of America Press, 1989.

Hibbert, Christopher, *Benito Mussolini*, London: Longmans, 1962.

Hughes-Hallett, Lucy, *The Pike: Gabriele D'Annunzio: Poet, Seducer and Preacher of War*, New York: Alfred Knopf, 2013.

Hilton-Young, William, *The Italian Left: A Short History of Political Socialism in Italy*, Westport, Conn.: Greenwood, 1975.

Holland, James, *Together We Stand: Turning the Tide in the West: North Africa, 1942-1943*, New York: HarperCollins, 2006.

Holland, James, *Italy's Sorrow: A Year of War, 1944-1945*, New York: St. Martin's Press, 2008.

Holland, James, *The Battle of Britain: Five Months That Changed History, May-October 1940*, New York: St. Martin's Griffin, 2012.

Holland, James, *The Savage Storm: The Battle for Italy, 1943*, New York: Atlantic Monthly Press, 2023.

Horne, Alistair, *To Lose a Battle: France 1940*, New York: Penguin, 2007.

Horney, Karen, *New Ways in Psychoanalysis*, New York: W.W. Norton, 1939.

Horney, Karen, *Our Inner Conflicts*, New York: W.W. Norton, 1945.

Horney, Karen, *Neurosis and Human Growth*, New York: W.W. Norton, 1950.

Hostetter, Richard, *The Italian Socialist Movement: Origins, 1860-1882*, New York: Literary Licensing, 2012.

Hughes, Stuart, *Prisoners of Hope: The Silver Age of the Italian Jews, 1924-1974*, Cambridge, Mass.: Harvard University Press, 1983.

Ipsen, Carl, *Dictating Demography: The Problem of Population in Fascist Italy*, New York: Cambridge University Press, 1996.

Jackson, Julian, *The Fall of France: The Nazi Invasion of 1940*, New York: Oxford University Press, 2004.

Jentz, Thomas, *Tank Warfare in North Africa: The Opening Campaigns*, London: Schiffer Military History, 1998.

Jonas, Raymon, *The Battle of Adwa: An African Victory in the Age of Empire*, Cambridge, Mass.: Havard University Press, 2015.

Kallis, Aristotle, *Fascist Ideology: Territory and Expansionism in Italy and Germany, 1922-1945*, New York: Routledge, 2000.

Kelman, Herbert and Lee Hamilton, *Crimes of Obedience: Towards of Social Psychology of Authority and Responsibility*, New Haven, Conn.: Yale University Press, 1989.

Kennedy, Paul, *The Rise and Fall of the Great Powers*, New York: Vintage, 1989.

Kirkpatrick, Ivone, *Mussolini: Study of a Demagogue*, New York: Odhams Books, 1964.

Kirkpatrick, Jeanne, *Dictatorships and Double Standards: Rationalism and Reason in Politics*, New York: Simon and Schuster, 1982.

Kitchen, Martin, *Fascism*, London: Macmillan, 1976.

Kitchen, Martin, *Rommel's Desert War: Waging World War II in North Africa, 1941-1943*, New York: Cambridge University Press, 2009.

Knox, MacGregor, *Common Destiny: Dictatorship, Foreign Policy and War in Fascist Italy and Germany*, New York: Cambridge University Press, 2000.

Knox, MacGregor, *Hitler's Italian Allies: Royal Armed Forces, Fascist Regime and the War of 1940-1943*, New York: Cambridge University Press, 2000.

Knox, MacGregor, *Mussolini Unleashed, 1939-1941: Politics and Strategy in Fascist Italy's Last War*, New York: Cambridge University Press, 2008.

Koon, Tracy, *Believe, Obey, Fight: The Political Socialization of Youth in Fascist Italy, 1922-1943*, Chapel Hill: University of North Carolina Press, 1985.

Lamb, Richard, *The War in Italy, 1943-1945: A Brutal Story*, London: John Murray, 1993.

Landy, Marcia, *Fascism in Film: The Italian Commercial Cinema, 1931-1943*, Princeton, N.J.: Princeton University Press, 1986.

Laqueur, Walter, ed., *Fascism: A Reader's Guide: Analyses, Interpretation, Bibliography*, New York: Penguin, 1979.

Larebo, Haile, *The Building of an Empire: Italian Land Policy and Practice in Ethiopia, 1935-1941*, New York: Oxford University Press, 1994.

Ledeen, Michael, *Universal Fascism: The Theory and Practice of the Fascist International*, New York: Howard Fertig, 1972.

Ledeen, Michael, *The First Duce: D'Annunzio at Fiume*, Baltimore: Johns Hopkins University Press, 1977.

Levitsky, Steven and Daniel Ziblatt, *How Democracies Die*, New York: Broadway Books, 2018.

Liddell Hart, Basil, *History of the Second World War*, Old Saybrook, Conn.: Konecky and Konecky, 1970.

Lubasz, Heinz, ed., *Fascism: Three Major Regimes*, New York: John Wiley, 1972.

Lurino, Maria, *The Italian Americans: A History*, New York: W.W. Norton, 2014.

Lyttleton, Adrian, ed., *Italian Fascisms from Pareto to Gentile*, New York: Harper Torchbooks, 1975.

Lyttleton, Adrian, *The Seizure of Power: Fascism in Italy, 1919-1929*, Princeton, N.J.: Princeton University Press, 1987.

Macdonald, John and Zeljko Cimpric, *Caporetto and the Isonzo Campaign: The Italian Front, 1915-1918*, London: Pen and Sword, 2015.

MacGregor-Hastie, Roy, *The Day of the Lion: The Life and Death of Fascist Italy*, New York: Macdonald, 1963.

Mack Smith, Denis, *Mussolini's Roman Empire*, New York: Penguin, 1977.

Mack Smith, Denis, *Mussolini as a Military Leader*, Reading: University of Reading Press, 1974.

Mack Smith, Denis, *Mussolini*, New York: Alfred Knopf, 1982.

Mack Smith, Denis, *Italy and Its Monarchy*, New Haven, Conn.: Yale University Press, 1989.

Mack Smith, Denis, *Modern Italy: A Political History*, Ann Arbor: University of Michigan Press, 1997.

Macmillan, Margaret, *The Peacemakers: The Paris Peace Conference and Its Attempt to End War*, New York: Hodder, 2003.

Madej, Victor, *Italian Army Handbook, 1940-1943*, Allentown, Penn.: Game Publishing Company, 1984.

Maier, Charles, *Recasting Bourgeois Europe: Stabilization in France, Germany and Italy in the Decade after World War I*, Princeton, N.J.: Princeton University Press, 1975.

Maier, Charles, In *Search of Stability: Explorations in Historical Political Economy*, Cambridge: Cambridge University Press, 1988.

Mallett, Robert, *The Italian Navy and Fascist Expansionism, 1935-1940*, New York: Routledge, 1989.

Mallett, Robert, *Mussolini in Ethiopia, 1919-1935: Origins of Fascist Italy's African War*, New York: Cambridge University Press, 2018.

Mancini, Elaine, *The Free Years of the Fascist Film Industry, 1930-1935*, Ann Arbor: University of Michigan Press, 1985.

Mangione, Jerre, *La Storia: Five Centuries of the Italian American Experience*, New York: Harper Perennial, 1992.

Marcus, Harold, *A History of Ethiopia*, Berkeley: University of California Press, 2002.

Mason, Timothy, *Nazism, Fascism and the Working Class*, New York: Cambridge University Press, 1995.

May, Ernst, ed., *Knowing One's Enemies: Intelligence Assessment before the Two World Wars*, Princeton, N.J.: Princeton University Press, 1984.

Menze, Ernest, ed., *Totalitarianism Reconsidered*, Port Washington, N.Y.: Kennikat, 1981.

Merloo, Joost, *The Rape of the Mind: The Psychology of Thought Control, Menticide and Brainwashing*, New York: Martino Publishing, 2015.

Michaelis, Meir, *Mussolini and the Jews: German Italian Relations and the Jewish Question in Italy, 1922-1945*, New York: Oxford University Press, 1978.

Milfull, John, ed., *The Attractions of Fascism: Social Psychology and Aesthetics of the 'Triumph of the Right'*, New York: Berg, 1990.

Millett, Allen and Williamson Murray, *Military Effectiveness: The First World War*, Boston: Allen and Unwin, 1988.

Millett, Allen and Williamson Murray, *Military Effectiveness: The Interwar Period*, Boston: Allen and Unwin, 1988.

Millett, Allen and Williamson Murray, *Military Effectiveness: The Second World War*, Boston: Allen and Unwin, 1988.

Mockler, Anthony, *Haile Selassie's War: The Italian-Ethiopian War, 1934-1940*, New York: Random House, 1984.

Moorehead, Alan, *The Desert War: The North African Campaign, 1940-1943*, New York: Penguin, 2001.

Morgan, Philip, *Italian Fascism, 1919-1945*, London: Macmillan, 1995.

Morgan, Philip, *Fascism in Europe, 1919-1945*, New York: Routledge, 2003.

Morgan, Philip, *The Fall of Mussolini: Italy, the Italians and the Second World War*, New York: Oxford University Press, 2009.

Moseley, Ray, *Mussolini's Shadow: The Double Life of Count Galeazzo Ciano*, New Haven, Conn.: Yale University Press, 2014.

Moseley, Ray, *Mussolini: The Last 600 Days of Il Duce*, Guilford, Conn.: Lyon Press, 2021

Mosse, George, *Nazism: A Historical and Comparative Analysis of National Socialism*, New Brunswick, N.J.: Transaction Publications, 1978.

Mosse, George, *Masses and Man: Nationalist and Fascist Perceptions of Reality*, New Brunswick, N.J.: Transaction Books, 1980.

Mosse, George, *The Fascist Revolution: Toward a General Theory of Fascism*, New York: Howard Fertig, 1999.

Mosse, George, *International Fascism, 1920-1945: New Thoughts and New Approaches*, New York: Harper Collins, 2000.

Negash, Tekeste, *Italian Colonialism in Eritrea, 1882-1941: Policies, Praxis and Impact*, Stockholm: Almquist & Wiksell International, 1987.

Nester, William, *Putin's Virtual War: Russia's Subversion and Conversion of America, Europe and the World Beyond*, London: Frontline, 2019.

Nester, William, *Land of War: A History of European Warfare from Achilles to Putin*, New York: Stackpole Books, 2023.

Nester, William, *Franklin D. Roosevelt and the Art of Leadership: Battling the Great Depression and the Axis Powers*, London: Frontline Books, 2024.

Neville, Peter, *Hitler and Appeasement: The British Attempt to Present the Second World War*, New York: Bloomsbury, 2006.

Nolte, Ernst, *Three Faces of Fascism: Action Francaise, Italian Fascism, National Socialism,* New York: Holt, Rinehart, Winston, 1966.

O'Brien, Paul, *Total State: Totalitarianism and How We Can Resist It,* New York: Wordwell, 2023.

O'Grada, Cormac, *The Hidden Victims: Civilian Casualties of the Two World Wars,* Princeton, N.J.: Princeton University Press, 2024.

O'Hara, Vincent, *The Struggle for the Middle Sea: The Great Navies at War in the Mediterranean Theatre, 1940-1945,* Annapolis, Maryland: Naval Institute Press, 2009.

O'Reilly, Charles, *Forgotten Battles: Italy's War of Liberation 1943-1945,* New York: Lexington Books, 2001.

Overy, Richard, *The Origins of the Second World War,* New York: Routledge, 2022.

Pansini, Anthony, *The Duce's Dilemma: An Analysis of the Tragic Events Associated with Italy's Part in World War II,* Waco, Texas: Greenvale Press, 1997.

Pauley, Bruce, *Hitler, Stalin and Mussolini: Totalitarianism in the Twentieth Century,* New York: Wiley Blackwell, 2014.

Pavlowitch, Steven, *Hitler's New Disorder: The Second World War in Yugoslavia,* New York: Columbia University Press, 2008.

Pavone, Claudio, *A Civil War: A History of the Italian Resistance,* New York: Verso, 2014.

Paxton, Robert, *The Anatomy of Fascism,* New York: Vintage, 2004.

Payne, Stanley, *Fascism: Comparison and Definition,* Madison: University of Wisconsin Press, 1987.

Payne, Stanley, *A History of Fascism, 1914-1945,* Madison: University of Wisconsin Press, 1995.

Payne, Stanley, *Fascism in Spain, 1923-1977,* Madison: University of Wisconsin Press, 1999.

Payne, Stanley, *The Spanish Civil War, the Soviet Union and Communism,* New Haven, Conn.: Yale University Press, 2004.

Payne, Stanley, *The Collapse of the Spanish Republic, 1933-1936,* New Haven, Conn.: Yale University Press, 2006.

Payne, Stanley, *Franco and Hitler: Spain, Germany and World War II,* New Haven, Conn.: Yale University Press, 2008.

Payne, Stanley, *The Franco Regime, 1936-1975,* Madison: University of Wisconsin Press, 2011.

Payne, Stanley, *The Spanish Civil War,* New York: Cambridge University Press, 2012.

Pearce, Jeff, *Prevail: The Inspiring Story of Ethiopia's Victory over Mussolini's Invasion, 1935-1941,* New York: Skyhorse, 2017.

Pearce, Jenny, *Under the Eagle: U.S. Intervention in Central America and the Caribbean,* Boston: South End Press, 1982.

Pickering-Iazzi, Robin, ed., *Mothers of Invention: Women, Italian Fascism and Culture*, Minneapolis: University of Minnesota Press, 1995.

Pinkus, Karen, *Bodily Regimes: Italian Advertising under Fascism*, Minneapolis: University of Minnesota Press, 1995.

Plan, Etienne, and Eric Lefevre, *La Bataille des Alps, 10-15, Juin: L'Armee Invaincue* (Paris : G. Lavanzelle, 1982.

Poggi, Christine, *Inventing Futurism: The Art and Politics of Artificial Optimism*, Princeton, N.J.: Princeton University Press, 2008.

Pollard, John, *The Vatican and Italian Fascism, 1929-1932: A Study in Conflict*, Cambridge: Cambridge University Press, 1985.

Pollard, John, *The Fascist Experiment in Italy*, New York: Routledge, 2005.

Pons, Silvio, *The Rise and Fall of the Italian Communist Party: A Transnational History*, Palo Alto, Calif.: Stanford University Press, 2024.

Preston, Adrian, ed., *General Staffs and Diplomacy before the Second World War*, New York: Routledge, 2021.

Preston, Paul, *The Spanish Civil War: Reaction, Revolution and Revenge*, New York: W.W. Norton, 2006.

Preston, Paul, *Franco: A Biography*, New York: Fontana Press, 2011.

Proctor, Raymond *Hitler's Luftwaffe in the Spanish Civil War*, Westport, Conn.: Praeger, 1983.

Quartermaine, Luisa, *Mussolini's Last Republic: Propaganda and Politics in the Italian Social Republic*, Exeter, Eng.: Elm Book Publications, 2000.

Reich, Wilhelm, *The Mass Psychology of Fascism*, New York: Farar, Straus and Giroux, 1980.

Reill, Dominique Kirchner, *The Fiume Crisis: Life in the Wake of the Hapsburg Empire*, Cambridge, Mass.: Belknap Press, 2020.

Rhodes, Ben, *After the Fall: The Rise of Authoritarianism in the World We've Made*, New York: Random House, 2022.

Ricci, Ralph, *Italian Tanks and Fighting Vehicles of World War 2*, London: Pique Publications, 1975.

Riccio, Ralph and Massimiliano Afiero, *Birth and Fall of an Empire: The Italian Army in East Africa*, New York: Helion Company, 2024.

Richardson, Dan, *Comintern Army: The International Brigades and the Spanish Civil War*, Lexington: University of Kentucky Press, 1983.

Ridley, Jasper, *Mussolini: A Biography*, New York: St. Martin's Press, 1998.

Roberts, David, *The Syndicalist Tradition and Italian Fascism*, Manchester: Manchester University Press, 1979.

Robertson, Esmonde, *Mussolini as Empire Builder: Europe and Africa, 1932-1936*, London: Macmillan, 1977.

Rodogno, Davide, *Fascism's European Empire : Italian Occupation during the Second World War*, New York: Cambridge University Press, 2006.

Roland, Seth, *Caporetto: The Scapegoat Battle*, London: Macdonald, 1965.

Rusinow, Dennison, *Italy's Austrian Heritage, 1919-1946*, Oxford: Clarendon, 1969.

Sachs, Harvey, *Music in Fascist Italy*, New York: W.W. Norton, 1988.

Sadkovitch, James, *The Italian Navy in World War II*, Westport, Conn.: Greenwood Press, 1994.

Salvemini, Gaetano, *The Fascist Dictatorship in Italy*, New York: Howard Fertig, 1967.

Salvemini, Gaetano, *Italian Fascist Activities in the United States*, New York: Centre for Migration Studies, 1977.

Sarfatti, Margherita, *The Life of Benito Mussolini*, London: Thorton Butterworth, 1926.

Sarti, Roland, *Fascism and the Industrial Leadership in Italy, 1919-1940: A Study of Private Power under Fascism*, Berkeley: University of California Press, 1971.

Sarti, Roland, ed., *The Ax Within: Italian Fascism in Action*, New York: New Viewpoints, 1974.

Sbacchi, Alberto, *Ethiopia under Mussolini: Fascism and the Colonial Experience*, London: Zed Books, 1985.

Scala, Spencer Di, *Mussolini, 1883-1915: Triumph and Transformation of a Revolutionary Socialist*, New York: Palgrave Macmillan, 2016.

Schapp, Jeffrey, *Staging Fascism: 18BL and the Theatre for Masses*, Stanford: Stanford University Press, 1996.

Schlesinger, Arthur, *The Vital Centre: The Politics of Freedom*, Boston: Houghton Mifflin, 1949.

Segre, Claudio, *Fourth Shore: The Italian Colonization of Libya*, Chicago: University of Chicago Press, 1975.

Seidman, Michael, *The Victorious Counter-Revolution: The Nationalist Effort in the Spanish Civil War*, Madison: University of Wisconsin Press, 2011.

Seldes, George, *Sawdust Caesar: The Untold History of Mussolini and Fascism*, New York: Harper and Brother's, 1935.

Seton-Watson, Christopher, *Italy from Liberalism to Fascism, 1870-1925*, London: Methuen, 1967.

Shapiro, Leonard, *Totalitarianism*, New York: Praeger, 1972.

Sharp, Alan, *The Versailles Settlement: Peacemaking in Paris, 1919*, New York: St. Martin's, 1991.

Sica, Emmanuelle, *Mussolini's Army in the French Riviera: Italy's Occupation of France*, Chicago: University of Illinois Press, 2016.

Slaughter, Jane, *Women and the Italian Resistance, 1943-1945*, Denver: Arden Press, 1997.

Sluga, Glenda, *The Problem of Trieste and the Italo-Yugoslav Border: Difference, Identity and Sovereignty in Twentieth Century Europe*, Albany: New York State University Press, 2001.

Smyth, Howard, *Secrets of the Fascist Era: How Uncle Sam Obtained Some of the Top-level Documents of Mussolini's Period*, Carbondale: Southern Illinois University Press, 1975.

Spackman, Barbara, *Fascist Virilities: Rhetoric, Ideology and Social Fantasy in Italy*, Minneapolis: University of Minnesota Press, 1996.

Spierenberg, Pieter, ed., *Men and Violence: Gender, Honor and Rituals in Modern Europe and America*, Columbia: Ohio University Press, 1998.

Stahel, David, *Operation Barbarossa and Germany's Defeat in the East*, New York: Cambridge University Press, 2009.

Stanley, Jason, *How Fascism Works: The Politics of Us and Them*, New York: Random House, 2018.

Steer, George, *Caesar in Abyssinia*, New York: Faber and Faber, 2011.

Stephenson, Charles, *Mussolini, Mustard Gas and the Fascist Way of War: Ethiopia, 1935-1941*, London: Pen and Sword, 2024.

Stille, Alexander, *Benevolence and Betrayal: Five Jewish Families under Fascism*, New York: Penguin, 1993.

Stone, Maria, *The Patron State: Culture and Politics in Fascist Italy*, Princeton, N.J.: Princeton University Press, 1998.

Strang, Bruce, *On the Fiery March: Mussolini Prepares for War*, Westport, Conn.: Praeger, 2003.

Synder, Timothy, *On Tyranny: Twenty Lessons from the Twentieth Century*, New York: Crown, 2017.

Synder, Timothy, *The Road to Unfreedom: Russia, Europe, America*, New York: Crown, 2019.

Tanenbaum, Edward, *Fascism in Italy: Society and Culture, 1922-1945*, London: Allen Lane, 1973.

Taylor, A.J.P., *The Origins of the Second World War*, New York: Simon and Schuster, 1996.

Taylor, Flagg, *The Great Lie: Classic and Recent Appraisals of Ideology and Totalitarianism*, New York: Regnery Gateway, 2023.

Taylor, Telford, *Munich: The Price of Peace*, New York: Doubleday, 1979.

Thomas, Hugh, *The Spanish Civil War*, New York: Penguin, 2001.

Thomas, Martin, *Britain, France and Appeasement: Anglo-French Relations in the Popular Front Era*, Oxford, Eng.: Berg, 1996.

Thompson, Mark, *The White War: Life and Death on the Italian Front, 1915-1919*, London: Faber and Faber, 2008.

Tormey, Simon, *Making Sense of Tyranny: Interpretations of Totalitarianism*, Manchester, U.K.: Manchester University Press, 1995.

Toscano, Mario, *The Origins of the Pact of Steel*, Baltimore: Johns Hopkins University Press, 1967.

Turner, Henry, ed., *Reappraisals of Fascism*, New York: New Viewpoints, 1975.

Urban, Joan Barth, *Moscow and the Italian Communist Party: From Togliatti to Berlinguer*, Ithaca, N.Y.: Cornell University Press, 1986.

Vaida, Mihaly, *Fascism as a Mass Movement*, London: Allison and Busby, 1976.

Vaquero, Rodrigo, *The Axis Conquers Greece*, London: Helion, 2025.

Villari, Luigi, *Italian Foreign Policy under Mussolini*, London: Devin Adair, 1956.

Villari, Luigi, *The Liberation of Italy, 1943-1947*, Appleton, Wisconsin: C.C. Nelson, 1959.

Ward, David, *Antifascisms: Cultural Politics in Italy, 1943-1946: Benedetto Croce and the Liberals, Carlo Levi and the 'Actionists'*, Madison, N.J.: Farleigh Dickinson University Press, 1996.

Whealey, Robert, *Hitler and Spain: The Nazi Role in the Spanish Civil War, 1936-1939*, Lexington: University of Kentucky Press, 1989.

Whittam, John, *Fascist Italy*, Manchester: Manchester University Press, 1995.

Wilhelm, Maria, *The Other Italy: Italian Resistance in World War II*, New York: W.W. Norton, 1988.

Williamson, David, *Poland Betrayed: the Nazi-Soviet Invasion of 1939*, Mechanicsburg, Penn.: Stackpole Books, 2011.

Willson, Perry, *The Clockwork Factory: Women and Work in Fascist Italy*, New York: Oxford University Press, 1994.

Wintr, Jerzy, ed., *The New Authoritarianism: Challenges to Democracy in the 21st Century*, New York: Verlag Barbara Budrich 2019.

Wiskemann, Elizabeth, *The Rome-Berlin Axis: A Study of the Relations between Hitler and Mussolini*, Oxford: Oxford University Press, 1949.

Wiskemann, Elizabeth, *Fascism in Italy*, London: Macmillan, 1969.

Woolf, S.J., ed., *The Nature of Fascism*, London: Weidenfeld and Nicolson, 1968.

Woolf, S.J., ed., *Fascism in Europe*, London: Methuen, 1981.

Zamagni, Vera *The Economic History of Italy, 1860-1990*, Oxford, Eng.: Clarendon, 1993.

Zuccotti, Susan, *The Italians and the Holocaust: Persecution, Rescue and Salvation*, New York: Basic Books, 1987.

INDEX

Acerbo, Giacomo 48, 63, 71
Acquarone, Pietro 135, 198
Africa 26, 106–07
Agnelli, Giovanni 77
Aksun, King Ezana 107
Albania 16, 51, 96–7, 130, 133–7, 168, 170, 174, 176, 194
Albert, King 74
Albertini, Luigi 54
Alcala-Zamora, Niceto 121
Alexander I, King 247
Alexander, Harold 186, 193, 194, 206, 218, 219, 225, 233
Alfieri, Dino 71, 89
Alfonso XIII, King 121
Algeria 187
Alighieri, Dante 88, 159
Almirante, Giorgio 255
Al-Muktar, Umar 100
Al-Sennusi, Mohammad ibn 100
Alvaro, Carrado 89
Alzana, Manuel 121, 12
Ambrosia, Vittorio 146, 158, 194–5, 198, 199, 209
Amedeo, Duke Savoia-Aosta, Luigi 177–8
Anderson, Kenneth 188
Anfuso, Filipo 120
Antonelli, Domenico 212
Anzar-Cabanas, Juan 121
Argentina 117, 247
Arnim, Hans-Jurgen von 189
Arpinati, Leandro 48
Ataturk, Mustafa Kemal 95, 247
Auckinleck, Claude 184, 185
Augustus, Emperor 106
Australia 4
Austria / Austria-Hungary 15, 17, 22, 23–4, 25, 26, 28, 30, 32, 36, 37–8, 41, 42, 43, 45, 46, 47, 51, 52, 98, 105–06, 124, 127–8, 136, 144

Bacci, Giovani 57
Baden, Max von 46
Badoglio, Pietro 4, 60, 100, 109, 110, 145, 146, 164, 169, 170–1, 190–1, 198, 201–02, 203, 204–05, 207, 208, 209, 220, 221, 228, 229
Bahamas 179
Balabanoff, Angelica 29–30
Balbo, Italo 59, 62, 65, 85, 146, 164, 166
Baratieri, Oreste 27
Barbaro, Umberto 88, 90
Barbone, Tito 28
Baselli, Paolo 42, 54
Bastianini, Giuseppe 84
Bastico, Ettore 125, 152, 177, 185, 188
Belgium 3, 25, 38, 94, 98–9, 102, 163
Benedict XV, Pope 59
Beneduce, Alberto 78
Beneš, Edvard 128–9
Berio, Alberto 204
Berlusconi, Silvio 255
Bermuda 179
Bertrand, Aristide 58
Bianchi, Michele 58, 59, 62, 65, 66
Biden, Joe 254
Bilenchi, Romano 89
Bismarck, Otto von 118
Blanqui, Louis 29
Blassetti, Alessandro 90
Bocchini, Arturo 73
Boccioni, Umberto 34
Bolin, Luis 122

Bolla, Luigi 230
Bombacci, Nicolo 53, 56
Bonaccorsi, Arconovaldo 121
Bonaparte, Napoleon 7, 22, 111, 120, 216–17
Bono, Michele 65
Bonomi, Ivanoe 54, 57, 59, 198–9, 204, 222, 223, 228, 230
Bordiga, Amadeo 56
Bosnia-Herzegovina 36
Bottai, Giuseppe 78, 88, 194, 198, 199, 207
Braun, Eva 233
Brazil 117
Briand, Aristide 102
Brignone, Giulio 90
Britain 3, 4, 22, 25, 26, 32, 37–8, 41–2, 44, 46, 47, 48, 51, 58, 68, 79, 83, 94, 95, 96, 98–9, 101, 102, 103, 104–05, 107, 108, 109, 110, 113, 114, 120, 123, 124, 128–30, 131, 139, 141, 143, 144, 147, 148, 149, 151, 153, 154, 155, 156, 157, 158, 162, 163–95, 179–81, 182–3, 184–5, 189–95, 203–04, 205, 218–19, 220, 223, 224, 228, 233, 236, 243, 253
Buffarini-Guidi, Guido 214
Bulgaria 167, 174, 175
Bulwer-Lytton, Victor 104
Burma 181
Burzagli, Ernesto 153

Caesar, Julius 7, 99, 106
Camazza, Gabrielo 63
Cambodia 247
Camerini, Mario 90
Campbell, Ronald 205
Campioni, Inigo 168
Canada 179, 263
Capello, Luigi 72–3
Carboni, Giacomo 203, 207
Cardona, Luigi 42
Cardona, Rafaele 42, 226, 231
Carl Albert, King 23
Carnaris, Wilhelm 123
Carra, Carlo 34
Caruso, Pietro 229, 330
Casalini, Armando 70
Casari, Ferdinando 168
Castano, Giuseppe 204–05
Castellano, Giuseppe 198, 199, 205, 207–08
Catholicism / Catholic Church / Papacy 7, 57, 100–01, 121, 166
Cavagnari, Domenico 145, 154
Cavallero, Ugo 146, 158, 170–1, 179, 188, 207
Cavazzoni, Stefano 63
Caviglia, Enrico 53, 198
Cavour, Camille Benso, Count 7, 22–3, 23–4, 222
Chamberlain, Austen 103
Chamberlain, Neville 128–9, 163
Charles IV, King 120
Chavez, Hugo 248
Chiang Kai-shek 4, 104
China 3, 4, 94, 103–04, 117, 118, 180, 226, 247, 248
Churchill, Clementine 9
Churchill, Winston 9, 103, 109, 162, 16364, 166, 173, 175, 179, 182–3, 184–7, 189–90, 191, 203, 204, 205, 207, 219, 220, 227, 228, 233, 238–9, 243
Cianetti, Tullio 226, 227
Ciano, Costanza 63, 117
Ciano, Galeazzo 71, 89, 113, 114, 116, 117, 118–19, 120, 126, 128, 129, 130–3, 134–7, 138, 139, 140, 141, 142, 143–4, 147, 160, 163, 164–5, 166, 167, 168, 169, 170, 173–4, 181, 182, 183, 192, 194, 198, 199, 207, 213, 226–7, 235, 241–2, 245, 249
Ciarlantini, Franco 88
Cimmaruta, Roberto 107
Cincar-Markovic, Dmitrijs 174
Cini, Vittorio 77
Cipriano, Amilcare 19–20
Cittadini, Auturo 60
Clark, Mark 5, 206, 219, 220
Clemenceau, Georges 41
Collins, John 168
Colonna, Giovanni 62, 63
Communist International (Comintern) 55, 56, 119–20, 124, 125–6, 223
Concert of Europe 22
Constantine, King 147
Coppola, Francesco 88
Corbino, Orso 63
Corradini, Enrico 48, 62
Cortese, Guido 111
Costa, Andrea 20
Croatia 174, 176, 215
Croce, Benedetto 228
Crispi, Francesco 26, 27
Cuba 247
Cunningham, Alan 178, 184
Cunningham, Andrew 167, 178

Curzon, George 96, 99
Cvetković, Dragisa 174
Cyprus 26, 124
Czechoslovakia 16, 17, 102, 128–9, 136

D'Ajeta, Blasco 204
Daladier, Edouard 129
Damtu, Ras Desta 109, 110
D'Annunzio, Gabriele 50, 52, 53, 99
Darlan, Jean 187
D'Arzago, Giuseppe 63
Dawes, Charles 99
D'Azeglio, Massimo 24
De Ambris, Alceste 52
De Bono, Emilio 62, 65, 108, 109, 226
De Ceasare, Nicolo 207
De Cespedes, Alba 89
De Chirico, Georgia 88
De Courten, Raffaele 228
De Gasperi, Alcide 68, 222, 228, 240
De Rivera, Primo 14
De Robertis, Francesco 90
De Ruggiero, Guido 228
De Stefani, Alberto 63
De Vecchi, Ferrucio 49, 54, 65
De Vecchio, Cesare 57, 59
Deng Xiao-ping 248
Denmark 233
Di Lauro, Raffaele 113
Di Revel, Paolo 62, 63
Di Revel, Thaon 96
Diaz, Armando 46, 62
Dietrich, Sepp 175
Djibouti 107, 110, 166
Dolfin, Giovanni 217
Dollfuss, Engelbert 105–06
Dollman, Eugen 207
Donegani, Guido 77
Dönitz, Karl 5, 233
Donovan, William 190
Douhet, Giulio 146
Ducci, Gino 154
Dulles, Alan 231, 233
Dumini, Amerigo 69, 70, 237
Duterte, Rodrigo 248

Eden, Antony 108, 109, 130, 191
Egypt 3, 4, 99, 114, 171
Eisenhower, Dwight 4, 185, 187, 188, 193, 204, 205, 208, 220, 233
Elena, Queen 110
Emmanuele, Santo 120
Emmanuelli, Enrico 88
Engels, Friedrich 25–6, 29
Eritrea 27, 99, 106, 107, 112, 113
Esterle, Carlo 41
Estonia 141
Ethiopia / Abyssinia 3, 16, 27, 81, 102, 107–14, 147, 171, 177, 178

Facta, Luigi 54, 59, 60
Falk, Giorgio 77
Farinacci, Roberto 48–9, 57, 62, 65, 66, 72, 113, 125, 137–8, 199
Favagrossa, Carlo 71
Federici, Riccardo 218
Federzoni, Luigi 61, 63, 70, 73
Fermi, Enrico 88
Filipelli, Filippo 69
Fini, Aldo 137
Fini, Gianfranco 255
Finland 142–3
First World War 12, 26, 36–8, 41–3, 44–5, 46–8, 94, 100, 105, 117, 151, 157, 236, 238
  Caporetto 45–6
  Piave 46
  Triple Alliance / Central Powers 36, 42, 46
  Triple Entente 26, 41–2, 48
  Vittorio-Veneto 46
Fitzgerald, Scott 117
Fitzgerald, Zelda 117
Ford, Henry 79
Foscini, Antonio 96
France 3–4, 17, 24, 25, 26, 32, 36, 37–8, 41–2, 44, 46, 47, 48, 51, 58, 68, 74, 83, 94, 95, 96, 98–9, 101, 102, 104–05, 107, 108, 109, 110, 113, 114, 123, 124, 129, 130, 131, 139, 141, 143, 144, 148, 149, 156, 157, 158, 163–5, 166, 167, 180, 183, 187, 203–04, 224, 243, 248, 253
Francis of Assisi, Saint 7
Francisci, Pietro 63
Franco, Francisco 3, 17, 122–5, 126, 133, 215, 247
François-Poncet, Andre 130
Franz-Ferdinand, Archduke 36
Fredeborg, Hans-Georg 233
Fredendall, Lloyd 187, 193
Frederick II, King 118

Gandhi, Mahatma 7, 102
Gardiner, William 208
Garibaldi, Giuseppe 22–3, 24

Gariboldi, Italo 146, 191–2
Gaspari, Pietro 101
Gaza 253
Geloso, Carlo 147, 168–9, 174
Genina, Augusto 90
Gentile, Giovanni 12, 14, 63, 89
George V 96
Germany 3, 4, 5, 15, 22, 25, 26, 29, 32, 36, 37–8, 41, 44, 46, 47, 51, 58, 67, 83, 95, 97, 98–9, 102, 103, 105–06, 108, 109, 113, 118, 119–20, 120, 122–5, 125–6, 127–8, 128–30, 130–3, 139, 140–1, 142, 143, 148, 149, 153, 154, 156, 157, 158–9, 162, 163–95, 211–34, 236, 238, 240, 243, 244–5, 246, 247, 248
  East Germany 249–50
  West Germany 250
Giani, Mario 78
Giani, Nicolo 91
Gibson, Violet 73
Gil-Robes y Quinones, Jose 121, 122
Giolitti, Giovanni 32, 35, 36, 53, 54, 56–7, 68
Giunta, Francesco 65, 66
Giurnati, Giovanni 63, 66, 241
Goethe, Johann 118, 245
Goldman, Cesare 44
Gonatas, Stylianos 96
Göring, Hermann 188
Gott, William 186
Gottardi, Luciano 226
Gramsci, Antoinio 56, 68, 73, 119
Grandi, Dino 57, 58, 62, 160, 194, 198, 199, 200
Graziani, Rodolfo 100, 108, 109, 110, 111, 145, 146, 171–2, 176, 214, 231, 233
Greece 3, 14, 51, 95, 96–7, 127, 137, 147, 168–71, 174–6, 186, 243, 247
Greenland 253
Guarnieri, Felice 71
Guerrini, Giovani 88
Guiana 179
Guzzoni, Alfredo 135, 146, 197–8

Harding, Warren 94, 99
Harris, Kamala 253
Hearst, William Randolph 182
Heinlein, Konrad 128–9
Henry II, King 237
Hindenburg, Paul von 105
Hirohito, Emperor 103
Hitler, Adolf 3, 4, 5, 7, 14–17, 89–90, 93, 95, 97, 103, 105–06, 109, 113, 116, 120–1, 122, 123, 126, 127–8, 128–30, 136, 139, 140–1, 142, 162, 164, 165–6, 167, 168, 169, 173, 174, 175, 176, 178, 181, 186, 187–8, 199, 201, 203–04, 207, 213, 215, 230–1, 233, 235, 244–5, 246, 247, 253
Hoare, Samuel 109, 204–05
Hoxha, Daut 169
Hull, Cordell 189–90
Hungary 5, 29, 51, 52, 167, 174, 247, 248
Hus, Jon 32

Ideologies
  Authoritarianism 235
  Communism 12, 25–6, 28–9, 45, 58, 101, 245, 247, 248, 249, 250
  Fascism 2, 11–14, 40–60, 61–92, 93–115, 116–44, 145–61, 162–95, 196–210, 211–34, 243, 245, 246–7, 248–56
  Futurism 33–5, 40
  Liberalism/Humanism 249
  National Socialism (Nazism) 12, 243
  Social Darwinism 12, 40
  Socialism 9, 25–6, 28–9, 32, 34, 39, 58, 101
  Totalitarianism 245
Imru, Ras 110
Indonesia/East Indies 181
International Organizations
  European Coal and Steel Community 241
  European Economic Community 241
  European Union 241, 248
  League of Nations 3, 51, 94, 95, 96–7, 103–04, 109, 112–13, 120, 143
  North Atlantic Treaty Organization 241, 248, 252
  Organization for Petroleum Exporting Countries 241
  United Nations 183
Iraq 171
Italy (Unification, Republic, 1848–1922): 18–27, 28–39, 40–60
  Big Business/Corporations 41, 44
  Carboni 23

Chamber of Deputies 2, 12, 20, 23, 26, 32, 35, 36, 42, 52, 53, 56–7, 62, 63–4, 68, 69, 70, 71, 73, 75
Communist Party 12, 56, 57, 65, 69, 70, 73, 74
Confederation of Industry (*Confindustria*) 55–6, 77
Conservative Party 54
Constitution 23, 70
Constitutionalist Party 69
Council of Miniters 23
Democratic Bloc 57
Democratic Liberal Party 57
Economy 3, 42–3, 47, 48
Elections 2, 24–5, 68, 75
Empire 26–7, 34–5
Foreign Policies 26–7, 34–5, 36, 41–2
General Confederation of Labor 32
Italian Workers Confederation 55–6
Italian Workers Federation 55–6
Liberal / Liberal Union Party 32, 36, 42, 53, 54, 59, 62, 68
Nationalist Association Party 62
National Unity Party 52
Parliament 63, 69
Peasant Party 68
People's Party 53, 55, 57, 68
Populist Party 69, 222
Radical / Social Democratic Party 36, 53, 54, 57, 62, 68
Republican Party 69
Senate 46, 57, 68
Socialist Party 26, 28–30, 35, 36, 39, 41, 53, 54, 55, 56, 57, 68, 69, 74
Surrender 4–5
Unification (*Risogimento*) 22–5
Unitary Socialist Party 68, 69
Italy (Fascism, 1918–45): 40–60, 61–92, 93–115, 116–44, 145–61, 162–95, 196–210, 211–34
Acerbo Law 68
Big Business / Corporations 41, 77
Blackshirts and Militant Groups 2, 40, 48–50, 63, 70, 111–12, 178, 231, 237
Chamber of Deputies 127
Chamber of Fasci and Corporations 2
Confederation of Fascist Organizations 78
Confederation of Industry (*Confindustria*) 77–8
Economy 2–3, 76–7, 78–90, 145–61
Empire 93–115, 133–7, 237–8, 244
Fascist Party and Movement 7, 10, 11–14, 40–1, 44, 48–50, 53–60
Grand Council 2, 4, 7, 64, 72, 74, 75, 114, 118, 134, 160, 199–201, 202, 203, 214, 215, 241
Intelligence Community 147
Italian Popular Union Party 198
Jews 137–9, 236–7
March on Rome (takeover) 2, 11, 13, 58–60, 87
Military 42, 64, 65, 66, 67, 68, 80–1, 124–5, 133, 145–61, 209–10, 214–15, 215–16, 225, 236, 243–4
Overthrow of Mussolini 2, 4, 5, 196–210
Organization for Vigilance and Repression of Anti-Fascism (OVRA) 73–4
Policies (domestic) 68–92
Policies (foreign) 84–5, 93–115, 116–44, 162–95
Rescue and Salo Republic 5, 211–34, 235
Senate 127
Special Tribunal 16, 73–4
Italy (Republic, 1943 – present):
Action Party 198, 222, 224–5, 228, 240
Brothers of Italy 255
Christian Democratic Party 198, 222, 228, 240
Communist Party 119–20, 198, 222, 223, 228, 240
Forza Party 255
Italian Social Movement 255
Labour Democratic Party 198, 222, 228
Liberal Party 198, 222, 228, 240
Military 225, 236
National Alliance 255
National Liberation Committee 222–3, 228, 231
Socialists of Proletariat Union Party 198, 222, 228
United Freedom Front 198, 204, 222, 228
War Crime Trials 229–30, 239–40

Jamaica 179
Japan 3, 5, 25, 94, 95, 101, 102, 103–04, 125–6, 128, 130–3, 148, 149, 156, 158, 167, 174, 180–1, 183, 190, 214, 215, 233–4, 240, 245, 247
Jews/Judaism 137
Jodl, Albert 209, 233
Joseph I, King 120
Joyce, Kenyon 221
Juarez, Benito 19
Jung, Guido 78, 137

Kant, Emmanuel 118
Kappel, Herbert 229–30
Kassa, Ras 110
Kautsky, Karl 29
Kellogg, Frank 102
Kelly, John 250–1
Kennan, George 205
Kenya 99, 177, 178
Kerensky, Alexander 45
Kesselring, Albert 187–8, 193, 209, 219, 220
Kim Il-sung 247
Kim Jong-un 253
Koryzis, Alexander 175
Kosovo 176
Kropotkin, Peter 20
Kurusu, Saburo 167

La Padula, Ernesto 88
Lachino, Angelo 178
Laos 247
Latin America 23
Latvia 141
Laval, Pierre 108, 109
Law, Andrew Bonar 96
Lazzari, Constantino 36
Lazzaro, Urbano 232
Le Bon, Gustav 86
Lease, Oliver 219–20
Leccisi, Domenico 255
Lenin, Vladimir 9, 45
Lerroux, Alejandro 121
Lessona, Alessandro 63, 113
Libya 16, 34–5, 99, 100, 106, 108, 114, 171, 176, 188, 187, 188
Limbaugh, Rush 250
Lithuania 141
Lloyd George, David 5, 58
Lombardi, Riccardo 231
Longanesi, Leo 90
Longoni, Attilio 49
Lucas, John 219
Luccetti, Gino 73
Luchaire, Julien 41
Luciano, Charles 'Lucky' 85
Ludecke, Kurt 97–8
Luther, Martin 118
Luzzatti, Luigi 54
Lvov, Michael 45

Macedonia 176
Mackensen, Hans Georg von 203
MacMillan, Harold 221
Madero, Francisco 248
Malacria, Augusto 69
Malaparte, Curzio 10
Malaya 181
Malta 134, 176, 186, 196–7
Mancini, Pasquale 26
Mao Zedong 247
Marazza, Achille 231
Marconi, Guglielmo 88
Marinelli, Giovanni 226
Marinetti, Filippo 34, 54, 88
Marrelli, Magneti 77
Marsich, Pietro 57, 58
Mason-MacFarlane, Noel 221
Marx, Karl 25–6, 29, 30–1, 33, 118
Mary, Queen 96
Mascagni, Pietro 88
Matteotti, Giacomo 68, 69, 70, 72, 227
Mazzini, Giuseppe 22–3, 40
Mecozzi, Amedeo 146
Meloni, Giorgia 255–6
Merlino, Lino 41
Messe, Allesandro 82, 171, 195
Messe, Giovanni 146, 179, 193–4, 221
Metaxas, Ioannis 15, 170, 247
Metternich, Clemens von 22
Mexico 19, 44
Michaels, George 86
Michelini, Arturo 255
Middle East 114, 171, 172
Miklas, Wilhelm 128
Milley, Mark 250–1
Millo, Enrico 53
Minilik II 27
Mola, Emilio 122
Molotov, Vyacheslav 141
Montagna, Gulio 96

Montenegro 176
Montgomery, Bernard 4, 1867, 189, 193, 194, 196, 197, 206, 208, 210
Moravia, Alberto 88, 89
Morgan, John Pierpont 181
Morgan, William 233
Morocco 187, 189
Muggeridge, Malcolm 119
Mulugeta, Ras Tadessa 109
Murat, Joachim 22
Murphy, Robert 221
Mussolini, Ada Dalser (first wife) 8, 9, 43–4
Mussolini, Alessandro (father) 19
Mussolini, Anna (daughter) 8, 44
Mussolini, Arnaldo (brother) 20, 91, 116–17
Mussolini, Benito
  Beliefs 1, 11–14, 26, 28, 33–4, 40, 48–9, 61, 70, 78–9, 85–7, 91–2, 100–01, 162
  Character 5–9, 19–21, 30, 242–3
  Childhood 19–27
  Death 17, 232
  Health 76, 184
  Hitler Relations and Comparison 3, 4, 14–17, 89–90, 95, 106, 126, 128, 129, 130, 139, 140–1, 144, 166, 167, 173, 183, 187, 199, 216, 244–5, 246
  Military Service 29, 30, 43–4
  Mistresses and Girlfriends 9, 29, 30, 35–6
  Political Appeal 9–11, 76–7, 242
  Socialist 28–30, 35, 36, 39, 41
  Writings and Journalism 28–9, 30–1, 32, 33, 35, 38–9, 41, 50
Mussolini, Bruno (son) 8, 44, 112, 184
Mussolini, Edda (daughter) 8, 31–2, 44, 117–18, 119, 126, 184, 207, 217, 226–7, 241–2
Mussolini, Evige (sister) 20
Mussolini, Rachele Guidi (second wife) 7, 30–3, 44, 75–6, 102, 110, 111, 181, 200, 207, 216, 217, 218, 230, 232, 241, 242, 255
Mussolini, Romano (son) 8, 44
Mussolini, Rosa Maltoni (mother) 19–20
Mussolini, Vito (nephew) 91, 113
Mussolini, Vittorio (son) 8, 44, 113, 117, 184, 217
Muti, Ettore 66, 207

Naldi, Filippo 41
Navale, Roberto 120
Neame, Philip 177
Nehring, Walter 188–9
Nenni, Pietro 119
Netherlands 3, 4, 94, 163, 233
Nicaragua 238
Nicholas I, Tsar 45
Nietzsche, Friedrich 9, 29, 33, 40, 86, 118
Nitti, Francesco 52, 53–4, 57
Nobili, Tito 68
North Korea 247, 253
Norway 17

Occhetto, Roberto 229–30
O'Connor, Richard 172, 177
Orban, Viktor 248
Orlando, Vittorio 42, 46–7, 51, 52, 53, 54, 68
Ortega, Daniel 248
Oviglio, Aldo 63
Oviletti, Adriano 77

Panama Canal 253
Panunzio, Sergio 39
Papagos, Alessandro 170
Papal States 22, 24
Papen, Franz von 105
Papini, Giovanni 48
Pareschi, Carlo 226
Pareto, Vilfredo 29
Pariani, Alberto 146, 148
Parri, Ferruccio 222
Pasella, Umberto 49, 66
Paul, Prince 174
Paulus, Friedrich 192
Pavelic, Ante 174, 215
Pavesi, Gino 196–7
Pavolini, Alessandro 66, 89, 170, 226
Patton, George 4, 187, 193, 194, 196, 197, 205
Peron, Juan 247
Pershing, John 44
Petacci, Carla 9, 17, 217–18, 232
Pétain, Philippe 4, 163, 165, 203–04
Peter I, King 52
Peter III, King 174
Philippines 248

Philips, William 181
Piedmont-Sardinia, Kingdom of 22, 23, 24, 74
Pilsudski, Josef 237
Pirandello, Luigi 88
Pirelli, Alberto 77
Pius IX 100
Pius XI / Ratti, Achille 58, 59, 101
Platt, William 178
Poincaire, Raymond 96
Pol Pot 247
Poland 17, 102, 139, 141, 142, 247
Poletti, Charles 220
Polvorelli, Gaetano 89
Portugal 23, 94, 205, 207
Poveromo, Amleto 69, 70
Prasca, Sebastiano 169, 170
Prezzolini, Giuseppe 33–4
Pricolo, Francisco 145, 151
Princep, Gavrilo 36
Prussia 22, 24, 118
Pugliese, Emanuele 60
Putin, Vladimir 248, 250, 252
Puyi, Emperor 104

Radetsky, Joseph 23
Radivoge, Aleksander 174
Rafanelli, Leda 9, 35–6
Rahn, Rudolf 215
Rathenau, Walter 58
Reynaud, Paul 163, 165
Ribbentrop, Joachim 139, 141, 167, 169, 181
Ricardi, Arturo 155
Riccardi, Raffaello 207
Ricci, Renato 214
Ritchie, Neil 184
Rivera, Jose 121
Rivera, Miguel de 121, 247
Roatta, Mario 120, 123, 146, 169, 171, 203, 209, 221
Rocco, Alfredo 62, 77–8
Rocco, Augustino 157
Röhm, Ernst 15
Romania 5, 25, 167, 169, 174
Romano, Mario 88
Romeo, Alfa 77
Rommel, Erwin 4, 153, 176–7, 184–7, 188, 193, 216
Roosevelt, Franklin 85, 124, 143, 146, 179–81, 182–3, 185, 189–90, 191, 205, 207, 220, 228, 233
Rosenberg, Alfred 14
Rosi, Ezio 197
Rosselli, Carlo 120, 222
Rosselli, Nello 120
Rossi, Teofino 63
Rossoni, Edmondo 88
Ryder, Charles 187

Sacchi, Ettore 36
Saint Lucia 179
Salandra, Antonio 41–2, 54, 60, 68, 97
Sanjurjo, Jose 121, 122
Saragatt, Giuseppe 229, 240
Sarfatti, Cesare 36
Sarfatti, Margherita 9, 36, 137
Schiller, Friedrich 118
Schleicher, Kurt von 105
Schmaltz, Wilhelm 198
Schopenhauer, Arthur 29
Schuschnigg, Kurt von 127–8
Schuster, Ildefonzo 231
Schweinitz, Victor von 233
Scorza, Carlo 66, 199
Sforza, Carlo 229, 230
Second World War, the Fronts, Campaigns, Battles 2, 3–4, 7, 236, 238, 247
  Albania 134–7, 147, 168–70, 184
  Atlantic Front 4, 180
  Balkans 17, 173, 176, 189, 209
  Bombing (Strategic) 5, 205–06, 234
  Britain 166–7
  East Africa 177–8
  Eastern (Soviet Union / Europe) Front 4, 17, 146–7, 167, 178–9, 184, 192, 209
  El Alamein 4, 173, 185–7, 188, 193
  Ethiopia / Abyssinia 3, 16, 27, 81, 107–15, 118, 153, 177–8
  Finland 142–3
  France / Low Countries (1940) 17, 141, 163–6
  France / Low Countries (1944) 5, 189, 209
  Greece 141, 147, 153, 168–71, 173, 174–6, 178, 186, 189
  Indochina 4
  Italy / Sicily Front 4–5, 17, 196–210, 211–34
  Manchuria 3, 103–04, 128
  Mediterranean Naval Front 155, 167, 168, 176, 178, 186, 196–7

North Africa Front 4, 17, 141, 147, 153, 170, 171–3, 176–7, 183, 184–7, 188–9, 191–4
Norway 17, 162
Pacific–East-Southeast Asia 4, 180–1, 233–4
Pearl Harbor 4, 17, 180–1
Philippines 17
Phoney War 162
Poland 17, 141, 142
Sudetenland 16
Tunisia 172
Western European Front 4, 5
Yugoslavia 168–70, 174, 178
Treaties and Conferences:
Atlantic Charter 180, 183
Axis / Anti-Comintern Pact / Pact of Steel 3–4, 125–6, 130–3, 139, 142, 167, 174
Argentia Conference 180
Casablanca Conference 189–90, 196
Destroyers for Bases Swap 179
Hitler-Stalin Pact 141
Lend-Lease 180
Selassie, Emperor Haile 107, 109, 112–13, 178
Senise, Carmine 73
Serbia 25, 36, 37–8, 53
Serpieri, Arrigo 82
Serena, Adelchi 48, 66
Severini, Gino 34
Seyoum, Ras 110
Seyss-Inquart, Arthur 127–8
Sheba, Queen of 107
Shiferra, Fitorari 107
Silvestri, Carlo 217
Singapore 181
Skorzeny, Otto 212–13
Slovakia 167, 174
Smith, Walter Bedell 205, 202–08
Soddu, Ubaldo 146, 169, 170–1, 207
Soleri, Marcello 228
Solomon, King 107
Somalia 99, 106, 113, 177, 178
Soninno, Sidney 26, 41–2, 54
Sophie, Grand Duchess of Austria-Hungary 36
Sorel, George 29, 86
Soviet Union / Russia 4, 5, 22, 25, 26, 29, 36, 37–8, 41–2, 44–5, 46, 47, 48, 56, 65, 82, 83, 95, 102, 104, 119–20, 123, 124, 125–6, 139, 141–2, 147, 148, 149, 150–1, 158, 167, 178–9, 180, 189, 223–4, 247, 248, 250, 252, 254
Spain 3, 14, 17, 23, 81, 120–5, 133, 205, 207, 215, 247
Speer, Albert 158
Sperle, Hugo 124
Stalin, Joseph 7, 16–17, 65, 119–20, 141–2, 224, 247
Starace, Achille 58, 66, 71, 207
Stauffenberg, Klaus von 216
Stimson, Henry 104
Strong, Kenneth 205
Student, Karl 312
Sturzo, Luigi 53, 57, 62, 222
Sudan 177
Sweden 3, 162
Switzerland 5, 21–2, 28–9, 30, 41, 45, 59, 117, 207, 232, 233
Szalasi, Frence 247

Tangono, Vincenzo 62
Taylor, Frederick 79
Taylor, Maxwell 208
Tebaldi, Adofo 98
Tellera, Giuseppe 172
Tellini, Enrico 96
Tito, Josip Broz 176
Togliatti, Palmiro 119, 222, 223, 224, 228, 240
Tojo, Hideki 167
Toscanini, Arturo 88
Treaties and Conferences: Pre-1939
Brest-Litovsk Treaty 45, 46
Cannes Conference 58
Dawes Plan 99, 143
Five Power Pact 94, 101, 102
Four Power Pact 94
Geneva Protocol 102, 113
Kellogg-Briand Pact 102
Lateran Treaty 101
Lausanne Conference 95–6
Lausanne Treaty 52
Locarno Treaty 102
London Conference 102
London Treaty 47
Munich Pact 129
Nine Power Pact 94
Non-Intervention Agreement 123–4
Paris Conference 50–1
Rapallo Treaty 53
Saint Germain Treaty 52
Sèvres Treaty 95

Trianon Treaty 52
Versailles Treaty 50–2, 84, 98, 120, 127, 143
Wachale Treaty 27
Washington Conference 94, 95, 143
Young Plan 143
Treccanti, Giovanni 89
Treves, Claudio 41
Trotsky, Leon 29
Trump, Donald 250–6
Truscott, Lucian 219–20
Tsolakoglou, Georgios 175
Tunisia 26, 108, 134, 172, 187, 188, 189, 195, 198
Turati, Augusto 78
Turati, Filippo 26, 66
Turkey / Ottoman Empire 26, 34–5, 38, 45, 52, 95, 99, 247
Two Sicilies, Kingdomof the 22, 23, 24

Ukraine 252, 254
Umberto I, King 32
Umberto II, King 111, 228
United States 4, 5, 17, 25, 42–3, 44, 45, 46, 47, 51, 79–80, 84–5, 90, 94, 98–9, 101, 102, 104, 107, 124, 143–4, 147, 148, 149, 150–1, 156, 157, 158, 167, 179–81, 182–3, 184–95, 203, 207, 218–19, 220, 223, 224, 228, 231, 233, 244, 250–6
Uruguay 130

Valle, Giuseppe 146
Valti, Luca 58–9
Vecchi, Aldo 227
Venezuela 248
Verdi, Giuseppe 21
Viola, Giuseppe 69
Victor Emmanuel II, King 23, 24, 100
Victor Emmanuel III, King 2, 4, 11, 13, 32, 36, 42, 43, 46, 53, 60, 64, 67, 69–70, 88, 98, 107, 110–11, 117, 127, 131, 134, 135, 136, 142, 146, 174, 190–1, 198, 199, 201, 202, 203, 204–05, 207, 207–08, 209, 210, 221, 228, 229, 240
Vidussoni, Aldo 66
Vietinghof, Heinrich von 210, 233
Vietnam 247
Vinci, Luigi 107
Virgil 106
Visconti, Luchino 90
Vittorini, Elio 89
Volpi, Albino 69, 70
Volpi, Giuseppe 77

Wagner, Richard 118
Wars and Battles (not WWI and WWII)
Adowa 27, 107
Cold War 247
Custoza 23
First Italian Independence War 23
Libya War 35, 42, 100
Novara 23
Second Italian Independence War 24
Spanish Civil War 3, 81, 115, 120–5, 133, 135, 153
Waterloo 22
Wavell, Archibald 172, 177, 184
Welles, Sumner 143–4
Wenner, Eugen 233
Wilson, Henry 175
Wilson, Woodrow 44, 46, 51, 84, 143
Wolff, Karl 215, 231, 233

Xi Jinping 253

Yeltsin, Boris 248
Yemen 107
Yohannes 27
Yugoslavia 5, 51, 53, 99, 134, 167, 169–70, 174, 224, 247

Zacharie, Georg 218, 230
Zaniboni, Tito 72–4
Zelensky, Vlodymyr 252
Zimmerman, Arthur 44
Zog I, King 134, 135, 136